Introduction to Christian Theology

CONTEMPORARY NORTH AMERICAN PERSPECTIVES

Roger A. Badham, *editor*

Westminster John Knox Press
Louisville, Kentucky

Scripture quotations, unless otherwise indicated, are from the New Revised Standard Version
of the Bible, copyright © 1989 by the Division of Christian Education
of the National Council of the Churches of Christ in the U.S.A.,
and used by permission.

All quotations from Martin Luther King, Jr.'s speeches are reprinted by arrangement with The Heirs
to the Estate of Martin Luther King, Jr., c/o Writers House, Inc. as agent for the proprietor. All
material copyright Martin Luther King, Jr., all material renewed by the Estate.

Grateful acknowledgment is made to the Society of Christian Ethics to reprint Emilie Townes's "To
Be Called Beloved," which first appeared in *The Annual*, 1993.

Grateful acknowledgment is made to Orbis Books for permission to reprint Ada María Isasi-Díaz's
essay from chapter 4 of Mujerista *Theology*, 1996.

Book design by Jennifer K. Cox
Cover design by Kevin Darst

First edition
Published by Westminster John Knox Press
Louisville, Kentucky

This book is printed on acid-free paper that meets the
American National Standards Institute Z39.48 standard. ∞

PRINTED IN THE UNITED STATES OF AMERICA
98 99 00 01 02 03 04 05 06 07 — 10 9 8 7 6 5 4 3 2 1

Library of Congress Cataloging-in-Publication Data

Introduction to Christian theology : Contemporary North American perspectives/Roger A.
Badham, editor. — 1st ed.
      p.   cm.
Includes bibliographical references and index.
ISBN 0–664–25674–0
1. Theology, Doctrinal—Introductions.   2. Theology—North America.   1. Badham,
Roger A.
BT65.I58   1998
230'.097—dc21   97-22794

For my wife, Beth,
a gift of God's gracious love

IN GRATITUDE

CONTENTS

ACKNOWLEDGMENTS

A multitude of colleagues and friends have offered encouragement and wisdom as I moved through the various stages of imagining, testing, and executing the vision for this volume: Robin Lovin and Robert Corrington offered the kind of support that kindles confidence in a project; Peter Ochs added his unique enthusiasm and helped in the shaping of the book; Roger Shinn was characteristically selfless in the time he gave on my behalf; Vanessa Ochs, Kelly Livingston, and Bill Elkins offered many invaluable suggestions; and Dale Irvin was both godly and enthusiast on behalf of the book's seeing it its first light of day. Also my thanks to Maureen Wallin, Sharon Betcher, Terry Baker, Maurice Davis, Joel Scandrett, and Michael Christensen.

I also want to thank David Tracy and George Lindbeck for their guidance, and Rachel Adler and Otto Maduro for their help. I am grateful to Westminster John Knox Press, especially Jon Berquist and Catherine Carpenter for their editorial support throughout the project, Richard E. Brown, and Stephanie Egnotovich.

My friend and former colleague at Cornell University, Robert L. Johnson, has been more helpful than he could possibly know by introducing me to so many leading theologians, several of whom are contributors to this volume. I want to thank Gary Phillips for his advice and for his collegiality that has grown out of this project. I would encourage readers to pay attention to his highly original biblical postmodernism. Thanks are due most of all to my wife, Beth, whose encouragement, advice, and patient support are unfailing.

It has been a privilege to work with the authors, who have so willingly contributed to this book. I am deeply grateful for their very fine work and their patience over the long period of time that such a volume takes from its inception to its publication. They join me in hoping that this text will achieve its goal as a valuable introduction to the wide variety of Christian theologies in North America today.

Where voices are omitted, I can only hope for the readers' understanding. I have sought to offer as broad a spectrum as is possible in a single volume, yet there will inevitably be gaps. I hope this book will serve as a map that will orient and guide readers, so that they may further explore the theological terrain with a fuller understanding of the contemporary debates.

The following chapters in *Introduction to Christian Theology* first appeared in the publications listed below and are reprinted with permission:

Chapter 15. Emilie Townes, "To Be Called Beloved," *Annual,* Society for Christian Ethics (1993): 93–115.

Chapter 17. Ada María Isasi-Díaz, "*Mujerista* Theology: A Challenge to Traditional Theology," in *Mujerista Theology: A Theology for the Twenty-First Century* (Maryknoll, N.Y.: Orbis Books, 1996).

Chapter 18. Mark C. Taylor, "The End(s) of Theology," in *Theology at the End of Modernity*, ed. Sheila Davaney (Valley Forge, Pa.: Trinity Press International, 1991).

CONTRIBUTORS

ROGER A. BADHAM is lecturer in the Department of Religious Studies at Drew University in Madison, New Jersey, and has served as cochair for programs in Jewish-Christian dialogue at Drew. He has written a number of articles, including "Windows on the Ecstatic: Reflections on Robert Corrington's Theonomous Naturalism," *Soundings* (forthcoming); "Redeeming the Fall: Hick's Schleiermacher *versus* Niebuhr's Kierkegaard," *Journal of Religion* 78:3 (July 1988); "World Spirit and the Appearance of the God: Philosophy of Religion and Christian Apologetics in Schleiermacher's Daily Thought," *The New Athenaeum* 5 (forthcoming); and "Conti's Reclamation of Farrer's Cosmological Personalism: A Pragmatist's Response," *The Personalist Forum* 12:1 (Spring 1996): 18–34. He is currently preparing a book focusing on the philosophical hermeneutics of Hans-Georg Gadamer and its relevance for Christian ethics. He is a member of the Episcopal Church.

RITA NAKASHIMA BROCK is Director of the Mary Ingraham Bunting Institute, Radcliffe College. She formerly held the Endowed Chair in Humanities at Hamline University in St. Paul, Minnesota, where she taught in the departments of both Religion and Women's Studies. She is the author of *Journeys by Heart* and coauthor with Susan Thistlethwaite of *Casting Stones: Prostitution in Asia and the United States*. She serves on the board of the Center for the Prevention of Sexual and Domestic Violence and is a member of the editorial board of the *Journal of Feminist Studies in Religion*. She is a member of the Christian Church (Disciples of Christ).

JAMES J. BUCKLEY is professor of theology at Loyola College in Baltimore, Maryland. He has written *Seeking the Humanity of God: Doctrines, Practices, and Catholic Theology*; and, with L. Greg Jones, he has edited *Spirituality and Social Embodiment*, as well as various articles and essays, including "Revisionists and Liberals," in *The Modern Theologians*, edited by David Ford. He is coeditor of *Modern Theology* and *Blackwell Readings in Modern Theology*. He is a member of the Roman Catholic Church.

JOHN B. COBB JR. is Ingraham Professor of Theology Emeritus at the School of Theology at Claremont and Avery Professor Emeritus at the Claremont Graduate School in Claremont, California. He was the director of the Center for Process

Studies at Claremont. He is author of *Reclaiming the Church*; *A Christian Natural Theology*; *Christ in a Pluralistic Age*; *God and the World*; *Process Theology as Political Theology*; *Process Theology: An Introductory Exposition,* with David Ray Griffin; *Is It Too Late?* and *The Liberation of Life: From the Cell to the Community*, with Charles Birch. He was a Fulbright professor at the University of Mainz and was elected fellow of the Woodrow Wilson International Center for Scholars in 1976. He is an ordained minister in the United Methodist Church.

JAMES H. CONE is Charles A. Briggs Distinguished Professor of Systematic Theology at Union Theological Seminary in New York. He is author of many books, eight of which have been translated into other languages. His more recent books include the two-volume *Black Theology: A Documentary History*; *Speaking the Truth: Ecumenism, Liberation, and Black Theology*; and the well-known *Martin & Malcolm & America: A Dream or a Nightmare?* Dr. Cone is on the editorial board of several major journals, including *The Journal of Religious Thought*; *Sojourners*; and *The Journal of the Interdenominational Theological Center*, as well as having published over one hundred articles. He has lectured at over five hundred colleges, universities, and divinity schools in America and around the world.

ROBERT S. CORRINGTON is associate professor of philosophical theology at the Graduate and Theological Schools of Drew University in Madison, New Jersey. He has written over forty articles and has been an editor or coeditor of five works. He is also author of *The Community of Interpreters*; *Nature and Spirit*; *An Introduction to C. S. Peirce*; *Ecstatic Naturalism*; *Nature's Self* and, most recently, *Nature's Religion*. He has written a full-length play, *Black Hole Sonata*. He has served on the executive boards of the Semiotic Society of America and the Highlands Institute for American Religious Thought. He is a member of the Unitarian-Universalist Church.

FR. CHARLES E. CURRAN is Elizabeth Scurlock University Professor of Human Values at Southern Methodist University in Dallas, Texas. He is author of *History and Contemporary Issues: Studies in Moral Theology*; *Contemporary Problems in Moral Theology*; *Politics, Medicine, and Christian Ethics: A Dialogue with Paul Ramsey*; *New Perspectives in Moral Theology*; and *The Responsibility of Dissent: The Church and Academic Freedom*. With Richard A. McCormick he has coedited the seven-volume series *Readings in Moral Theology*. He has served as president of the Catholic Theological Society of America and of the American Society of Christian Ethics. He is an ordained priest in the Roman Catholic Church.

STANLEY HAUERWAS is the Gilbert T. Rowe Professor of Theological Ethics at Duke University in Durham, North Carolina. With Alasdair MacIntyre he is coeditor of the *Revisions* series published by the University of Notre Dame Press. His books include *Vision and Virtue: Essays in Christian Ethical Reflection*; *A Community of Character: Toward a Constructive Christian Social Ethic*; *Dispatches from the Front: Theological Engagements with the Secular*; and, most recently,

Wilderness Wanderings: Probing Twentieth Century Theology and Philosophy. He has also edited, with Nancey Murphey and Mark Nation, *Theology without Foundations: Religious Practice and the Future of Theological Truth.* He is a member of the United Methodist Church.

CARL F. H. HENRY has served as editor and editor-at-large of *Christianity Today*, and was full professor at Northern Baptist Theological Seminary, Fuller Theological Seminary in Pasadena, California, and Eastern Baptist Seminary, successively. He served World Vision International from 1974 to 1986. He continues as a visiting professor at Trinity Evangelical Divinity School, and as a lecturer-at-large. He has been the recipient of six honorary doctoral degrees and has received, among others, the Distinguished Service Award of the Christian Life Commission of the Southern Baptist Convention. He is the author of thirty-eight books, including the six-volume work *God, Revelation and Authority.* He is a member of the Baptist Church.

JOHN HICK is H. G. Wood Professor of Theology at the University of Birmingham, England, and Danforth Professor of the Philosophy of Religion Emeritus at the Claremont Graduate School. He has received two Guggenheim Fellowships, and has lectured in Germany, Italy, Spain, Sweden, Canada, Japan, India, and Sri Lanka. He is the author of fourteen books, including *Faith and Knowledge*; *Philosophy of Religion*; *Evil and the God of Love*; *Death and Eternal Life*; and *Disputed Questions in Theology and the Philosophy of Religion.* He is editor or coeditor of ten more volumes. Several of his books have been translated into eleven languages. He gave the Gifford Lectures at Edinburgh in 1986–1987, which were published as *An Interpretation of Religion* and received the Grawemeyer Award in 1991. He was awarded an honorary doctorate by the University of Uppsala, Sweden. He is ordained in the Presbyterian Church.

ADA MARÍA ISASI-DÍAZ is professor of Christian ethics and theology at Drew University in Madison, New Jersey. Her latest books are *En La Lucha / In the Struggle* and *Mujerista Theology: A Theology for the Twenty-first Century*, and she has edited, with Fernando F. Segovia, *Hispanic/Latino Theology: Challenge and Promise.* She was born in Havana, Cuba, and her main theological enterprise is the development of *mujerista* theology: a Latina women's liberation theology. She is a member of the Roman Catholic Church.

WERNER G. JEANROND has been professor of systematic theology at the University of Lund in Sweden since 1994. Prior to that he was head of the school of theology and professor of theology at Trinity College in Dublin. Born in Germany, he received his Ph.D. from the University of Chicago, where he worked closely with David Tracy. His publications include *Text und Interpretation als Kategorien theologischen Denkens*, which is also in English translation, *Theological Hermeneutics: Development and Significance* (Swedish and German translations forthcoming); *Call and Response: The Challenge of Christian Life* (also published in Swedish and German), and numerous articles. He has also edited in collaboration two other books, one on the theology of David Tracy. He is a member of the editorial boards of the *Journal of the American Academy of Religion*; *Biblical Interpretation*; *Svensk Teoloisk Kvartalskrift*; *Hermathena*; and *Beiträge zur Geschichte der biblischen Exegese*.

CATHERINE KELLER is associate professor of constructive theology at Drew University in Madison, New Jersey. She is the author of *From a Broken Web* and *Apocalypse Now and Then: A Feminist Guide to the End of the World*. She is the author of numerous articles and essays, including "The Jesus of History and the Feminism of Theology," in *Jesus and Faith*, edited by J. Carlson et al.; "Chosen Persons and the Green Ecumenacy," in *Ecotheology*, edited by D. Hallman; and "Eschatology, Ecology, and a Green Ecumenacy," in *Reconstructing Christian Theology*, edited by Rebecca Chopp et al. She is a member of the United Methodist Church.

THOMAS C. ODEN is the Henry Anson Butz Professor of Theology and Ethics at Drew University in Madison, New Jersey. He received a Danforth Foundation Fellowship for research at the University of Heidelberg. He is the author of numerous articles and over thirty books, including *The Promise of Karl Barth: The Ethics of Freedom*; *Contemporary Theology and Psychotherapy*; *After Modernity—What?* and *Requiem: A Lament in Three Movements*. He is currently the general editor of the multivolume *Ancient Christian Commentary on Scripture*, the first volumes of which will appear in 1998. He has served as a member of the Ethics and Public Policy Center in Washington, D.C., and was a member of the White House Dialogue on Urban Initiatives in 1985. He is an ordained United Methodist minister.

CLARK H. PINNOCK is professor of theology at McMaster Divinity College in Hamilton, Ontario. He is the author of *Tracking the Maze: Finding Our Way through Modern Theology from an Evangelical Perspective* and *Flame of Love: A Theology of the Holy Spirit*. Articles and essays include "Evangelicalism and Other Living Faiths: An Evangelical Charismatic Perspective," in *All Together in One Place*, edited by H. Hunter et al.

MARK C. TAYLOR is Preston S. Parish Third-Century Professor of Religion at Williams College in Williamstown, Massachusetts. He has served as director of the Center for the Humanities and Social Sciences at Williams College. He is author of *Hiding*; *Journals to Selfhood: Hegel and Kierkegaard*; *Erring: A Postmodern A/Theology*; *Altarity*; and *Disfiguring: Art, Architecture, Religion*, as well as writing numerous articles, including "Denegating God," *Critical Inquiry* 20:4. He has served as the chair of the Research and Publications Committee of the American Academy of Religion and is the recipient of fellowships from both the Guggenheim and the Fulbright foundations.

EMILIE M. TOWNES is associate professor of Christian social ethics at Saint Paul School of Theology in Kansas City, Missouri. She is author of *Womanist Justice, Womanist Hope* and *In a Blaze of Glory: Womanist Spirituality as Social Witness*. She has authored articles and essays, including "Washed in the Grace of God: African Americans and Sexism," in *Violence against Women and Children*, edited by C. Adams et al. She is editor of *A Troubling in My Soul: Womanist Perspectives on Evil and Suffering*. She is an ordained minister in the American Baptist Church.

CLARK M. WILLIAMSON is professor of Christian thought at Christian Theological Seminary in Indianapolis, Indiana. He is the author of numerous articles and books, including *God Is Never Absent; When Jews and Christians Meet; The Teaching Minister;* and *A Guest in the House of Israel*. He has served as president of the Association of Disciples for Theological Discussion. He has served as a member of the Holocaust Memorial Council. He is an ordained minister in the Christian Church (Disciples of Christ).

—PART I—

THE CONTEMPORARY SETTING FOR THEOLOGY

THE LANDSCAPE OF
TWENTIETH-CENTURY THEOLOGY

ROGER A. BADHAM

THE SETTING FOR CONTEMPORARY
CHRISTIAN THEOLOGY

As an introduction to the variety of theological positions current within Christianity in North America today, this book presents a wide spectrum of theological positions and religious commitments, with chapters that may be antithetical to one another and exhibit widely differing starting points and purposes. The current state of theology appears to some as a disastrous fragmentation, a loss of constructive focus for the church, while others view it as an opportunity for boldly recasting the role of theology and of the church, an opportunity only belatedly achieved.

Denominational commitments play a far smaller role here than would have been the case in a similar volume in previous generations. Most denominations are finding themselves to be somewhat latitudinarian reflections of the dynamic currents swirling through both church and culture as we approach the third millennium. New and old lights, as it were, vie side by side in attempts to define future direction. The question, What is God doing in our midst? becomes a highly charged theological question where there is little consensus whether *God* as referent is real, a linguistic symbol, or a necessary idea; whether supernatural, natural, or humanly constructed; whether transcendent being, immanent being-itself, or product of nature. Christian theology is in crisis insofar as the diverse theologies that still take upon themselves the name *Christian* increasingly appear on the surface to share nothing in common; conservative theologies can appear to hold to untenable premodern beliefs; progressive theologies can appear to care nothing for traditional beliefs. Deep currents of fear and distrust run through the defensive and aggressive postures of diverse theological positions, and yet each seems equally imbued with its own hopes and anticipations that its discoveries will bring something salvific.

These tensions are real, and no student of theology who wishes to understand contemporary currents can afford to ignore them. This book brings together some of the most important voices in Christian theology today as a means to provide the reader with an undistorted presentation of each position *from the horse's mouth*, as it were. Each theologian describes and analyzes his or her own theological position. All are highly respected within their respective schools of thought and are major contributors to their theological position. Nearly all the chapters have been written expressly for this book.

As divergent as these theological positions are, there are, I believe, three inter-linking realities that are fundamental for all theological thinking in North America today. These realities may be described under the rubrics of modernism, pluralism, and the Holocaust. For those engaged in theological reflection the effect of ignoring these three massive realities is worse than simply risking irrelevance. It is to respond with silence and to act as if nothing has happened to change the way Christians should think about God and the world. To ignore the third heading, for example, is to act as if the church and Christian theology have had no influence on the thinking and acting that permitted the threefold holocausts of African slavery, Native American tribal decimation, and Hitler's "final solution" of attempting to annihilate the Jews. Christian theological justifications were used for all three, just as Christian voices were lifted up prophetically against all three. The pretense that Christian theology has had no complicity in these acts is a denial of the considerable influence of the church on society over the last four hundred years.

Modernism

In the light of modernity, many traditional Christian beliefs have become deeply problematic for Christians, whose worldviews are at least partially, if not mostly, formed according to scientifically oriented naturalistic patterns of reasoning. Christian tradition has become increasingly problematic to its own devotees over the last two hundred years, or as Thomas Oden conveniently frames it in his chapter, from 1789 to 1989—the fall of the Bastille to the fall of the Berlin Wall. Paul Ricoeur argues that "a tradition raises no philosophical problem as long as we live and dwell within it in the naïveté of the first certainty. Tradition only becomes problematic when the first naïveté is lost."[1] Modernism has moved Western Christian thinking beyond any possible first naïveté, although fundamentalism may be interpreted as a movement attempting to nurture that possibility. But even as early as the fourth century, Augustine found it necessary to defend the hiddenness of God and the passing of the age of miracles. What was different for him than for us, however, is that he was still confident that all moderately intelligent people believed in the immortality of the soul, the existence of a spiritual realm, and the miraculous character of God's work of regeneration in the soul.[2]

Liberal and progressivist Christians argue that to attempt to believe in a premodern manner, as if we can ignore the discoveries and insights of modernity, as if we can continue thinking theologically with a quasi–pre-Copernican cosmology, is perhaps more an act of self-deception than it is of faith. Such an attempt (fideism) fails to admit to the realities of human discovery. The tendency to literalize and absolutize language about God, for example—as king, as judge, as male—represents a refusal to admit to the metaphorical character of biblical description and all descriptive language about God. Similarly, the continued defense of a metaphysic with God as a supernatural being beyond nature leads to a vast and growing dichotomy between most persons' religious beliefs and their scientific understandings. It also is to defend a kind of scriptural literalism rejected by

Augustine so long ago.[3] In fact, Augustine strongly rejects the literal reading of personalist figures about God: "There are others," he writes of some theologians of his day, "whose concept of God, such as it is, ascribes to God the nature and moods of the human spirit, a mistake which ties their arguments about God to distorted and misleading rules of interpretation."[4] This is to suggest that present-day theologians who attempt to be faithful to the biblical texts in a literalist manner are, ironically, being faithful to postbiblical methods of interpretation more characteristic of the Middle Ages and modernity than to an earlier period of biblical understanding. Instead of avoiding modernity, such a hermeneutic chooses to read scripture by applying a nonbiblical scientific reasoning (with its strong demand for literal truth and its antipathy to metaphor and poetry). The modernist movement toward literalism has been mapped in Hans Frei's book *The Eclipse of Biblical Narrative.*

On the other hand, evangelical and conservationist Christians argue that the liberal tendency to accept the scientific and secular assumptions of modernism as if unassailable is to dismantle the gospel. We fail to enter the meaning of the tradition if we view Christianity from the outside simply as a social construct or an archive for historical criticism, or if we view God as nothing but that which it bears upon us naturalistically in the world (whether considered as a symbol, as with Gordon Kaufman, or as real, as with James Gustafson). Expressing something of the crisis that modernism has brought, Abraham Heschel wrote in 1943 that "we ridiculed superstition until we lost our ability to believe."[5] For this reason, Ricoeur argues, we have to enter through a second naïveté to believe through an appropriation of the tradition as it discloses itself to us in our own time.[6] For many, the attempts of liberal Christianity to accommodate to the views of modernity, a tendency seemingly toward ever-greater secularism, has been at least as problematic as the conservative attempt to freeze theology in past time against the tides of secularism.

Pluralism

The second of the three interlinking realities requiring emphasis is pluralism. Through vastly expanded global communication and increasingly multicultural societies, in the United States more than anywhere else, pluralism is a new and lasting reality in the consciousness of all who are attempting the work of theology. However imperfectly, all except the most conservative Christian theologian are aware of making truth claims that admit to no easy defense when judged against the competing claims of a world that comprises many other ancient indigenous and worldwide historical religions. Christian theologians have attempted a variety of interpretative solutions to traditional doctrines of the church to understand them in the light of pluralistic claims. For example, one can discover a spectrum of interpretations of the Trinitarian claims that Jesus Christ is God and that salvation comes only through Christ. Reduced claims have included that Jesus Christ was no more than a man, though unique, and his particular efficacious significance is only for the church; arguing from that theologically liberal point of view, Christian theologians will reason that all religions potentially point toward spiritual truth (Hick; see his chapter, which follows), *or* salvation comes through all other religions but in a less developed manner (Friedrich Schleiermacher).[7] A more conservative but pluralist answer continues to assert the divinity of Christ, and that salvation always comes through the atonement of Christ even if believers in other religions are unaware of his efficacy for them (Rahner's anonymous or hidden Christians), *or* that there is no salvation except through the church or faith in Christ.[8] Of course, the concept of salvation, so central to Christianity, is itself problematic today in the face of both modernism and pluralism, no longer having its obvious reference to the enjoyment of eternal life for many Christians who consider it a mythic concept or interpret it in temporal and liberationist ways.

Part of the sense of crisis for some is that there is no part of the tradition uncontested, no doctrine exempt from radical critique, for in a postcolonial world, which is nevertheless an increasingly Western-dominated world, the exclusive truth claims of the historical church as the vessel of salvation have been attacked from inside and out as no different from any other ideological rhetoric and no purer in motive.

Pluralism has also led to increasing ecumenical and interreligious dialogue, including irenic dialogue among conservatives of different faiths. Conservative Catholics are in dialogue with conservative Jews, for example.[9] In many ways they find greater mutual understanding than with liberal groups, just as liberal groups are in dialogue together across previously insurmountable boundaries. Shared social and ethical concerns, such as the abortion issue, become litmus tests for a way of viewing society that transcends significant religious differences. Evangelicals join with conservative Catholics and Jews and conservative secularists to oppose abortion; liberals join with other liberal religious, nonreligious, and even antireligious groups to defend women's rights to abortion. These changing realities profoundly challenge the ways in which we do theology and cannot be honestly avoided.

The Holocaust

The third linked reality is closely identified with the second, but stands out as the starkest judgment on the assumptions of the Christian West. The Holocaust, perpetrated as it was by a nation historically at the heart of pre-Reformation Christendom and post-Reformation Europe, has forever changed the way the church may properly interpret its own history. It brings into sharper focus the prior evils of Christian complicity in African slavery and the annihilation of Native Americans, as well as the long, deeply ingrained injustice of anti-Semitism within the church from the late first century to the present. It cries out to us never to forget the demonic powers unleashed from within Christendom itself, that political entity which shaped Europe from the Middle Ages onward and which was previously hailed as the great monument to the triumph of the gospel and the providence of God.

If there was ever such a thing as a Christian culture, it was that of Germany, and its capitulation to Hitler stands as a reminder of the dangers of idolatry and compromise that have become characteristic of Christian relationships to its society and culture. These compromises, too, have both liberal and conservative expressions: the liberal tendency has been to desire close ties with its society and to downplay the differences between Christian beliefs and secular beliefs; the conservative tendency has been to assume the Christian roots of American culture and to adopt a form of nationalism whereby America (at its *Christian* best) stands for the good, for freedom, and for democracy.

The Holocaust raises profound questions of Christianity's denial of its own Jewish heritage and the church's pathological blame of the Jews as a people corporately responsible for the crucifixion and forever under the judgment of God for it. Christian supersessionism has permitted the church to appropriate to itself the name of Israel, while simultaneously stripping Jews of their dignity and heritage through two thousand years. The church took the honorific, covenant title and the promises adhering to Israel, but left God's judgments as falling on the Jews. Hearing the words of Jesus against hypocrisy, the church has too often preferred to interpret them as being aimed for all time against the Jews rather than against the deep currents of hatred running below the Christianized surface of Europe. Jews were often forced to dress distinctively and live in ghettos to maintain the appearance of being the other. Neither of these features was original with Hitler. Nor has anti-Semitism gone away since: John Pawlikowski, O.S.M. and Clark Williamson have both pointed to the continuing anti-Judaism in many schools of current theology, including, surprisingly, the liberation theology of Gustavo Gutiérrez and Jon Sobrino. A Jewish feminist theologian, Judith Plaskow, has also pointed to feminist forms of Christian anti-Judaism, as when feminists portray Jesus as advocating the liberation of women from the yoke of the Jewish law.[10]

If we read portions of the New Testament (which theologian Paul van Buren prefers we rename the "Apostolic Writings"), we discover harsh words against the Jews, particularly in John's Gospel. Many interpreters have too literally maintained the antipathy that existed at the time of its writing, when two marginal groups, the Christian churches and the diaspora Judaism, were in competition and conflict with each other, not unlike theologies today. But the political ascendance of the church as the established religion of Europe changed the reality. Lacking an appropriate interpretative theory, the church continued to believe that the harsh words of first-century sibling rivalry were therefore inspired and sanctioned by God for all times and places. Defective hermeneutical methods have been the means of incalculable damage throughout history, and, in tandem with other factors, led directly to the massive unleashing of evil against the Jews in the *Shoah*. How can Christians oppose anti-Jewish interpretations of John's Gospel unless our own hermeneutical theory can demonstrate the distortion of that interpretation and simultaneously display that our own theory is less distorting?

A central question that haunts both Jewish and Christian post-Holocaust theology is that of theodicy. Why, if God acts in history, was the Holocaust permitted to happen? A God who has the power to intervene, but who does not, surely stands indictable of injustice?[11] There are many attempted solutions: The classical Greek model of God is of a Being beyond time, an unrelated Absolute, immutable and static. Immutability and omnipotence remain at the heart of Augustine's doctrine of God, but he stresses that God is in all parts of creation, and is by no means removed from it. Schubert Ogden claims that God's "body is the whole universe of nondivine beings"; therefore, all creatures are effected by God and effect God, and experience levels of freedom.[12] Paul van Buren, adopting this process model, argues for the self-limiting character of God through the creation of self-determining agents, after which event power is social—shared between God and humanity in covenant together.[13] God's power is not absolute, but is relational and persuasive, and can therefore be profoundly frustrated. Because God is relational, God is affected by, and suffers with, creation. Tillich's Kierkegaardian approach is compatible: If moral freedom is an inseparable trait of being human, for God to restrain evil would be synonymous with taking away our humanness. God has provided us already with every gift possible by which the Holocaust was to be prevented. Tillich moves away from personalist or supranaturalist assertions about God as a superbeing or agent, and speaks instead of God as the ground of Being and as Being itself. God is therefore perceived as the ground of agency rather than as an agent, which profoundly changes one's theological view of God. Put differently, H. Richard Niebuhr insists that "responsibility affirms—God is acting in all actions upon you. So respond to all actions upon you as to respond to [God's] action."[14]

The Holocaust stands as a marker to the death of political Christendom. Whether God's own death must follow is a question affecting many of the theologies represented in this volume. The death-of-God theologians may see deconstructionism and Mark C. Taylor's cleverly named a/theology as their most immediate progeny. Their effect, however, has been more widespread, raising questions about the necessity of the idea of God. The Episcopal bishop of Newark, John Spong, has written with pastoral concern, "We wonder if God has died. Certainly the God defined by yesterday's world has lost power, but does yesterday's definition exhaust the reality of God?"[15] It is a live question: Many departments of religion and even divinity schools and seminaries are increasingly treating God as an outdated concept. Whether this represents a bold and necessary move away from outmoded premodern ways of thinking or a devastating defeat by the powers of secularism is again left to the reader's own theological investigations.

Finally, it must be remembered that equally sincere Christians argued from the same Bible for or against slavery, for or against Native American rights to survive. It is surely vital that theologians in their praxis and reflection at the end of the twentieth century be able to confess the complicity of their own theological legacy in radical evil if they are to have a prophetic voice for good in the future. Unfortunately, the tendency too often remains that we consider our own theological school of thought exempt from our own critiques.

THE CHAPTERS IN THEIR
THEOLOGICAL CONTEXT

The issue of modernism, pluralism, and the Holocaust are reflected in various ways in the chapters of this text. John Hick focuses brilliantly on the issues of pluralism that challenge Christian theology. He considers that Christianity is in transition from assuming its superiority over other religious expressions to a new self-understanding, having begun to learn of the wisdom and dignity of other faiths. Most people remain in the religion to which they were born and assume it as normative and superior to all others, but pluralism is forcing us to consider the merits of other religions. Hick identifies three *inclusivist* types of theology within contemporary Christian thought. He discusses Rahner, Dinoia, and Lindbeck as providing us with forms of inclusivism whereby salvation comes to individuals within other religions yet through Christ. The other religion is not considered the bearer of salvation. A further type of inclusivism, however, extends farther, validating the efficacy of those other religions "as alternative mediators or contexts of salvation." This view accepts that each world religion has its own way of turning men and women from a natural self-centeredness to a new orientation "centered in the Ultimate, the Real, as conceived and experienced within one's own tradition." Another religion has its own linguistic framework for this reorientation that will be very different from that of Christianity's. Understood theocentrically, the same God is at work through the linguistic and cultural framework of each religion. Hick draws on philosophical resources, particularly Kant, to argue this last position, whereby an ultimate reality is knowable to us only through our cultural interpretations and constructions of it. God will therefore be understood in one religion as personal, in another as impersonal, but in both as that which is Ultimate or Real.

Clark Williamson addresses the issue of Christian-Jewish relations through a typology of two broad categories of people and groups: those who are *protean*, lacking fixed identities, and those who are *closed-off*, with rigid identities in their relations with otherness. He echoes H. Richard Niebuhr's concept of closed societies in this latter group.[16] Neither of these groups can engage with otherness; protean theologies fail because of their "emptied-out inclusivism," and closed-off theologies fail for being absolutist. Williamson leads toward an Aristotelian mean between these two positions, whereby boundaries are held as important for identity and self-understanding, yet without rigidness and exclusivity. Citing Tillich, Cobb, and Brock, Williamson suggests the importance of boundaries. He argues his thesis through a number of case studies: Paul "sought to transcend the boundary between Jews and Gentiles in order to create one new community of the two," but many of the church fathers sought to replace Paul's permeable boundary with anti-Jewish boundaries created to delegitimize Jewish worship and interpretation, and cast the Jews as the older brother who must serve the younger, the church—for example, Chrysostom's fourth-century attack on the Jews as "wild animals . . . suited only for slaughter," and "Christ-killers." Williamson argues for an understanding between Jews and Christians as that of *chaverim*, as traditional study-partners of Torah, open to one another while respecting the boundaries of each religion. Post-Holocaust theology "is a form of liberation theology," and "it is committed to freeing Christian theology from its inherited anti-Jewish ideology." The Holocaust calls for a complete reinterpretation of Christian theology, one that establishes an open Christian identity that is neither protean nor closed.[17]

Evangelical and Conservationist Theologies

Carl F. H. Henry has been described as the dean of evangelical theology, a staunch defender of the inerrancy of the Bible against liberalism.[18] He emphasizes that a Christian belief in inerrancy is neither new nor marginal, although its critics often cast it that way. Only the term, not the idea, is recent. Fundamentalists and evangelicals claim that they stand in the historic line of the Reformation, upholding its classic doctrines against incursions of liberal theologies. The rejection of biblical inerrancy has led to "a selective and partisan approach to biblical teaching [which] leads to fantastic diversity," and its *forfeiture* leads to a serious undermining of "the classic creeds of Christendom." Henry argues that many claims of higher or *destructive* criticism regarding the Bible's accuracy have been shown to be erroneous, while much textual criticism has strengthened confidence in the accuracy of the biblical text. He criticizes the Roman Catholic Church in that it subordinates the authority of the Bible to the teaching authority of the church, although he argues that Catholicism from the Fathers to the Reformation held to a doctrine of inerrancy. Following from Jesus' and Paul's views of the authority of scripture, Henry argues that there is no better model for the church, and that "no one can convincingly claim to stand in the tradition of Jesus and the apostles who views Scripture as merely a human product." The Reformed tradition makes the distinction between inerrancy and infallibility, whereby the latter speaks of the Bible's unfailing truths in matters of faith and salvation. As a result, the Bible is not assumed infallible in matters of historical record or scientific fact. Henry rejects this view because of the historical nature of the incarnation. He also criticizes narrative theologies for failing to uphold what is "historically factual, cognitively true and ontologically real outside the text." However, Henry does not think that these differences mean that inerrantists need to avoid relationships with errantists. Dialogue is important, although some minimal doctrinal confession is necessary, he concludes.

Thomas Oden, in his theological sea change from a leading liberal voice in the 1960s to his current *postmodern paleoorthodoxy*, displays in dramatic form the religious search for an authority that can be trusted. Oden's position differs from Henry's inerrantism in that its locus of authority is placed on the patristic period of the first eight centuries as the time of the development of a Christian orthodox position that is definitive for future Christian expressions of faith and doctrine. Oden's version of what it means to be postmodern is an ideological position opposed both to two hundred years of modernity and to what he calls *ultramodernity*, which he defines as that avant-garde movement that describes itself as postmodern, but which actually continues the secular and antireligious assumptions of modernity. Oden would certainly consider Mark C. Taylor's a/theology ultramodern. Against the despairing characteristics of Foucauldian and Derridean ultramodernity, Oden pits his own postmodern orthodoxy as "evangelically more hopeful, culturally more realistic, and providentially more circumspect." In ways that may appear to the reader as less than circumspect, however, he strikes out at "media elites" and "liberal investigative journalists . . . too intimidated to investigate" the claims and key values of "corrupted modernity," which he considers an amalgam of the ideologies of Marx, Freud, Nietzsche, Feuerbach, and Bultmann that "are now falling synchronously down like tottering dominoes . . . [with] their wholly owned ecclesial subsidiaries, their theological hirelings and flunkies." Whatever else readers may conclude, they will hardly charge Oden with blandness. It is especially to the Greek church fathers that he looks, for their work is less distorted by speculative scholasticism than those of Western medieval Catholicism. Those who are making this return, dubbed "young fogys" by Oden, are finding a refreshing alternative to modernity as they develop a suitable hermeneutic for adapting the primitive apostolic testimony to new historical challenges and languages. Authority resides in the testimony of the apostles. If not there, there is nowhere that the church can learn the truth.

Clark Pinnock's evangelicalism appears to breathe a very different air from Henry's or Oden's. At once more moderate and more irenic, he is critical of the "conservative, postfundamentalist subculture," which has appropriated the name *evangelical* to refer only to itself. Carl Henry is postfundamentalist in Pinnock's account, by which he means that group who were thoroughly antiliberal but nevertheless wanted to resist the anti-intellectualism of fundamentalism. Pinnock argues that evangelicalism represents more of a movement than a theology in that its theology "is a patchwork quilt," for the term includes Reformed, Arminian, charismatics, Pentecostals, and neoorthodox, among others. For Pinnock, though perhaps not for Henry, this has created "a wonderful mixture of vitality amid diversity," held together more by a piety than by a creed, more by witness than by scholarship. Therefore, those within the movement who wanted to define it creedally were in that sense acting contrary to the spirit of the movement, except insofar as it remains antiliberal in its attitude. Pinnock considers that evangelicalism is largely defined by liberalism, as a protest against it. As such, its general features tend to be the divinity of Christ, the authority of the Bible, the lostness of humanity, and the priority of grace. However, he moves gently away from the doctrine of the inerrancy of the Bible as a central tenet of evangelicalism. In his book *Tracking the Maze* he wrote, "We are not bound to deny the Bible the possibility of playful legend just because the central claim is historical."[19] Pinnock suggests that the success of the evangelical movement could easily be shared by the mainline denominations if they realized that "the liberal experiment was a mistake." Evangelicalism arose to preserve historic Christianity, and if the churches returned to their roots the need for the movement would disappear. Pinnock therefore shares Oden's conservationist concerns, though not his patristic focus.

Narrative and Postliberal Theologies

"In general, the Enlightenment tends to accept no authority and to decide everything before the judgement seat of reason. Thus the written tradition of Scripture . . . can claim no absolute validity; the possible truth of the tradition depends on the credibility that reason accords it."[20] Hans-Georg Gadamer's negative assessment of the Enlightenment and his retrieval of the importance of tradition as the means whereby truth emerges within a coherent and meaningful context is a mode of thinking shared by many who might loosely be described under the banners of narrative or postliberal theologians.[21] H. Richard Niebuhr expresses very similar concerns. If Gadamer is correct, modernity has privileged a reductive empiricism based in technical reason largely unsuited for the pursuit of knowledge in the humanities and theology, yet the scientific approach has dominated in all areas of theological and religious studies, evangelical or liberal.

In 1977, Stanley Hauerwas wrote ironically that "stories are prescientific, according to the story legitimizing the age which calls itself scientific."[22] Narrative and postliberal theologies seek to recover the spiritually formative power of the story, exhibiting a cultural-linguistic sensitivity to narrative in response to the linguistic turn of Wittgenstein and Heidegger. The narratives of our historical traditions form and shape our ways of seeing the world. We are embedded within narrative traditions and have no means of transcending our historical contingency. Our knowledge is therefore always partial and from our own particular standpoint. Protestant and Catholic theologians have found this approach a way to reassert particularity and identity in the expression of Christian faith without making foundationalist, triumphalist, or supersessionist claims. Indeed, Peter Ochs, a Jewish postcritical philosophical theologian, works closely with Christians in this school of thought and trained under George Lindbeck. Two quite different forms of neoorthodoxy, those of Karl Barth and H. Richard Niebuhr, are formative for this movement. George Lindbeck and the late Hans Frei, who were both at Yale, as was Niebuhr, have exerted enormous influence in this sphere.[23]

James Buckley offers a Catholic reading of a postliberal position. He describes nineteenth-century Catholicism as offering the most effective resistance to modernity by attempting to recover the sources of faith that nourished the tradition.[24] But in the early twentieth century it was Barth who most opposed modernity, while simultaneously opposing conservative attempts "to repristinate a premodern era." Like Barth, postliberals take scripture as a crucial source for all meaningful Christian theology, but it is scripture understood more in terms of biblical narratives, rather than doctrinal propositions characteristic of both pre-Enlightenment Protestant orthodoxy and contemporary conservative evangelicalism. Because any reading of the text as narrative implies one's theories of interpretation, hermeneutics has become a central concern to postliberal theology. The particularity of Jesus Christ is also far more central to postliberal theology than to most liberal theologies. H. Richard Niebuhr's view again accords with many postliberals. He opposed Barth's Christocentrism as leading to idolatry, and stressed instead a strong theocentrism which nevertheless saw theologically through the lens of the existential occasion of Jesus Christ. Hans Urs von Balthasar, whom Buckley cites as perhaps the leading Catholic postliberal, speaks in terms of Jesus as the central character of the biblical narrative, or *theo-drama*.

Buckley argues (like Frei) that both liberal and conservative theologies are philosophically foundationalist and to that extent remain modernist. Liberal theologies have used human reason and experience as foundational, while evangelicals have used scripture as inerrant and supernaturally revealed and most Roman Catholics have used an infallible teaching office. Postliberal theology, as nonfoundationalist, is based rather on what John Henry Cardinal Newman described as *cumulative* arguments for the faith.[25]

Hauerwas writes a story of Protestant Christian ethics that shows the dominant trajectory from the social gospel of Walter Rauschenbusch to the theocentric ethics of James Gustafson. It is a story critical of a once confident liberal Christian movement that lost its way because its focus was on the nation rather than the church—it considered its task to articulate an ethics for everyone. This remains largely the expectation for Christian ethics.[26] But as a result, as the nation has become less Christian, Christian ethicists like Gustafson, seeking to effect change in public policy, have largely had to suppress their particularity. Gustafson, in turn, charges Hauerwas, his former student, with sectarianism when he writes that "Hauerwas's God becomes the tribal God of a minority of the earth's population."[27] Hauerwas stands much closer to Gustafson's own teacher, H. Richard Niebuhr (whom nobody would charge with tribalism), than is Gustafson at this point. Niebuhr considered that theology existed for the sake of clarifying the thought of the church, and though Hauerwas is critical of Niebuhr's continuing liberalism, Niebuhr shares many theological features with the ethicist most admired by Hauerwas, John Howard Yoder, whose Mennonite understanding is straightforwardly that Christian ethics is for Christians. In his book *Dispatches from the Front*, Hauerwas expresses himself characteristically when he writes that "Protestantism, at least the mainstream variety, is dying in America. I prefer to put the matter more positively, that is—God is killing Protestantism in America, and we deserve it."[28]

Liberal and Progressivist Theologies

Liberal and progressivist theologies are those which, far more than those addressed so far, have intentionally embraced the philosophical discoveries of the Enlightenment, and most particularly the encompassing significance of Kant's critiques. Kant's *Critique of Pure Reason* discredited theological claims that God could be known directly, and it therefore appeared to undermine the doctrinal systems of "positive" or revelation-based religions vis-à-vis a more general natural religion. Adopting these insights led to a theological crisis which was met most profoundly in the *via media* solutions of Friedrich Schleiermacher, whose influence has therefore been seminal for successive generations of modern theologians. Following Kant, Schleiermacher rejected orthodox propositionalism and the speculation characteristic of religious metaphysics, yet contra Kant, insisted on the continuing significance of positive religion (and the effectual nonviability of natural religion) through his turn toward the empirical characteristics of religious experience. By focusing on the ways in which religion is expressed within the religions and in the life of the believer, Schleiermacher was able to treat doctrines as creative cultural developments, articulations of religious experience, rather than as timeless truth propositions.

There is no doubt that Kant's and Schleiermacher's thought had a deeper impact on Protestant than on Catholic theology in the nineteenth century, but, as Charles Curran's chapter makes clear, there has been a move away from a rather general "condemnation of liberalism and the Enlightenment" toward a more inductive and historically conscious approach by Catholic theologians as a result of

Vatican II, a move especially reflected in Bernard Lonergan's work. *The Declaration of Religious Liberty* (Vatican II) draws on Enlightenment themes of the dignity of the human person, and the prior Catholic insistence on Thomism has given way to a more ecumenical consciousness. Curran lays out the contemporary tensions that have arisen since Vatican II (1962–1975) and the pivotal papal encyclical *Humanae vitae* (1968). He describes the reasons for tension between revisionist moral theologians and the more conservative and hierarchical papal authority represented by the encyclical and supported by successive popes since Paul VI.[29] Curran offers an incisive analysis of four major areas of conflict arising from the encyclical—sexual ethics, natural law, the grounding of norms (physicalism versus proportionalism), and the issue of dissent within Catholicism. Curran analyzes two methodologies at work in contemporary magisterial teachings, one on sexual and medical moral teachings, the other on social teachings. Curran is a dissenter on the former while generally supportive of the church's current teachings on the latter. He points to liberationist, feminist, and ecological concerns as being crucial for the future development of Catholic moral theology and maintains the importance of the church's commitment to a communitarian rather than a more Protestant modernist, individualistic ethic.

Curran has often been described as a liberal Catholic theologian, yet it is clear that his liberalism breathes a different air than that of most Protestant liberal theologies. A commonplace might be to assume that liberal theologies all tend toward dissolving the division between Catholicism and Protestantism, but this proves not to be the case: For example, process and empirical theologies (represented respectively in this book by John B. Cobb Jr. and Robert S. Corrington) can be shown to be naturalistic movements developing out of strongly Protestant roots, which tend to move beyond the liturgical and communitarian commitments of most Catholic theologians. Correlational theology, on the other hand, truly spans the Catholic–Protestant divide, albeit at the revisionist pole of each. Catholics Hans Küng, Edward Schillebeeckx, and David Tracy and Protestants Paul Tillich and Langdon Gilkey can be described as having a correlational approach. Because of the link with Tillich, Gilkey, and Tracy the correlational approach has often been identified as the "Chicago School." Werner Jeanrond writes that Tillich was the first to use the term *correlational*, in his *Systematic Theology*, as a means of describing "a one-way movement from existential questions to Christian answers." But contemporary approaches have enlarged the methodological framework and now promote "a mutually critical dialogue" between theology and all other forms of self-knowledge in the world. Gilkey applied a hermeneutical and phenomenological methodology and explored the presence of the divine in secular culture and other religions, thereby offering a significant reinterpretation of Christian faith. His theology aims at linking "an interpretation of human existence under the conditions of modernity with a reinterpreted Christian message." Theology must speak in the cultural terms of its day as it interprets the human situation in the light of faith. Tracy continues this commitment to mutuality and openness, especially to other academic disciplines, although his more recent works have been markedly more critical of modern secularism and the ambiguities of the Enlightenment project. The earlier optimism displayed in his *Blessed Rage for Order* (1975) has been tempered, notably in *Plurality and Ambiguity* (1987). Both Gadamer's and Ricoeur's hermeneutical-linguistic sensitivities are important to Tracy, and have brought him to a greater appreciation of the cultural-linguistic approach even while he remains a critic of Lindbeck's methodology.

Just as process philosophy is synonymous with philosophers Alfred North Whitehead and Charles Hartshorne, so process theology is synonymous with theologian John B. Cobb Jr., whose chapter further shows the powerful influence of the University of Chicago for twentieth-century liberal theology. Under the influence of evolutionary biology, the human was no longer seen as *above* nature, so the movement toward a theological naturalism developed, which sought to overcome the strong Kantian division between the human and the natural sciences. An openness to the findings of the natural sciences marks both process and empirical theologies.[30] Cobb shows how Hartshorne broke with Aristotelian categories like immutability and omniscience, which had introduced irresolvable tensions into the doctrine of the reality of God. Hartshorne argues, rather, that God is in process in and through the evolution of the cosmos. Cobb, a Whiteheadian, also shows how Hartshorne's metaphysics differs significantly from Whitehead's, the latter with its intriguing indebtedness to ideas of Jamesian continuity and flux and its Leibnizian discreteness of atomistic occasions. Whitehead also subordinates God to creativity. Radical reassessments of the divine have led to process theologians such as Marjorie Suchocki's adopting feminist perspectives without abandoning earlier commitments to process thought, while others, like Catherine Keller and Rita Brock, are firstly feminists who are strongly influenced by process, Cobb suggests. Cobb's own theology has become ecologically and economically conscious as he has remained faithful to a process naturalism.[31]

Empirical theologian Nancy Frankenberry suggests that while for process theology the concept of nature is included in God, for empirical theology the concept of God is understood as one kind of process within nature. As such, she would include herself under the heading of empirical rather than process theologian, yet there is no doubt that the boundaries between the two are especially porous. While process thought springs largely out of either Whitehead's or Hartshorne's metaphysics, empirical theology looks more to nineteenth-century Protestant liberalism flowing from Schleiermacher and to the American pragmatism of James and Dewey. In his chapter, Robert Corrington additionally identifies a more recent strain of Peircean influence through Robert Neville, Michael Raposa, and his own work.[32] Nature is not understood over against anything else but rather as a precategory that encompasses all else. God may be synonymous with the totality of nature or of an aspect of nature, but may not be external to nature. (Peirce's pragmaticism would have added: God may not be external to nature *in any knowable or meaningful sense to us*.) The radical consequences of a thoroughgoing naturalism lead to a recasting of Christian concepts like sin and grace, whereby both are understood as naturally occurring; so a life-threatening virus is as much sustained by natural grace as is the human life so threatened. Corrington suggests that empirical theology, with its sense of authority deriving from finite human experience, is split in its relationship to traditional forms of Christian (or Jewish) worship. Neville's "quasi-process naturalism" represents that wing of empirical theology most at home within the Trinitarian Christian church, while Corrington himself has migrated to Unitarian-Universalism, and many others, highly skeptical of ecclesial doctrine and authority, express a strongly individualistic Kantian universalism that stands at a far remove from the communitarian impulses of postliberal and narrative theologies. But even the least ecclesial forms of empirical theology derive "their driving categories and metaphors . . . from both Judaism and Christianity, even if they are stretched, or even broken," Corrington writes.[33] William James once wrote, "Let empiricism once become associated with religion, as hitherto, through some strange misunderstandings, it has been associated with irreligion, and I believe that a new era of religion as well of philosophy will be ready to begin."[34]

Liberationist and Feminist Theologies

If, broadly speaking, liberal and progressivist theologies have tended to place their authority in individualistically realized forms of experience and reason, and conservative and evangelical theologies have tended to place it more in scripture, and postliberals have stressed the importance of a communitarian understanding of tradition, where is the emphasis among feminist and liberationist theologies? They are *generally* highly critical of enlightenment individualism, yet they are equally critical of the tendency to locate authority in scripture or tradition, while constructing strong communities which nevertheless remain highly resistant to any heteronomous authority. It is at this point, in fact, that the issue of authority emerges in its full force as a central tension between contemporary theological positions. How are issues of identity, so important to feminists and liberationists as well as to narrativists, to be negotiated communally yet without abusive totalities of identification emerging? How is integrity possible without a homogeneous integration and assimilation for the historically marginalized? As with Foucault, a hermeneutics of suspicion is cast on all teleologies, totalizations, and false unities by liberationist and feminist theologies. A profound questioning of the Euro-American theological and philosophical tradition is brought to the center, an impulse largely unnoticeable in most empirical and process theologies. This is accompanied by a replacement of the metaphysical speculations of empirical and process theologies with a much stronger sociological and politicoethical concentration on the features of particularity that adhere to the marginalized groups. Theology therefore becomes a discipline that has a strongly developed praxis and advocacy function.[35]

Rita Brock, citing Fumitaka Matsuoka, writes that "holy insecurity rests partly in a different sense of selfhood than the Western autonomous individual." Matsuoka found in Asian American religious communities an emphasis on the "intrinsically social and collective character of selfhood and the irreplaceable character of community for the well-being of Asian-American Christians."[36] If European existentialism has focused on the alienation of the individual, then the liberationist and feminist theologies represented here focus no less existentially on the alienation of whole groups through a critique of dominance. This alienation is not created by the group itself, but imposed through a complex of dominant norms and structures into which these groups are not permitted to fit. Brock traces her own cultural ambiguities to her dual heritage—a Japanese American, from a culture where the female is submissive to the male, confronted with Western dualistic either/or expressions of Christianity, which has historically emphasized autonomy over community, male over female, reason over emotion, mind over body, and so on. Brock articulates, through her concept of *interstitial integrity*, what she finds missing in Eurocentric and androcentric theological categories. Primarily, she is developing a methodology for exploring identity beyond the dualistic definitions of oneself and community only in relationship to a dominant paradigm. For Asian Pacific Americans, this means living in the interstices between, for example, the practice of silence familiar to Asian spiritual practices and the words of Protestant Christianity, without the either/or of a Protestant exclusivism.

"Double-consciousness" was the term given by W. E. B. Du Bois for the struggle within African Americans between, for example, integration and nationalism, between being African and being American. James Cone, one of the foremost African American theologians of our day, writes that black religious thought lies, as it were, in the interstices between African beliefs and the Christian theology of white Christians. The reality of God as a God of justice and the refusal to decouple religion from politics have been themes central to black theology, and the church has been at the heart of the African American understanding of justice. "Our rejection of European metaphysical speculations and our acceptance of an apparently crude anthropomorphic way of speaking of God is black theologians' way of concretizing" a gospel of liberation. Cone draws on the rich heritage from Du Bois and the accommodationism of Booker T. Washington, through preachers Adam Clayton Powell and Howard Thurman, to Martin Luther King Jr. King brought the traditional black Christian themes of justice, liberation, love, hope, and suffering into a creative synthesis with the democratic tradition, a synthesis that refused to be co-opted by hatred. His theopolitical position, a combining of the exodus-liberation, the cross-love, and the resurrection-hope themes of scripture, brought King to oppose the Vietnam War, as one of the interconnected evils of war, racism, and poverty. Cone also traces the stream of black nationalism and black power from Marcus Garvey to Malcolm X and the discovery that a gospel of liberation must begin with the people whom God is seeking to liberate, rather than with European theological contexts and methodologies. This is currently leading toward a growing *Afrocentric perspective* for today's theologians.

Emilie Townes provides just that in her "theo-ethical concerns for wholeness," in which the issue of African American women's learning to love themselves is a central concern. Womanism received its name and a rich description from Alice Walker, and signaled a move away from forms of feminist analysis that had lacked sufficient attention to race and class oppression. Like Cone, Townes emphasizes the African elements that remained significant aspects in African American Christianity. Black women's spirituality and theology was "forged from

African cosmology, evangelical piety, and revival fervor." Its sociology reveals a more organic relationship between private/domestic and public/religious roles than often experienced in the past by white women. Relationality lies at the heat of womanist spirituality. Womanism, too, is strongly critical of "modernist inadequacies," and sees "the theoretical intent of postmodern thought" as a potential discourse for legitimating otherness. However, Townes considers those forms of postmodernism which remain individualistic, which continue to privilege epistemology and aesthetics and ignore vital political and ethical dimensions, to remain deeply problematic. Perhaps she too would describe that species of postmodernity *ultramodern*. Womanist theology is a twofold response, "to the sexism in black theology and the racism in feminist theology," and it calls for a broadening of the liberationist messages of both movements and a recognition of the wide variety of women's experiences. Of course, black and feminist theologies are closer to contemporary womanist thought than any preliberationist theologies in their concerns, so her critique needs to be understood within that broad context.

Catherine Keller's concerns in her chapter, "Burning Tongues: A Feminist Trinitarian Epistemology" suggests that, in order to arrive at a new *way* of knowing (as distinguished from a new body of knowledge), we "treat the divine attributes . . . as adverbs of human knowing rather than as mere substantives of divine substance." Through a Trinitarian feminist lens this means that, for example, the First Person of the Trinity is a symbol that teaches us "to seek to know first of all personally." We do not so much "gaze at the divine personae, the 'masks of God'; we look through them at our existence." In so doing, we discover the importance of the interpersonal—the relational. Similarly, looking through the mask of God as creator, as "the divine matrix of life," as Ruether calls it, theology and ecological crisis come together as ecofeminism, a movement profoundly influenced by the early Whiteheadian work of Keller's teacher, John Cobb. These new ways of knowing are contrasted against the dualistic epistemology of the Enlightenment. Acknowledging the neoorthodox move in this direction, Keller nevertheless considers its influence to be purely intraecclesial ("ecclesiocentric") and therefore of limited potential, for it fails to engage the complexities of cultural, multicultural, and ecological conversations. Secondly, Keller offers an analysis of Christology, the "great thorn in the flesh" of Christian feminism, and criticizes Elisabeth Schüssler Fiorenza's tendency toward poststructuralist antireferentialism. Keller argues for the importance of affirming the referential power of language to describe a suffering world. Thirdly, the suppression of a nonandromorphic Spirit, with its fertile possibilities, under the *filioque* clause of the Western tradition allowed it "to flap around within . . . private pietisms," but disallowed it the possibility of reshaping "the operative epistemologies of mainline faith and culture."

Ada María Isasi-Díaz, representing the *mujerista* theology of Hispanic women engaged in primarily Roman Catholic liberation struggle, again makes the theme of community central. Like womanist theology, *mujerista* theology is strongly praxis-oriented, without any divorce between theological and sociopolitical concepts of liberation. Unlike more liberal theologies and sharing some of the sensitivities already met in Cone's chapter, Isasi-Díaz is comfortable with more traditional theological and scriptural language stemming from the community it-self, like sin, conversion, and revelation, but her *mujerista* reinterpretation repre-sents the pluralism resulting from the mixing of African, Amerindian, and European races into a pluriform multiethnic culture in North America. The em-bracing of racial diversity is understood ethically as virtue over against the sin of racism, liberation functioning as a moral norm. The professional *mujerista* the-ologian is understood as being in service to her community and its liberation, "rather than at the service of institutional churches." The communities have their own key religious figures which they celebrate, not only Christian but also African and Amerindian, and their own "way of knowing." Isasi-Díaz adopts Georgene Wilson's fine term *kin-dom* to redefine the concept of the kingdom of God in re-lational and nonpatriarchal terms.

Deconstructionist A/Theology

Derrida is the name most connected with the term *deconstruction*. Mark C. Taylor has carried many of Derrida's concerns and those of contemporary literary theory into his own very distinctive mode of theology which, following the death-of-God impulses of Nietzsche and, in the '60s, Thomas J. J. Altizer, he imagina-tively names *a/theology*. Taylor's approach is itself literary, embracing a playfulness with the ambiguities of language drawing theology toward a poetics in ways resembling both the late Heidegger and Derrida. "The End(s) of Theol-ogy" therefore plays on themes of death, of consummation, and of goal in the strange interstices between the theological proclamation of the death of God in the 1960s and the birth of liberation theologies and televangelists since then—a pe-riod of "disenchantment with disenchantment." Taylor remarks on the worldwide phenomenon of a reactionary fundamentalism as a search for sure foundations in an uncertain world. Their solution to modernism is erroneous, Taylor claims, and so he seeks another. Like Keller, he sees Barth's neoorthodoxy, his antifounda-tional *No!* to modernity as crucial to twentieth-century theology. And he sees Al-tizer's *No!* as a rejection of the transcendent God of Barthianism and as issuing in a new immanentism which has dominated theology since then, and which has cer-tainly been a central feature of the liberationist and feminist theologies discussed above. Liberal Protestant theologies would perhaps dispute Taylor's reading that immanental theological views had to await Altizer's appearance. They would more likely suggest that immanentism has been the central theological theme since Schleiermacher two hundred years ago, suffering only a temporary setback at the hands of Barth and neoorthodoxy. Nevertheless, Taylor seeks to explore the Der-ridean *unthought* between transcendence and immanence—a nondialectical third, which he calls *altarity*. But is this religion at all? he asks, and beginning with God as Alpha and Omega, he plunges into a/theology's struggle "to inscribe the failure of religion." Thus Taylor, the a/theological writer, "strives to restage the sacrifice of the Word" as part of a movement against the assertions of religious truth that erupt continually in the violence of mastery over otherness.[37] Many theologians of the past, including Barth, have engaged in linguistic play with the Johannine Logos doctrine, with Christ as preexistent Word and as Word incarnate, with the

Bible as the Word of God, with the synthesis of Christ and the scriptures as God's Word of truth. Similarly, written words are the incarnations of the spoken word, bearers of truth. Derrida's critique on logocentrism has been against oppression by the word, the assertions of truth which, as means of power, are strategies of mastery over otherness. Thus Taylor's attempt "to restage the sacrifice of the Word" can be read variously as an attempt to continue the sacrifice of Christ in order to bring redemption, as the need for Christianity to die in order that it might, in altered form, experience resurrection, as a sacrifice of religion's own mastery, its giving up of its own truth claims, as the necessary death of the failed god without resurrection—Taylor negates and attempts to avoid the Christian tendency to always negate the negation. Instead, he seeks to explore what lies beyond the possible end of theology.

AUTHORITY AND HERMENEUTICS

Too much will certainly have been left out of the account that this text attempts to provide. There are important theologians and ethicists left unmentioned. But comprehensiveness is impossible. One of the noticeable and perhaps disturbing features of contemporary theology is the number of independent claims made and reportedly owned by a particular school of thought which actually turn out to be much larger currents of thought shared by a variety of differing groups. Part of the sense of fragmentation could be diagnosed as a result of solipsism, whereby theologians are aware only of their own tribal group's theology, considering its discoveries quite unique.

As has already become apparent, the issue of authority is inscribed indelibly on all sides. Edward Farley speaks of the collapse of the house of authority and Linell Cady wonders whether theology's "new found freedom in relation to the past easily slips into an ahistorical isolation from all previous theological interpretations." But she simultaneously notes that evangelical feminist scholars like Virginia Ramey Mollenkott have concluded that a positivistic conception of revelation "inevitably sanctifies the patriarchal distortions of the ancient Near East."[38] Elisabeth Schüssler Fiorenza criticizes Mollenkott and Ruether for holding a neoorthodox orientation toward the authority of scriptural texts and instead suggests a move behind the texts to reconstruct the life situation from which the texts emerged. This is a hermeneutical move that many find unacceptable for various reasons. For narrative theologians this represents a characteristic modernist approach whereby the narrative itself is devalued and provides only the "stuff" for historical-critical constructions. This criticism is true for many liberationists too, who find in the narratives the powerful themes of deliverance and justice so vital to marginalized peoples. For propositional theologians the move behind the text tends to dismantle the value of the doctrines that are drawn from the text. Yet, propositionalists are criticized for using the texts instrumentally for the purpose of constructing propositional doctrines. For process and empirical theologians whose focus is not so scriptural, the historical reconstruction may simply be too tied to antiquarian powers of origin instead of being free to reconstruct according to the best knowledge available to us in the present.

Each of these positions represents a different approach to and use of authority, as mentioned above. Hermeneutical strategies thus become central to the problem. First, the subject matter that we consider important for interpretation, and then the methods we use to interpret that subject matter—both differ enormously among the theologies represented here. How do we weight the relative importance of scripture, tradition, reason, and experience, of different biblical themes, of different themes in the church's history, of how we even define reason or experience? Is there a correct weighting, is there a correct interpretative method? By what authority do we claim ours is the correct weighting or method? The multiplicity and complexity of the questions should at the very least cause us to argue our positions with a certain humility.

In the face of the complexity of arriving at shared meaning, Gadamer calls for the centrality of *conversation* between differing ideological positions. Each conversation partner is called on to maintain an openness to the other in the ethical face-to-face relationality of an *I* and a *thou* as the necessary condition within which truth can emerge. This book is an attempt to enrich conversation by providing competing voices that can speak truthfully of their own theological positions, to provoke further conversation among readers who will find voices here with which they are in concert and others that may appear entirely cacophonous. Augustine calls for a hermeneutics of charity: perhaps truth will emerge far more fully within theology as each theologian subjects his or her hermeneutics of retrieval and suspicion to a Christian hermeneutics of charity. Only this, it seems to me, can overcome the either/or mentalities that so many theologies seek to overcome in theory, yet which cling to us like old habits. Augustine, after all, hardly applied a hermeneutics of charity to the Donatists and the Pelagians.

NOTES

1. Paul Ricoeur, *Interpretation Theory: Discourse and the Surplus of Meaning* (Fort Worth, Tex.: Christian University Press, 1976), 44.
2. Augustine, *De Trinitate* 3. 10–11.
3. Ibid., 1–2 and passim.
4. Ibid., 1.
5. Abraham Heschel, "The Meaning of This Hour," in *Man's Quest for God: Studies in Prayer and Symbolism* (New York: Charles Scribner's Sons, 1954), 150.
6. Paul Ricoeur, *Hermeneutics and the Human Sciences*, ed. and trans. John B. Thompson (Cambridge: Cambridge University Press, 1981), 185.
7. For a reading of Schleiermacher's 1799 *Speeches to the Cultured Despisers of Religion*, see Roger A. Badham, "World Spirit and the Appearing of the God: Philosophy of Religion and Christian Apologetic in Schleiermacher's Early Thought," *New Athenaeum* 5 (Summer 1997).
8. See chapter 2, below, for an exploration of these possibilities in depth.
9. For example, John Richard Neuhaus and Leon Klenicki, *Believing Today: Jew and Christian in Conversation* (Grand Rapids: Wm. B. Eerdmans Publishing Co., 1989).

10. Judith Plaskow, "Christian Feminism and Anti-Judaism," *Cross Currents* (Fall 1978): 59–75, cited in John T. Pawlikowski, O.S.M., "Christology, Anti-Semitism, and Christian-Jewish Bonding," in *Reconstructing Christian Theology,* ed. Rebecca S. Chopp and Mark L. Taylor (Minneapolis: Fortress Press, 1994), 245–68, esp. p. 250.

11. See Clark Williamson, *A Guest in the House of Israel: Post-Holocaust Church Theology* (Louisville, Ky.: Westminster/John Knox Press, 1993), 218–19.

12. Schubert Ogden, *The Reality of God* (New York: Harper & Row, 1966) quoted in Williamson, *A Guest in the House of Israel,* 221.

13. See Paul M. van Buren, "A Theology of the Jewish-Christian Reality," part 2 of *A Christian Theology of the People Israel* (San Francisco: Harper & Row, 1983).

14. H. Richard Niebuhr, *The Responsible Self* (New York: Harper & Row, 1963), 126.

15. John S. Spong, "Sing the Lord's Song in This Strange Land," *The Voice* 43:5 (June 1995).

16. H. Richard Niebuhr, *The Meaning of Revelation* (New York: Macmillan Co., 1941).

17. For Christian theologians other than Williamson paying attention to the Holocaust, see works by Paul van Buren and Peter Haas, *Morality after Auschwitz: The Radical Challenge of the Nazi Ethic* and Darrell J. Fasching, *Narrative Theology after Auschwitz: From Alienation to Ethics.* From a Jewish theological perspective, Marc H. Ellis, *Ending Auschwitz: The Future of Jewish and Christian Life* and *Unholy Alliance: Religion and Atrocity in Our Time.*

18. Apart from the evangelical writers represented in this text, see works by conservatives Richard Lints and David Wells and more moderate evangelicals, Stanley Grenz, Mark Noll, Elizabeth Achtemeier, Richard Mouw, Gabriel Fackre, and Anthony Thiselton.

19. Clark A. Pinnock, *Tracking the Maze: Finding Our Way through Modern Theology from an Evangelical Perspective* (New York: Harper & Row, 1990), 161. For a discussion of Pinnock's book, see Roger A. Badham, "Infirma Terra," *Harvard Divinity Bulletin* 20:4 (1990–1991): 22–23.

20. Hans-Georg Gadamer, *Truth and Method,* 2d rev. ed., trans. Joel Weinsheimer and Donald G. Marshall (New York: Continuum, 1994), 272.

21. Writers who fall in this broad category include the late Hans Frei, George Lindbeck, Ronald F. Thiemann, Alasdair MacIntyre, William Placher, George Hunsinger, L. Gregory Jones, Nancey Murphey, David Burrell, Kathryn Tanner, William Willimon, Robert Wilken, and James McClendon. From a Jewish perspective, see works by Peter Ochs.

22. Stanley Hauerwas, Richard Bondi, and David Burrell, *Truthfulness and Tragedy* (Notre Dame, Ind.: University of Notre Dame Press, 1977), 25; cited in James Wm. McClendon, *Ethics: Systematic Theology* (Nashville: Abingdon Press, 1986), 1:334.

23. George A. Lindbeck's *The Nature of Doctrine: Religion and Theology in a Postliberal World* (Philadelphia: Westminster Press, 1984) is a key work for understanding contemporary cultural-linguistic postliberal theology.

24. For a nuanced discussion of nineteenth-century conflicts over Catholic Americanization, see R. Laurence Moore's account in his *Religious Outsiders and the Making of Americans* (Oxford: Oxford University Press, 1986).

25. For a comparison of Newman and Gadamer, see two recent studies, Joseph Dunne's remarkable *Back to the Rough Ground: "Phronesis" and "Techne" in Modern Philosophy and in Aristotle* (Notre Dame, Ind.: University of Notre Dame Press, 1993); and Thomas K. Carr, *Newman and Gadamer: Toward a Hermeneutics of Religious Knowledge* (Atlanta: Scholars Press, 1996).

26. See, for example, Catherine Keller's rejection of *ecclesiocentrism* in chapter 16, below.

27. James M. Gustafson, "A Response to Critics," *Journal of Religious Ethics* 13:2 (Fall 1985): 185–209; quote, p. 196.

28. Stanley Hauerwas, *Dispatches from the Front: Theological Engagements with the Secular* (Durham, N.C.: Duke University Press, 1993).

29. More conservative American Roman Catholic approaches can be found by the late Cardinal Bernardin, Cardinal O'Connor, and Richard John Neuhaus.

30. Other leading process theologians include David Ray Griffin, Lewis Ford, Charles Birch, Ian Barbour, Schubert Ogden, and Catholic theologian Ewart Cousins. Huston Smith is also strongly influenced by Whitehead's thought. Cobb's typology includes process thought under the larger rubric of empirical theology, so many theologians may be described under either.

31. John B. Cobb Jr., *Is It Too Late?* and, with Charles Birch, *The Liberation of Life: From the Cell to the Community* (Cambridge: Cambridge University Press, 1981). Ecotheologians from a variety of perspectives include Rosemary Radford Ruether, Catherine Keller, Dieter Hessel, William Gibson, James M. Gustafson, Sallie McFague, Paul H. Santmire, Matthew Fox, Wesley Granberg-Michaelson, Larry Rasmussen, Jay McDaniel, and Wendell Berry. See also Roger A. Badham, "Images of Creation: An Ecological Theology," in *Becoming Persons*, ed. Robert N. Fisher (Oxford: Applied Theology Press, 1994).

32. For an analysis of Corrington's ecstatic naturalism, see Roger A. Badham, "Windows on the Ecstatic: Reflections on Robert Corrington's Theonomous Naturalism," *Soundings* (forthcoming).

33. Other empirical theologians include Randolph Crump Miller, William Dean, Bernard Lee, Tyron Inbody, Marjorie Hewitt Suchocki, and Frederick Ferré.

34. William James, quoted in *Empirical Theology: A Handbook,* ed. Randolph Crump Miller (Birmingham, Ala.: Religious Education Press, 1992), 3.

35. African American liberationist theologians not mentioned in the text include, for example, Garth Baker-Fletcher and Peter J. Paris and womanist theologians Cheryl J. Sanders and Katie Cannon; see also *Stony the Road We Trod*, edited by Cain Hope Felder. Feminist theologians include Virginia Ramey Mollenkott, Phyllis Trible, Susan Brooks Thistlethwaite, Mary McClintock Fulkerson, Kathleen Sands, Sharon Welch, Constance Buchanan, Rosemary Radford Ruether, and Sallie McFague. Not surprisingly, these women's writings represent a wide spectrum of theological positions, but their theologies are approached from a distinctly feminist perspective which is an irreducible part of their theology, hence the importance of feminism as a general category.

36. Fumitaka Matsuoka, *Out of Silence: Emerging Themes in Asian American Churches* (Cleveland: Pilgrim Press, 1995), 64.

37. Other deconstructionist, poststructuralist, or a/theological writers include Gary Phillips, Stephen D. Moore, Frank Kermode, and Robert Scharlemann.

38. Linell Cady, "Hermeneutics and Tradition: The Role of the Past in Jurisprudence and Theology," *Harvard Theological Review* 79:4 (1986): 439–63; quotes, pp. 440, 451. She mentions the importance for this discussion of theologians Hans Frei, Gordon Kaufman, Edward Farley, van Harvey, and David Tracy and moral philosopher Alasdair MacIntyre.

2

THE THEOLOGICAL CHALLENGE OF RELIGIOUS PLURALISM

JOHN HICK

In our own time a new challenge to the structure of Christian belief has come from our awareness, not merely of the existence of the other great world faiths—there is nothing new about that—but of their spiritual and moral power. The challenge is to the traditional assumption of the unique superiority of the Christian gospel, or faith, or religion. If I am right, we are in the early stages of an adjustment that may take another fifty or more years. This is the transition from a view of Christianity as the one and only true religion to a new Christian self-understanding as one true religion among others. This will certainly mean a considerable restructuring of Christian theology.

I shall for the most part confine what I say here about other religions to the *great world faiths*, meaning those traditions that have existed for upward of a thousand years, which have profound scriptures and have produced great saints and thinkers, and which have provided the foundations of civilization for many millions of people. Oral primal traditions, and the many smaller and newer religions, and also the modern secular faiths, are not intrinsically less important, but in the case of the great world religions one can assume a certain common background of knowledge that can facilitate discussion. If we can achieve a viable Christian view here, it will then be easier to cope with the further problems posed by the yet wider religious life of the world.

Christians have, of course, always been aware of other religions. However, during the second half of the present century a new kind of awareness has developed. The cause that I would single out here has been the large-scale immigration from the East to the West, bringing millions of Muslims, Sikhs, Hindus, Taoists, and Buddhists into a number of European and North American cities. The population of the Los Angeles area, for example, includes the third largest Jewish community in the world, the biggest Buddhist temple in North America, supported by a large Buddhist population, and quite large Muslim and Hindu, and smaller Sikh and Taoist, communities. And when one meets some of one's neighbors of these other faiths, and gets to know individuals and families, and is invited to their weddings and festivals and community events, one discovers that, while there are all manner of fascinating cultural differences, Muslims and Jews and Hindus and Sikhs and Buddhists in general do not seem to be less honest and truthful, or less loving and compassionate in family and community, or less good citizens, or less religiously committed, than are one's Christian neighbors in general. The ordinary people of these other faiths do not generally seem to be better human beings, morally and spiritually, than Christians, but neither do they seem to be worse human beings. Further, reading a fair amount of the literature of these other faiths, and encountering several outstanding individuals of the kind whom we call saints, confirms the impression that these other traditions are, to about the same extent as Christianity, contexts of a salvific human transformation from natural self-centeredness to a new orientation centered in the divine or the transcendent. And, although this is another dimension of the subject which there is not time to go into here, I think we have to conclude that the civilizations in which these faiths have been expressed, although very different, have been more or less on a par with Christendom as regards their moral and spiritual fruits.[1]

I appreciate that these last statements can be contested. Indeed, probably most Christians assume as a matter of course that Christian religious life and Christian civilization exhibit a manifest superiority. Rather than debate this here, I would like to focus attention on the procedural issue. Just as it has been asked whether Christianity stands or falls by historical evidence concerning that which of the Gospel accounts of Jesus, so also it can be asked whether it stands or falls by historical evidence concerning the moral quality of Christian civilization. And I imagine that just as there have been theologians (such as Kierkegaard, Barth, Tillich, Bultmann) for whom knowledge about the historical Jesus does not affect the core of their faith, so also there will be theologians for whom the superiority of Christianity is accepted a priori, without depending on historical evidence.

Indeed, such an a priori judgment comes very naturally to us all. It is where we most naturally start. But it evokes a "hermeneutic of suspicion," arising from the fact that in perhaps 99 percent of cases the religion to which one adheres (or which one specifically rejects) is selected by the accident of birth. When someone is born into a devout Muslim family in Pakistan or Egypt or Indonesia, it will nearly always be a safe bet that he or she will become a Muslim, either observant or nonobservant. When someone is born into a devout Christian family in Italy or Mexico, it will nearly always be a safe bet that he or she will become a Catholic Christian, again either observant or nonobservant. And so on. And of course it normally seems obvious that the religion that has been part of one from infancy is normative and basically superior to all others.

This relativity of religious conviction to the circumstances of birth and upbringing is so obvious that we seldom stop to think about it. But it nevertheless has immense significance. If there is a religious "plus," a spiritual gain, advantage, benefit, in being a Christian rather than a Jew, Muslim, Hindu, or Buddhist, then there is a corresponding "minus," a spiritual loss or disadvantage, in being a Buddhist, Hindu, Muslim, or Jew. It then becomes a proper question why only a minority of the human race, something like one-fifth, have been awarded this religious "plus." For if the "plus" is a reality, divine providence has favored those born into a Christian society over those born in non-Christian countries. And the greater the religious "plus" for Christians, the greater the "minus" for everyone else and the greater the discrimination that needs to be accounted for in our theology. Should we conclude that we who have been born within the reach of the gospel are God's chosen people, objects of a greater divine love than the rest of the human race? But then, on the other hand, do we not believe that God loves *all* God's creatures with an equal and unlimited love?

There is obviously a problem here, and yet it is very rare to find it discussed. I am aware of only two responses to it. One is to stress the imperative of evangelization, the duty to bring all humankind to enjoy the religious "plus" of knowing Christ. But the general failure of the Christian mission to Jews, Muslims, Hindus, and Buddhists leaves the original problem very largely intact. (The Christian population of the entire Indian subcontinent, for example, after two hundred years of fairly intensive missionary activity, is about 2.5 percent.) The other response is the horrific suggestion, based on the concept of middle knowledge—the idea of a divine knowledge of what everyone would freely do in all possible circumstances—that God knows concerning all those who lack any real access to the Christian gospel that they would reject it if they heard it. They thus deserve the religious "minus" under which they suffer, which, according to the evangelical Christian philosophers who propound this theory, consists of eternal damnation.[2] This theory declares completely a priori that each one of the hundreds of millions of men and women in each generation who have lived without knowledge of the Christian gospel are depraved sinners who would have rejected it if they had heard it. This is a priori dogma carried to terrifying lengths.

Suppose, then, we accept (1) that most of us are not Christians as a result of a deliberate choice resulting from a comprehensive study and evaluation of the religions of the world, but because we were born into a Christian rather than some other society; and (2) that the moral and spiritual fruits of faith seem to be more or less on a par within the different world religions. The question that I am then raising is, How should this affect our inherited Christian belief-system?

It might at this point be said that our belief-system has already been adjusted to take account of all this. The older exclusivist position was, in its Roman version, that outside the church there is no salvation or, in its Protestant version, that outside Christ (that is, outside a personal faith in Christ as our Lord and Savior) there is no salvation. But through the discussions and debates of the last thirty or so years a new majority consensus has emerged, which is generally known as Christian inclusivism. This is both continuous and discontinuous with the previous exclusivism. The continuity is in the claim that salvation is, exclusively, Christian salvation, made possible solely by the atoning death of Jesus. The new element however, the discontinuity, is in the claim that this Christian salvation is not limited to Christians but is available to all human beings without restriction.

I should perhaps remind us at this point that the question of salvation for non-Christians as well as Christians is distinct from the question of universal or restricted salvation, which is not the issue here. The inclusivist position is that all who are saved, whether they constitute the whole human race or only part thereof, are saved by Christ, but that this is not dependent on their accepting Jesus as their Lord and Savior, at least not in this life.

INCLUSIVIST TYPE OF THEOLOGY

This inclusivist type of theology of religions takes three forms. The first (in the arbitrary order in which I shall discuss them) is based on the idea developed within Catholic thinking of implicit faith, or the baptism of desire, the idea that at least some individuals of other faiths, and indeed of no faith, may be so rightly disposed in their hearts that they *would* respond to the Christian gospel if it were properly presented to them. But they have in fact never encountered it, or only in inadequate ways, and have thus had no real opportunity to respond to it. Such people, who may be said to have an implicit faith in Christ, have been dubbed by Karl Rahner anonymous Christians. Only God knows who they are; but we can at least know that non-Christians who in their hearts sincerely desire to know the truth and to serve the good are not excluded from salvation by the fact that, through no fault of their own, they are not presently Christians. This was the view of some of the early church fathers concerning persons who lived before Christ. But Rahner and others have now gone farther in applying this principle to people of the other world religions since the time of Christ. Not only those who lived B.C.E. (Before the Common Era), but also non-Christians today, may be anonymous Christians.

The second form of inclusivism holds that salvation does require a conscious personal faith in Christ but that although this is not possible for hundreds of millions in the present life, it will be possible in or beyond death. Thus the devout Muslim living, let us say, in Pakistan and insulated from the gospel by a powerful Islamic faith, will encounter Christ after or in the moment of death and will thus have an opportunity to receive salvation.

Among contemporary Catholic theologians perhaps the most explicit recent expression of this idea is Father J. A. Dinoia's "Christian theology of religions in a prospective vein."[3] Father Dinoia, who is the secretary for doctrine and pastoral practice of the National Conference of Catholic Bishops in the United States, rejects Rahner's suggestion that some non-Christians can now, in this present life, be accepted as having an implicit faith in virtue of which they are anonymous Christians. "Rather," he says, "than attributing an implausible implicit faith in Christ to the members of other religious communities, theology of religions in a prospective vein contends that non-Christians will have the opportunity to acknowledge Christ in the future. This opportunity," he says, "may come to them in the course of their present lives here on earth or in the course of their entrance into the life to come."[4] And he invokes the doctrine of purgatory, adding that the interval in which the necessary purification or transformation takes place "may be thought of as instantaneous and coterminous with death."[5] Thus, he says, "The doctrine of purgatory permits Christians a wide measure of confidence about the salvation of non-Christians."[6]

Among Protestant theologians George Lindbeck is probably the most influential proponent of what he calls "an eschatologically futuristic perspective."[7] Like Dinoia, he is critical of the Rahnerian idea of implicit faith. He speaks of "the temptation to religious pretentiousness or imperialism implicit in the notion that non-Christians are anonymously Christians,"[8] and says that, "saving faith cannot be wholly anonymous, wholly implicit, but must be in the same measure explicit: it comes, as Paul puts it, *ex auditu*, from hearing."[9] His alternative theory is eschatological. "The proposal is," he says, "that dying itself be pictured as the point at which every human being is ultimately and expressly confronted by the gospel, by the crucified and risen Lord. It is only then that the final decision is made for or against Christ; and this is true not only of unbelievers but also of believers. . . . Thus it is possible to be hopeful and trusting about the ultimate salvation of non-Christians no less than Christians."[10]

The difference between the theories, on the one hand of the prospective or eschatological salvation of non-Christians, and on the other hand of their present anonymous salvation, is however not as great as it might seem. For Rahner also presumably holds that ultimately the implicit faith of the anonymous Christian will become explicit. I shall therefore not play these two kinds of inclusivism off against each other but shall bracket them together in the composite view that (1) salvation is in Christ alone, and (2) non-Christians may nevertheless receive this salvation by being related to Christ either implicitly in this life and explicitly beyond it or, as an alternative version, only explicitly and beyond this life.

It is to be noted that this kind of inclusivism, in either form, does not regard other religions as such as channels of salvation, but is a theory about individuals within them. A third form of inclusivism, however, validates those religions themselves as alternative mediators or contexts of salvation; and this is a large step closer to the position at which I think we must eventually arrive. But before coming to that, let me comment on the individualistic inclusivism of the "anonymous Christians" and the eschatological salvation theories.

The appeal of inclusivism is, of course, that it retains the unique centrality of Christ as the sole source of salvation, and yet at the same time avoids the morally repugnant idea that God consigns to perdition the majority of the human race, who have not accepted Jesus as their Lord and Savior. It is thus a comfortable and comforting package, enabling Christianity to go on regarding itself as superior while at the same time being charitable to the people of other religions.

But there are nevertheless two problems. One is its sheer arbitrariness. I referred earlier to the "hermeneutic of suspicion" evoked by the presumed centrality and normativeness of the religion into which one was born. If I, who was born in England and who as a student experienced an evangelical Christian conversion, had instead been born in India or Egypt or Tibet, my religious awakening would almost certainly have taken a Hindu or a Muslim or a Buddhist form. Of course this is a misleading way to put it, because it would not then be the same I, since we are all so largely formed by our surrounding culture, including our religious culture. But when someone, anyone, is born as an Indian or an Egyptian or a Tibetan the belief-system that he or she internalizes will very likely not be Christian but Hindu, Muslim, or Buddhist, as the case may be. And just as it seems obvious to most devout Christians, without any argument being needed, that their familiar Christian set of beliefs is true and any incompatible beliefs therefore false, so likewise it seems obvious to devout people of the other world religions that *their* inherited beliefs are true and any incompatible beliefs false. They can also, if they wish, fit sincere and devout Christians into their own belief-system as anonymous Hindus, Muslims, or Buddhists, or as to be converted to one of those faiths beyond death, as indeed some of the thinkers of these traditions do. But is not the sheer arbitrariness of this procedure, whoever is using it, glaringly evident?

One can of course "bite the bullet" and say, Yes, it is arbitrary; but why not? It so happens that the beliefs that were instilled into me by my Christian upbringing are true, while those instilled into Hindus, Muslims, Buddhists, and so on, insofar as they are incompatible with mine, are false. As Karl Barth wrote, "The Christian religion is true, because it has pleased God, who alone can be the judge in this matter, to affirm it to be the true religion."[11] This is a theological cover for the fact that, having been brought up as a Christian, Barth assumed that Christian revelation is revelation and that other "revelations" are not. And if this seems unilaterally dogmatic in a way that is difficult to defend rationally, one can add that happily the situation is not as harsh as it might seem, because we can believe that God is also able in the end to save by some indirect route those who presently lack the one true revelation.

This kind of armor-plated belief-system is logically invulnerable. What we normally do when faced with someone else's armor-plated conviction is to look at its practical fruits. In the case of major world religions, we have to make discriminations, recognizing both good and evil elements. Some Christian beliefs, for example, have in the course of history proved extremely harmful to others. Thus the belief that the Jewish people are guilty of deicide authorized the medieval persecution of the Jews and created a prejudice that continued in the secular anti-Semitism of the nineteenth and twentieth centuries, culminating in the Nazi Holocaust of the 1940s. The belief, during the European wars of religion, that Protestants, or Catholics, are heretics who have forfeited divine grace, validated slaughter on a massive scale. The belief that white Christian colonists stood on superior religious ground to that of the pagan natives of what today we call the third world, and were accordingly justified in conquering them, validated their enslavement and the exploitation of their natural and human resources. The belief that, because Jesus and his apostles were all men, women cannot serve the church as ordained priests, still continues to validate the ecclesiastical oppression of women. And similar discriminations have to be made within each of the other great world faiths. The belief that the caste system of India is divinely ordained; the belief that God has given the entire area of Israel and Palestine to the Jewish people; the belief that God demands the death of Salman Rushdie, are obvious examples of beliefs that validate evil. Thus while claims to be the sole possessors of the truth may start out as pure and innocent, they can all too easily become a cloak for human prejudice and self-interest, and their arbitrariness properly evokes, as I have suggested, a "hermeneutic of suspicion." In the case, to take recent examples, of such cults as the People's Temple of the 1978 Jonestown mass suicide, or the Branch Davidians of the 1993 Waco massacre, or the Order of the Solar Temple of the 1994 Swiss mass suicide, the fruits were manifestly evil, and we condemn their arbitrary dogmatism.

The other main criticism of Christian inclusivism turns on what we mean by salvation. If this means being forgiven and accepted by God because of the atoning death of Jesus, then salvation is by definition Christian salvation and it is a tautology that Christianity alone knows and proclaims its possibility. Either an exclusivist or an inclusivist theology of religions then becomes virtually inevitable. But suppose we think of salvation in a much more concrete and empirically observable way as an actual change in men and women from natural self-centeredness to, in theistic terms, God-centeredness, or in more general terms, a new orientation centered in the Ultimate, the Real, as conceived and experienced within one's own tradition. Salvation in this sense is the central concern of each of the great world religions. Within Christianity it is conceptualized and experienced as the state in which Paul could say, "It is no longer I who live, but Christ who lives in me" (Gal. 2:20, RSV). Within Judaism it is conceived and experienced as the joy and responsibility of life lived in accordance with God's Torah. Within Islam it is conceived and experienced as a personal self-surrender to God in a life lived according to God's revealed commands. With Advaitic Hinduism it is conceived and experienced as a transcending of the ego and discovery of unity with the eternal reality of Brahman. Within Buddhism it is conceived and experienced as a loss of the ego point of view in a discovery of the Buddha nature of the universal interdependent process of which we are all part. And in each case this transformation of human existence from self-centeredness to Reality-centeredness is reached by a moral and spiritual path. The Golden Rule is taught by all the great traditions, as are love and compassion, justice and fair dealing, and a special concern for the vulnerable—in the societies within which the scriptures were produced, the widows and orphans. Within Buddhism, for example, much of the Noble Eightfold Path to enlightenment is ethical, including among its requirements kindness, truthfulness, abstaining from stealing, from dishonesty, from cheating, from illegitimate sexual intercourse, from intoxication, and from earning one's living by trading in arms or by killing animals. And each of the other world religions has its own overlapping though not identical moral requirements.

So if we understand by salvation the transition to a life centered in the Divine, the Ultimate, the Real, we can properly look about us for the signs of it. To what extent is this transformation actually taking place among Christians, among Jews, among Muslims, among Hindus, among Buddhists? I suggest that, so far as we can tell, it is taking place to much the same extent within each of these traditions. It is true that we have no organized evidence or statistics to establish this. But we can properly put the issue the other way round. If anyone asserts that Christians in general are morally and spiritually better human beings than Jews, Muslims, Hindus, or Buddhists in general, the onus is on them to produce the evidence for this. It cannot simply be affirmed a priori, without regard to the concrete realities of human life.

My conclusion, then, so far is that the salvific transformation seems to be taking place more or less equally within all the great world religions, including Christianity, and that for any one of them to assert that it alone is the source of this change within all the others is an arbitrary claim that cannot be refuted but on the other hand cannot be rationally justified.

But there is also a third kind of inclusivism. This goes farther than the other two in speaking, not only of non-Christian individuals, but of the other world faiths as such. It sees the divine Logos, or cosmic Christ, or Holy Spirit as at work within these other religious histories. It holds that God, whether as second or third member of the Holy Trinity, has been and is savingly present within them. There are different ways of developing this thought. One is the Christocentric version, which gave rise to the idea of the unknown Christ of Hinduism, and likewise by implication the unknown Christ of Islam, and so on. Since Hinduism and Buddhism (and also Taoism, Confucianism, Zoroastrianism, and Jainism) all long predate Christianity, the Christ who has been at work within them from the beginning cannot be the God-man Jesus, but must be the cosmic Christ or eternal Logos who later became incarnate as Jesus of Nazareth. And so we are in effect talking about a worldwide and history-long divine presence to and within the religious life of humanity, while insisting that this be named and thought of in exclusively Christian terms. The inevitable criticism of this insistence is, once again, its arbitrary and religiously imperialistic character. To claim that Christ is the real though hidden source of saving grace within other religions is a way of asserting the unique centrality of one's own tradition. The hermeneutic of suspicion that I referred to earlier is inevitably brought into play here.

The other version is the much more radical idea that the same God who saves Christians through their response to the incarnate Christ also saves Jews through their response to the Torah, and saves Muslims through their response to the Qur'an, and saves Hindus through their response to the Vedic revelation and the various streams of religious experience to which it has given rise, and saves Buddhists through their response to the Dharma. This view validates the other world religions as alternative channels or contexts of divine salvation. One can then stress their complementarity, and the possibility that they may in the future converge as a result of friendly dialogue.

There are two comments to be made about this more promising theory. The first is a clarification. The test question for this position is whether it involves a renunciation of the missionary ideal of converting Jews, Muslims, Hindus, Buddhists to Christianity. Does it entail the conclusion that there is an equal possibility of salvation within whichever of the great world religions one has been born into, so that there is no salvific "plus" in being a Christian rather than a Jew or a Muslim, for example? If it does not accept this implication, then it is only an elaborate maneuver for preserving belief in the unique superiority of Christianity. But if it does entail a renunciation of that supposed religious superiority, it then comes close to the kind of pluralism that I want to recommend.

There is, however, at this point a qualification to be made to the idea that no religious "plus" is involved in being born into one rather than another of the great world faiths. Each tradition has its own distinctive religious "pluses" and "minuses," for each is a different and unique mixture of good and evil. But this fact does not amount to one of these complex mixtures' being superior as a totality to the others. If any of them claims this for itself, that claim must be established by objective evidence. Nevertheless, for the individual who has been spiritually formed by a particular tradition, that tradition does normally have an overall "plus." For our religion creates us in its own image, so that it fits us and we fit it as no other can. It is thus for us the best, truest, most naturally acceptable faith, within which we rightly remain. This is the point made by Ernst Troeltsch, at the beginning of the modern discussion of the problems of religious plurality, when he said, "We cannot live without a religion, yet the only religion that we can endure is Christianity, for Christianity has grown up with us and has become a part of our very being."[12] There are, of course, and will always be, individual conversions in all directions, for individual reasons. But broadly speaking we do best to live within the religion that has formed us, though with an awareness that the same holds for those who have been formed by a different tradition from our own.

My other comment on the idea that the Christian God is at work saving people through the medium of each of the world religions is that it does not take adequate account of the nontheistic traditions, most particularly Buddhism. If we are to proceed inductively from the actual religious experience of humanity, rather than deductively from an arbitrarily adopted premise, then we must see theism as one form, but not the only form, of religious thought and experience. And if we accept that the fruits in human life of Buddhist faith are on a par with the fruits of the monotheistic faiths, we have to expand our theory to take account of this fact.

Such an expanded understanding of religion has been forming in many minds during the last seventy or so years and has come to be known as religious pluralism. This is the view that the great world faiths, both theistic and nontheistic, are different culturally formed responses to the Ultimate, and thus independently valid channels or contexts of the salvific human transformation. The general conception is ancient and widespread—from the basic Vedic declaration that "the Real [sat] is one, but sages name it variously";[13] to the edicts of the Buddhist emperor Ashoka affirming and supporting all the religions of his empire; to the Sufis of Islam, with Rumi, for example, saying of the religions of his time, "The lamps are different, but the Light is the same";[14] to the Christian Nicholas of Cusa's statement that "there is only one religion in the variety of rites."[15] The problem comes when we try to spell out this basic insight in a philosophically coherent way. Some who take a broadly pluralist view think that it is not possible, or not necessary, or not desirable to spell it out. There are indeed many good Christians who in practice treat people of other religions on the implicit basis that it is perfectly acceptable in the sight of God for them to be, and to remain, Jews, Muslims, Hindus, or Buddhists, but who shrink from making explicit the implications of this. If they are ecclesiastical officials, they probably do so to avoid controversy and division within the church. If they are lay people, they probably shrink from it because it would be unacceptable to the church leaders. All this is readily understandable. We are in an interim situation in which theological theory lags behind our practical religious insights. But it is the task of Christian theologians and philosophers to think through the implications of these insights. And so as a contribution to this I will now very briefly outline a positive suggestion.

A POSITIVE SUGGESTION

This rests on two basic principles. One is the view, widespread in philosophy since Kant, and confirmed by cognitive psychology and the sociology of knowledge, that consciousness is not a passive reception of the impacts of our environment but always an active process of selecting, ordering, integrating, and endowing with meaning in accordance with our human systems of concepts. I suggest that this applies to awareness of our divine, or supranatural, environment as well as of our physical environment. The other basic principle is consequent on this: the discussion between something as it is in itself, independently of human observation, and as it appears to us, with our specifically human perceptual equipment and conceptual resources. This also, I suggest, applies to our awareness of the Ultimate.

To avoid using a string of alternative terms, such as the Divine, the Transcendent, the Ultimate, Ultimate Reality, the Real, I shall arbitrarily employ the last. The distinction then is between, on the one hand, the Real in itself and, on the other hand, the Real as variously conceived and experienced and responded to within the different world religions. There fall into two main groups. One group thinks of the Real in personal terms, as a great transcendent Thou, further specified as the Adonai of Judaism, or more complexly as the Holy Trinity of Christianity, or as the Allah of Islam, or as the Vishnu or Shiva of theistic Hinduism, and so on. The other thinks of the Real in nonpersonal terms, as Brahman, or the Tao, or the dharmakaya, and so on. According to this pluralistic hypothesis, the status of the various God-figures is as personae of the Real, that is, the Real as variously perceived by the personifying human mind, while the various nonpersonal absolutes are *im personae* of the Real, that is, the Real as variously manifested in nonpersonal terms to a nonpersonifying religious mentality. Both are joint products of the universal presence of the Real above, below, around, and within us, together with the distinctive set of concepts and accompanying spiritual practices of a particular religious tradition.

The Real in itself lies beyond the range of our entire network of concepts, other than purely formal ones. We therefore cannot experience it as it is in itself but only as we conceptualize it in our human terms, organizing its impact on us in a particular form of religious experience. The religious traditions thus stand between us and the Real, constituting different "lenses" through which we are aware of it. As Thomas Aquinas wrote, in a foreshadowing of the Kantian insight, "Things known are in the knower according to the mode of the knower."[16] And in relation to the Real or the Divine the mode of the knower is differently formed within the different religious traditions.

Here, then, are the bare bones of a pluralistic hypothesis. It is open, as probably all large-scale hypotheses are, to a variety of objections, and I will now in conclusion look briefly at a few of these.

First, is not the concept of the ineffable Real so featureless as to be redundant, incapable of doing any work? Reply: The concept of the Real does do vital work. For the Real is that which there must be if religious experience in its variety of forms is not purely imaginative projection but a response to a transcendent reality. The difference between affirming and not affirming the Real is the difference between a religious and a naturalistic interpretation of religion in its variety of forms.

But, second, how can we worship the noumenal Real? Surely an object of worship must have some definite characteristics, such as being good, loving, and so on. Reply: We do not worship the Real in its infinite transcendent nature, beyond the scope of our human categories, but the Real as humanly thought and experienced within our own tradition. In religious practice we relate ourselves to a particular "face" or appearance or manifestation of the ultimate divine reality.

But, third, do not the different traditions make many mutually contradictory truth claims—that the divine reality is personal, that it is nonpersonal; that it is unitary, that it is triune; and so on? Reply: These different and incompatible truth claims are claims about different manifestations of the Real to humanity. As such they do not contradict one another. That one group conceives and experiences the Real in one way is not incompatible with another group's conceiving and experiencing the Real in another way, each described in its own theology. There is contradiction only if we assume that there can be only one authentic manifestation of the Real to humanity.

Fourth, in seeing the various objects of worship and foci of religious contemplation as not being themselves ultimate, but appearances of the ultimate to human consciousness, does not this hypothesis contradict the self-understanding of each of the religions? And is this not gross presumption? The reply here is a counterquestion: Does not the traditional Christian view contradict the self-understanding of every religion except itself? And is it not a lesser presumption to apply the same principle to one's own religion also?

Fifth, on what basis can we judge that the figure of the Heavenly Father, for example, is indeed an authentic manifestation of the Real? Answer: On the basis of its capacity to promote the salvific transformation of human life.

But then, sixth, if we say that the figure of the Heavenly Father is a manifestation of the Real because it is salvific, and that it is salvific because it is a manifestation of the Real, are we not moving in a circle? Reply: Yes, the hypothesis is ultimately circular, as indeed every comprehensive hypothesis must be. The circle is entered, in this case, by the faith that human religious experience is not purely imaginative projection but is also a response to a transcendent reality. The hypothesis should be judged by its comprehensiveness, its internal consistency, and its adequacy to the data—in this case, the data of the history of religions.

But, seventh, surely in denying that the Real in itself is personal, is one not asserting that it is nonpersonal, and thus arriving at a Hindu or Buddhist conclusion? Reply: The suggestion is more radical than that, namely, that these dualisms of human thought—personal/impersonal, good/bad, substance/process, and so on—do not apply to the Real in itself. Its nature is beyond the scope of our human conceptual systems.

Eighth, so the Real is not properly thought of as being good or loving? Reply: No, these human concepts do not apply to the Real in itself. But we have found, within all the great world religions, that the Real is good, or benign, from our human point of view, as the ground of our highest good, which is the transformed state that we speak of as eternal life, or nirvana, or moksha, and so on.

Ninth, can we not, however, modify the ineffability of the Real in itself by saying that it has analogous attributes to those of its *personae* and *impersonae*? Thus, if the Heavenly Father of Christian belief is an authentic manifestation of the Real, must not the Real in itself be loving and fatherlike, at least in an analogous sense? The reply is again a counterquestion: What could it mean for the Real to be both analogically personal and analogically nonpersonal, both analogically conscious and analogically not conscious, both analogically purposive and analogically not purposive, both analogically a substance and analogically a nonsubstantial process? Would this not be a mass of contradictions? If, however, these mutually incompatible attributes are attributes of different manifestations of the Real to human consciousness, the contradictions disappear.

Tenth, why postulate *one* Real? The different religions report different realities, so why not affirm all of them? Reply: For two reasons. One is the difficulty of making sense of the relationship between a plurality of ultimates. Does the Holy Trinity preside over Christian countries, Allah over Muslim countries, and so on? And what about those parts of the world where people of different religions live mixed together? And, more fundamentally, if there exists a God who is the creator *ex nihilo* of everything other than God, how can there also be the eternal uncreated process of *pratitya samutpada*?

The other reason is that the moral and spiritual fruits produced by response to the different experienced ultimates are so essentially similar, within the cultural differences of their different traditions, that it seems more reasonable to postulate a common source of this salvific transformation.

There are many other issues, and a growing literature about them.[17] But the task of this chapter has been the relatively modest one of introducing the newly perceived global context within which Christian theologians will increasingly feel obliged to think in the future.

NOTES

1. For more about this see, for example, John Hick, "The Non-Absoluteness of Christianity," in *The Myth of Christian Uniqueness*, ed. John Hick and Paul Knitter (New York: Orbis Books; London: SCM Press, 1992).
2. For example, William Lane Craig, " 'No Other Name': A Middle Knowledge Perspective on the Exclusivity of Salvation through Christ," *Faith and Philosophy* 6:2 (April 1989).
3. J. A. Dinoia, O.P., *The Diversity of Religions* (Washington, D.C.: Catholic University of America Press, 1992), 104.
4. Ibid., 107.
5. Ibid., 105.
6. Ibid.
7. George Lindbeck, *The Nature of Doctrine: Religion and Theology in a Postliberal Age* (Philadelphia: Westminster Press; London: SPCK, 1984), 63.

8. Ibid., 61.

9. Ibid., 57.

10. Ibid., 59.

11. Karl Barth, *Church Dogmatics*, II/2 (English translation; Edinburgh: T. & T. Clark, 1956), 350.

12. Ernst Troeltsch, "The Place of Christianity among the World Religions" (1923), in *Christianity and Other Religions*, ed. John Hick and Brian Hebblethwaite (London: Collins; Philadelphia: Fortress Press, 1980), 25.

13. *Rig-Veda*, I, 164. 46.

14. *Rumi: Poet and Mystic*, trans. R. A. Nicholson (London and Boston: Unwin Mandala Books, 1978), 166.

15. Nicholas of Cusa, *De Pace Fidei*, 6, trans. James Biechler and Lawrence Bond, in *Nicholas of Cusa on Interreligious Harmony* (Lewiston and Lampeter: Edwin Mellon Press, 1990), 7.

16. Thomas Aquinas, *Summa Theologica*, 2-2 q.1, art. 2.

17. See, e.g., John Cobb, *Beyond Dialogue* (Philadelphia: Fortress Press, 1982); Paul Knitter, *No Other Name? A Critical Survey of Christian Attitudes toward the World Religions* (New York: Orbis Books, 1985); Alan Race, *Christians and Religious Pluralism* (London: SCM Press; New York: Orbis Books, 2d ed. 1993); Hans Küng et al., *Christianity and the World Religions: Paths of Dialogue with Islam, Hinduism, and Buddhism* (New York: Doubleday, 1986); John Hick and Paul Knitter, eds, *The Myth of Christian Uniqueness* (New York: Orbis Books; London: SCM Press, 1987); Gavin D'Costa, ed., *Christian Uniqueness Reconsidered* (New York: Orbis Books, 1990); John Macquarrie, *Mediators between Human and Divine: From Moses to Muhammad* (New York: Continuum, 1996); John Hick, *An Interpretation of Religion* (New Haven, Conn.: Yale University Press; London: Macmillan Publishers, 1989, and idem, *A Christian Theology of Religions* (Louisville, Ky.: Westminster John Knox Press, 1995); S. Mark Heim, *Salvations: Truth and Difference in Religion* (New York: Orbis Books, 1995); Peter Byrne, *Prolegomena to Religious Pluralism* (London: Macmillan Publishers; New York: St. Martin's Press, 1995).

3

DOING CHRISTIAN THEOLOGY WITH JEWS

The Other, Boundaries, Questions

CLARK M. WILLIAMSON

The historical relation of the church to the synagogue can be analyzed into two periods. The first is that of the church within Judaism, or of the church as one of the Judaisms of the early first century of the Common Era. The second is that of the Gentile church against the Jewish people. Post-Holocaust or post-*Shoah*[1] theology challenges the church to become the church *with* the Jewish people, to work out our self-understanding—our theology—in a relationship of conversation and critical solidarity with the Israel of God.[2] The post-*Shoah* question before the church is whether it will come to terms with Karl Barth's claim:

> Why do we so dislike to be told that the Jews are the chosen people?
> Why does Christendom continually search for fresh proof that this is
> no longer true? In a word, because we do not enjoy being told that the
> sun of free grace, by which alone we can live, shines not upon us, but
> upon the Jews, that it is the Jews who are elect and not the Germans,
> the French or the Swiss, and that in order to be chosen, we must, for
> good or ill, either be Jews or else be heart and soul on the side of the
> Jews. . . . They have the promise of God; and if we Christians from
> among the Gentiles have it too, then it is only as those chosen with
> them, as guests in their house, as new wood grafted on to their old tree.[3]

The proposal made here, in the light of the long teaching and practice of contempt for Jews and Judaism and the complex relation between that tradition and the Nazi attempt to make the world *Judenrein*, is that the church must effect a critical solidarity with the Israel of God and begin working out its theological self-understanding in conversation with Jews.[4]

Doing so requires us to think about our Christian identity and its boundaries. What shall be the contours of our self-understanding and our community? Robert Jay Lifton distinguishes two types of personalities and, by analogy, two types of ecclesial identity: (1) Protean people lack fixed identities or boundaries and are marked by fluidity. (2) Closed-off people have a clear, if rigid, identity and a constricted self-process. They are reluctant to allow any alien influence into their lives.[5] Neither protean nor closed-off churches can engage in conversation with the stranger. To the closed-off theology of an absolutist church, strangers and their questions are dismissed except as targets for conversion. To the emptied-out inclusivism of protean theologies, there is no stranger because there is no self-identity to which the other stands in contrast. To a post-*Shoah* theologian in conversation with Judaism, these two positions offer no hope for conversation.[6]

Closed-off churches are constricted in their capacity for relationship. They need learn nothing from anybody else, least of all the Israel of God, and construct ideologies of displacement to rationalize their exclusion of the other from contributing to or questioning their self-understanding. Non-closed-off churches might congratulate themselves on being open if they did not reflect the protean trait. Open to all influence, taking diversity as a norm, they lack identity and centeredness. If there is little they are willing to stand for lest they seem "exclusive," they have difficulty recognizing that some things are incompatible with the gospel. Averse to critical theological reflection, they fail to be authoritative teachers of the Christian faith.

Hence, our topic is that of "boundaries" or limits and the difficulties that we encounter in trying to think about them. We will approach the topic by reference to the history of relations between Jews and Christians, in which different kinds of boundaries and different attitudes toward them play important and diverse roles. The thesis is that boundaries protect what is at the heart of the matter for a community of faith, that an assault on boundaries is an assault on the heart of the matter, that transcending boundaries is the work of God and Christ, that erecting the wrong kind of boundaries resists that work, and that the right understanding of boundaries can facilitate it.[7]

The question of boundaries is inescapably pragmatic. Is respect for others who differ from us also respect for boundaries and an acceptance of our limits? Does respect for boundaries permit conversation across the border? Does it require it? Does the wrong attitude toward boundaries result in fear toward what is on the other side of a boundary, with the concomitant urge to destroy it? Is failure to know where the boundaries of a tradition are located also failure to understand what is at the heart of a tradition? Do boundaries inhibit creativity, or are they the condition of its possibility?

Theologians who cut their theological teeth on Paul Tillich's theology of correlation, and who believe that a chastened method of correlation (one in which we *can be questioned*) is the best way to do theology in a pluralistic religious context, think it is critically important to know where the boundaries are. We can hardly do our theology "from the boundary" if we do not know where it is.[8] Nor can we take advantage of John Cobb's approach to interfaith relationships, that of "passing over and coming back," if the boundaries are so invisible that we know neither when we are at home in our own tradition nor when we have crossed over into another.[9] Nor can we know, in the language of Rita Brock, what is at the "heart" of Christianity's iconoclastic capacity for empowerment and liberation unless we know what its limits are and that those demonic aspects of historic Christianity that leave people "brokenhearted" are outside those normative limits.[10] Boundaries are theologically critical.

We shall look at the question of boundaries in relation to Judaism through a number of case studies. Case study #1 has to do with the apostle Paul and his attitude toward the "boundary markers" separating the Israel of God from the Gentile peoples. The term *boundary markers* partakes of the detached, academic vocabulary of outsiders. What an outsider names "boundary markers," an insider may refer to as "sacraments" or *mitzvoth*, commandments of God. In an age in which boundaries and limits tend to be treated pejoratively, spiritually incorrect because "exclusivist," this may be a difficult point to see.

Paul's theology on this point is complex. Consider a hypothesis at odds with the standard view of Paul. The inclusion of Gentiles in the church without requiring them to be circumcised does *not* seem to have been Paul's contribution to the early church. At least some synagogues allowed Gentile "God-fearers" to participate in services without making any ritual demands on them, allowing them to study and discuss Torah, to participate in conducting the synagogue's charitable works, while these same Gentiles, as members of the city council, performed "the public sacrifices required of their office."[11] With the later rabbis, Paul "stood within the 'liberal' stream of Deutero-Isaiah. The Kingdom of God would include two peoples: Gentiles, redeemed from idolatry, and Israel, redeemed finally from exile."[12] The earliest church seems to have admitted Gentiles to enter it without their having to "convert" to Judaism. The old distinction between "Jewish-Christians" and Paul is not helpful. Paul described himself as "circumcised on the eighth day, a member of the people of Israel, of the tribe of Benjamin, a Hebrew born of Hebrews; as to the law, a Pharisee; as to zeal, a persecutor of the church; as to righteousness under the law, blameless" (Phil. 3:5–6). The term *Christian* is anachronistic when used of this period. It is not part of Paul's vocabulary and can prematurely suggest two separate religions.[13]

Paul's introduction to the church took place in the context of the Hellenistic-Jewish Gentile mission movement, during which time he participated in the Damascus and Antioch churches, living with and learning from these Christians. "Paul lived in a gentile community during his formative years as a convert."[14] He did not require Gentiles to submit to Jewish boundary markers for admission to the community, but this was not his doing.

Paul preached his understanding of the gospel to Gentiles for sixteen or seventeen years (Gal.1:18; 2:1) before giving an account of himself to the "pillars" of the church. Titus, a Greek, was not required to be circumcised (Gal. 2:3) and, according to Paul, the Jerusalem authorities agreed "that we should go to the Gentiles and they [James, Cephas, and John] to the circumcised" (Gal. 2:9). The dispute discussed in Jerusalem was about "whether the gentiles who *had* joined the followers of Jesus at Antioch must *now* undergo the normal rite of incorporation into the Jewish community."[15] The question is not why Paul broke from traditional Jewish practice, but why the earlier consensus broke down at this time.

To this question, there are two answers, one arising from within the early church, the other from outside pressures. First, while the church was predominantly Jewish, Gentile participation was a welcome affirmation of the gospel. As it became increasingly Gentile, it compromised its identity as a renewal movement within Judaism and its chances for success among Jews. Hence, the "circumcision party" urged Gentiles in the church to become *converts* to Judaism. So they pressed upon the Antioch congregation, the first to include Gentiles, to have these Gentiles observe circumcision and the dietary laws.

Second, Jews in and out of Palestine again felt Roman heat; many regarded their very existence as being at stake. Caligula instigated a crisis over his insistence that a statue of himself be erected in the Temple (40 C.E.). Inept Roman governors inflicted indignity and suffering on the people. Fadus required that the high priest's vestments be returned to Roman custody and put down the rebellion of Theudas; Tiberius Julius Alexander crucified the sons of Judas the Galilean, on charges that they agitated against Rome. Josephus calculates that twenty- to thirty-thousand people were killed in a Jerusalem riot against Cumanus. There was a series of disorders involving Zealots in Samaria.[16] Jewish heritage, identity, national and religious rights, and prerogatives were under siege. Jews in major cities throughout the empire also suffered from mob violence and local governmental misrule.[17]

Hence, the practice of including Gentiles without the halakic requirements of circumcision and the dietary laws was perceived by many Jews to be a threat to Jewish existence.[18] The conservative followers of Jesus raised the stakes on the practices in which Paul and his fellow Christians in Antioch had been engaged. Paul's response was to write letters (which postdate this time) arguing for the full inclusion of Gentiles in the community without their having to take on Jewish boundary markers. His argument was that the grace of God was surely not limited to those who possessed Jewish boundary markers. Among Christians he prevailed, as long as we leave out of account the dissenters (such as the community for which Matthew was written).

Paul represents a victory for "inclusive Judaism" over "exclusive Judaism" (using these terms descriptively and not pejoratively). The church developed without Jewish identity markers' getting in the way of its missionizing Gentiles. But was this an unambiguous victory for Paul? Christians typically assume that Paul was utterly right on this question and his opponents clearly wrong. They presume, however, that Paul also argued that Jews should cease retaining their own boundary markers. Yet Paul's argument was directed, as his authentic letters make clear, at Gentiles (e.g., Thess. 1:9; 1 Cor. 8:7; Rom. 1:5–6, 13). Paul nowhere says that Jews should give up their identity markers. He does argue, as one of his students put it, that this boundary should not be "a dividing wall, . . . hostility" (Eph. 2:14), but that Gentile Christians and Jews should be "fellow citizens . . . of the household of God" (Eph. 2:19, RSV). To say that the grace of God is not limited to possessors of Jewish boundary markers does not imply that these boundary markers should be eliminated. It is compatible with saying that they should be transcended, that Jewish identity has *always* meant, since the time of Abraham, that through the Jews "all the families of the earth shall be blessed" (Gen. 12:1–3). Indeed, the letter to the Romans addresses the problem of Christian *Gentile* exclusivism. Paul admonishes his Gentile audience: "Do not boast over the branches" (Rom. 11:18)[19] and urges his Gentile audience to observe some kind of Jewish boundary markers: "Do not let what you eat cause the ruin of one for whom Christ died" (Rom. 14:15).

The heart of the matter for Paul, the gospel, was that in Jesus Christ the good news of God's unconditional love was made manifest. Jesus Christ is the free and unconditional gift to us of God's love. We cannot take the gift of God's unconditional love and make it into a condition apart from which God is not free to love. Hence, if God's unconditional love is not true for both Jews and Gentiles, it is true for neither, and if it is not true for Jews who do not believe in Jesus Christ, it is not true for those who do (Romans 9—11). At the heart of Paul's attitudes toward boundaries is a prior attitude toward what is at the center—the good news of God's love graciously given, of God's grace lovingly given.

Case study #2 shows that while Christianity was developing without the hindrance of Jewish boundary markers, Judaism paid serious attention to its boundaries. The opening paragraph of the *Pirke Aboth* ("The Teachings of the Fathers") reads:

> Moses received the Law from Sinai and committed it to Joshua, and Joshua to the elders, and the elders to the Prophets, and the Prophets committed it to the men of the Great Synagogue. They said three things: Be deliberate in judgment, raise up many disciples, *and make a fence around the Torah.*[19]

This striking statement makes three claims. First is that a tradition from God's revelation to Moses at Sinai continues beyond the scriptures of Israel to "the men of the Great Synagogue." There is an oral Torah alongside the written Torah. Second is that this oral Torah comes down through the generations of teachers and disciples. Third, what is stated is not a citation of scripture but a saying that stands on its own two feet. It is a part of the oral, not the written, Torah.

The *Pirke Aboth* is central to the Mishnah, which was later included in the Babylonian Talmud and the Talmud of the *eretz Yisrael*. Unlike the Talmuds, the Mishnah almost never cites or exegetes scripture in support of its statements. The "fence" that it sought to put around the Torah did not require coming to terms with a canon. The Talmud confesses the supremacy of scripture, but insists on interpreting it in ways that will be life-giving to the community. Scripture is authoritative, yet subordinate to the needs of the community interpreting it.[21] The drafters of the Mishnah had their own context and their own questions. They turned to the Priestly Code because it had asked and answered similar questions. This code was worked out during a time of exile, dislocation, and bifurcated identity. For the framers of the Mishnah, dispersed among Gentiles in the Land of Promise and under Roman occupation, the questions "Who are we?" and "What are we to do?" arose with new urgency. They reinterpreted the Priestly Code in a way that would serve God and the well-being of the community.

The authoritative interpreters of scripture derived from it: (1) a new form of religion based on study of scripture, not on Temple ritual; (2) a new religious institution, the synagogue (the house of the people of God), no longer the Temple (the house of God); (3) a new type of religious leader, the lay scholar (rabbi), not an ordained priest; and (4) new religious concepts, such as resurrection. None of these results of the authoritative interpretation of the Torah can be found in the Torah. Putting a fence around the Torah generated creativity, perhaps a revolution, but in no sense stagnation.[22] Sometimes a limit can be a moving horizon within which revolutionary expansion takes place.

At the same time, the framers of the Talmud provided an answer to what Christians were saying in their anti-Jewish tracts (to which we turn next). Here is the way Jacob Neusner puts it:

> Everything we hear from sages turns inward upon Israel. There is no explicit confrontation with the outside world: with the Christian emperor, with the figure of Christ enthroned. It is as if nothing happened to demand attention. Yet the stress for sages is on the centrality of the keeping of the laws of the Torah in the messianic process. Keep the law and the Messiah will come. This forms an exact reply to Chrysostom's doctrine: do not keep the law, for the Messiah has come.[23]

Case study #3 takes us to the church fathers. We will look at two such fathers and at one council. The writer of the Epistle of Barnabas was concerned with the behavior of Christian lay people in Alexandria. They socialized with Jews and said, "The covenant belongs to us and them; it is both theirs and ours."[24] Barnabas's response was to build a wall between his Christian congregation and the Jewish community. He produced a displacement ideology, according to which "they" had the covenant but lost it and "we" got it. He undercut Jewish interpretations of the Hebrew Bible by using a typological exegesis that made of everything "old" a shadowy prefiguring of something in the "new" testament. Thus he sought to empty Jewish worship, particularly the sabbath, of all legitimacy. He articulated the "two peoples" allegory, in which Christians become the younger brother served by the elder brother. We now are the people of inheritance; they are not, having "proved themselves unworthy" of the covenant.

Late in the fourth century, Chrysostom of Antioch faced a similar situation. To understand Chrysostom, we have to set him in context. Not long before, Julian became emperor of Rome and tried to reverse the development initiated by Constantine of increasing Christian rights and privileges. Although Julian tolerated all religions, he disliked Christianity. Familiar with the claim that the destruction of the Temple was a sign of God's displacement of the people Israel with the church, Julian started to rebuild it, an attempt that failed. But to Chrysostom, the security of Christianity was far from assured.

In addition, members of his flock failed to observe the proper boundary between themselves and their Jewish neighbors. As he said, "The festivals of the wretched and miserable Jews are about to take place. And many who belong to us . . . attend their festivals. It is this evil practice I now wish to drive from the church."[25] So he inveighed against the synagogue, urging Christians not to join the ranks of the "Christ-killers."

As in Alexandria three centuries earlier, the laity was theologically more generous and socially more gregarious than the clergy. Chrysostom could not look calmly on the fact that his flock were frequenting synagogues and Jewish homes, sharing presents on festival occasions. Jews are the broken-off branches, whereas we have borne the fruit of piety. Chrysostom descended to calling Jews "dogs, wild animals . . . suited only for slaughter." Drunken and gluttonous, said Chrysostom, the Jews "murder your master."[26]

Our first evidence of a church council's legislation concerning relations between Jews and Christians is found in Spain. In 306 the Council of Elvira passed four canon laws pertaining to Jewish-Christian relations. Canon 16: "Catholic girls may not marry Jews." Canon 49: "Landlords are not to allow Jews to bless the crops they have received from God and for which they have offered thanks." Such action "would make our blessing invalid and meaningless." Canon 50: "If any cleric or layperson eats with Jews, he or she shall be kept from communion as a way of correction." Canon 78: "If a Christian confesses adultery with a Jewish or pagan woman, he is denied communion for some time."[27] Later councils of bishops would require all Jews in Christendom to wear distinctive dress (1215: the fourth Lateran Council), ban Jews from Christian universities (1432–1449: the Council of Basel), permit the kidnapping of Jewish children that they may be raised as Christians (633: Council of Toledo IV), and ban Jews from the streets during Christian holidays (538: Synod of Orleans III). All the West a joint would look canon law as their establishing precedent; for example, the law barring Jews from dining cars on trains cited Elvira.[28]

Polemic against socialization between Jews and Christians means that such activity was occurring, that laws against Jews and Christians doing everything from sleeping and eating together to mixing in universities were aimed at stopping behavior that was taking place. The insistence on a complete separation of Christians from Jews followed lines of power and authority in the church and served the interest of those who wielded power and authority. Hence their strategy needs to be put under the microscope of ideology critique and made to answer the question, Cui bono? Who benefits from this?

We have seen three approaches to the reality of boundaries: that of Paul the apostle, who sought to transcend the boundary between Jews and Gentiles in order to create one new community of the two; that of the framers of the Mishnah, who built a fence around the Torah to protect what was at the heart of Jewish faith and who sparked off a movement of remarkable religious creativity; and that of the church fathers, who sought to replace Paul's semipermeable boundaries with impermeable ones.

Since post-*Shoah* theologians argue that we should do our theological thinking in conversation with Jews, let us derive a constructive suggestion from that conversation. We recur to the *Pirke Aboth* where, five paragraphs after our prior quote, Joshua ben Perahyah says: "Provide thyself with a teacher and get thee a fellow-disciple [student]."[29] In a later development of this tradition of studying Torah *with one another*, "The Teachings of Rabbi Natan" say: "A person should set himself a companion, to eat with him, drink with him, study Bible with him, study Mishnah with him, sleep with him, and reveal to him all his secrets, secrets of Torah and secrets of worldly things."[30]

Rachel Adler argues that this rabbinic text describes a distinctively Jewish kind of intimacy: the study-companion relationship, that of the *chaverim*.[31] The *chaverim* do not simply study texts; the structure of their relationship and the nature of its boundaries present a Jewish model for the relation between the self and the other. In it, people experience each other as wholes, not as fragmented beings. Companionship is physical, emotional, intellectual, and spiritual. *Chaverim* study together by *questioning* each other. They question lovingly and love questions.

Such an understanding of boundaries seems to lie at the heart of Paul's theology. The root of *chaver* means to join together at the boundaries. Boundaries define the shape and extent of an entity, and distinguish between what is inside and what is out. They maintain its integrity and keep it from dribbling out into everything else. Being "joined together at the boundaries" is the kind of relationship reflected in Paul's approach to boundaries—that they should be transcended without being destroyed. God's gracious love overflows boundaries and requires its recipients not only to love God in return, but to love the neighbor and the stranger as we love ourselves.

Some boundaries are like the Berlin Wall—fronted by land mines, topped with barbed wire, guarded by machine guns. Others serve to facilitate interaction with the environment. Adler points out that a cell membrane, for example, is part of the living substance of the cell. It is the perimeter at which the cell works out its reciprocity with other cells—the relations that maintain its life within its context. This Torah of self and other grounds our capacity to be *chaverim* and our capacity to create *tzedek*, justice-as-righteousness, to embody the Torah of self and other in a social matrix that allows all human beings to flourish.

This understanding of boundary as elastic and semipermeable, that both defines the self and requires bonding with the other, points to the reality of mutual interconnectedness. Such communion attests that we inhabit a single context, and within that context we live deeply within one another's boundaries. The only way to in-habit is to co-habit. The fantasy of the impermeable self or religious boundary is a snare and a delusion.

Such an understanding of boundaries might encourage those willing to cross over and return, and create the conditions for *shalom* between traditions long separated from each other, dissipating the anxiety that leads to fear of what lies beyond the boundary and the will to eliminate it.[32] It may also address the concerns of those whose experience with the ideologically constructed boundaries of historic traditions leads them to legitimate fear of all boundaries as oppressive. A moving, semipermeable boundary protects the authentic identity of an entity and generates creativity and community.

What is at stake in this for Christians is the heart of the matter, the gospel of Jesus Christ as the gift to us of God's unconditional and gracious love. This singular gift of God's justifying love brings with it a singular command: that we who can understand ourselves in any ultimate sense in terms of and only in terms of God's love graciously offered to us, are given and called to understand ourselves as those who are to love God with all our selves and our neighbors as ourselves.

What we now need to make clear, in this post-*Shoah* period, is what "love of the neighbor" means. For much of Christian history, Jews have not been included within the Christian "universe of moral discourse." They have not been moral patients whom Christians, as moral agents, particularly had to take into account. Christians could say anything about Jews that served their ideological purposes. And while Christians were not supposed to do just anything to Jews (who were the only legally protected religious minority in Christendom), nonetheless such restraints were all too often violated, to horrendous effect. After the *Shoah*, as in principle they should always have been, Jewish strangers are those neighbors whom God has given us to love. Christian understanding and commitment to the gospel of God's all-inclusive love will now be measured by our ability to welcome strangers and to defend their dignity and well-being. Doing theology with *chaverim* from other traditions, doing theology as Christians with Jewish *chaverim*, will open us to seeing ourselves through the eyes of another. We will become more self-questioning. Doing theology as women and men, *chaverim* of each other, will accomplish the same. The theology of a closed-off church will be an ethnocentric theology that can tolerate the stranger, if at all, only as a potential candidate for conversion to sameness. That such a theology ends up walking down the apocalyptic path to Auschwitz, bearing in mind all the complexities involved in getting there, is not surprising. Such a closed-off theology cannot finally account for the existence of others in the world, others whose way of being human, by its sheer contrast with ours, causes us self-doubt and self-questioning. Openness to strangers requires openness to questions, because strangers are questions to us and bring their questions with them. Jews are among those strangers whom God commands us to love and are necessary to our Christian self-understanding; we cannot be Christian until we are prepared to welcome them and their questions into our life.

The alternative to the absolutism of an ethnocentric theology is not relativism. Relativism, the view that all faiths are equally important and equally unimportant, takes no particularities seriously, neither ours nor anyone else's. It is as destructive of the otherness of the other as is absolutism.[33] The alternative is the method of questioning at the heart of the relationship between *chaverim*. The self-complacency at the heart of absolutism and relativism is replaced by the act of self-transcendence that results from openness to questions and to the other. After Auschwitz, "nothing dare evoke our absolute, unquestioning loyalty, not even our God, for this leads to the possibility of SS loyalties."[34]

Jacques Ellul was one of those infrequent Christian theologians who "takes the Jewish experience of faith seriously in its own right."[35] He argued that "there is only one political endeavor on which world history now depends: that is the union of the Church and Israel."[36] He has in mind a conversion of the church to share the same hope so as to support Israel "in its long march through the same night and toward the same Kingdom."[37] His work illuminates our problem with boundaries. He treats the terms *sacred* and *holy* as antonyms rather than synonyms. The sacred performs the sociological function of integration and legitimation. It creates a sense of order within which human life can be carried on. But its demonic propensity is to create a "closed" order that prevents the continuing transformation of self and society. Without such a self-transcending openness to the future, life ceases to be either human or free.

For human life to be creative, the claims of the social order to be sacred and unalterable must be rendered proximate by its opposite—the holy. The holy is that which is "other" than our closed-off social order. Whereas the sacred demands integration and closure, the holy demands openness to transformation.[38] Yet freedom requires transcending a limit. If there are no limits, as is the case with the relativist church, there can be no freedom. Freedom requires the establishment of a limit where there is none, for both the limit and the revolt against it must be present if freedom is to be actual.

Theology that is responsible to the contagious love of God that lies at its heart needs a movable, semipermeable boundary, one that will let it bond with *chaverim* beyond that boundary, without which it cannot recognize the "other" because it cannot recognize itself, one that is open to and requires the presence of strangers, questions, and self-transcendence. The best way for Christians to come to understand something of the God of Israel is in conversation with the Israel of God. Whether such conversation will shape the self-understanding of the church in the future we cannot know. That it ought to is the promise and challenge put before the church by its long history with the God of Israel and the Israel of God.

Post-*Shoah* theology is a form of liberation theology. It is committed to freeing Christian theology from its inherited anti-Jewish ideology, an ideology that has misconstrued the understanding of the Christian faith and reflected and reinforced social practices that have wreaked untold havoc on the Israel of God. Anti-Judaism is inappropriate to the Christian faith, and immoral. More than a theme running through the history of the church, it is a systematic hermeneutic that structures the interpretation of every Christian teaching. It can be replaced only by an equally systematic post-*Shoah* reinterpretation.

The spectrum of theologians working in post-*Shoah* theology embraces feminists on one end, evangelicals on the other, and many possibilities between them.[39] Several Jewish scholars participate in the dialogue with Christians, as well as in post-*Shoah* efforts at reconstruction of their theological tradition.[40] Christology is the fulcrum doctrine in post-*Shoah* theology, hence we have several attempts to restate this doctrine.[41] Other doctrines, such as that of the Holy Spirit, receive concentrated attention.[42]

It is the comprehensive task of Christian systematic theologians to address the full range of issues brought to the forefront of our awareness by the light that the *Shoah* sheds on its own prehistory of contempt for Jews and Judaism.[43] These theologians stipulate that the covenant between the God of Israel and the Israel of God is the one context in which Christian language makes sense, thus reversing the Christian tendency to regard Jews as the disconfirming other. The church is that community called by God's grace to join the Israel of God on its way along the way (*torah*) of faith. Taking the covenant between God and Israel as the primary context of theology implies that the covenant with Israel remains in place, that Jews as Jews today participate in it. Our theological conversation is not with a fossil, but with our living Jewish neighbors.

Post-*Shoah* theology differs from other theologies by proposing a new paradigm in which everything looks different and in which doctrines have a different cash value. Whereas the Trinity typically has stood for a sign of what Jews do not believe, now it is the church's way of articulating that the God by whom it is met in Jesus Christ is the God of Israel. Whereas Jesus Christ was interpreted as having lived in conflict with Jews and Judaism, having taught against Jews and Judaism, having been crucified at the hands of Jews and Judaism, only to be raised by God in victory over Jews and Judaism, now every proper Christological statement must make clear that it affirms the covenant between God and Israel.[44]

In pre-*Shoah* theology, anything could be said as long as it served the interests of the institutional church and rendered Jews invisible or scapegoated them as the old, bad, carnal, ethnocentric antitheses of all things good, new, Christian, spiritual, and universal. God became the God who displaced Israel with the church, who gave Israel an inferior covenant and then punished Israel for being faithful to it. Christ became the kind of mediator who would negotiate the displacement. Scripture became a hyphenated, Marcionite scripture with a "New" Testament that fulfills and cancels the "Old." The Holy Spirit became a Christian possession, who unites believers to Christ but is absent from carnal Israel. The church is the replacement people who get the benefit of all this; the doctrine of the church is where the cash value of the anti-Judaism of all the other doctrines in cashed out.

In post-*Shoah* theology, God is reenvisioned as the faithful One of Israel who seeks out covenant partners for the redemption of the world. Jesus Christ, the representation of *torah* (Romans 10), is a gift to the church from both the God of Israel and the Israel of God in whom he took shape. The Spirit is now Shechinah/Spirit, active among Jews and all people to bind our hearts in love to God and one another. The covenant becomes genuinely inclusive, not only of Jews and Christians, but the basis for authentic pluralism. Scripture, in which the New Testament or "Apostolic Writings" are reinserted into the rest of the Bible, becomes useful light for walking the way of faith. The rule of God remains ahead of both Jews and Gentiles as a destabilizing sign that God is not yet finished with the church, the synagogue, or human history.

NOTES

1. *Shoah* is used here in place of "holocaust," because the latter refers to a whole burnt sacrifice offered to the Lord, which was hardly the intent of the Nazi effort to render the world "clean" of Jews. *Shoah* connotes destruction.
2. "Critical solidarity" is an alternative to criticism without solidarity (the *adversus Judaeos* tradition) and to an uncritical solidarity. As Jews are rightly free to criticize Christian praxis as it bears on Jews, so Christians who demonstrate solidarity with Jews are free to criticize Jewish or Israeli practices. See Clark M. Williamson, ed., *A Mutual Witness* (St. Louis: Chalice Press, 1992), 119–43.
3. Karl Barth, *Against the Stream* (London: SCM Press, 1954), 199–200.
4. I begin to work out what this means in Clark M. Williamson, *A Guest in the House of Israel: Post-Holocaust Church Theology* (Louisville, Ky.: Westminster/John Knox Press, 1993).
5. Robert Jay Lifton, *Boundaries: Psychological Man in Revolution* (New York: Vintage Books, 1970), 37–38, 43–44, 51.

6. See Williamson, *Guest in the House of Israel*, 9–14.
7. This chapter was inspired by a reading of Delwin Brown's *Boundaries of Our Habitations: Tradition and Theological Construction* (Albany, N.Y.: State University of New York Press, 1994).
8. See Tillich's autobiographical sketch, *On the Boundary* (New York: Charles Scribner's Sons, 1966).
9. John B. Cobb Jr., *Beyond Dialogue* (Philadelphia: Fortress Press, 1982), esp. chaps. 4 and 5.
10. See Rita Nakashima Brock, *Journeys by Heart* (New York: Crossroad, 1988), xv.
11. J. Reynolds and R. Tannenbaum, *Jews and God-fearers at Aphrodisias: Green Inscriptions with Commentary* (Cambridge: Cambridge University Press, 1987), 56–58.
12. Paula Fredricksen, *From Jesus to Christ* (New Haven, Conn.: Yale University Press, 1988), 166.
13. See the discussion of this point in Krister Stendahl, *Paul among Jews and Gentiles* (Philadelphia: Fortress Press, 1976), 7–23; Philip A. Cunningham, *Jewish Apostle to the Gentiles* (Mystic, Conn.: Twenty-third Publications, 1976), 21–30; and Clark M. Williamson, *Has God Rejected His People?* (Nashville: Abingdon Press, 1982), 47–50, 60–62.
14. Alan Segal, *Paul the Convert* (New Haven, Conn.: Yale University Press, 1990), 26.
15. Wayne A. Meeks, *The First Urban Christians* (New Haven, Conn.: Yale University Press, 1983), 112 (emphasis mine).
16. James D. G. Dunn, *Jesus, Paul, and the Law* (Louisville, Ky.: Westminster/John Knox Press, 1990), 133.
17. See Philo of Alexandria's petition to Caligula in this regard, cited in Williamson, *Has God Rejected His People?* 38.
18. Segal, *Paul the Convert*, 150, 223.
19. See Mark D. Nanos, *The Mystery of Romans* (Minneapolis: Fortress Press, 1996), 10–31, for a discussion of Romans as addressing Christian-Gentile exclusivism.
20. *Pirke Aboth* 1.1 trans. Herbert Danby (London: Oxford University Press, 1933), 446 (emphasis mine).
21. Jacob Neusner, "Scripture and Mishnah: Authority and Selectivity," in *Scripture in the Jewish and Christian Traditions*, ed. Frederick E. Greenspahn (Nashville: Abingdon Press, 1982), 65.
22. That revolution was the result of the work of the Pharisees and rabbis is the argument of Ellis Rivkin, *A Hidden Revolution* (Nashville: Abingdon Press, 1978), esp. chap. 5.
23. Jacob Neusner, *Jews and Christians: The Myth of a Common Tradition* (Philadelphia: Trinity Press International, 1991), 64.
24. "The Letter of Barnabas," vol. 1, in *The Ante-Nicene Fathers*, ed. A. Roberts and J. Donaldson (Grand Rapids: Wm. B. Eerdmans Publishing Co., 1950-51), 145, 138, 141.
25. Wayne A. Meeks and Robert A. Wilken, *Jews and Christians in Antioch* (Missoula, Mont: Scholars Press, 1978), 93–100. Two of Chrysostom's sermons are in this book.
26. Ibid., 87–89.
27. The canons of the Council of Elvira are found in Jan L. Womer, ed., *Morality and Ethics in Early Christianity* (Philadelphia: Fortress Press, 1987), 75–82.
28. See Raul Hilberg, *The Destruction of the European Jews* (New York: Harper & Row, 1979), 5–6.
29. *Pirke Aboth* 16.
30. *Avot d/Rabbi Natan*, 8.

31. Rachel Adler, a Jewish feminist theologian, made clear this understanding of *chaverim* and an alternative Jewish understanding of boundaries in "Breaking Boundaries," *Tikkun*, 6/3 (1991): 43–46, 87.

32. See Paul Tillich, "Boundaries," in *Theology of Peace*, ed. Ronald H. Stone (Louisville, Ky.: Westminster/John Knox Press, 1990), 163.

33. For a feminist critique of relativism as inimical to the concerns both of women and of interfaith conversation, see Pamela Dickey Young, *Christ in a Post-Christian World* (Minneapolis: Fortress Press, 1995), 33, 69, 86.

34. Irving Greenberg, "Cloud of Smoke, Pillar of Fire: Judaism, Christianity, and Modernity after the Holocaust," in *Auschwitz: Beginning of a New Era?* ed. Eva Fleischner (New York: KTAV Publishing House, 1977), 38.

35. Darrell J. Fasching, *Narrative Theology after Auschwitz: From Alienation to Ethics* (Minneapolis: Fortress Press, 1992), 154–64. I follow Fasching's argument here in relation to Ellul.

36. Jacques Ellul, *Hope in Time of Abandonment*, trans. C. Edward Hopkin (New York: Seabury Press, 1973), 290–91, 297. Cited in Fasching, *Narrative Theology*, 157.

37. Ibid., 305; cited in Fasching, 157.

38. Jacques Ellul, *The Ethics of Freedom*, trans. and ed. Geoffrey W. Bromiley (Grand Rapids: Wm. B. Eerdmans Publishing Co., 1976), 345; discussed in Fasching, 155.

39. Evangelical theologians working for the rapprochement between Jews and Christians include Marvin Wilson, *Our Father Abraham* (Grand Rapids: Wm. B. Eerdmans Publishing Co., 1989), and David A. Rausch, *Building Bridges* (Chicago: Moody Press, 1988). Rosemary Ruether's *Faith and Fratricide* (New York: Seabury Press, 1974) was an early contributor to post-*Shoah* theology, while Katharina von Kellenbach's *Anti-Judaism in Feminist Religious Writings* (Atlanta: Scholars Press, 1994) is a thorough criticism of feminist theologians for largely ignoring the ways in which feminist theology renders Jews and Judaism as scapegoats for patriarchy and antithetical to feminist concerns.

40. See, e.g., Eugene R. Borowitz, *Contemporary Christologies: A Jewish Response* (New York: Paulist Press, 1980); Jacob Neusner, *Telling Tales: The Urgency and Basis for Judeo-Christian Dialogue* (Louisville, Ky.: Westminster/John Knox Press, 1993), and *Jews and Christians: The Myth of a Common Tradition* (Philadelphia: Trinity Press International, 1991); and David Novak, *Jewish-Christian Dialogue: A Jewish Justification* (New York: Oxford University Press, 1989). Rabbi Irving Greenberg has profoundly influenced many Christian theologians. See his "Cloud of Smoke, Pillar of Fire," 7–55.

41. See, for example, Michael B. McGarry, C.S.P., *Christology after Auschwitz* (New York: Paulist Press, 1977); A. Roy Eckardt, *Reclaiming the Jesus of History: Christology Today* (Minneapolis: Fortress Press, 1992); and Jürgen Moltmann, *The Way of Jesus Christ*, trans. Margaret Kohl (New York: Harper & Row, 1989).

42. For example, Michael Lodahl, *Shekhinah Spirit* (Mahwah, N.J.: Paulist Press, 1992).

43. These systematic theologians include Paul M. van Buren, *A Theology of the Jewish-Christian Reality*: pt. 1, *Discerning the Way* (New York: Seabury Press, 1980); pt. 2, *A Christian Theology of the People Israel* (New York: Seabury Press, 1983); pt. 3, *Christ in Context* (New York: Harper & Row, 1988); Williamson, *A Guest in the House of Israel*; and R. Kendall Soulen, *The God of Israel and Christian Theology* (Minneapolis: Fortress Press, 1996).

44. See van Buren, *Christ in Context*, xviii–xix.

PART II

EVANGELICAL AND CONSERVATIONIST THEOLOGIES

4

INERRANCY AND THE BIBLE IN MODERN CONSERVATIVE EVANGELICAL THOUGHT

CARL F. H. HENRY

The doctrine of the inerrancy of the Bible has roots in scripture's valuation of itself, in Jesus' attitude toward scripture, in the teaching of the apostles, in the writings of church fathers, in Roman Catholic tradition, and in the view of the Protestant Reformers.

It is reaffirmed in statements of faith characterizing the conservative evangelical denominations, including the fifteen-million member Southern Baptist Convention, as well as by the 1949 founding statement of the Evangelical Theological Society[1] and by the extensive 1978 *Chicago Statement on Biblical Inerrancy*.[2]

Multitudes of devout believers affiliated even with critically compromised ecumenical churches and congregations subscribe to scriptural inerrancy. In 1910, the Presbyterian Church in the United States of America issued a doctrinal summary, reaffirmed in 1916 and in 1923, that identified the inerrancy of the Bible as among Christianity's essential beliefs.

CRITICS OF BIBLICAL INERRANCY

Biblical inerrancy means that the original manuscripts of the Hebrew-Christian scriptures are truthful in all that they affirm and teach nothing contrary to truth and fact. All tributes to the Bible, even as great literature, are subordinate to a view that defers to the biblical text in terms of divine revelation and inspiration. This high view predominates among evangelical theologians, being expounded and defended as recently as 1994 by Wayne Grudem.[3]

The notion that scriptural inerrancy is an apologetic artifice or ploy promoted by American fundamentalists, as some critics contend, has no legitimacy. Nor is it historically accurate to say that the doctrine of the inerrancy of the Bible has its lifeline in the "Princeton School" of Charles and Alexander Hodge and B. B. Warfield, although in the first part of the twentieth century they were assuredly among its influential champions in North America.

The doctrine of inerrancy is curiously ridiculed by critical scholars who cling unqualifiedly to their own extensive dogmatisms. Critical writers ridiculing the doctrine of inerrancy sometimes show little disposition to question their private authority; indeed, some critical theorists seem rather to be obsessed by it. To insist, as others do, that pervasive fallibility and sinfulness necessarily defaces all human experience and communication has negative implications not only for human omniscience in general but for the intellectual significance of Jesus of Nazareth as well.

The multiplex consequences of a denial of biblical inerrancy are attested by the variety and conflict of views reflected by contributors to this present volume. A selective and partisan approach to biblical teaching leads to extensive diversity. Forfeiture of biblical inerrancy involves a modification of scriptural inspiration and authority. It leads also to creative reconstructions of divine revelation and its implications. One after another the classic creeds of Christendom are undermined by kaleidoscopic combinations and recombinations of doctrinal affirmations and denials.

The record of higher critical claims that affirm the errancy of the Bible contrasts unimpressively with the insistence by evangelical scholars that patient exploration will vindicate the scriptural teaching. Destructive critics have been demonstrably mistaken not only with regard to minutiae of the biblical record but in their questioning of principal elements as well.

Among the erroneous claims once seriously made by critics—issuing in contrabiblical views that no reputable scholar would hold today—are such notions as that the Hittites of the patriarchal era never existed, that Moses could not have written the Pentateuch because writing was assertedly then nonexistent, that the Bible grossly overstates the power, wealth, and fame of Solomon's kingdom, that the Hebrew captivity in Babylon is a literary fiction. Few would now hold that John's Gospel—and many of the Pauline epistles as well—are really second- and third-century products.[4] Such claims deal not merely with the details of scripture but with basic aspects of the biblical account.

Meanwhile, in contrast to reckless and discredited critical views, the number of questionable or disputed biblical passages is continually being reduced as evangelical scholars continue to probe confirmatory evidence. Radical critical theories multiplied as concessions were made to speculative liberalism, secular humanism, liberation theory, feminism, and other novelties. But alleged errors in scripture dematerialized from decade to decade as misunderstandings were dispelled.[5]

It is assuredly the case that some religious cults have affirmed biblical inerrancy only to expound subbiblical and nonbiblical doctrines. But the question of interpretation must not be confused with that of objective authority. If scripture is not inerrant, no objectively verbal criterion exists whereby to distinguish authentic from unauthentic doctrines.

BIBLICAL AUTHORITY IN
THE ROMAN CATHOLIC CHURCH

The dogma of papal infallibility is often injected into the debate over the authority of scripture. Early in Christian history the title *papa* (Latin for "father") was applied affectionately to bishops or overseers of the churches, and sometimes even to simple priests. But from about the ninth century the term was applied in the

West solely to the bishop of Rome. From the time of Innocent III (1161–1216) the pope of Rome laid claim to be the vicar of Christ. As such the pope claimed supreme sovereignty over both the church and the Western world, exercise of earthly power being entrusted to the emperor and to his princes subject to papal sanction.

By virtue of the pope's declared primacy of jurisdiction in ecclesiastical matters he was considered the supreme doctrinal authority. In view of his asserted apostolic authority as pastor and teacher of all Christians, his pronouncements were regarded as infallible through divine assistance.

Appeal is made to some early church fathers, notably Irenaeus, to support the claim that the see of Rome was early considered to be the center of doctrinal and disciplinary unity for the entire church. But Thomas Aquinas (1225–1274) first discussed papal infallibility as an integral aspect of systematic theology. Pope John XXII declared that Thomas had written by inspiration of the Holy Spirit and Thomistic theology thereafter became official. In support of the doctrine of papal infallibility, Roman Catholic theologians assert the necessity of a central and final supreme authority in faith and morals—one easily accessible in times of dispute and providing a guarantee of the unity of faith.

Like Eastern Orthodoxy, Roman Catholicism emphasizes scripture alongside other authorities. Catholic representatives often appeal to scripture to attest papal primacy and infallibility (especially Matt. 16:18; Luke 22:31ff.; John 21:15ff.), a deduction that non-Catholics dispute. Yet in practice and even in commentary, Rome qualifies the primacy of scripture. The Tridentine Profession of Faith apparently affirms it in its identification of scripture as the "norm which governs and is not governed." This is modified, however, by a two-source communicated revelation and by the role of the magisterium. In the final analysis, tradition gains equivalence with scripture, not only through the expansion of canonical books but through the prominence of the magisterium as well. The Roman Catholic view is that authentic interpretation of the Word of God is entrusted solely to the pope and to the bishops in communion with him.

Gabriel Fackre notes the ambiguity of Catholic teaching on biblical authority.[6] The deposit of revelation is found in scripture and in tradition; the church's living tradition supplements and clarifies the Bible. "The definition of the dogmas of the church established directly or traceable to Scripture is in the hands of the magisterium," he comments.[7] Many Roman Catholics emphasize that the church first identified the Bible as authoritative and that the Bible is therefore subject to interpretation by the church. To this claim Calvin replied that "they speak as if the daughter gave birth to the mother."

After the Protestant Reformation some Roman Catholic spokesmen insisted that error permeated and corrupted the available translations, and emphasized that the Roman church is the ongoing locus of divine revelation and authority. Until Vatican II (1962–1965) the Latin Vulgate was the Roman Catholic Church's official translation. The Reformation promoted translation of the scriptures into the language of the people. Roman Catholic editions followed fast on Protestant editions. Calvin noted that some Romanists commonly depicted scripture as "a nose of wax" that can be "formed into all shapes."8 In recent years Roman Catholic agencies have cooperated in Bible translation and distribution, their editions always including apocryphal books. Yet in principle the Catholic believer receives even the scriptures from the infallible teaching authority of the church.

Both Hans Küng and Karl Rahner contend that the Holy Spirit's guidance promised by the Lord remains continuously present in the teaching hierarchy. Yet both Küng and Rahner consider dogma as a historically conditioned formulation of absolute divine truth. Rahner correlates the developing refinement of dogma with the errorlessness of church teaching; Küng has held that the Spirit's guidance is compatible with error in church teaching and that the church's teaching has in fact included error.9

JESUS' VIEW OF SCRIPTURE
AND SCRIPTURE'S SELF-VALUATION

There can be no doubt that Jesus invoked scripture as divinely authoritative and inspired, and that he viewed scripture as the Word of God given in written form. Jesus' response to Satan in the wilderness is based entirely on an appeal to scripture: "It is [stands] written" (Matt. 4:4ff.). He attributes the theological error of the Sadducees to their ignorance of the power of God and of the scriptures: "Ye do err, not knowing the scriptures, nor the power of God" (Matt. 22:29, KJV). The Sadducees disbelieved in a future resurrection and held that both body and soul perish at death. Their question to Jesus presupposed levirate marriage, a custom prescribed by the Mosaic code, whereby a dead man's brother was obliged to marry the widow if there were no sons. Suppose a woman successively married six husbands after the death of her first husband. In the resurrection to come, which of them would be her spouse? To this hypothetical question Jesus replies that the Sadducees are ignorant of the power of God, who raises the dead in circumstances quite different from those involved in this life and in which marriage claims no longer exist. The question: "Have you not read?" is a rebuke that appeals to the teaching of Exodus 3:6, in which God is ongoingly present in living relationships to the patriarchs and to Moses.

In the familiar words of the Sermon on the Mount, Jesus warns that not a "jot" or "title" of the entire Old Testament scriptures will be nullified as D. A. Carson comments, "Jesus here upholds the authority of the OT Scriptures right down to the 'least stroke of a pen.' "10 In another context Jesus affirmed that "scripture cannot be broken" or invalidated (John 10:35, KJV). Merrill C. Tenney appropriately comments that throughout the Fourth Gospel "the constant assumption is that the Scripture is the revelation of God."11

The apostle Paul expressly declares that "all scripture is God-breathed" (*theopneustos*)—in short, that the sacred writings are produced by the breath of God and hence are divinely authoritative (2 Tim. 3:16). This primary witness to the divine spiration of the scriptures is paralleled by many passages affirming that the sacred writings, although given *through* chosen human writers, are to be understood basically in terms of a *divine activity and element* (Ps. 119; Luke 24:25–27; John 10:34–35; Heb. 1:1–2; 2 Peter 1:21). Although New Testament references to the written word of God are mainly to the Old Testament, they anticipate also the New Testament writings (2 Peter 3:15–16).

In one of the earliest New Testament epistles, the apostle Paul commends the Thessalonians for honoring the apostolic word not simply as the word of humans but rather "for what it really is, the word of God" (1 Thess. 2:13, RSV). In the classic passage 2 Timothy 3:16, Paul emphasizes that divine inspiration is not simply an activity of God's "inbreathing" into chosen prophets and apostles; it is rather a matter of God's "*theopneustos* or outbreathing"—not indeed of humans but of the scriptural text ("all scripture is God-breathed"), so that divine inspiration is a quality of the text. The apostle Peter (2 Peter 1:21) indicates how scripture was produced: it involved a dual authorship (cf. 2 Sam. 23:2; Jer. 1:7, 9). The writers were carried along by the Holy Spirit.

No one can convincingly claim to stand in the tradition of Jesus and the apostles who views scripture as merely a human product, or who only selectively adheres to its teaching. Not only did Jesus honor every "jot" and "tittle," but the apostle Paul deferred to its very detail, even to the distinction between the use of a singular noun rather than plural (cf. Gal. 3:16).

Critics of scripture are prone to dismiss inerrancy as a fanciful modern appendage of historic church doctrine. Although the term "inerrancy" has commonly been used of scripture only since the nineteenth century, the view was not alien to the Reformers or the church fathers and, as already noted, is implicit in Jesus' statement "Ye do err, not knowing the scriptures" (Matt. 22:29, KJV).

INERRANCY:
ANCIENT OR MODERN?

Until the rise of destructive criticism in the modern era, the church considered the Bible to be God's infallible Word. Distrust of scripture in contemporary critical circles differs so strikingly from traditional deference to scripture that critical scholars understandably strive to show that their concessions are akin to views of the Reformers and of the medieval church fathers. But competent scholars engaged in Luther studies and in Calvin studies clearly range the Reformers on the biblical side of the debate.[12]

For more than a thousand years the Roman Catholic Church propagated the doctrine of biblical inerrancy. *The New Catholic Encyclopedia* in 1967 stated that "the inerrancy of Scripture has been the constant teaching of the Fathers, the theologians, and recent Popes in their encyclicals on Biblical studies."[13] The encyclopedia states that "Catholic doctrine maintains that, because the books of the Bible have God as Author they are free from error. Any theory that detracts from Biblical inerrancy is reprobated." The clearest statement of Catholic doctrine is found in the encylical *Providentissimus Deus*, issued in 1893 by Leo XIII (1878–1903). It states that "inerrancy is an inescapable corollary of divine inspiration. . . . So far is it from being possible that any error can coexist with inspiration, that inspiration not only is essentially incompatible with error, but excludes and rejects it as it is impossible that God Himself, the Supreme Truth, can utter that which is not true." He adds that "those who maintain that error is possible in any genuine passage of the sacred writings must either pervert the Catholic notion of inspiration or make God the author of such error."

It is the case that to the somewhat ambivalent statement "the books of Scripture . . . without error teach that truth which God . . . wished to see confided to Sacred Scripture" the New Catechism (1994) adds the qualification "for the sake of our salvation." This seems to entertain the possibility of error in historical or scientific matters. Yet orthodox Catholic scholars insist that the Catechism cannot contradict the express repudiation by Pius XII (1939–1958) of the notion that "inerrancy pertains only to religious sections of the Bible" or the denunciation by Benedict XV (1914–1922) of opinions "that regard historical sections to be without foundation in reality."

Although he is personally hostile to the view, Hans Küng notes that "from the time of Leo XIII, and particularly during the modernist crisis, the complete and absolute inerrancy of Scripture was explicitly and systematically maintained in papal encyclicals."[14]

George Duncan Barry's survey concludes that the church fathers stress the inspiration and authority of scripture, but not its inerrancy.[15] But the distinction was not an epistemological issue among the fathers. Barry remarks that "the fact that for fifteen centuries no attempt was made to formulate a definition of the doctrine of inspiration of the Bible, testifies to the universal belief of the Church that the Scriptures were the handiwork of the Holy Ghost." My own survey of the teaching of the fathers concerning the nature of scripture is found in *God, Revelation and Authority*.[16]

Augustine (354–430), the supreme theological influence prior to the Reformation, wrote to Jerome:

> I have learnt to ascribe to those Books which are of canonical rank, and only to them, such reverence and honour, that I firmly believe that no single error due to the author is found in any of them. And when I am confronted in these Books with anything that seems to be at variance with truth I do not hesitate to put it down either to the use of an incorrect text, or to the failure of a commentator rightly to explain the words, or to my own mistaken understanding of the passage.[17]

In view of the claims of some contemporary theologians that Luther held a critical view of scripture, it is noteworthy that Luther expressly identifies himself with Augustine's view: "St. Augustine, in a letter to St. Jerome, has put down a fine axiom — that only Holy Scripture is to be considered inerrant."[18]

More than one student of world religions has made the striking observation that only within the Christian movement has a cadre of scholars, supposedly speaking for the church rather than against it, devoted its energies to undermining the fundamentals of that movement, including its decisive epistemic authority, while all the while they were salaried by the sacrificial giving of devout believers.

Wayne Grudem corrects some common misconceptions of the inerrancy doctrine. The notion that inerrantists presuppose divine dictation is no longer entertained by critical scholars in view of the strenuous disavowal of that theory by evangelical writers. But not a few critics have contended that the Bible's use of ordinary rather than scientific or technical language precludes inerrancy, or that loose or free quotation falsifies inerrancy, or that unusual or uncommon grammatical construction falsifies truthfulness. But if the Bible were to use technically precise scientific language, the technical language of what generation should it employ in order to avoid being swiftly outdated? Quotation marks and other linguistic devices were not yet in use in the biblical era, and thesis-summary statements can be as accurate as precise vocabulary usage.

Critics have argued that the term "inerrant" is capable of multiple meanings and nuances, and should therefore be avoided. But many terms have a variety of meaning. Dictionary definition will readily distinguish between competing usages. Language would be greatly impoverished if all terms were restricted to but one meaning.

It has sometimes been argued that resort to the doctrine of biblical inerrancy is evasive because the original manuscripts are inaccessible. The objection that "no body has seen the inerrant autographs" is wide of the mark, however. No critic has seen errant autographs; the prophets and apostles provided divinely inspired inerrant originals. When they mount circuitous argument, critics evasively assume what they allege to prove.

The difference between autographs and copies must not, however, be exaggerated. The identification of variants by textual criticism has not undermined the propositional truth of scripture. Just as then-current texts of the Hebrew Old Testament were fully serviceable in Jesus' day, and the Nazarene insisted that "scripture cannot be invalidated" (John 10:34–35), so presently available Hebrew and Greek scholarly texts reflect an evident continuity with the original manuscripts. Deviations do not involve any alteration of doctrinal or ethical content but are mainly matters of tense, conflicting uses of singular or plural, or in a few cases of statistics (which are notably vulnerable in copying). One unintended achievement of textual criticism is that it has at times heightened confidence in the accuracy of the text.

In view of the vocational care exerted by scribes, it is more likely than not that their copies were meticulously accurate. Before the Qumran discoveries in 1947 the earliest copies of the Hebrew scriptures preserved in our century had been translated (with scant exception) at the end of the ninth and beginning of the tenth centuries of the Christian era. But Qumran manuscripts went back almost a millennium earlier, to the first Christian century, thereby antedating by a thousand years the earliest manuscripts of the Masoretic text on which our Old Testament translations have been based. Scholars were amazed how few scribal errors—and relatively unimportant at that—had found their way into the text in the course of a thousand years. F. F. Bruce commented that the Bible reader can rely on the long familiar text with "increased confidence in its essential accuracy."[19]

The historic view, remarks Grudem, is that scripture is "completely true and without error in any part."[20] The Bible's authority is therefore not limited to matters of "faith and practice" but extends also to whatever it affirms that bears on historical and scientific matters.

Critics who disparage the inerrancy claim are involved in a curious array of counterclaims and contradictions. Jack Rogers contends that English and Scottish scholars who wrote the Westminster Confession article on scripture held that the Bible is not wholly trustworthy.[21] Clark Pinnock views the Bible as the supreme norm and eminent authority, yet refuses to equate the Bible with divine revelation.[22] J. Kenneth Grider, in his *A Wesleyan-Holiness Theology*,[23] concedes that John Wesley wrote that "if there be one falsehood in that book, it did not come from the God of truth."[24] Yet Grider contends that inerrancy is not the Wesleyan position. Grider insists scripture is not inerrant except in doctrinal or ethical matters and that it would be inconsequential even if Jesus erred.[25] He affirms that scripture "is thought-inspired generally, although it might well be verbally inspired at certain special points. . . . Inconsequential errors on matters such as geography, mathematics or history may have existed even in the autographs."[26] In a foreword, Thomas C. Oden gives tribute to Grider's perspective as reflecting "a high view of scriptural authority without being trapped in wooden conceptions of the inspiration of the sacred text."[27]

Given Grider's view, the possibility remains that scripture narrates "story" rather than history. According to Grider not even very broad theological error is spiritually disqualifying, for he assures us that "if our sins are forgiven at the time of our death, we will be taken to heaven, even if our theology is off base a thousand miles."[28] Apparently almost no amount of theological error is spiritually devastating. Elsewhere Grider assures us that "what is reasonable is not a special interest of Scripture." Many "Christian understandings" are "not reasonable."[29] Such attempts to compensate for theological fallacy by emotive or experiential considerations are usually found in nonevangelical circles.

Other mediating scholars seek to compensate for supposed error in scripture by appealing to the Holy Spirit's empowerment, frequently at the expense of rational criteria. Donald Bloesch contrasts rational theism with biblical revelation.[30] Bloesch thinks confidence in logic and reason belongs to Enlightenment rationalism and not to the intelligibly revealed Logos and Wisdom of God.[31]

Some Reformed commentators prefer to speak of biblical infallibility rather than of biblical inerrancy, and they expound this to mean not the unrestricted truthfulness of scripture but rather that scripture salvifically escorts the attentive reader to the redemption that is in Christ Jesus. But this emphasizes volitional more than cognitive concerns and does not adequately grasp the prophetic or apostolic teaching about scripture, including the emphasis that objective inspiration is a quality of the text. The Bible cannot "find us" salvifically, moreover, apart from the historical factuality of certain events, centrally the incarnation and bodily resurrection of Jesus Christ. This has implications, moreover, for one's view of nature, since scientific theory predicated on naturalism precludes incarnation and resurrection.

There is some justification both for identifying infallibility with inerrancy and for distinguishing them, depending on definition. The two terms are indeed widely used as synonyms, and some languages do not distinguish them. Yet the term "infallible" is used not only to mean inerrant, but also for "not prone to err." In accord with this distinction, the present writer distinguishes inerrancy of the prophetic-apostolic autographs from the infallibility of the copies. The copies, while not necessarily inerrant, are not prone to err. This distinction accords also with the emphasis of the Protestant Reformers, who associated infallibility not with the pope but rather with the sacred writings.

Discussion of scriptural inerrancy, inspiration, and authority gains a diversionary orientation through the widening contemporary interest in narrative theology. Once scripture is understood essentially in terms of narrative, developed by exponents in a diversity of ways, Christian faith is faced with the problem of what remains historically factual, cognitively true, and ontologically real outside the text. If the biblical narrative is a projection of the imagination of the community of faith, it makes little difference ultimately whether the narrative is inspired and inerrant. There is room in Christian literature, of course, for writing that integrates biblical "wisdom" into human reflection and life. But if one shrivels scripture to this category, one imposes on the writers a genre that is more modern than apostolic and clouds the intention of the biblical writers.

The attempt to restate Christianity in terms of "myth" —as a category for experiencing a transcendent world apart from rational and historical referents—is but one step removed from some "narrative" interpretations. Postmodernists, who deny that there is an objective world, objective truth, objective morality, and an objective self are then again not far removed from such reconstructions of Christian faith, and should be confronted initially with their own insistence that no view is more true than any other.

INERRANCY IN
AMERICAN EVANGELICALISM

Across the century and a half of its existence, the massive Southern Baptist Convention has only thrice affirmed a statement of faith: the *Abstract of Principles* (1858), the *Baptist Faith and Message* statement (1925), and a revision of the latter in 1963. The *Abstract* asserts the divine inspiration of the scriptures, as "the only sufficient, certain and authoritative rule of all saving knowledge." By 1925 the conflict over evolution and then the Convention's rejection in 1963 of Ralph Elliott's *The Message of Genesis* (1961) and later of the introductory volume of *The Broadman Bible Commentary* (1969) were signposts of crystallizing attitudes against Darwinism and higher critical views of scripture. The Convention at no time moderated its confidence in the inspiration and authority of scripture. But the 1925 statement spoke of inerrancy only in regard to religious or doctrinal matters. The 1963 statement viewed inspired scripture as "the record of God's revelation of Himself to men" and added, as a hermeneutical guide, that "the criterion by which the Bible is to be interpreted is Jesus Christ."

C. H. Toy more than any other Southern Baptist scholar promoted higher critical views of the Bible. In 1879 he was forced to resign from the faculty of Southern Seminary. Reaffirmation of the full inerrancy and authority of the Bible followed by the leading Convention scholars, including A. T. Robertson and John R. Sampey, and discussion of scriptural authority thereafter frequently dominated Convention activities.

David S. Dockery's volume *Christian Scripture*[32] provides an insightful overview of relevant Southern Baptist developments. He notes that despite limited concessions to critical theories by one or another scholar, "the historic Southern Baptist position during the first century of its existence was primarily the commonly held conviction that the Bible is the inspired, written, reliable, and authoritative Word of God."[33] But in the 1950s more and more seminary and college faculty openly championed historical-critical studies, until a decade later controversy erupted publicly over the nature of scripture. Mediating efforts to combine belief in biblical inspiration with biblical criticism and theistic evolution were challenged. Critical scholars became increasingly aggressive until, as Dockery comments, "the doctrine of inerrancy was virtually absent in academic circles from the mid-twenties to the eighties, usually being relegated to obscurantist thought and falsely equated with a mechanical dictation view."[34]

In 1983 the Baptist Sunday School Board focused on the inerrancy controversy by selecting the doctrine of scripture for theological study. Books were appearing on both sides of the inerrancy debate. The National Association of Baptist Professors of Religion sought to repudiate inerrancy while affirming scriptural authority and inspiration. Others limited inspiration to matters of faith and morals, a view adopted by Fuller Theological Seminary in its transition from historic evangelical orthodoxy.

The Convention deliberately elected to its presidency and to the headship of denominational agencies leading clergy who affirmed inerrancy. Seminary boards came under increasing pressure to reflect the Convention's historically evangelical conservative affirmations.

Dockery summarizes the majority belief of Southern Baptists as that "the Bible is God's truthful written word" and that it should be "trusted in all matters."[35] The focal point of differences has been biblical inerrancy.

> The SBC of the nineties has clearly decided that inerrancy cannot be ignored, de-emphasized or eliminated from the discussion. It is the focus of the developing new theological center in the SBC. It has now been heartily affirmed, but it must be carefully clarified since the issue remains an emotional one, often misunderstood and misrepresented by progressives, moderates and even many traditionalists as well.[36]

Clarification of the doctrine of biblical inerrancy against misrepresentations and misunderstandings was provided by the 1978 *Chicago Statement on Biblical Inerrancy*[37] and the 1982 *Statement of Biblical Interpretation*,[38] both produced and signed by over one hundred evangelical scholars.

Kenneth S. Kantzer writes that "evangelicals today assert the truthfulness and divine authority of the Scripture—all of it."[39]

The inerrancy of scripture therefore remains the official commitment of the largest Protestant denomination of the United States (Southern Baptists, number fifteen million), of the Roman Catholic Church, of millions of believers in inter-denominational churches identified with the National Association of Evangelicals, and of many Christians whose churches are uneasily identified with the ecumenical leadership of the National Council of Churches. It has been the view of this century's world-renowned evangelist Billy Graham, of pastors of most of the nation's largest churches, and of many of the most gifted and productive young theologians of our time.

Commendation of the Bible as wholly trustworthy by those who reject its inerrancy violates logic and overstretches truth. Trust concerns volition more than cognition. But even if we correlate trust and truth and fact, the difficulty remains. Dr. J. Walter Carpenter, a Houston attorney, pointedly asks how one would react were a travel agency to provide a flight schedule containing some false departure times and a marginal note that some flights may be unpredictably canceled.

Among a ventriloquist's most disconcerting deceptions would be a projection of the person's voice as the Word of God. Such illusion becomes a pastime among theologians who affirm the errancy of scripture, yet insist on its divine authority and inspiration. Once divine authority and inspiration are correlated with scriptural fallibility and fallacy, the insistence on divine authority and plenary textual inspiration is inevitably qualified. It is unsurprising that so many critical theories have their glorious half-day only to perish. Nowhere are contemporary religionists more inconsistent than when they deny the inerrancy of the biblical autographs and simultaneously insist that scripture is the written Word of God. Something in the way of semantic confusion is obviously involved here that does violence to the law of noncontradiction. Only self-delusion can accommodate the view that a sovereign and loving God inspires an assertedly fallible text and that devout humans are to cherish it as divinely authoritative.

Compromise of biblical inerrancy must not, for all that, be translated into the necessary unregeneracy of those who defect from that doctrine, or into the necessary spiritual superiority of those who espouse inerrancy. What is at stake is the believer's logical consistency in relation to the inspired text. Some verbally orthodox humans have disowned the Lord, while some who disavow orthodoxy have lived commendable lives. God alone knows the human heart and the many factors that shape human decision. Inerrancy need not be the first thing said about scripture, which itself gives priority to scripture's divine authority and inspiration.

Nor does the Bible's inerrancy assure accuracy of interpretation, although there can be no objectively normative interpretation of a fallible text. Yet even some marginal cults that espouse unorthodox doctrine have had to acknowledge that the Bible teaches its divine authority, inspiration, and inerrancy.

When critical scholars partition or revise or reject textual teaching while they cling to fragments of it, the question must indeed be pressed on what epistemic ground they retain elements of a text that they otherwise consider unreliable.

Nor does it follow that inerrantists need to avoid relationships with errantists; surely they can dialogue over theological, ecclesial, and social issues. But without minimal doctrinal confession, one puts in jeopardy one's salvific faith in Christ the Redeemer. The denial of inerrancy can be and often is a crucial first step in disengagement from other revealed truths that are definitive of evangelical orthodoxy.

NOTES

1. "The Bible alone, and the Bible in its entirety, is the Word of God written, and therefore inerrant in the autographs."
2. "*Inerrant* signifies the quality of being free from all falsehood or mistake and so safeguards the truth that Holy Scripture is entirely true and trustworthy in all its assertions."
3. Wayne Grudem, *Systematic Theology: An Introduction to Biblical Doctrine* (Grand Rapids: Zondervan Publishing House, 1994), 90–102.
4. See Carl F. H. Henry, *God, Revelation and Authority*, vol. 4: *God Who Speaks and Shows* (Waco, Tex.: Word Books, 1979), 77ff.
5. See Gleason L. Archer, *Encyclopedia of Bible Difficulties* (Grand Rapids: Zondervan Publishing House, 1982).
6. Gabriel Fackre, *The Christian Story*, vol. 2 (Grand Rapids: Wm. B. Eerdmans Publishing Co., 1987), 125ff.
7. Ibid., 127.
8. John Calvin, *Tracts and Treatises* 3:69.
9. Cf. the discussion in Henry, *God, Revelation and Authority*, vol. 4, 225ff.
10. Frank E. Gaebelein, ed., *The Expositor's Bible Commentary*, vol. 8 (Grand Rapids: Zondervan Publishing House, 1984), 145.
11. Frank E. Gaebelein, ed., *The Expositor's Bible Commentary*, vol. 9 (Grand Rapids: Zondervan Publishing House, 1981), 113.
12. Cf. M. Reu, *Luther and the Scriptures* (Columbus, Ohio: Wartburg Press, 1944); and James Packer, "Calvin's View of Scripture," in *God's Inerrant Word*, ed. John Warwick Montgomery (Minneapolis: Bethany Fellowship, 1974).
13. *The New Catholic Encyclopedia*, ed. Catholic University of America (New York: McGraw-Hill, 1967) 2:384.
14. Hans Küng, *Infallible? An Inquiry*, trans. Edward Quinn (Garden City, N.Y.: Doubleday, 1972), 174.
15. George Duncan Barry, *The Inspiration and Authority of Holy Scripture: A Study in the Literature of the First Five Centuries* (New York: Macmillan Co., 1919), 10.
16. Henry, *God, Revelation and Authority*, vol. 4, 370–73.
17. Augustine, *Epistolae*, 82. i.3.
18. Martin Luther, *Weimar Ausgabe*, 24:1, 347, sermon on John 16:16–23.
19. F. F. Bruce, "New Light from the Dead Sea Scrolls," in *The Holman Study Bible*, ed. Carl F. H. Henry (Philadelphia: A. J. Holman Co., 1962), 1175.
20. Grudem, *Systematic Theology*, 90.
21. Jack Rogers, *Confessions of a Conservative Evangelical* (Philadelphia: Westminster Press, 1974).
22. Clark Pinnock and Delwin Brown, *Theological Crossfire: An Evangelical-Liberal Dialogue* (Grand Rapids: Zondervan Publishing House, 1990), 40–47.
23. J. Kenneth Grider, *A Wesleyan-Holiness Theology* (Kansas City, Mo.: Beacon Hill Press, 1994).
24. John Wesley, *The Journal of the Rev. John Wesley*, A.M., ed. Nehemiah Curnock, (London: Epworth Press, 1938), 6:117.

25. Grider, *Wesleyan-Holiness Theology*, 75–79.

29. Ibid., 99.

27. Ibid., 13.

28. Ibid., 100.

29. Ibid., 547.

30. Donald Bloesch, *A Theology of Word and Spirit* (Downers Grove, Ill.: InterVarsity Press, 1992), 255.

31. Ibid., 253.

32. David S. Dockery, *Christian Scripture* (Nashville: Broadman & Holman, 1995).

33. Ibid., 199.

34. Ibid., 205.

35. Ibid., 208.

36. Ibid.

37. See Norman Geisler, *Inerrancy* (Grand Rapids: Zondervan Publishing House, 1979).

38. See Robert Preuss, *Hermeneutics, Inerrancy, and the Bible* (Grand Rapids: Zondervan Publishing House, 1984).

39. "Evangelicals and the Inerrancy Question," in *Evangelical Roots*, ed. Kenneth S. Kantzer (Nashville: Thomas Nelson, 1978), 95f.

5

POSTMODERN PALEOORTHODOXY

THOMAS C. ODEN

M*odernity* is the period, the ideology, and the malaise of the time from 1789 to 1989, from the storming of the Bastille to the fall of the Berlin Wall. The gawky, ungainly term *postmodern* points ironically to the course of actual hazardous history following the death of modernity. The period after modernity is a required course for Catholics and evangelicals who attest the risen Lord amid a dying culture.

ON KICKING THE POST
OUT OF ULTRAMODERNITY

When nostalgic ultramodernity poses as trendy postmodernity, what apologetic responses are fitting for evangelicals? At what point will evangelicals learn to kick the post out of a fatigued ultramodernity camouflaging as postmodern?

The term *postmodern* is still being used by ultramoderns as if the assumptions of modernity were going to continue forever. Postmodernity in their sense simply refers to an intensification of the despairing messianisms of modernity.

When evangelicals today hear reckless talk of postmodernity by avant-garde academics, there is no longer any reason to break out in a sweat. The cure is easy: just quietly strike out the *post* and mentally insert *ultra*. That is what I call kicking the post out of ultramodernity.

Where postmodern has become a euphemism for ultramodern, paleo-Christians do not mind making a little jest over the difference. Where the value assumptions of modernity are nostalgically idealized, and where ancient wisdoms are compulsively disparaged, you have only a thinly veneered ultramodernity, even where it calls itself postmodernity. It is like a moth winging frantically and circling ever closer to the flame of instant fad death.

The ploy is to make modern value assumptions appear eternal by co-opting them in what is called *postmodernity*. The nameplate may say postmodern, but the *intellectus* was patented in the Enlightenment. The subterfuge is based on the deceit of trying to make the key values of corrupted modernity appear permanent by endowing them with the fake label postmodern. It is a cover-up that the liberal investigative journalists have not even begun to grasp, and are too intimidated to investigate.

The Catholic-evangelical position on postmodernity was well established long before 1980, long before many in America had heard of Derrida or Foucault. Already by the late '70s, before the postmodern fad of the 1980s, some of us were looking toward the emergence of a

> postmodern orthodoxy, having been immersed in the deteriorations of later stage modernity, now reawakened to the power and beauty of classical Christianity, seeking to incorporate the achievements of modernity into an ethos and intellectus that transcends modernity under the guidance of ancient ecumenical Christianity.[1]

That, in fact, was the "agenda for theology," as I saw it, in 1979 and remains so for many more today than in 1979.

> This is what I mean by postmodern orthodoxy. Its spirit is embodied in the student who has been through the rigors of university education, often through the hazards of the drug scene, through the ups and downs of political engagement, through the head shrinks and group thinks of popular therapies, and through a dozen sexual messianisms, only to become weary of the pretentious motions of frenetic change. Finally they have come on Christ's living presence in the world in an actual community of Christians and now have set out to understand what has happened to them in the light of the classical texts of scripture and tradition.[2]

> The agenda for theology in the last quarter of the twentieth century, following the steady deterioration of a hundred years and the disaster of the last two decades, is to begin to prepare the postmodern Christian community for its third millennium by returning again to the careful study and respectful following of the central tradition of classical Christianity.[3]

It was not until after this that the secular expressions of postmodern theology began to be formed, in response to the work of Foucault, Derrida, and Rorty, when their weaker, thinner, chic definition of postmodernity caught the imagination of ultramodern (not postmodern!) academics in literary and hermeneutic theory. It was only then that the popular press caught sight of the concept of postmodernity according to this later, despairing, ultramodern definition. Since the media elites have controlled this definition since the early 1980s, it has intruded itself belatedly upon theological dialogue as if normative. I continue to return to the pre-1980 definition of postmodernity, which is evangelically more hopeful, culturally more realistic, and providentially more circumspect.

WHITHER POSTMODERN PALEOORTHODOXY?

Postmodernity in its truer, paleoorthodox definition is simply that period that follows the time span from 1789 to 1989 which characteristically embraced an enlightenment worldview that cast an ideological spell over our times, now in grave moral spinout.

The spinout phase of later modernity is epitomized by the reductive naturalism of Freud, which is no longer marketable as an effective therapy, the idealistic historical utopianism of Marx, which is now internally collapsing from St. Petersburg to Havana, the narcissistic assertiveness of Nietzsche, which is drastically cutting life expectancy on urban streets, and the modern chauvinism typified by Feuerbach, Dewey, and Bultmann, which imagines the ethos of late modernity to be the unquestioned cultural norm that presumes to judge all premodern texts and ideas. Under the tutelage of these once brave modern ideologies so touted by the liberal media elites, sex has been reduced to orgasm, persons to bodies, psychology to stimuli, economics to planning mechanisms, and politics to machinery. These malfunctioning ideologies are today everywhere in crisis, even while still being fawned over by isolated church bureaucratic elitists.

These tired, fading modern illusions are woven together in an ideological temperament that still sentimentally shapes the old-line liberal Protestant ethos, especially its politicized bureaucracies and academies, who remain largely unprepared to grasp either their own vulnerability or their divine calling and possibility within this decisive historical opportunity.

The Marxism-Leninism of the Soviet era is now gone; the Freudian idealization of sexual liberation has found it easier to make babies than to parent them morally; the children of the postpsychoanalytic culture are at peril; the truculence of Nietzschean nihilism has spread to the bloody banks of Nazi, Soviet, and Cambodian rivers with a trail of genocide along the way; the modern chauvinism of once-confident Bultmannians is now moribund, since the modernity they expected never arrived.

These once-assured ideologies are now unmasked as having a dated vision of the human possibility; for none has succeeded in engendering a transmissible intergenerational culture. Since each of these ideological programs has colluded to support the other, they are now falling synchronously down like tottering dominoes: the command economies, the backfiring therapeutic experiments, the patient-abusing therapists, the mythic fantasies of demythology, the interpersonal fragments of drug experimentation, the exploding splinters of narcissism, and their wholly owned ecclesial subsidiaries, their theological hirelings and flunkies. If the Freudian project, the Bultmannian project, the Marxist project, and the Nietzschean project are all functionally morose, then later-stage modernity is dead in the regenerative sense. That is what is meant by the phrase "terminal modernity." In a despairing search for a social utopia, we have blundered our way into the black hole of a social counterutopia.

Renewing classic Christians are now being awakened and energized by this dawning realization: the Holy Spirit is determined to continue making alive the body of Christ. It is only on the falsely hypothesized premise of the default of the Holy Spirit that the called-out people might seem at times to be coming to nothing. The demise of the church is the least likely premise in the Christian understanding of history.

Those who willingly enslave themselves to passing idolatries should not be surprised when these gods are found to have clay feet. When beloved modern systems die, the idolaters understandably grieve and feel angry and frustrated. Meanwhile the grace-enabled community can celebrate the passage through and beyond modernity, and celebrate the intricate providences of history in which each dying historical formation is giving birth to new forms and refreshing occasions for living responsively in relation to grace.

What is happening today is a profound rediscovery of the texts, apologetic methods, and pastoral wisdom of the long-neglected ancient Christian exegetical tradition. For many evangelicals this means especially the Eastern church fathers of the first five Christian centuries, which never suffered as deeply as did Western medieval Catholicism from the distortions of speculative scholasticism.

What is happening amid this historical situation is a joyful return to the sacred texts of Christian scripture and the consensual exegetical guides of the formative period of scriptural interpretation. The *postmodern paleoorthodox* pioneers are those who, having entered in good faith into the disciplines of modernity, and having become disillusioned with the illusions of modernity, are again studying the Word of God made known in history as attested by prophetic and apostolic witnesses whose testimonies have become perennial texts for this worldwide, multicultural, multigenerational remembering and adjudicating and reconciling community of pardon.

IS THE HISTORY OF EXEGESIS RECOVERABLE
AFTER A CENTURY OF REDUCTIONIST HISTORICISM?

The Holy Spirit has a history. When this history is systematically forgotten, it is incumbent on evangelical guardianship to recover it by new, rigorous historical effort. This is why the apologetic task for biblical studies in our time must focus in a deliberate way on the early history of exegesis. We have a right to learn from the reasonings and arguments that have sustained Christian textual interpretations and spiritual formation through many previous modernities, especially in their earliest prototypical forms. The canonical text has a history of interpretation, which has been systematically ignored in the last century of historicist investigation.

Evangelical scholarship is already sorely tempted to become too much co-opted by reductionist nineteenth-century historicist models of interpretation that approach the text by disavowing that it could be the revealed Word of God. To overcome this amnesia, Catholic evangelicals are conspicuously taking the lead in recovering the history of exegesis among the guild of biblical scholars.

This is why most of the rest of my life will be primarily devoted to editing a twenty-seven volume *Ancient Christian Commentary on Scripture*. Its goals are the renewal of Christian preaching based on classical Christian exegesis, the intensified study of scripture by laypersons who wish to think with the early church about the canonical text, and the stimulation of Christian historical, biblical, theological, and pastoral scholars toward further inquiry into the exegesis of the ancient Christian writers.

This verse-by-verse commentary will consist of carefully chosen selections in dynamic equivalent English translation from the ancient Christian writers of the first eight centuries. Texts are now being selected by an international team of experts out of the ancient Christian tradition from Clement of Rome to John of Damascus, ranging through the early centuries of Christian exegesis (100–750 C.E.).

This work stands in the early medieval catena tradition of patristic exegesis, and will benefit by utilizing and adapting that tradition in appropriate ways. This after-modern effort has antecedents in Eastern Orthodox and in seventeenth-century Lutheran and Reformed inheritors of the tradition of the *glossa ordinaria*.

On each page the scripture text will be presented in the center, surrounded by well-referenced direct quotations of comments of key consensual early Christian exegetes. The most succinct way to visualize this is to picture the printed text of the Talmud, a collection of rabbinic arguments and comments of the same period as the patristic writers, surrounding and explicating the texts of the sacred tradition.

HAVE EVANGELICALS OUTLIVED
THE DISSOLUTION OF MODERNITY?

The turning point we celebrate today is: the enduring called-out community has in fact outlived the dissolution of modernity. It is a fact: Catholic and evangelical spirituality, scholarship, preaching, pastoral care, and institutional life have, against all odds, already weathered the waning winter of modernity.

We are witnessing an emerging resolve in worldwide Protestant, Catholic, and Eastern orthodoxy to renew familiar, classic spiritual disciplines: daily scripture reading, prayer, mutual care of souls, and intensive primary-group accountability that lives out of its baptism and is constantly nurtured by the Eucharist.

Having been disillusioned by the illusions of modernity, the faithful are now engaged in a low-keyed, quiet determination unpretentiously to return to the spiritual disciplines that have profoundly shaped our history and common life together, and in fact have enabled our survival.

As amid any cultural death, gracious gifts of providential guidance are being proffered to human imagination, along with precipitous risks. Human folly and sin are being curbed by the quiet hedging of God in history.

Those made alive by the Spirit, whose lives are hidden in Christ, enter the postmodern ethos confidently. Those enlivened by the reemergent vitality of classic Christian forms of pastoral care, preaching, worship, and spiritual formation are now living and breathing in a refreshing atmosphere, in a fecund, volatile, potentially pivotal period of apostolic opportunity and consequential witness. Long-set-aside possibilities and aptitudes for spiritual formation that have had a history of being repeatedly disdained by modernity are at last viable. We need not be driven to despair by the pressures and melancholy that the modern visions of history pretend authoritatively to thrust on us. Their vulnerability offers the witnessing community an unparalleled opportunity.

The faithful who are surviving modernity are each year less and less intimidated by the supposed potency of modernity. Many pilgrims in evangelical spirituality have already doubly paid their dues to modernity, and now search for forgotten wisdoms long ruled out by the narrowly fixated dogmas of Enlightenment empiricism and idealism.

This does not prevent the faithful from appreciating the technological, economic, political, and social achievements of modernity. This can be done precisely while soberly recognizing that the ideological underpinnings of modernity now face radical crisis. Modernity lacks the power to regenerate itself intellectually and morally and continue its genetic imprint into another generation. The gene pool is too thin for reconceiving modernity. The reigning metaphor is impotence. That is the central effect of late-modern aspirations.

WHY ARE THE EMERGING AUTHENTICALLY POSTMODERN EVANGELICALS CALLED YOUNG FOGYS?

To all who suffer in despair over decadent modernity, I bring joyful greetings on behalf of young classicists within the postliberal underground who abide patiently in the crevices of our despairing modern culture. Despair is the least appropriate response of well grounded culturally aware believers to these times. Classic Christianity has in fact healthily survived the death of modernity and joyfully flourishes in this spirited after-modern environment.

Against all prognostications of modern chauvinists, disciplined Christian spirituality is spontaneously flourishing all over postmodernity. I speak of the impassioned commitment of an emerging group of young born-again, classic Christian cultural renovators who, having analyzed the methods of analysis of modernity are now applying an evangelical critique to those analyses. Having been disillusioned by the emptiness of those methods of modern inquiry (psychoanalytic, nihilistic, naturalistic, Marxist, and historicist), having turned in horror from their social consequences, they are now turning in earnest to the texts and ideas and liturgies of classic Christianity. They are young in spirit because they are not the least intimidated by modernity.

When I affectionately dubbed them "young fogys" over two decades ago, I intended merely to point ironically to their youthful, impassioned vitality amid modern disillusionments, and their energetic determination to ground themselves scripturally and classically. The term has stuck. They are young because they have not been made old by modernity's skewed dreams. They are young because they are enlivened by the Holy Spirit. They are fogys only in the comic sense of being freed to laugh heartily at the inner contradictions of pretentious modernity. They are sharply distinguished from the "old fogys" who remain ideologically bogged in liberal pietism. These young believers are wrongly imagined to be outdated fogys by a hypermodern messianism, which fantasized the continuing power of the assumptions of modernity. They are made youthful and energetic precisely by becoming firmly grounded in the apostolic tradition.

So here's to a whole school of emergent classicists who are discovering in the ancient Christian exegetes of the early Christian centuries the most brilliant hermeneutics and doctrinal reflection. In the company of Irenaeus, Athanasius, and Jerome, they have found a surer basis for critiquing modern historicist pretenses to hermeneutical superiority.

Anyone who has discovered the dialectical joy and vitality of that critique is a young fogy. The young fogys are grass-rooted, risk-capable, street-smart, populist, pragmatic renovators of the apostolic tradition. They are mostly recent graduates of celebrated universities, yet tough-minded critics of the ideological tilt of those universities. They understand that the surest form of cultural renovation begins one by one with personal religious conversion, the turning of the heart away from arrogance and folly and toward faith in God. They are the newest work of the Holy Spirit.

The emerging young classical Christians are astute critics of my generation's modern chauvinism that so blithely assumed that newer is better, older is worse. As I behold this spiraling emergent generation of young classic Christian women and men, I find myself entering into a kind of resistance movement in relation to my own generation of moral relativists, who have botched up our society pretty absolutely. These young believers know that time is on their side, and so far as time goes, God has plenty of it.

WHY IS PALEOORTHODOXY
SO CROSS-CULTURALLY AGILE?

The most salient feature of orthodoxy is not its rigidity, but its flexibility centered in life in the Lord, its willingness to enter freely into this and that culture on behalf of its all-embracing redemptive mission. Apostolicity does not imply a rigid lack of adaptability to emergent cultural formations. The glory of the apostolic tradition is precisely its readiness to reach out, meet, confront, and dialogue with different cultures, to become all things to all on behalf of Christ (1 Cor. 9:19–22).[4]

The Holy Spirit speaks all languages. Paleoorthodoxy has not survived twenty centuries by being unresourceful or unable to make clever responses. Rather, it is freed to variable cultural responsiveness by being centered in the eternal Word—the incarnate and risen Lord. The living body of Christ lives by penetrating and embracing each new culture and language and symbol system as God's special providential gift.

Because cultures and languages are constantly changing, and because the apostolic testimony must be attested in ever-new languages, it is a necessary feature of the apostolic tradition that it both guard the original testimony and make it understandable in emergent cultural formations. Failing either is to default on the apostolic mission. Far from implying unbending immobility, apostolicity requires constant adaptation of the primitive apostolic testimony to new historical challenges and languages, yet without altering or diluting the primitive witness.

CAN WE RETRIEVE THE CANON?

Contemporary witnesses are called to take every thought captive to Christ, to appraise every argument or explanation by its correspondence with the received testimony of the apostles. The working premise is that the Holy Spirit would not allow a truly debilitating or defective testimony to be transmitted permanently to the church.

It is not we who creatively decide what is apostolic, but the apostles. The contemporary apostolate exists only because it has decided that the testimony of the apostles is true and will always remain trustworthy. If the apostles' testimony is fundamentally flawed or defective, there is no way the church can begin to learn the truth, for the truth about God's own coming is attested only by original eyewitnesses, namely, those called the apostles.

Surely the Holy Spirit would not leave an important matter as the intergenerational transmission of the truth up to the jaded imagination of tired, tenured radicals speculating about form criticism or social location analysis. The academic cartel of selected guild scholars who sat for decades on the Dead Sea Scrolls has only recently been broken up. Now it is time to say to the guild scholars who pretend to serve a guardianship function with the New Testament text: Give us back our canon.

There is nothing to fear from solid historical inquiry into the tradition of transmission of apostolic testimony. There is only the task of improving historical inquiry and bringing it ever closer to the facts of the incarnate, risen Lord and his body, the church.

WHAT ABOUT THOSE WHO CHOOSE
TO BE LIBERATED FROM CLASSIC CHRISTIANITY?

The liberated form of ecclesial imagination that has attached itself to modernity is expiring as modernity expires. The church that weds itself to modernity is already a widow within postmodernity.

Those who view themselves as most liberated think of themselves as most freed from traditional constraints of all sorts, all past oppressions, and old ideas. Yet they are often unaware of their own continuing debt to premodern wisdoms.

The fantasy of liberation is not a metaphor applied externally to accommodators from outside their own self-understanding, but a term they insist on applying to themselves. By liberated they usually imply: doctrinally imaginative, liturgically experimental, disciplinarily nonjudgmental, politically correct, ethically situationist, and, above all, sexually lenient, permissive, uninhibited. I am not speaking merely of liberation theology in the best sense, as argued by Gustavo Gutiérrez or Jürgen Moltmann or Theodore Runyon, but rather an engulfing attitude that we have been liberated from our classic Christian past, from the patriarchalism of Christian scriptures, from benighted Jewish and Christian traditions. As a former full-time liberator, I know from experience how mesmerizing this enchantment can be.

When the liberated have virtually no immune system against heresy; no defense whatever against perfidious teaching, no criteria for testing out the legitimacy of counterfeit theological currency, it is time for the faithful laity and clergy to enter the arena of bureaucratic church reform and reinvent church governance, polity, and theological education. Laity are coming to grasp that they have a decisive interest in the apostolicity of the ministries they are asked to trust.

What is now clear is that a worldview is ebbing, perhaps not yet wholly extinct, but numb in emergent vitality and only awaiting a lingering expiration process of these failed ideologies: autonomous individualism, narcissistic hedonism, reductive naturalism, and absolute moral relativism. Others may call that world something other than terminal modernity, but I have no better way of naming it.

Young fogys, the mod-surviving, postmodern paleoorthodox, are those who, having entered in good faith into the disciplines of the modern university, and having become disillusioned with its illusions, are again studying the texts of the ancient Christian tradition that point to the Word of God revealed in history, as attested by prophetic and apostolic witnesses whose testimonies have become perennial authoritative scripture for this worldwide, multicultural, multigenerational, remembering and celebrating community.

NOTES

1. Thomas C. Oden, *Agenda for Theology* (New York: Harper & Row, 1979), passim.
2. Ibid., 5.
3. Ibid., 31.
4. Martin Luther, *Luther's Works* (Philadelphia: Fortress Press, 1955), 27:202.

[6]

EVANGELICAL THEOLOGY
IN PROGRESS

CLARK H. PINNOCK

Many are acquainted with evangelicalism as a religious phenomenon but few know much about it as a theology. This is because it is not really a theology at heart but a spirituality or way of being Christian. Such theology as there is within it is usually practically, not academically, oriented. Serious theology is not a big seller in the evangelical market. Nevertheless, serious theology is done on the edges of the movement, and this chapter will attempt to offer the reader access to it. Even the meaning of evangelical theology is contested and you will find several versions of it in this very book. The particular version presented here comes from one who views evangelicalism as a spirituality, not a creed, a point of view that allows for more theological pluralism than might have been expected.[1]

The noun *evangelical*, like Christian, belongs to the whole church (it means "gospel" people), but has been removed from general usage and applied to a particular group choosing to call itself evangelical. No longer a general word, it has become the property of a conservative, postfundamentalist, subculture in the church. With help from the media, this group managed to expropriate it and make it refer only to themselves. Indeed (to be candid), some would like to narrow the reference more if they could and have it refer to their subset of the subculture. For example, many of the Reformed do not consider Arminians evangelical, and there are similar suspicions among Wesleyans, Pentecostals, and Anabaptists. Being evangelical today, in this new sense, is a marriage of convenience, not necessarily of love. It refers to a conglomeration of conservative Protestants thrown together in something called evangelicalism. The theft of the word is not a happy business either—it is hard to explain what it means, others are deprived of its use, and those who grabbed it carry the burden of being the only "gospel" people, a claim hard to justify and harder to live up to. So before I'm done, I will write about the possibility of giving the word back when circumstances permit.[2]

MOVEMENT NOT THEOLOGY

Evangelicalism is a diverse religious movement without a specific confession. Within it jostle a confusion of traditions, all crowded together. What we call evangelicalism today spun off from American fundamentalism as a movement to reform it.[3] Its early leaders liked the doctrinal solidity of fundamentalism as opposed to a culturally accommodated and unorthodox liberalism, but they also wanted to change it in certain ways. Men like Ken Kantzer, Carl Henry,[4] and Harold Ockenga liked the antiliberal posture of fundamentalism but disliked other features of it, such as antiintellectualism, loss of tradition, the tendency to separatism and disengagement from society. Though most of the founders of the National Association of Evangelicals (1943) were northern white Calvinist males and often Baptists, they managed to rally numbers of people from other traditions around their postfundamentalist agenda. They created a large and dynamic movement, but its theology is a patchwork quilt.[5]

Over three or four decades, the success of the venture led to a large increase in numbers, and consequently also to a greater theological diversity. To the original neofundamentalists were added varieties of charismatics, confessionalists, neoorthodox, and self-styled Catholic evangelicals. As a result, the movement has become something like a large and extended family. Religiously speaking, it is like a vast tent, and theologically speaking, like a kaleidoscope. Though from one point of view this is confusing, from another point of view it has created a wonderful mixture of vitality and diversity, which lies at the heart of the appeal of evangelicalism and which contains the promise, at least, of theological fruitfulness. So often vitality goes with narrowness and diversity with tepidity, but here you have a movement broad and vital at the same time. On such branches good theological fruit may come to hang.

My own experience may illustrate the rise of evangelicalism in its current form. Though my parents attended a mainline church, I was converted as a teen in the early fifties through the testimony of "born again" Christians and was nourished by the radio ministries of Billy Graham and Donald Grey Barnhouse. Soon I found myself attending Toronto Youth for Christ on Saturday nights, washing dishes at Canadian Keswick Conference in the summers, participating in Intervarsity Christian Fellowship at university, and attending mammoth Urbana missionary conventions at New Year. Like so many others, I was caught up in a religious awakening and became involved in an explosion of parachurch structures. It happened to hundreds of thousands of people like me, who suddenly found themselves in a network of like-minded persons.[6]

What I got swept up in was a religious movement that overflowed with vitality without being theologically defined beyond a few simple points. Spiritually and missiologically, it was and it is a powerhouse, but theologically there was and is only a simple set of convictions and not much inclination to deepen or broaden them. Certain leaders like Carl Henry wanted theological depth and specificity of a certain kind, but they labored in vain because most people just wanted vital Christianity with a simple theology. This made it possible for members of many traditions to come together around the evangelical banner—Lutheran, Reformed, Wesleyan, Baptist, dispensational, Pentecostal, Adventist, Campbellite, and more. It was possible because this was a movement, not a theology, and it was a piety that held it together, not a creed.

Inevitably there were tensions: between Calvinist and Arminian, dispensational and covenantal, charismatic and cessationist, high and low church, and (most important) between those who define evangelical creedally and those who define it spiritually. The founding leaders viewed it creedally in the context of orthodoxy, and they wanted to keep it as close as possible to the Reformed traditions, but they were not able to because people flooded into evangelicalism as a spiritual family transcending any confession. What defines evangelicalism for them is its warm biblical faith, its vital spiritual experiences, and its passion for mission and evangelism. Unwittingly, it tapped into the desire in people for faith that would be ecumenical and nonaligned and would bypass the tired, old denominational and theological barriers. Evangelicalism, like Pentecostalism, its high voltage sister, is part of the ecumenical surge of our century. People want Christ to be central, not the sectarian debates that led to wars of religion in the past.[7]

Evangelicalism is a spirituality that links people with others with whom they feel a religious affinity as if members of the same spiritual family. Some of its features include warm personal faith, love of the Bible, the desire to spread the gospel, delight in testimony, love of singing, and valuing of the quiet time. You know when you are in an evangelical setting the same way you know when you are in a Pentecostal or Roman Catholic grouping. Creed is not the key to recognizing it. Central is the vision of what it means to be a Christian. It includes a degree of doctrinal consensus, but much more in the style of religious experience.

Donald G. Bloesch captures the spirit:

> An evangelical is one who affirms the centrality and cruciality of Christ's work of reconciliation and redemption as declared in the Scriptures: the necessity to appropriate the fruits of this work in one's own life and experience; and the urgency to bring the good news of this act of unmerited grace to a lost and dying world. It is not enough to believe in the cross and resurrection of Christ. We must be personally crucified and buried with Christ and rise with Christ to new life in the Spirit. Yet even this is not all that is required of us. We must also be fired by a burning zeal to share this salvation with others.[8]

Being an evangelical theologian is different from being a process theologian or a feminist theologian because it does not refer to beliefs except tangentially. A good deal of it is sociological—it means that one identifies with this way of being Christian and networks with people in this spiritual family. One cannot deduce from this many details of what such theologians believe beyond a few essentials, because the network is theologically so inclusive. It is a bit like being a Catholic theologian—you know he or she belongs to the Catholic Church but do not know what this one espouses in detail because the church too is a large and diverse network. Actually evangelicalism is less theologically defined than that, and does not endorse Calvin or Luther, Wesley or Wimber, Rome or Canterbury, though it includes followers of them all. It is like an ecumenical river of traditions without a specific confession.

For that reason (ironically) a theologian may hold precisely the same views as an evangelical theologian and not be called one, simply because being one has mainly to do with networking, not with content (aside from simple convictions). Why is Bloesch called evangelical and Wainwright not? The answer is that Bloesch uses evangelical publishers and Wainwright does not. Were Wainwright to do so, he would inherit the label, because in every other respect he deserves it in terms of his own piety. Maybe he is happy just to be Methodist. When he wants to be ecumenical, he can work with the World Council of Churches or dialogue with the Roman Catholics; he doesn't need the peculiar ecumenism called evangelical.[9]

There is within evangelicalism a lot of room to encounter many theological options and much opportunity to try them out. The vitality and diversity of evangelicalism make theological creativity a real possibility. It is an enjoyable experience to live under this tent with so many who love God sincerely and want to share their faith. In their company, it is possible to grow as hearers of the word of God. Defining evangelical as a spirituality has advantages over earlier attempts to align it with Reformed theology. It is less restrictive theologically and more open ecumenically.

THE THEOLOGICAL ETHOS
OF EVANGELICALISM

Though evangelicalism is more a movement than a theology, it does have theological interests. It began as neofundamentalism, and its impulse was antiliberal from the start. Like Karl Barth, it takes a stand against liberalism in the church. Its theology protests against the forces of revision. One could say that liberals created the movement and that they hold evangelicals together. If liberals disappeared, evangelicals would fall to bickering among themselves again. Insofar as evangelicalism has one, it has a theology that is dictated by the liberal opposition, which determines what is included in it. Convictions like biblical authority, justification by faith, the deity of Christ, the lostness of humanity, the priority of grace, the necessity of new birth, and so on, which appear on typical evangelical doctrinal statements without elaboration are on them because they are felt to be under threat from liberalism. They are not listed to give a coherent picture of evangelical theology, but to point out features of classical theology that are being threatened.[10]

Evangelicalism has a conservative theological tendency and locates itself on the side of historic Christianity in the debates of our time. Evangelicals consistently oppose revising traditions laid down in scripture and creed and object to making them palatable to the cultured despisers of faith. The goal theologically is to train disciples in theologies in continuity with the faith once delivered to the saints.[11]

Evangelicalism does not have a theological vision, but adopts the defensive posture required by the current liberal threat. The threat keeps it focused theologically despite its own diversity of traditions. It always favors what is seen as orthodox Christianity over against what is seen as revisionist. Liberals force evangelicals to think theologically. Seeing classical faith under siege, evangelicals sally forth to defend it, and this feature serves them well. Many appreciate evangelicalism for this very reason. It appeals to a widespread desire for continuity with what theology has been in the past. As it has grown in numbers and self-confidence, however, its theologians feel ever freer to think about topics not dictated by the liberal threat and in ways not so predictably conservative.[12]

At first, evangelicalism's antiliberal, protest theology was narrowly conceived and crudely mounted. After all, the movement was dominated at first by paleo-Reformed elements. But owing to success over the decades, it has become much more inclusive, to the point that orthodoxy can no longer be equated with theology from the old Princeton Seminary. It sounds quaint now, but I was taught to look at it that way when I was converted. The early leaders mostly understood theology to be rational, propositional, and Reformed. But success spoiled their plans and a greater inclusivity set in. Now evangelicalism has to be defined as a spirituality—it has proved itself to be such.[13]

Not only will this mean a good deal more theological liberty, it may even allow for a better response to liberalism itself. With a greater appreciation of experience (for example), a more sympathetic judgment even of liberalism can be rendered. It will also make it easier for others than it was for me to transcend the theology that dominated in the early days. It took me the whole struggle free of the shackles of old Princeton, but this is a diminishing problem for younger people.

Evangelical theology has great promise due to its diversity coupled with vitality, a mix that creates a fruitful hermeneutical situation. Mixing with brothers and sisters from dozens of traditions and sharing with them a warm evangelical faith creates a great opportunity for growth in understanding. All evangelicals want to negotiate their identity in relation to the Bible and none want to go down the liberal path, but their diversity makes possible great mutual enrichment. How fruitful it can be to reflect theologically from an orientation that is vital, classical, and ecumenical!

TWO THEOLOGICAL CONTRIBUTIONS

One contribution arises out of the nature of the evangelical movement, whose identity theologically is to hold up the standard of sound teaching and guard the treasure of God's Word (2 Tim. 1:14ff.). In its simple theological way, it has been self-conscious about contending for the faith once for all delivered to the saints (Jude 3). Therefore, its first and chief contribution is bound to be one of conservation. Instinctively it rises to the defense of endangered traditions. Like Barth, though in a simpler way, evangelical theology sets itself against the liberal impulse, asserting the truth and importance for the modern world of doctrines that have been central to orthodoxy. The Word of God deposited in the scriptures must be heard. Human speculation must not dominate the biblical themes.[14]

In a movement whose instincts are conservative and antiliberal, it follows that a good deal of the time and energy of its theologians will go into a defense of the faith. Volumes will be written for the sole purpose of reasserting older beliefs against newer proposals. Great effort will be put into recovering biblical faith with its classical interpretations. The spirit of this conserving function is this: Let's go forward to the fathers, to the Reformers, to the Puritans, to Wesley, to the pietists, to Edwards, and to Hodge. Let's keep them in print and let's publicize their ideas. Evangelicals do not lack energy for this enterprise. The efforts leave much to be desired. They perpetuate some traditions perhaps better forgotten, and they commonly operate with an unadmitted paleo-Reformed hermeneutic. An amusing example is Grudem's subtitling his theology "An Introduction to Christian Doctrine," as if he had lifted it right out of the Bible and not filtered it through a paleo-Calvinist screen. At the same time, though out of step with the present diversity, this tendency actually reflects the original direction of the movement, which privileged the Reformed impulse.[15]

There was much lacking in these efforts: for example, theological determinism is left largely uncritiqued, the resurrection is slighted theologically owing to the prominence of the theory of penal substitution, the scope of salvation is narrowed to individual justification, and the charismatic dimension is suppressed. So one cannot praise such theology for independence and creativity, but perhaps credit can be given to it for standing up for the historic faith against forgetful and aberrant trends in modern theology. Modern theology has often fallen into grievous error, and somebody needs to call it back to its foundations in divine truth. In my judgment, God raised up and uses the evangelical movement (despite its many limitations) to preserve the gospel in our time. It matters not if we see it as a case of God's using the foolish to confound the wise—for in truth the quality of work has not been uniformly excellent.

Some speak of the scandal of the evangelical mind, meaning the lack of quality in evangelical thinking.[16] No doubt this is true, but it does not worry me much because I think God raised up the evangelicals to be witnesses, not scholars. Do we protest the undoubted lack of learning among Mother Teresa's nuns? Of course not—it is not their vocation. Being faithful, not profound, has been the calling of evangelicalism. If you want deep theology, look to Lutherans and Catholics. Mother Teresa's strength was a simple faith in the gospel, which also explained her appeal. People are weary of substitutions and want the living Word. There may be few scholars among us, but they are not essential when the real aim is to stop neo-paganism with an undiluted gospel. Of course, eventually depth must be added to proclamation for it to have staying power, but if the purpose of evangelicalism was to hold the fort until the reinforcements arrive, it is not fatal that the evangelical mind has been undeveloped. As a matter of fact, the reinforcements are arriving in numbers.[17]

With the passage of years, a second theological contribution has become possible. As the quality of theology has improved with practice, it has been able to add reform to the original function of conservation. A measure of innovation and creativity has begun to crop up because, in the course of defending the faith, the theologians have begun to notice ways to reform evangelical thinking as well. Reform was not something we thought was needed when we started out, but it was forced on us. Over time it has become apparent to many of us that there is room, not only for change among liberals, but for us to grow in understanding too. An increasing number of theologians are less sure about some of the traditions they used to think themselves duty-bound to defend, and they are reopening certain issues that had been thought closed.

I think I can explain how this happened, since it happened to me. We began to ask ourselves why we were defending certain traditions, some of which made little sense and seemed to have outlived their usefulness. It was all right to have admired fundamentalism for courage in standing up to modernism, but do we have to stop with the fundamentalist theology and method? Isn't evangelical theology potentially bigger, grander, and older than that? Therefore, we began to ask what evangelical theology is and what it might be: perhaps there are profounder accounts than reside in the current version shaped by Carl Henry and Billy Graham. William J. Abraham boldly spoke of the collapse of modern evangelicalism with its rationalism and its obsession with inerrancy. A large number of people have been hurt by the way theology has been handled. Jack Rogers looks back with love and anger to his experience in the movement. Alister McGrath refers to the dark side of evangelicalism, while Bloesch talks about its pathways to oblivion. Let us not be so flushed with success that we are blind to our foibles. We will not make a contribution to the renewal of theology if we are glued to being reformed ourselves.[18]

As a result, we are beginning to see a number of theologians who resemble, not settlers with a fortress mentality as before, but pilgrims searching for more truth. It is a bit unnerving, since evangelicals have always assumed that they had everything straight. Some do not want to hear about it. They regard openness to change as the slippery slope down which liberalism plunged, and they try to marginalize the new thinkers. But others appreciate fresh light being shed on aspects of God's Word. Nowadays, if you want to find the two types, the settlers tend to congregate at the Evangelical Theological Society, while the pilgrims like to gather in various sections of the American Academy of Religion. Fortunately, for those like myself who want to mix with both types, the societies meet back to back in the same cities.[19]

One result of the reforming impulse is the appearance of volumes in systematic theology that do not just defend past formulations but actually break new ground. (The biblical scholars have been doing this for years, but the theologians have been slower to catch up.) The best example, in my opinion, is Stanley J. Grenz, a native son of the movement, a student of Pannenberg, and a most productive scholar. He has just issued a notable systematic theology called *Theology for the Community of God*, which carries forward the program he sketched in *Revisioning Evangelical Theology*.[20] It is unique in many ways: it places theology in the postmodern setting, it adopts the motif of community, it integrates theology and apologetics, it works with narrative, not with timeless propositions, it is nonrationalist in method, it discusses scripture under pneumatology, and so on. The book marks a new phase and, I think, shows us the way forward.

Grenz is not alone as an innovative evangelical systematic theologian. Bloesch has joined the movement from the neoorthodox side of mainline Protestantism, and is presently writing a seven-volume set of dogmatics for InterVarsity Press in the Barthian style. He is an example of the way in which superb talent is joining the movement and deepening it. At the same time, the fideistic tone and other Barthian features are bound to temper its influence. The same would be true of Gabriel Fackre, who also adds depth but operates more in the mainline church context. Thomas Finger is another theologian who enriches the movement, but does so from the Mennonite fringe. As a result his excellent work is not widely noticed.[21]

The reforming function also appears in individual topical contributions. One interesting phenomenon has been a series of "four view" books, including *Predestination and Free Will: Four Views of Hell*, and *More than One Way? Four Views on Salvation in a Pluralistic World*. They bring to the surface a considerable diversity of evangelical opinion and break down the smugness that can stand in the way of growth in understanding. Our thinking about the theological situation has deepened.[22] Our thinking about scripture has become wiser in terms of the human aspects.[23] Our thinking about God has advanced in a more dynamic manner.[24] Our thinking about theology and science is going deeper in terms of integration.[25] Our thinking about salvation is opening out to embrace social action in it.[26] Our thinking about access to salvation and about God's generosity has enlarged.[27] We are even thinking well of the Roman Catholics:[28] Where will it stop! Certainly theology among evangelicals is improving. Perhaps it will even reach the point where it will be of help not only to us but even to others.

GIVING THE WORD BACK

Evangelicalism, like its sister Pentecostalism, has become a powerful form of twentieth-century Christian faith. It even has the potential of becoming a dominant form alongside Catholicism. This is likely if the Protestant mainline churches continue to refuse to listen to their people and act irrationally. The success of evangelicalism is due in large measure to their irresponsibility. If the denominations would only wake up and take account of reasons why evangelicalism has an appeal, they could stop the decline and make their proper and needed contribution. The liberal experiment was a mistake in so many ways, and the evangelical movement arose to preserve historic Christianity. But nothing prevents churches from returning to their roots and making evangelicalism unnecessary. The movement calls for reform. As soon as it happens, the need for evangelicalism as something separate disappears. Let's get together on the basis of a living faith in mere Christianity in a holy catholic church.[29]

When reform takes place, the word *evangelical* can be returned to the churches, because it will really describe them. The movement exists only for the good of the whole church and its goal is to be integrated back in. The time will surely come when the Word will be returned, when the evangelical witness will no longer be needed. The day will dawn when it will be normal to do theology classically. As we wait for that day, let us join forces with all others who want it together with us. Let us continue to build a larger and ever more ecumenical coalition. You are all invited to join in.

NOTES

1. For background, see Leonard I. Sweet, ed., *The Evangelical Tradition in America* (Macon, Ga: Mercer University Press, 1984), chap. 1; Alister McGrath, *Evangelicalism and the Future of Christianity* (London: Hodder & Stoughton, 1994); and Donald G. Bloesch, *The Future of Evangelical Christianity: A Call for Unity amid Diversity* (Colorado Springs: Helmers & Howard, Pubs., 1988).
2. Mark Ellingsen addresses the issue of word theft in a gracious way: *The Evangelical Movement: Growth, Impact, Controversy, Dialog* (Minneapolis: Augsburg, 1988), 46.
3. On the background movement, see George M. Marsden, *Fundamentalism and American Culture: The Shaping of Twentieth Century Evangelicalism 1870–1925* (New York: Oxford University Press, 1980). For the Canadian dimension, see John G. Stackhouse, *Canadian Evangelicalism in the Twentieth Century: An Introduction to Its Character* (Toronto: University of Toronto Press, 1993).
4. See Carl Henry's "Inerrancy and the Bible in Modern Conservative Evangelical Thought," chap. 4, above.
5. This is a description of Richard Lints, *The Fabric of Theology: A Prolegomenon to Evangelical Theology* (Grand Rapids: Wm. B. Eerdmans Publishing Co., 1993), 54–56.
6. On defining the movement, George Marsden, editor of *Evangelicalism and Modern America* (Grand Rapids: Wm. B. Eerdmans Publishing Co., 1984), calls it "The Evangelical Denomination," chap. 1. Robert K. Johnston calls it a family in "American Evangelicalism: An Extended Family," in *The Variety of American Evangelicalism*, ed. Donald W. Dayton and Robert K. Johnston (Knoxville, Tenn: University of Tennessee Press, 1991), chap. 15.
7. On defining evangelicalism as a spirituality, see Stanley J. Grenz, *Revisioning Evangelical Theology: A Fresh Agenda for the 21st Century* (Downers Grove, Ill.: InterVarsity Press, 1993), chaps. 1–3.
8. Bloesch, *The Future of Evangelical Christianity*, 17. Bloesch came to the movement, not from fundamentalism, but from an older evangelicalism of German pietism in the Protestant mainline. He illustrates the success of neofundamentalism in attracting such eminent scholars.
9. Southern Baptists too can be unsure as to whether they want to call themselves evangelical. Isn't their own identity good enough? James Leo Garrett, E. Glenn Hinson, and James E. Tull, *Are Southern Baptists "Evangelicals"?* (Macon, Ga: Mercer University Press, 1983); and David S. Dockery, *Southern Baptist and American Evangelicals: The Conversation Continues* (Nashville: Broadman & Holman, 1993).
10. On the themes, Alister McGrath, *Evangelicalism and the Future of Christianity*, chap. 2; and Mark Ellingsen, *The Evangelical Movement*, pt. 3.
11. In this respect, evangelical theology is more Catholic than it realizes: see Clark Pinnock, *Tracking the Maze: Finding Our Way through Modern Theology from an Evangelical Perspective* (San Francisco: Harper & Row, 1990), chap. 2.
12. Roger E. Olson, "Postconservative Evangelicals Greet the Postmodern Age," *Christian Century* (May 3, 1995): 480–83. Olson is also seeing a parallel with postliberalism out of Yale and even suggesting a strategic alliance. See "Whales and Elephants Both God's Creatures but Can They Meet? Evangelicals and Liberals in Dialogue," *Pro Ecclesia* 4 (1995): 165–89.
13. John Gerstner equated evangelical theology with his own paleo-Calvinism in "The Theological Boundaries of Evangelical Faith," in *The Evangelicals: What They*

Believe, Who They Are, Where They Are Changing, ed. David F. Wells and John D. Woodbridge (Nashville: Abingdon Press, 1975), 21–37.

14. In his last book, Bernard Ramm saw evangelical theology as being strengthened by recognizing Barth as ally, not as foe, in the struggle with liberalism. The title suggests also that Barth might help us escape fundamentalism at the same time: *After Fundamentalism: The Future of Evangelical Theology* (San Francisco: Harper & Row, 1983).

15. Among lengthy works of this kind: Millard J. Erickson, *Christian Theology*, 3 vols. (Grand Rapids: Baker Book House, 1985); James Leo Garrett, *Systematic Theology: Biblical, Historical, and Evangelical*, 2 vols. (Grand Rapids: Wm. B. Eerdmans Publishing Co., 1990, 1995); Gordon R. Lewis and Bruce A. Demarest, *Integrative Theology*, 3 vols. (Grand Rapids: Zondervan Publishing House, 1994); Thomas C. Oden, *Systematic Theology*, 3 vols. (San Francisco: Harper SanFrancisco, 1992); Wayne Grudem, *Systematic Theology: An Introduction to Christian Doctrine* (Grand Rapids: Zondervan Publishing House, 1994); and (more briefly) Alister E. McGrath, *Christian Theology: An Introduction* (Oxford: Basil Blackwell Publisher, 1994).

16. Mark A. Noll, *The Scandal of the Evangelical Mind* (Grand Rapids: Wm. B. Eerdmans Publishing Co., 1994).

17. Thomas C. Oden loves to blow the trumpet of orthodoxy: *Requiem: A Lament in Three Movements* (Nashville: Abingdon Press, 1995); and Carl E. Braaten and Robert W. Jensen are two excellent reinforcements standing in the gap on behalf of the mind: *Either/Or: The Gospel or Neo-Paganism* (Grand Rapids: Wm. B. Eerdmans Publishing Co., 1995). Names like these illustrate the fact that the evangelical impulse continues to attract talented fellow travelers.

18. William J. Abraham, *The Coming Great Revival: Recovering the Full Evangelical Tradition* (San Francisco: Harper & Row, 1984); Jack Rogers, *Confessions of a Conservative Evangelical* (Philadelphia: Westminster Press, 1974), 122f.; Alister McGrath, "The Dark Side of Evangelicalism," in *Evangelicalism and the Future of Christianity,* chap. 6; and Donald E. Bloesch, "Pathways to Evangelical Oblivion," in *The Future of Evangelical Christianity*, chap. 5. Having such critics gives me hope for the future.

19. Michael Bauman, *Pilgrim Theology: Taking the Path of Theological Discovery* (Grand Rapids: Zondervan Publishing House, 1992). Despite his open stance, Bauman sticks with the Evangelical Theological Society because he wants to keep ties with the settlers, as I do.

20. Stanley J. Grenz, *Theology for the Community of God* (Nashville: Broadman & Holman, 1994).

21. Donald Bloesch's volumes so far (all published by InterVarsity Press): *Theology of Word and Spirit* (1992), *Holy Scripture* (1994), and *God the Almighty* (1995). His wife, Brenda, is a superb researcher and theologian, and this helps explain how Don can produce so much so good so fast. Gabriel Fackre wrote one volume to be followed by seven others fleshing it out: *The Christian Story: A Narrative Interpretation of Christian Doctrine* (Grand Rapids: Wm. B. Eerdmans Publishing Co., 1984); Thomas N. Finger, *Christian Theology: An Eschatological Approach*, 2 vols. (Nashville: Thomas Nelson Publishers, 1985; and Scottdale, Pa.: Herald Press, 1989).

22. Stanley J. Grenz and Roger E. Olson, *Twentieth Century Theology: God and the World in a Transitional Age* (Downers Grove, Ill.: InterVarsity Press, 1992); and Pinnock, *Tracking the Maze.*

23. James D. G. Dunn, "The Authority of Scripture according to Scripture," in *The Living Word* (London: SCM Press, 1987); John Goldingay, *Models for Scripture* (Grand Rapids: Wm. B. Eerdmans Publishing Co., 1994); and Clark H. Pinnock, *The Scripture Principle* (San Francisco: Harper & Row, 1984).

24. Pinnock, Rice, Sanders, Hasker, Basinger, *The Openness of God: A Biblical Challenge to the Traditional Understanding of God* (Downers Grove, Ill.: InterVarsity Press, 1994).

25. John Polkinghorne, *Serious Talk: Science and Religion in Dialogue* (Valley Forge, Pa.: Trinity Press International, 1995); and Howard J. Van Till, *The Fourth Day* (Grand Rapids: Wm. B. Eerdmans Publishing Co., 1986).

26. Ronald J. Sider, *Onesided Christianity? Uniting the Church to Heal a Lost and Broken World* (Grand Rapids: Zondervan Publishing House, 1993).

27. John Sanders, *No Other Name: An Investigation into the Destiny of the Unevangelized* (Grand Rapids: Wm. B. Eerdmans Publishing Co., 1992); and Clark H. Pinnock, *A Wideness in God's Mercy: The Finality of Jesus Christ in a World of Religions* (Grand Rapids: Zondervan Publishing House, 1992).

28. Charles Colson and Richard J. Neuhaus, eds., *Evangelicals and Catholics Together: Toward a Common Mission* (Dallas, Tex.: Word Publishing, 1995).

29. Another surprise is the passion for unity in the newer evangelical thinking: Rex A. Koivisto, *One Lord, One Faith: A Theology for Cross-Denominational Renewal* (Wheaton, Ill.: Bridgepoint Books, 1993); and John M. Frame, *Evangelical Reunion: Denominations and the Body of Christ* (Grand Rapids: Baker Book House, 1991).

—PART III—

POSTCRITICAL AND CULTURAL-LINGUISTIC THEOLOGIES

7

POSTLIBERAL THEOLOGY:
A Catholic Reading

JAMES J. BUCKLEY

Postliberal theology (for purposes of this chapter) challenges "liberal" or "modern" theology's engagement with God and the world by proposing alternative ways of using biblical texts, justifying Christian truth claims, and articulating God's triune identity. The aim of this chapter is to give the reader a sense of this postliberal theology, including the ways it has been criticized.

This is, as the subtitle says, "a Catholic reading." It is a "reading" because the label "postliberal" has to a good is used in a variety of ways. I will be particularly interested in the way the label "postliberal" came into frequent use after George Lindbeck's *The Nature of Doctrine: Religion and Theology in a Postliberal Age* (Westminster Press, 1984).[1] But labels like "postliberal" are abstractions from the specific persons in particular circumstances who do theology; I am less interested using or defending such labels than in dealing with their ingredients. (Something similar could be said about other labels sometimes used for what I am calling "postliberal theology." For example, "postliberal theology" is sometimes called "the Yale School" because so much of it emanated from Yale University, especially from Hans Frei, George Lindbeck, and their students; it is also sometimes called "narrative theology" because of its stress on biblical narrative. On the reading to be offered here, however, particular "schools" and individuals will be read as part of a larger story—and the focus will be less on narrative in general than specifically biblical narrative.)

More important, this is a "Catholic" reading. Theologies dubbed "postliberal" have often seemed "Protestant" or "evangelical" (especially Lutheran or Reformed, but also Anabaptist) rather than "Catholic" (whether Orthodox, Episcopal, or Roman Catholic, like myself). But it has rarely been noticed how often postliberal theologies have drawn on a broad Catholic tradition in articulating their theology. One result is that many Catholics have treated postliberal theology as essentially alien—and many Protestants have ignored its Catholic dimensions. One of my aims is to read "Protestant" postliberal theologians as part of a Catholic movement, without denying that postliberals are obviously critics of some or many features of that tradition.

I will begin with a narrative of our circumstances, then propose some common grounds among postliberals, and conclude with the debate within and around postliberal theology.

THE MALAISE OF MODERN THEOLOGY

On a postliberal reading, modern theology confronts problems not faced by earlier theologies—Catholic or Protestant. This means that the differences between Catholic or Protestant theologies, "while far from resolved, have been considerably rearranged" in modern theology.[2] One reason the old disputes are not completely "resolved" is that the sixteenth-century divisions between Catholics and Lutherans, Reformed and Anglicans, Anabaptists and other radical Reformers yielded separate histories for each of these groups in subsequent centuries. On the other hand, a major reason the disputes have been "rearranged" is that, as Christians fought with one another, the Western world was turning from the Christian tradition that, along with Jerusalem and Greece and Rome, had created it. Consider some of the different ways Christian traditions confronted this situation, often passing each other like ships in the night, with guns blazing.

Liberal and Preliberal Theologies

Beginning in Anglican England and Catholic France and climaxing in Protestant Germany, academic elites as well as more ordinary folk began redefining themselves as free or autonomous (and in this sense "liberal") nation-states and individuals. For example, toward the end of the eighteenth century Immanuel Kant (1724–1804) said that enlightenment meant "man's exodus from self-incurred tutelage," including the tutelage of orthodox theological traditions. It is especially when modernity is taken to be characterized by such freedom or autonomy that we can speak of the creation of "liberal" or "modern" theology. Scripture and traditions would have to be fitted within the limits of reason—or at least what the enlightened found reasonable. "The modern world" would provide the common ground for humanity that traditional religion could not. Although not always executed with Kant's depth and intelligence, liberal or enlightened theology (as I shall call it) remains an important kind of modern theology.

In the face of this enlightened humanity, some Christians sought the repristination or recovery of some part of Christendom as a countertradition to the modern world. There were Protestant varieties of such theologies—"premodern" or "preliberal" theologies, they are sometimes called. But most intellectually and institutionally effective resistance to modernity in the nineteenth century was official Roman Catholic theology. The Catholic theology that prevailed by century's end was articulated at the First Vatican Council, a meeting of Roman Catholic bishops at the Vatican City in 1869–1870 especially noteworthy for advocating "natural theology" and "papal infallibility." Enlightened theologies and some Catholics read Vatican I as exclusively an effort to repristinate premodern Christendom. But Vatican I was also an effort to recover (rather than repristinate) the sources of the faith. Pope Leo XIII (1878–1903) extended Vatican I, urging a revival of the medieval theology of Thomas Aquinas and an extension of medieval principles of social justice to the injustices created by modern capitalism and socialism. Other popes continued to nurture the repristination or recovery of traditional theologies and liturgies, while fighting against what they came to call "modernism"—"the synthesis of all heresies," said Pius X (1835–1914). The name for such opponents to the "modernists" was "integralists" (because they insisted that one had to accept the faith as an integrated whole, or not at all) or "ultramontanes" (those who lived "beyond the mountains"—that is, the Alps, beyond which was Rome).[3]

Revisionists and Outsiders

But it is important not to think that these were the only options. In fact, still others adopted what was sometimes called a "mediating" strategy, trying to adjust the Christian tradition to modern circumstances. Catholics such as Johannes Sebastian Drey (1777–1853) and his successors at the University of Tübingen in Germany engaged in a critical conversation with modernity. They were sometimes called, or called themselves, "liberal Catholics" or "reform Catholics," and they are the ancestors of later "revisionist" and "liberation" theologies.[4]

But the main story of nineteenth-century Catholic theology was the story of resistance rather than dialogue with modernity, while it was a form of Protestant theology that conducted the main dialogue with modernity. The most exemplary academic practitioner of this dialogue was the German Reformed theologian, Friedrich Schleiermacher (1768–1834). But there were a variety of practitioners of this "mediating" theology—"apologists" located in the academy as well as "activists" located in nation-states.[5]

There was also another nineteenth-century group, which did not fit easily into the previous categories—"outsiders" to nineteenth-century theology, Karl Barth called them.[6] Barth mentions thinkers like Søren Kierkegaard, Hermann Kutter, and Franz Overbeck—all, for different reasons, rejecting the liberal or mediating alliance between theology and culture, church and nation-state. Others might think of Catholics like John Henry Cardinal Newman and Maurice Blondel as well, who are hard to categorize as premodern, modernist, or revisionist theologians.

But the most important theological "outsider" of the early twentieth century was Karl Barth himself (1886–1968). Barth was a Swiss Reformed pastor who emerged in public with a commentary on Paul's epistle to the Romans (1919). In the second edition of this commentary (1922), Barth declared that the modern world was in "crisis"—the dialectical crisis of judgment and grace in the death and resurrection of Jesus Christ. Barth rejected modern theology in both its enlightened and its mediating forms. And yet he had even less patience with conservatives who aimed to repristinate a premodern era. He found more truth to Catholic than liberal Protestant theology, but rejected both as versions of the same mistake: truncated recognition of the wonder of God's revelation in Jesus Christ. In the 1930s, he not only was a leader of the Confessing Church in Germany (the segment of the church that opposed Hitler) but also began a project that would later become his multivolume *Church Dogmatics*. Debates over how to interpret Barth are an important part of postliberal theology.[7]

Vatican II and the Death of God

In the meantime, in the first half of this century, Catholic theology on the surface continued its antimodernist life and thought. Beneath the surface, however, reforming forces acquired momentum. Those interested in dialogue with modernity (*aggiornamento*, updating the church) and those interested in recovery of authentic tradition (*ressourcement*, the recovery of the true sources of faith in scripture and tradition) conspired to form what was sometimes called *la nouvelle théologie*, "the new theology," embracing Catholic theologians as diverse as Pierre Teilhard de Chardin (1881–1955) and Henri de Lubac (1896–1991).[8] This reform movement broke the surface in the Second Vatican Council (1962–1965). This Council eventually produced sixteen documents, sometimes repeating but more often refashioning Catholic traditions.[9]

In the meantime, as Catholics entered the mainstream of modern theology, Protestants began proclaiming the end of neoorthodoxy in its Barthian or other forms. In the late 1960s there was a short-lived movement in the United States called the "death of God theology," demanding that theology finally appropriate Nietzsche's proclamation of the death of God. In reality, Protestant theology had begun its own version of Nietzsche's eternal recurrence, reliving its eighteenth- and nineteenth-century history.

Something similar happened in Catholic theology after the Council as the Catholic reformers grew increasingly apart. Some advocates of aggiornamento replayed turn-of-the-century disputes over modernism; but most were less liberal Protestants than "revisionists," seeking critical correlations between theology and culture—particularly (as "liberation theologians" argued) correlations with the lives of the poor and oppressed. In turn, few advocates of *ressourcement* were old-fashioned "ultramontanes" or "integralists"; however, they did argue and work for traditional positions on controversial issues such as the identity of God and Jesus Christ, marriage (against birth control), and ordination (against priestly ordination of women). Revisionists thought Catholic theology was reliving its nineteenth-century opposition to modernity, while advocates of *ressourcement* thought that revisionists were reliving the nineteenth-century Protestant accommodations to modernity. What was once an argument between Catholic and evangelical theologies has been "rearranged" into a debate within them.

Five Modern Theologies

Thus, from one point of view, late twentieth-century theology is theology *déja lu*, a rereading of the existing options in modern theology: (1) liberal or enlightened theologies aimed at the replacement of Christian doctrine with more enlightened beliefs and practices; (2) repristinators aimed at revivals of premodern theologies (whether they continued the confessional orthodoxies and spiritual theologies inherited from the Reformation or aimed to revive a patristic or medieval synthesis); (3) Protestant or Catholic mediating or revisionist theologians aimed at revision of Christian life and thought in light of modern life and thought; (4) theologians like Barth, whether their theology is characterized as "dialectical" or in some other ways, and (5) Catholic theologians who followed in the footsteps of Vatican II—advocates of *ressourcement* now threatened with the reduction of their position to repristination, advocates of aggiornamento threatened with the reduction of their position, if not to liberal or enlightened theology, then to mediating or revisionist theology.

Students interested in reading further in the persons, movements, and concepts mentioned above will want to consult standard dictionaries and encyclopedias for further discussion.[10] But the point of this story of modern theology here is that a first definition of postliberal theology is that it is a theology that hopes to do more than repeat these premodern/modern options. How?

ISSUES

Biblical Narrative, and Jesus Christ

What do postliberals share in common? First, scripture is a crucial "source" for most Catholic and Protestant theologies. I say "most" because what I earlier called enlightened theologies have challenged the unity, reliability, and practical value of scriptures in ways more massive than any since the formation of the biblical canon. If we wish neither to avoid nor capitulate to this challenge, how can we take the Bible seriously? Postliberal theology insists on the importance of biblical narrative, especially the Gospels, for answering this question.

As Hans Frei (1922–1988) in particular noticed, taking the biblical narratives "literally" is not taking them as collections of propositions about historical facts or ideal states of affairs. Taking biblical narratives "literally" was traditionally taking them seriously, precisely as narratives, that is, stories of the interaction of ordinary as well as powerful characters and their circumstances over time.[11] Further, the many biblical stories traditionally were read as a single story, moving from creation to consummation, held together by interpreting earlier biblical stories as "figures" of later stories. Finally, these narratives were thought to render the world intelligible and livable—hence, what Christians traditionally called "the fourfold sense of scripture" (literal, typological, moral, and anagogical). The point was not to fit the Bible into our world, but to fit our world into what Barth had called "the strange new world of the Bible."

In modernity, Frei argued, these convictions collapsed. Most Christians did not deny that large parts of the Old and New Testaments were narratives with which they were vaguely familiar from personal Bible reading or communal Liturgy of the Word. But it always seemed to be something else other than, and outside, the biblical narrative that determined how the narrative was read—something extratextual, rather than intra- and intertextual.

The importance of the postliberal concern with the particularity of biblical narratives is most apparent in its focus on the Gospel narratives of Jesus Christ as rendering and identifying a particular person of universal significance in his life, death, and resurrection. Modern theology, the postliberal argument goes, either rejects the importance of the particularity of Jesus Christ (usually by dismissing it as "exclusivist") or insists that it is only important once correlated with our ideas or experiences. However, postliberals argue, this is to substitute a different narrative for the biblical one—or to risk confusing Jesus' identity with our own. Instead, Jesus' narrated particularity has priority over all attempts to locate Jesus' meaning or meaningfulness in some prior intellectual or practical context "outside" the Gospels.[12] As Hans Urs von Balthasar (1905–1988; perhaps the most important Roman Catholic postliberal theologian) put it, Jesus Christ is the central character of the biblical narrative or "theo-drama," the unnormed norm of world history precisely in his particularity, even unto the particularity of his death as our vicarious representative.[13]

Nonfoundationalism and Revelation

But how can Christians justify such narratives and teachings in a world that rejects or (more often) ignores such sources of life and thought? One way of posing this question is to consider a traditional paradox involved in our claims to know anything (e.g., ourselves, our world, God).[14] Faced with a challenge to our claim *that* we know someone or something, we can respond by giving the reasons or "sources" for *how* we know; however, no matter what reasons for "sources" we offer, our challenger can ask us how we know *that*. There seems to be a vicious circle between the questions "What do we know?" and "How do we know?" Each question seems to presume the other.

We can, of course, refuse to respond to such questions—either by admitting we do not know anything, or by claiming to know without being able to offer any reasons. Or we could discover or construct one thing we are certain we know (something, say, intuitively evident) and use it as a sort of foundation (a relatively certain ground, source, and starting point) for explaining how we know other things. This last strategy is sometimes called "foundationalism."

Most of modern theology has been thus "foundationalist," even when its practitioners have disagreed over what the foundation ought to be. For example, enlightened theologies have tended to argue that, since the world has turned from the church and since the church must find common ground with the world if it is to humanely preach the gospel, we need to find a foundation in common human thought, experience, or practice for preaching the gospel. On the other hand, Catholic ultramontanes and Protestant confessionalists have argued that, since the world has turned from the church, and since the church must preserve its own identity in an inhospitable world, we need to find a sure foundation within faith for preaching the gospel—for example, an unconditionally inerrant Bible, infallible teaching office, or arbitrarily posited revelation. For all the differences between such neo-Protestants or liberals and such ultramontanes and preliberals, they are all "foundationalists."

Postliberals are "nonfoundationalists," as were most premodern theologians.[15] They do not think that we need to agree on any single or all-purpose ground, source, or starting point for theological knowledge. For example, take the case of the Christian conviction that God reveals who God is. Enlightened theologies jettisoned this conviction since it transcends our natural reason—and conservative Christians respond that revelation provides the indubitable foundation for reason. But Ronald Thiemann rejects both these options by proposing that the doctrine of revelation is a crucial "subtheme of the doctrine of God"—that is, it is "an account of God's identifiability" as a God who is graciously "prevenient" (for example, "comes before" us, or loves us first) in matters of knowledge as well as everything else. Thiemann makes his case using what he calls "nonfoundationalist or holistic justification," centered on a reading of the Gospels as narratives of "the promising God."[16]

Catholics can recognize in such arguments something akin to what Cardinal Newman called a "cumulative" argument for the faith, over against those abandoning reasoned arguments as well as those seeking indisputable foundations for their arguments.[17] Such cumulative arguments do not provide a single way of correlating our faith with our world. Indeed, postliberals like Hans Frei argued that all defenses of the faith (apologetics) ought to be ad hoc—that is, context-specific and highly variable. To use the vocabulary of the Roman Catholic theologian Frans Jozef van Beeck (perhaps the most noteworthy Catholic postliberal theologian in North America), there needs to be a "fit" between church and world, and it ought to be a "discretionary fit"; that is, exactly how a Christian engages the modern world is "a matter of *discernment* not principle."[18]

God's Triune Identity and Identification

What, we rightly ask at this point, does all this have to do with God? Here we have a third common ground: postliberal theologies are participants in the renewal of Trinitarian theology in the twentieth century.[19] For postliberal Catholics and evangelicals, the doctrine of the Trinity is an identity description of the God narrated in the Bible and articulated in classic Christian creeds. Traditionally, God is the unbegotten Father from whom proceed the Son and the Spirit; God is three persons (in Greek, *hypostases*) in one nature (in Greek, *ousia*). This doctrine was formulated in the early history of Christianity and presumed in both Greek and Latin as well as Catholic and almost all of Protestant Christianity until it was challenged in modernity.

A fulcrum of the modern critique of the traditional doctrine of the Trinity was the liberal claim that the traditional doctrine separated who God is *in se* (God's "immanent" Trinitarian being, to use one traditional vocabulary) from who God is in relation to us *ad extra* ("economically," to use another traditional formula). The metaphysics ingredient in describing Father, Son, and Spirit as three "Persons" in one "nature" was rejected—as was eventually the very Trinitarian name (God as "Father, Son, and Spirit"). This "enlightened" modern theology was and is unitarian rather than Trinitarian.

Those I have been calling "preliberals" simply reasserted the doctrine, unperturbed by its irrelevance. The standard "mediating" alternative was to argue that the doctrine of the Trinity was a sort of primitive version of some higher truth (see, e.g., Hegel) or that, while it had no "immediate" significance for theology, it could provide a sort of "capstone" (Schleiermacher, Tillich). The result was, if not a complete eclipse of the triune God, at least a thorough "marginalization" of the Trinity.[20]

On the Protestant side, it was Karl Barth who initiated the renewal of Trinitarian theology in the twentieth century by insisting that God reveals himself *as* triune. There is no gap between who God is *in se* and who God is in relation to us, because God's (immanent) being is enacted for and with and in us (economically) in Jesus Christ and his Spirit. On the other hand, Catholic theology's participation in Trinitarian renewal began as a recovery of premodern liturgical and theological sources in the early church and climaxed in the crucial role the triune God played in many of Vatican II's central documents; this Trinitarian renewal developed after the Council, especially in dialogues with Eastern Orthodoxy.

However, as in the first two areas of agreement, it is important not to overemphasize the thickness (as it were) of postliberal agreement on the doctrine of the Trinity. Many Christian theologians clearly confess the triune God but without postliberal theology's commitment to nonfoundationalism or its insistence that the doctrine of the Trinity depends on dramatic readings of biblical narratives. And postliberal theologies can hardly be said to agree on the detailed grammar relating the doctrine of the Trinity to the biblical narrative (or the immanent and the economic Trinity)—or to the world of other religions and unbelief. It would even be difficult to get postliberal theologians to agree on exactly what features of the traditional doctrine of the Trinity are and are not open to revisions (e.g., the ancient abstractions of *hypostasis* and *natura*, or the concrete names of Father and Son).

DEBATES WITHIN AND
OVER POSTLIBERAL THEOLOGY

Postliberal theology, I proposed in the section "The Malaise of Modern Theology" above, hopes to do more than repeat "premodern" or "modern" theologies. However, having surveyed three central issues raised by postliberal theology in the next section, "Issues," we can now see that postliberal theology shares some key features of three of the five kinds of modern theologies discussed above. That is, postliberal theology shares a kind of "nonfoundationalism" with some revisionist theologies (without agreeing with most of their revisions of classic Christology and Trinitarian theology). Further, postliberal theology shares Barth's narratively christological exegesis (although not always Barth's dialectical reflections on that exegesis). Finally, postliberal theology shares much with those aspects of Vatican II centered on *ressourcement* (although not when such *ressourcement* becomes the effort to repristinate past eras). In still other words, postliberal theology is part of a history or genealogy at once Catholic and evangelical. Debates within and over postliberal theology, I suggest, are arguments over whether this combination of features results in a fruitful or fruitless set of tensions. Consider some of the debates over the common grounds of the previous action.

Narratives and Other Worlds

I earlier suggested that postliberals share a deep interest in the biblical narratives of Israel and Jesus Christ. But it is also true that there is no clear consensus on how this strange new world of the Bible relates to other worlds. For example, what do scriptural narratives have to do with what is "outside" them? Does Barth's strange new world of the biblical narrative take the place of our world, or does it illuminate it from within? Does Balthasar's theo-dramatic interpretation of scripture call us out of the theater of our world into God's theater, or does it show us the true and good and beautiful shape of our Trinitarian world-to-come? How is Frei's early insistence on the irreducibility of biblical *texts* related to his insistence later in life that such texts acquire literal sense only *in community*? How does what Lindbeck calls "intratextual" faithfulness relate to what he calls postliberal theology's applicability and intelligibility?[21]

These, it seems to me, are fair questions. They help explain why postliberal theology is sometimes charged with "fideism" (relying on faith to the exclusion of reason), "sectarianism" (advocating a church separated from the world), and "conservativism" (granting uncritical authority to scripture). These charges are ultimately more smoke than fire, however, if we take into account the variety of ad hoc ways postliberals address such questions.

For example, Catholics and Protestants address these questions in different and even opposed ways. In contrast to Barth's insistence on the written word as a crucial form of the Word of God, Balthasar seems almost suspicious of the letter of scripture, insisting that scripture is only scripture as it is the body of Christ, especially as it is consumed in the eucharistic church. Again, unlike Frei and Lindbeck, van Beeck's theology seems more interested in the narrative shape of eucharistic *worship* (including the Liturgy of the Word) than the narrative shape of the biblical *text* outside the context of such prayer. Such differences are partly differences over how to relate "the literal sense" of scripture to its other "senses" (allegorical or typological, moral, and anagogical).[22] But such differences, the argument might go, are even more marked when we consider competing Catholic and Protestant ways of ordering the community beyond scripture and worship (for example, issues of priestly ordination and papacy).

However, before turning such genuine differences into oppositions that divide churches from one another, Catholic and Protestant postliberals would insist that there is no *necessary* competition between scripture and eucharistic worship, between liturgy of the eucharistic word and the broader life of the Christian community, or between our identity as Christians in a specific community called church and God's revelation in Word and Spirit. Indeed, those postliberals who agree that our circumstances are no longer those of the sixteenth century argue that a common recognition of the importance of biblical narrative can provide one lever for raising up the common ground Catholic and evangelical theologies share in late modernity—common ground invisible before the modern era. We do not have to deny differences and oppositions between such theologies to argue that such differences and oppositions do not have to be (as George Lindbeck often puts it) "Church-divisive."

Even further, some postliberal theologians would argue for an emerging ecumenical consensus on the whole range of issues that previously divided Christians—justification, Eucharist, priestly and episcopal ministry, and even papal infallibility.[23] If postliberal theology is to continue being more than a new name for ignoring or perpetuating old disputes, it will have to continue to pursue such ecumenical convergences.

Natural Knowledge of God, Other "Religions," and Israel

Another set of arguments among postliberals has less to do with patterns of relationships between biblical narratives and the church than with patterns of relationships to a wider world. For example, the story of Paul's encounter with the "unknown god" of Athens (Acts 17:16–34) and Paul's teaching that God's "eternal power and divine nature, invisible though they are, have been understood and seen through the things he has made" (Rom. 1:20), were central to the way premodern Christians interacted with those who believed in other gods. Sometimes Christians found in such stories and teachings a strategy for addressing nonbelievers; more often they found in them the presuppositions of their own faith.[24]

But modern Christians have been tempted to see in them the assertion of a "natural" knowledge of God that is the foundation for "revealed" knowledge—or the expressions of a religious experience all religions supposedly shared in common. Where enlightened and revisionist theologies usually presumed that Christian faith was simply a species of the larger genus "religion," Barth argued that revelation "sublated" (preserved and abrogated) such religions, including Christianity. Vatican II's "Declaration on Non-Christian Religions" opened a broader dialogue with world religions.

George Lindbeck's *The Nature of Doctrine* went a step farther, arguing for the theological importance of a particular "theory of religion" he called "cultural-linguistic." Relying on cultural anthropologists such as Clifford Geertz and philosophers of religion such as William A. Christian, Lindbeck proposed that religions are like languages, embedded in forms of life with continuous and changing grammatical rules. Such a comprehensive theory of religion provides a way (Lindbeck implied) to link the liturgically ensconced biblical narrative to the broader religious world.

Even postliberals who have agreed with Lindbeck in other respects have worried that Lindbeck's theory of religion remains too bound to modern notions of religion, despite the fact that his theory of religion subordinates itself to the importance of attention to particular religions. For example, Hans Frei cautioned Lindbeck to keep his theory of religion ad hoc, lest postliberal theology veer toward Schleiermacher's mediating theology—and Anglo-Catholic John Milbank worries that Lindbeck's proposals have not become fully "ontological" and "political."[25] Defenders of Lindbeck have argued that his proposals bear more resemblance to the theology of Thomas Aquinas than to Schleiermacher—a reading of Thomas as a theologian that even closes the gap between him and Barth.[26]

Despite these differences, postliberals agree that Christian theology ought to deal with other gods and other religions primarily one by one rather than a lump-sum called "religion." Indeed, the postliberal model here is Christian interaction with the Jewish people—no mere "other religion," but the elect people of God

(Romans 9—11). Jewish thinkers like Peter Ochs have argued that Jewish and Christian thinkers share a mode of interpreting scripture he calls "postcritical scriptural interpretation," and Ochs draws explicit parallels to the work of George Lindbeck and Hans Frei.[27] Christian postliberal theology will be a theology for the nations only as it first listens again, in repentance and joy, to the story of Israel.

God Pre- and Postmodern

One could extend the circles of comprehensiveness wider and wider still, challenging postliberals to relate the biblical narratives of Israel and Jesus to the conflicting philosophies of our intellectual world, the politics and economies of our social world, and the particularities of our spiritual lives as embodied (and gendered) creatures. So far, postliberal theology has no single strategy for engaging these worlds, although those who share the common grounds discussed above are working on all these fronts to formulate a "discretionary fit" between scripture, church, and world.

But perhaps even more crucial for the future than any issues raised thus far is whether the third shared postliberal confession of the triune God promises insight not only into scripture, church, and world but into the distinctive subject matter of theology, God. Some of those whom I have called "postliberal" have focused on developing a theology that deals with the separation between Greek and Russian Orthodox theologies (on one side) and "Western" (Catholic or Protestant) theologies on the other side. An important part of this dispute is whether Catholic and Protestant theologies have done full justice to the Holy Spirit. Hans Urs von Balthasar is representative of a number of Catholic theologians who have argued that Orthodox and Catholic theologies of the Spirit are complementary rather than opposed. The Lutheran Robert Jenson has gone even farther, arguing that only a renewal of an Orthodox theology of the Spirit can overcome the Catholic-Protestant divide—but an Orthodox theology purged of the "churchly immobility" engendered by thinking that "being" is unchangeable.[28]

The Catholic philosopher Jean-Luc Marion, who has deep sympathies with the theology of Balthasar, has developed his position with explicit attention to "postmodernism." His *God without Being* is a set of essays suggesting that both theists and atheists have constructed idols of God that do not represent the God of pure love, incarnate in Jesus Christ and celebrated at the eucharistic table. But this orthodox postmodern theology is thus far being attended to more in Anglo-Catholic England and Europe than in the North America that is the focus of this chapter.[29]

Perhaps someplace between premodern and postmodern alternatives are those exploring the philosophical and theological issues raised by the biblical narrative's rendering of a triune God who acts in history. Thomas Tracy has proposed that we can think about God acting in history by thinking about persons like ourselves engaging in intentional actions over the course of time, and then stripping away the limitations of our embodied agency until we arrive at God's agency as "the perfection of agency." Kathryn Tanner, on the other hand, emphasizes that the theological claim that God acts in history "fractures" our ordinary ways of thinking about what it means to act in history, and this leads her to rank the Reformers' emphasis on creaturely freedom under God over the more Catholic emphasis on creaturely freedom (without denying that the latter is necessary as a "second step").[30]

External critics of postliberal theology might, at this point, wonder if it constitutes a coherent entity, for it stands Janus-faced toward the (premodern) past as well as the (postmodern) future, or toward human freedom and God's grace. Perhaps we should simply recognize that postliberal theology has made some important contributions, while not providing the fully comprehensive vision that we need. Then again, perhaps these tensions are the necessary part of any interesting theology, and postliberal theology is pointing, like a crooked line, beyond merely liberal or modern theology.[31] If so, it will be a theology for Catholics and evangelicals, open to Israel and the nations in humble trust that God can make all things work for the good.

NOTES

1. William Placher, "Postliberal Theology," in *The Modern Theologians*, ed. David Ford, 2d ed. (Oxford: Basil Blackwell Publisher, 1997); George Schner and John Webster, eds., *Theological Method after Liberalism* (Oxford: Basil Blackwell Publisher, forthcoming).

2. Frans Jozef van Beeck, S.J., *God Encountered: A Contemporary Catholic Systematic Theology*, vol. 1, *Understanding the Christian Faith* (San Francisco: Harper & Row, 1988; and Collegeville, Minn.: Liturgical Press, 1989), 56.

3. Norman P. Tanner, S.J., *Decrees of the Ecumenical Councils* (Kansas City, Mo.: Sheed & Ward; and Washington, D.C.: Georgetown University Press, 1990), vol. 2: 800–16 (Vatican I); Alasdair MacIntyre, *Three Rival Versions of Moral Inquiry: Encyclopedia, Genealogy, and Tradition* (Notre Dame, Ind.: University of Notre Dame Press, 1990), chap. 3 (on Leo XIII).

4. James J. Buckley, "Revisionists and Liberals," *The Modern Theologians*, 2d ed. (Oxford: Basil Blackwell Publishers, 1997).

5. William A. Clebsch, *Christianity in European History* (Oxford: Oxford University Press, 1979), chap. 6.

6. Karl Barth, "Evangelical Theology in the Nineteenth Century," in *The Humanity of God*, trans. Thomas Wieser et al. (Atlanta: John Knox Press, 1960), 13; Eberhard Busch, *Karl Barth: His Life from Letters and Autobiographical Texts*, trans. John Bowden (Philadelphia: Fortress Press, 1976), 173.

7. George Hunsinger, *How to Read Karl Barth: The Shape of His Theology* (Oxford: Oxford University Press, 1991); Bruce McCormack, "Beyond Nonfoundational and Postmodern Readings of Barth: Critically Realistic Dialectical Theology," *Zeitschrift für dialektischer Theologie* (forthcoming); John Webster, ed., *Cambridge Companion to Barth* (Cambridge: Cambridge University Press, forthcoming).

8. For example, Hans Urs von Balthasar, *The Theology of Karl Barth: Exposition and Interpretation*, trans. Edward Oakes, S.J. (German original 1951; San Francisco: Ignatius Press, Communion Books, 1992); chap. 2.

9. Tanner, *Decrees of the Ecumenical Councils*, 2:817–1135; Giuseppe Alberigo and Joseph Komanchak, eds., *The History of Vatican II, 1959–1965* (Maryknoll, N.Y.: Orbis Books, 1996–), 5 volumes planned.

10. For example, Alister McGrath, ed., *Encyclopedia of Modern Christian Thought* (Oxford: Basil Blackwell Publisher, 1993).

11. Hans Frei, *Theology and Narrative: Selected Essays*, ed. William Placher and George Hunsinger (Oxford: Oxford University Press, 1993); Stanley Hauerwas and L. Gregory Jones, eds., *Why Narrative? Readings in Narrative Theology* (Grand Rapids: Wm. B. Eerdmans Publishing Co., 1989).

12. Hans W. Frei, *The Identity of Jesus Christ: The Hermeneutical Bases of Dogmatic Theology* (Originally published 1967; Philadelphia: Fortress Press, 1975); Bruce Marshall, *Christianity in Conflict: The Identity of a Saviour in Rahner and Barth* (Oxford: Basil Blackwell Publisher, 1987).

13. Hans Urs von Balthasar, *Theo-Drama*, trans. Graham Harrison, vols. 1–4, 1988–1990 (San Francisco: Ignatius Press, 1988–); idem, *My Work: In Retrospect*, trans. Roxanne Mei Lum (San Francisco: Ignatius Press, 1990); Edward Oakes, S.J., *Pattern of Redemption: The Theology of Hans Urs von Balthasar* (New York: Crossroad, 1994).

14. Roderick Chisholm, *Theory of Knowledge*, 3d ed. (Englewood Cliffs, N.J.: Prentice-Hall, 1989).

15. John Thiel, *Nonfoundationalism* (Minneapolis: Fortress Press, 1994); Nicholas Wolterstorff, "The Migration of Theistic Arguments," in *Rationality, Religious Belief, and Moral Commitment*, ed. R. Audi and W. J. Wainwright (Ithaca, N.Y.: Cornell University Press, 1986), 38–81; Eugene F. Rogers Jr., *Thomas Aquinas and Karl Barth: Sacred Doctrine and the Natural Knowledge of God* (Notre Dame, Ind.: University of Notre Dame Press, 1995).

16. Ronald Thiemann, *Revelation and Theology: The Gospel as Narrated Promise* (Notre Dame, Ind.: University of Notre Dame Press, 1985).

17. See John Henry Newman, *An Essay in Aid of a Grammar of Assent* (Oxford: Clarendon Press, 1985); Balthasar, *Theo-Drama*, 2:130–36; *Catechism of the Catholic Church* (Collegeville, Minn.: Liturgical Press, 1994), para. 31 (where Newman is quoted but without reference); cf. Lindbeck, *Nature of Doctrine*, 131.

18. Hans Frei, "Karl Barth: Theologian," in *Theology and Narrative*, 167–76; William Werpehowski, *Ad Hoc* Apologetics," *Journal of Religion* 66 (1986): 282–301; William Placher, *Unapologetic Theology* (Louisville, Ky.: Westminster/John Knox Press, 1989); van Beeck, *God Encountered*, 1:42; 2, pt. 1, "The Revelation of the Glory" (Collegeville, Minn.: Liturgical Press, 1993), 270 n. m, 279, 283.

19. Lewis Ayres, *A Trinity Reader* (Oxford: Basil Blackwell Publisher, forthcoming).

20. William Placher, *The Domestication of Transcendence: How Modern Thinking about God Went Wrong* (Louisville, Ky.: Westminster John Knox Press, 1996), chap. 10.

21. Mark I. Wallace, *The Second Naiveté: Barth, Ricoeur, and the New Yale Theology* (Macon, Ga.: Mercer University Press, 1990); Kevin J. Vanhoozer, *Biblical Narrative in the Philosophy of Paul Ricoeur* (Cambridge: Cambridge University Press, 1990); Gerard Loughlin, *Telling God's Story* (Cambridge: Cambridge University Press, 1996); Bradford E. Hinze and George P. Schner, S.J., "Postliberal Theology and Roman Catholic Theology," *Religious Studies Review* 21 (#4, October 1995): 299–310; Timothy R. Phillips and Dennis L. Okholm, eds., *The Nature of Confession: Evangelicals and Postliberals in Conversation* (London: SPCK, 1996); William Placher, "Postliberal Theology" (note 1 above).

22. See *Catechism of the Catholic Church*, paras. 115–118.

23. George Lindbeck, *The Nature of Doctrine*, chap. 5; Robert Jenson, *Unbaptized God: The Basic Flaw in Ecumenical Theology* (Minneapolis: Fortress Press, 1992).

24. Jaroslav Pelikan, *Christianity and Classical Culture: The Metamorphosis of Natural Theology in the Christian Encounter with Hellenism*, Gifford Lectures at Aberdeen, 1992–1993 (New Haven, Conn., and London: Yale University Press, 1993).

25. Hans Frei, "Epilogue," in *Theology and Dialogue*, ed. Bruce Marshall (Notre Dame, Ind.: University of Notre Dame Press, 1990), 279–80; John Milbank, *Theology and Social Theory* (Oxford: Basil Blackwell Publisher, 1990), 382–88.

26. Bruce Marshall, "Thomas as Postliberal Theologian," *The Thomist* 53 (1989): 353–401.

27. Joseph DiNoia, O.P., *The Diversity of Religions* (Washington, D.C.: Catholic University of America Press, 1992; David Burrell, *Freedom and Creation in Three Traditions* (Notre Dame, Ind.: University of Notre Dame Press, 1993); Paul Griffiths, *On Being Buddha* (Albany, N.Y.: State University of New York Press, 1994); Peter Ochs, "An Introduction to Postcritical Scriptural Interpretation," in *The Return to Scripture in Judaism and Christianity: Essays in Postcritical Scriptural Interpretation*, ed. Peter Ochs (Mahwah, N.J.: Paulist Press, 1993), 3–51; Bruce Marshall, "The Jewish People and Christian Theology," *The Cambridge Companion to Christian Doctrine* (Cambridge University Press, 1997).

28. Rowan Williams, "Eastern Orthodox Theology," in *The Modern Theologians*, 2d ed. (Oxford: Basil Blackwell Publisher, 1997); Hans Urs von Balthasar, *Theologik*, vol. 3, *Der Geist der Wahrheit* (Basel: Johannes Verlag, 1987); Jenson, *Unbaptized God*, 142– 43.

29. Jean-Luc Marion, *God without Being: Hors-texte*, trans. Thomas A. Carlson (Chicago: University of Chicago Press, 1991); John Milbank, "Can a Gift Be Given? Prolegomena to a Future Trinitarian Metaphysic," in *Rethinking Metaphysics*, ed. L. Gregory Jones and Stephen E. Fowl (Oxford: Basil Blackwell Publisher, 1995), 119–61; Graham Ward, *The Postmodern God* (Oxford: Basil Blackwell Publisher, 1997).

30. Thomas F. Tracy, *God, Action, and Embodiment* (Grand Rapids: Wm. B. Eerdmans Publishing Co., 1984); Kathryn Tanner, *God and Creation in Christian Theology* (Oxford: Basil Blackwell Publisher, 1988), 161–62, 167; Thomas F. Tracy, ed., *The God Who Acts: Philosophical and Theological Explorations* (University Park, Pa.: Pennsylvania State University Press, 1994).

31. My thanks to Roger Badham, Frederick Bauerschmidt, Michael Baxter, David Dawson, George Hunsinger, Gregory Jones, William Placher, and Avihu Zakai for forceful and utterly incompatible criticisms of an earlier draft.

8

CHRISTIAN ETHICS IN AMERICA:
A Promising Obituary

STANLEY HAUERWAS

CHRISTIAN ETHICS IN AMERICA:
BEGINNING WITH AN ENDING

This chapter is an outline for a book meant to tell the story of the emergence of Christian ethics as a discipline in America.[1] It is a story of the emergence, development, and flourishing—but also the present exhaustion—of the discipline of Christian ethics. The reasons it is so exhausted, I believe, teach us much not only about the odd little area called Christian ethics, but more generally about the fate of Protestant Christianity in liberal democratic societies. Indeed, I hope to show how the story I tell has important implications for the practice of theology and our understanding of the church in the peculiar context we call America.

Christian ethics as a generalized subject existed prior to the development of a specialized discipline bearing that name. Beginning with the social gospel, we see the development of a self-consciousness about the activity of Christian ethics that is new. That "newness" produced some quite powerful intellectual and practical expressions, which we must understand if Christians are to know better how to go on in the world that they have created, but which now threatens to destroy them.

The story I tell takes place almost entirely in the twentieth century—the Christian century, according to the journal that bears that name. It is not by accident that the *Christian Century* became the magazine of record for those who became ethicists in the social gospel mold. It continued to be such even when the social gospel was no longer thought to be viable. The nature of "ethics" may have changed, yet "ethics" remained the way mainstream liberal Christianity negotiated what was thought to be the responsibility Christians had for society.

I will tell the story by focusing on the primary actors whose work in effect constituted the discipline. I begin with Walter Rauschenbusch, who is generally acknowledged to be the most articulate proponent of the social gospel. I then treat in succession Reinhold Niebuhr, H. Richard Niebuhr, Monsignor John Ryan, John Courtney Murray, Paul Ramsey, James Gustafson, and John Howard Yoder. Their lives as well as their work overlap one another in complex and mutually illuminating ways. Yet by treating them in the above order the theological motifs so important to the story can best be developed. As we shall see, Reinhold Niebuhr is a commanding figure that dominates the story.

By setting forth the plot of the narrative thus, I am as much constructing the discipline as I am reporting on it. Although each major figure tries to take account of his predecessor—Reinhold Niebuhr comments on Rauschenbusch, Ramsey tries to make use of both Niebuhrs, and Gustafson becomes the great cartographer of the discipline—it remains the case that the discipline has never been very clear about its subject matter. The account I provide, therefore, cannot help but make matters seem more coherent than in fact they were or now are. I am in the odd position of telling the story of the development of a discipline precisely at that juncture in its history at which I think the intellectual and social presuppositions that at another time appeared to make the discipline coherent are no longer intelligible.

Though I will take a critical perspective on much of the story I tell, my understanding of theology as a social practice owes much to those whom I criticize. Of course, for them the social character of theology meant the privileging of the social sciences—in contrast, I believe, with John Milbank, that theology is "itself a social science, and the queen of the sciences for the inhabitants of the *altera civitas*, on pilgrimage through this temporary world."[2]

"Christian Ethics in America: A Promising Obituary"? I believe that the story I tell of the discipline of Christian ethics has now come to an end. How could a tradition that began with Walter Rauschenbusch's *Christianizing the Social Order* end with a book by James Gustafson called *Can Ethics Be Christian?*[3] My answer is equally pointed: The subject of Christian ethics in America has always been America. Accordingly, just to the extent that Protestants in America got the kind of society and politics that the social gospel desired, Christianity became unintelligible not only to non-Christians, but more importantly to itself.

In so telling the story, I do not pretend to tell it in an "unbiased" fashion. As will become clear, the hero of the story is John Howard Yoder—a Mennonite. He stands as an outsider to the tradition that produced Christian ethics as a discipline. Yet by ending with Yoder I hope to suggest in what ways we shall all be poorer if we lose the story of the rise and fall of Christian ethics. Just as Walter Rauschenbusch could not help but be read differently after Reinhold Niebuhr, even if such a reading may be in some ways "unfair," I hope to show that Yoder provides a way to renarrate this tradition so that its theological significance is not lost.

For example, in 1978 James Gustafson wrote an article called "Theology Confronts Technology and the Life Sciences." He begins the essay by observing that much of the material concerning ethical issues raised by medicine and science is being produced by people with theological training. Yet he also notes that it is less than clear whether *theology* has anything to contribute to these areas. For a few, such as Paul Ramsey, their ethical principles and procedures receive explicit theological authorization; but, he says,

> for others, writing as "ethicists," the relation of their moral discourse to any specific theological principles, or even to a definable religious outlook, is opaque. Indeed, in response to a query from a friend (who is a distinguished philosopher) about how the term "ethicist" has come about, I

responded in a pejorative way, "An ethicist is a former theologian who does not have the professional credentials of a moral philosopher."[4]

Gustafson notes that much of the writing in the field is by persons who describe themselves as "religious ethicists," though it is by no means clear what the adjective "religious" modifies or qualifies. The term "religious" works primarily as a means of distinguishing those who invoke that term, for reasons of university location, from those holding cards in the philosopher's unions. "Religious" is also useful as a generic term, since many of the issues addressed in the realm of ethics contribute to the formulation of policy, thereby making any particularistic identifications a matter of acute embarrassment. If Christian ethicists are to be players within the constraints of a liberal social order for the drafting of public policy, then the "Christian" qualifier must be suppressed.

A quick perusal of an annual program of the Society of Christian Ethics will confirm Gustafson's point.[5] Most of the sessions are focused on "problems" or advocacy questions that may or may not involve theological claims. The kind of theological questions that were at one time at the heart of the work of Rauschenbusch and the Niebuhrs now seem, for most who currently "do ethics," to be a secondary concern. Even the liberal theology that gave birth to Christian ethics as a discipline now seems too "theological." The irony of Gustafson's complaint, as I will try to show, is that his own work has prepared the way for the development he presently appears to deplore.

This state of affairs at once creates the dramatic character of the story I want to tell, but at the same time it makes that story problematic. Again, Gustafson succinctly articulates the matter in the article referred to above. By trying to indicate in what ways theology might illuminate issues in science and medicine, Christian ethicists attempt to justify the importance of theology or "religious writing" for the practice of the discipline. This apologetic, however, is often directed to people who couldn't care less if theological justification is adequate or not. For example, Gustafson confesses that "I worked for years on a book *Can Ethics Be Christian?* with the nagging sense that most persons who answer in an unambiguous affirmative would not be interested in my supporting argument, that a few fellow professional persons might be interested enough to look at it, and that for those who believe the answer is negative the question itself is not sufficiently important to bother about."[6]

This present chapter is itself "an attempt," an effort, to produce the kind of readership that warrants—and in that sense recognizes itself as suited for, because it is disciplined by—the narrative shape of argument presented herein. Most of the actors who comprise my story thought that they could do Christian ethics for anyone. They did so under the not so unreasonable assumption (at the time) that Americans were in general Christian—hence their appeals to the "Judeo-Christian tradition." In contrast, Yoder's "ethics" is built on the assumption that Christian ethics is for Christians.[7]

Yoder's claim rests on the theological presumption that a broad American readership is different from, or at least not identified with, people who are disposed by "the resources of love, repentance, the willingness to sacrifice, and the enabling power of the Holy Spirit, within the supporting fellowship of the church."[8] Yoder is simply acknowledging the presumption that Christian discourse, like all discourse, is inescapably rhetorical.[9] That the Christian ethicist prior to Yoder would find such a claim indicative of the abandonment of the truth of Christianity denotes their presumption that Christian discourse is in principle a discourse for anyone.

The acknowledgment that this theological position governs my telling of the story of Christian ethics will seem to many a damning admission. Does that mean that non-Christians have no access or way to understand what I do and, even more, no reason, as Gustafson suggests, to be interested in this story? I see no reason why I am committed to answering affirmatively to either of those questions. Of course, non-Christians can understand the argument I develop. I just do not expect them to agree with it.

In that respect, however, I have to say that most Christians in America are in no better position than non-Christians to understand, much less agree with, the argument. For the story at once reflects and is created by the decline of mainline Christianity in America. As a result, most Christians in America cannot recognize any difference between themselves and their non-Christian neighbors. Indeed, in many ways the story I tell is but the intellectual expression of the loss of confidence, so evident in much of mainline Christianity, concerning what it means to be Christian in America. Therefore, this is about the end of a tradition; but it is also about the possibility of a new beginning if only Christians, as Yoder suggests, can rediscover that the true subject of Christian ethics is not America, but the church.

AMERICA AS THE GREAT EXPERIMENT
IN PROTESTANT CHRISTIANITY

Whether someone who does not share my theological agenda may be interested in the story I tell, I cannot anticipate. I should certainly hope many might, since I think that the account I provide not only illuminates the development of Christian ethics as a discipline but also casts light on a number of significant changes in America society in this century. Though my primary interests are theological, many may find my account to be but a footnote to the story of American progressivism. For there can be no question that the same movements that created what we now call the progressivist era also produced Christian ethics.

To be sure, it is hard to separate Protestantism and the spirit of progressivism. As George Marsden observes in his *Religion and American Culture*, the nineteenth century was one in which political power was firmly held by white Protestants who had no intention of giving it up. They could seek national legislation prohibiting the sale of alcohol as well as "blue laws," for example, with little regard for how such practices might appear to Catholics or Jews.[10] America in fact became the great experiment, in what Max Stackhouse happily describes as constructive Protestantism.[11]

Stackhouse argues that Rauschenbusch and the progressive Protestantism he represented in fact constituted a new Christian social philosophy, which Stackhouse calls "conciliar denominationalism." Following Ernst Troeltsch's account in *The Social Teaching of the Christian Churches*, Stackhouse states that only two major Christian social philosophies had ever been developed—the Catholic and the Calvinist. The former was a vision of an "organic, hierarchial order sanctified by objectified means of grace," while the latter centered around the ideal of "an established theocracy of elect saints who are justified by grace through faith."[12] Both these forms of "Christendom" have now ended, never to be resurrected.

Yet Protestantism in America, according to Stackhouse, has provided a third alternative which combines two conflicting motifs from the Calvinist and the Catholic visions: sectarianism and Christendom. These came together in the life of Rauschenbusch who, on the one hand, came

> from an evangelical background from which he gained a sense of intense and explicit faith that could only be held by fully committed members. On the other hand, Rauschenbusch lived in the age of lingering hope for a catholic "Christian culture" and in an age that, especially through the developing social sciences, saw the legitimacy of secular realms. He, like the developing "conciliar denominations," saw the necessity of the select body of believers anticipating the Kingdom in word and deed in good sectarian fashion, and of taking the world seriously on its own terms, as did all visions of Christendom. These motifs conspire in his thought to produce a vision of a revolutionized responsible society for which a socially understood gospel is the catalyst.[13]

Protestants would thus come to dominate American civilization, particularly in the nineteenth century, but without a sense that they were ruling. Robert Handy observes in his wonderful book *A Christian America: Protestant Hopes and Historical Realities*, that although American Protestants had hoped from the beginning that someday American civilization would be fully Christian, that hope only gained its most characteristic expression in the nineteenth century. Indeed,

> such expressions usually assumed that while the primary concern of true evangelicals would be for religion itself, devotion to the progress of civilization followed closely. Committed to the principle of religious freedom and to the voluntary method, the leaders of the thrust to make America Christian usually failed to sense how coercive their efforts appeared to those who did not share their premises.[14]

That Protestants failed to see the coercive nature of their attempt to create a Christian civilization was partly due to the presumption that what they wanted was not significantly different from what anyone would want for America. As Marsden points out, they were proud of the civilization they were sure was being created in America. The United States represented a model society, where people of many nationalities could live in peace and economic prosperity.

Whatever injustices, discriminations, and poverty were in the United States, one could find far worse in other quarters of the globe. Among the essential premises of the dominant American thought of the era were: (1) the superiority of Western civilization, (2) that Anglo-American democratic principles were the highest political expression of that civilization, (3) and that these principles were bound to triumph throughout the earth.[15]

The presumption of "American exceptionalism" that shapes so much of the story of the development of Christian ethics as a discipline finds a parallel in the discipline of American church history. In fact, throughout much of this period it is difficult to separate "ethics" from "history." As we shall see, Rauschenbusch also thought of himself as a historian. H. Richard Niebuhr's *The Kingdom of God in America* is as influential among those writing the history of religion in America as it is among "ethicists."[16] Reinhold Niebuhr's *The Irony of American History* was equally, if not more, influential.[17] It should not be surprising, therefore, that Reinhold Niebuhr becomes the paradigmatic "public theologian" in Martin Marty's historical account on the relationship between religion and the republic.[18]

The close relationship between Christian ethics and American church history is not surprising insofar as they were each given birth by the same spirit of progressivism. James L. Ash traces the beginnings of American church history to the deanship of Shailer Matthews at the Divinity School of the University of Chicago (1907–1933). Ash notes that in Matthews's book, *Spiritual Interpretation of History*, Matthews asserted that history manifests a general trend toward spiritual progress. Accordingly, he sought to attract scholars to Chicago who shared his views, namely,

> that religion was an integral part of society and therefore ought to be studied in the context of its social environment. He also believed that the empirical and inductive methods of "scientific" history, when properly pursued, would separate the essential elements of the Christian faith from their particular manifestations in individual societies and would enable modern people to use them most fruitfully. Matthew's "socio-historical method" became the hallmark of what is now known as the "Chicago school" of historians and theologians, a remarkably prolific and gifted group of scholars.[19]

Twenty years later when William Warren Sweet was brought to Chicago to begin the "field" of American church history, the discipline was no longer considered the province of seminary professors who thought the subject a manifestation of providential forces. Indeed, apart from their concentration on the church, church historians were methodologically indistinguishable from other historians. But as Ash observes,

> ironically, it was precisely this view of history which kept Sweet and other scientific historians from examining critically the assumptions about history which they embraced. Because history was conceived as morally and philosophically neutral, a science rather than a creative art, the scientific

historians felt no need to scrutinize their own presuppositions. Thus Sweet was able to become a highly skilled practitioner of his craft without having to recognize and question the assumptions of Protestant hegemony upon which his historical synthesis of American religion was based.[20]

The story that American church/religious historians tell about the relation between America and religion has become increasingly complex since the time of Sweet. No longer is the story told as if Jews, Catholics, evangelicals, as well as nonbelievers, do not exist. Works such as Nathan Hatch's *The Democratization of American Christianity* and Jon Butler's *Awash in a Sea of Faith: Christianizing the American People* make us aware that the thing called Christianity in America often contained elements and practices that many contemporary Christians would find odd at best.[21] As indicated above, Robert Handy helps us understand the interrelation of Protestantism and American exceptionalism.[22] Yet American church historians continue to explore the interrelation between Christianity and America with what can only be described as an apologetic intent.[23]

The seemingly never-ending debate about "secularization," or the decline of American Christianity, is but an aspect of this general project. But as Roger Finke and Rodney Stark point out, often claims about the "decline" of religion in America are really complaints about the loss of the kind of Christianity thought preferable. In contrast, they make no normative judgments about church or nation, but rather maintain that the churching of America has remained relatively constant, the only change being who is winning and who is losing. Winners and losers, it seems, have little to do with the quality of theological positions or religious practice, but with which form of Christianity is most aggressive in the market.[24] It is not my purpose to assess the accuracy of their account but rather to suggest how they illuminate the normative, if not the ideological, character of much of the work done as American religious history.

Of course, I cannot pretend to be free of the same problems as they afflict the development of the discipline called Christian ethics. For in constructing my narrative I am reliant on, and in many respects indebted to, the very historians I criticize above. Moreover, I am doing theology in a historical-like manner, just as H. Richard Niebuhr and Reinhold Niebuhr did. In all that, of course, I think they were right. The difference, as I indicated above, is who is taken to be the primary subject of the narrative and how the story is told. In other words, what finally distinguishes what they were doing from what I am doing cannot be described in terms of an opposition between history and theology—as if what they were writing was "history" while what I am doing is "theology." Rather, what distinguishes us is the peculiarly different shape and content that our respective kinds of theological histories take. By making the church, rather than America, the source, I am not thereby claiming to offer a more objective account. Rather, I think I am giving a more truthful account for Christians, whose task it is to live lives faithful to the God manifest in Jesus of Nazareth.

In his *The Nature of Doctrine*, George Lindbeck observes that the kind of theology that does not have a promising future is one that begins with the integrity of theological discourse for "reading" the world. Even if such theology were to become theoretically persuasive, it would simply remain "talk" in the absence of the practice of such readings.

> Disarray in church and society makes the transmission of the necessary skills more and more difficult. Those who share in the intellectual high culture of our day are rarely intensively socialized into coherent religious languages and communal forms of life. This is not necessarily disastrous for the long-range prospects of religion (which is not dependent on elites), but it is for theology as an intellectually and academically creative enterprise capable of making significant contributions to the wider culture and society. Further, theology (in the sense of reflection in the service of religion) is being increasingly replaced in seminaries as well as universities by religious studies. There are fewer and fewer institutional settings favorable to the intratextual interpretation of religion and of extrascriptural realities. Perhaps the last American theologian who in practice (and to some extent in theory) made extended and effective attempts to redescribe major aspects of the contemporary scene in distinctively Christian terms was Reinhold Niebuhr. After the brief neoorthodox interlude (which was itself sometimes thoroughly liberal in its theological methodology, as in the case of Paul Tillich) the liberal tendency to redescribe religion in extrascriptural frameworks has once again become dominant.[25]

I think Lindbeck largely right about his judgment concerning the viability of postliberal theology, even though my own theological perspective might be so characterized. Whether he is right about Reinhold Niebuhr, however, is a complex issue. That Niebuhr was one of the last theologians to command attention in circles of power and influence in America is certainly the case. The extent that Niebuhr's influence resulted from his ability to redescribe the contemporary scene "in distinctive Christian terms," however, remains doubtful. Niebuhr was, no less than Tillich, "thoroughly liberal" in his theological method, and that enabled him to approach the political world with theological discourse already well disciplined by the categories of the "world."

Yet Lindbeck's characterization is important since I hope to do exactly what he thinks Reinhold Niebuhr did—namely, redescribe the American narrative in distinctively Christian terms. I have in effect been trying to do that for over twenty years without notable success. That project has resulted in my being described as a "sectarian, fideistic tribalist" for my refusal to take a "responsible" position toward the American project.[26] One of the reasons for my lack of success is the continued presumption, held by most readers, that the narrative constructed by those whom I mention in this chapter remains normative. Thus, my attempt to provide a different narrative is an attempt not only to change the terms of the debate in my favor, but also to reclaim the power of Christian discourse so as to properly "place"—and in that sense "replace"—American liberal democracy with Christian economy.

Focusing on the development of the discipline of Christian ethics thus becomes a way to tell the story of the displacement of Christian convictions and practices in America. Protestant Christians set out to make America Christian and ended by making Christianity American. I tell the story in a way that I hope makes clear that there are no villains. Indeed, quite the opposite is the case, as I have nothing but deepest admiration for the people who are the central characters of this narrative. They did, I believe, as well as they could given their theological resources and their time. It is our task to be as courageous as they were in facing up to the theological challenge of our own time.

WHAT TO TELL? WHERE TO BEGIN?
WHOM TO INCLUDE? METHODOLOGICAL CONSIDERATIONS

The "rise of the Social Gospel" had much to do with the urbanization of Protestant Christianity. The role of the First and Second World Wars had dramatic impact on the story. It is not my intention, however, to try to account for every influence that might "explain" the development of Christian ethics. I am fortunate that the people whose story I tell were engaged with the issues of their day. So the "background" can, I trust, be displayed through their own work.[27]

The fact that both Rauschenbusch and Reinhold Niebuhr could read German was more important than the way they individually negotiated being German-American.[28] They were therefore able to read German theologians well before they were translated into English. The academic advantages of such a skill, particularly for the Niebuhrs, is apparent. Yet more important is *whom* they read—namely, Ernst Troeltsch. For if the subject of Christian ethics in America has always been America, then it is nonetheless equally true to say that the script, as is evident even in Stackhouse's account above, was written by Ernst Troeltsch. It is no doubt wrong to suggest as Whitehead does that the history of Western philosophy is a footnote to Plato; but it is certainly closer to the truth to suggest that Christian ethics in America is a footnote to Troeltsch.

The Niebuhrs were clearly more directly and differently influenced by Troeltsch than was Rauschenbusch. The latter, for example, saw little difference between Ritschl and Troeltsch.[29] Reinhold Niebuhr read the *Social Teachings* as early as during his years as the pastor of Bethel Evangelical Church in Detroit (1915–1927).[30] His course on the history of Christian ethics, which he taught often at Union Seminary, was basically structured on Troeltsch's *Social Teachings*.[31] Troeltsch was, of course, H. Richard Niebuhr's primary conversation partner from the time he completed his dissertation on Troeltsch in 1924 until his death.[32]

The recognition of Troeltsch's significance is important, as it clearly locates the narrative as part of the ongoing development of Protestant liberal theology.[33] That Troeltsch is *the* liberal Protestant theologian for Christian ethics, as I hope to show, helps us understand how a movement that took as central the social significance of Christianity was epistemologically wedded to an ahistorical and asocial account of religious knowledge.[34] That peculiar combination, however, proved to be a perfect fit for underwriting the kind of political ethic necessary if Christians were to be significant social actors in a society increasingly shaped by the presuppositions of liberal political theory. For, as we shall see, one of the dominant themes in the work of these men is that Christianity has a stake in the development of democratic social orders and governments.

It may seem odd to suggest that the story I tell is but a subplot to the more general story of Protestant liberalism, given the reputation of the Niebuhrs as "neoorthodox" theologians. Such a designation, as they both knew, is a profound mistake. They remained, as those who followed them, deeply committed to the project of subjecting Christian discourse to the criteria of modernity. Though there was and is a great variety of religious liberalism, Sydney E. Ahlstrom helpfully suggests that liberalism "denotes both a certain generosity or charitableness toward divergent opinions and a desire for intellectual 'liberty.' Liberal theologians also wished to 'liberate' religion from obscurantism and creedal bondage so as to give man's moral and rational powers scope."[35]

Reinhold Niebuhr is often identified as the American theologian who brought an end to this liberal project by challenging the optimistic views of human nature and history thought to be at the heart of Protestant liberalism. Thus even William Hutchison presents both Niebuhrs as challengers to the liberal faith in progress.[36] What such a characterization fails to see is that though the Niebuhrs, and in particular Reinhold, may have challenged the kind of anthropology characteristic of an earlier liberalism, they remained fundamentally within liberal presuppositions just to the extent that they assumed the issues were anthropological.[37] The essential liberalism of Rauschenbusch through Gustafson can only be seen in the light that Yoder casts over the whole history. For Yoder does not believe that he must secure an unproblematic starting point in order to begin his work as a Christian theologian. You do not need to have a theory of human nature if you have a church.

Why begin with Walter Rauschenbusch rather than Newman Smyth? After all, Smyth actually wrote his *Christian Ethics* prior to Rauschenbusch's own literary output.[38] Moreover, in some ways Smyth represents a more philosophically sophisticated position and certainly a more systematic presentation than Rauschenbusch. The simple reason for beginning with Rauschenbusch, however, is that when Reinhold Niebuhr began to distance himself from the social gospel he made Rauschenbusch the object of his attack. Furthermore, Rauschenbusch represents in his person the social gospel as a popular movement better than does Smyth. By concentrating on Rauschenbusch I do not mean to demean the many representatives of the social gospel that preceded him, but, rather, I focus on Rauschenbusch exactly because he was so representative.

A more profound objection than whom I treat and where I begin could well be how the narrative is told. In other words, it is a mistake to focus the story primarily on people rather than on institutions and issues. Edward Long and James Gustafson have written quite good studies along such lines.[39] Yet the story I tell has been dominated by these men, whose personalities are crucial for the story. I do not intend, however, to try to provide extensive biographical accounts, but will discuss their lives only as that is necessary to illuminate their work. That will differ from individual to individual, as biographical considerations are obviously much more important for figures like Rauschenbusch and Reinhold Niebuhr than for the others. That such is the case, of course, is telling, since the more "academic" these men become, the less necessary it is to depict their lives.

I am aware, moreover, that all those I treat are men, but then that is part of the story. There is, of course, the remarkable Georgia Harkness, whose life and work intersected with the story I tell, but she did not think of herself as contributing to the development of Christian ethics per se. Perhaps more glaring than the omission of Professor Harkness is the whole school of Boston personalism from which she sprang, and, in particular, the work of Walter Muelder.[40] Though the Boston liberals are not wrongly identified within the social gospel movement, they developed quite distinct emphases, which are interesting but I think not crucial for the story I wish to tell.[41] It is simply the case that after Reinhold Niebuhr the work of those at Boston was not seen as crucial for the central issues developing in the emerging "field" called Christian ethics.[42]

I suspect, for example, that few reading this chapter will think it necessary for me to offer any justification for the inclusion of the Niebuhrs as crucial actors in the story of Christian ethics. There are, of course, a few other important figures, such as John Bennett and Paul Lehmann, who will be mentioned along the way. Yet it was the Niebuhrs who set the terms of the discussion which continue their dominance to this day. They did so, moreover, in quite distinct ways, which helps make clear that even though my story focuses on people, it never does so without carefully considering the contributions of these individuals within their respective institutional settings.

Christian ethics began as a movement of the churches that found its intellectual home in seminary culture. In fact, the very distinction between university and seminary culture was quite blurred at the height of the social gospel's influence.[43] From such a perspective, Reinhold Niebuhr is much closer to the social gospel than is H. Richard Niebuhr. H. Richard, in contrast to Reinhold, represents the beginning of the professionalization of the discipline, a professionalization that is most fully expressed in the work of James Gustafson. For it has been one of Gustafson's projects to write about Christian ethics in a manner acceptable to the developing canons of knowledge underwritten by the modern university.[44] Put differently, beginning with H. Richard Niebuhr and developed by Gustafson, Christian ethics becomes the problem to be studied. The issue is no longer the transformation of America, but how do you move from theological claims to ethical principles and policy? Reinhold Niebuhr was never bothered with the question of whether Christian convictions embodied ethical commitments. His question was their realization. Now Christian ethics becomes the study of itself.

These are gross generalizations, to be sure, but ones that are not unfounded. Of course, the Niebuhrs are important for many reasons other than the ones just mentioned. How Reinhold Niebuhr's "realism" chastened the task of Christian ethics, plus preparing the way for its development into a discipline, is obviously a significant part of my account. H. Richard Niebuhr's preoccupation with relativism is a necessary part of the story if we are to understand why some who continue to work in Christian ethics cannot let go of epistemological issues.

Catholic developments in America, too, are vital, even though mine is predominantly a Protestant story. The most important justification for treating Catholic thinkers, such as Ryan and Murray, is that they provide counterpoint to Reinhold Niebuhr. Yet the Catholics are also necessary in order to understand the work of Paul Ramsey. Ramsey was the student of H. Richard Niebuhr, but in many ways his perspective was more determined by the work of Reinhold. Nevertheless, aspects of Catholic moral theology became indispensable for Ramsey, if only to control the kind of utilitarian calculus that at least some aspects of Reinhold Niebuhr's thought seemed to invite—particularly Niebuhr's tendency to embrace the lesser-of-two-evils argument. Joseph Fletcher, of *Situation Ethics* fame, is also important to Ramsey's work.

Of course, the Catholics are important because they exemplify in many ways the primary story line of my account of the development of Christian ethics in America. Catholic moral theology was quite different from the normative kind of Christian ethics developed in this century in America. It was a casuistry designed for very specific ecclesial purposes; namely, penitential practice. Moral theologians were, first, officers of the church whose "personal" theology was of little consequence in these matters. Yet those who occupy the office of moral theologian have been steadily transformed into Christian ethicists in the American context. Therefore, part of my story is to show how Protestant Christian ethicists, such as Ramsey and Gustafson, were drawn to Catholic moral theology exactly because it offered a casuistry for dealing with issues that were simply not part of the agenda inherited from the social gospel, while at the same time Catholics were attracted to "Christian ethics" exactly because of its promised openness.[45]

Although both Paul Ramsey and James Gustafson were students of H. Richard Niebuhr, they represent quite different sides of his work. Ramsey was influenced just as strongly by Reinhold Niebuhr, but Ramsey also represents the attempt by people in the field to deal with issues such as abortion, sexual ethics, and medical ethics. Such issues were not so pressing for Rauschenbusch and the Niebuhrs, inasmuch as they could continue to assume the hegemony of Protestant practices. Once those practices began to disappear, many assumed that the task of Christian ethics should be to supply the rationale for what at one time was agreed-upon ways of acting. In an interesting way, the project to Christianize America assumes a new form.

Ramsey was Gustafson's older contemporary, who spent almost his whole academic career at Princeton University. Yet he remained a figure much more determined by church culture than by the culture of the university. Gustafson, who spent much of his life at Yale and Chicago divinity schools, has always felt more at home in the university. While I would not want to suggest that their respective theologies were determined by the tensions between their institutional homes and their deepest convictions, I think Gustafson's work in particular is illuminated by his profound respect for the university. In an odd way, Gustafson is, with the possible exception of H. Richard Niebuhr, the most theological of any of these figures, if by "theological" one means focused on God. As we shall see, however, the crucial issue concerns what relation there may be, if any, between the God at the center of Gustafson's work and the God Christians know as Father, Son, and Holy Spirit.

As I suggested at the beginning, John Howard Yoder represents a figure outside the tradition of Christian ethics in America. It would be a mistake, however, to think that he is outside this tradition because he is a Mennonite, though obviously it is not unimportant that he is such. Nor is his defense of nonviolence the crucial difference, though the king of nonviolence he represents does, I hope, point up the importance of the issue of violence for shaping the kind of Christian ethics done in America. Yoder simply brings to the discussion a different way of structuring the relation between the church and the world, a difference with which I am in deep sympathy insofar as it casts fresh light on the story of Christian ethics in America. As will become obvious, the way I tell the story is dependent on how Yoder has taught me to think of theology and ethics or, more accurately, why one cannot distinguish between theology and ethics.

Yet, in an odd way, in order to appreciate Yoder you need to know the story I tell. For only when you appreciate the power of Reinhold and H. Richard Niebuhr's work can you understand why Yoder is such an important alternative to the project of making Christian ethics a distinctively American discipline—that is, a project for the furtherance of America. Any optimism inferred from the subtitle, "A Promising Obituary," is only because the "promise" might be found in Yoder's account of Christianity as practice.

The lives and work of the figures that I have mentioned overlap in complex ways. That Ramsey was an early student of H. Richard Niebuhr, and Gustafson a late student, is surely important. They each studied with the same H. Richard Niebuhr, but it was also a quite different H. Richard Niebuhr since the emphases in his theology were quite different at various times. There are some passages, for instance, in his earlier writings that could easily have been written by John Howard Yoder.[46]

The students, of course, overlapped with the teacher, such that the work of the students themselves became part of the resource for the then current work in Christian ethics. Thus, H. Richard Niebuhr would begin to make Paul Ramsey's *Basic Christian Ethics* a suggested reading in the syllabus for his own famous course in Christian ethics at Yale Divinity School. Even if I believe the story of Christian ethics in America is at an end, which I do, it does not make me any less indebted to these men. My own way of doing theology is what it is because of what I have learned from them.

NOTES

1. The reader will accordingly find some text written in a promissory form suggesting arguments to be made that cannot be made here. Though I hope to fulfill the promises in the proposed book, I hope some readers will find them suggestive enough to test them for themselves.
2. John Milbank, *Theology and Social Theory: Beyond Secular Reason* (Oxford: Basil Blackwell, Publisher, 1990), 380; see also Dorothy Ross, *The Origins of American Social Science* (Cambridge: Cambridge University Press, 1991).
3. Walter Rauschenbusch, *Christianizing the Social Order* (New York: Macmillan Co., 1921); James Gustafson, *Can Ethics Be Christian?* (Chicago: University of Chicago Press, 1975).

4. James Gustafson, "Theology Confronts Technology and the Life Sciences," *Commonweal* 105; 12 (June 16, 1978): 386.

5. See Edward LeRoy Long Jr., *Academic Bonding and Social Concern: The Society of Christian Ethics, 1959–1983* (publication of the Society of Christian Ethics, 1984).

6. Gustafson, "Theology Confronts Technology and the Life Sciences," 392.

7. John Howard Yoder, *The Christian Witness to the State* (Newton, Kans.: Faith and Life Press, 1964), 28–29.

8. Ibid., 29.

9. For a beginning of the exploration of the rhetorical character of theology, see David Cunningham, *Faithful Persuasion: In Aid of a Rhetoric of Christian Theology* (Notre Dame, Ind.: University of Notre Dame Press, 1991).

10. George Marsden, *Religion and American Culture* (New York: Harcourt Brace Jovanovich, 1990), 96.

11. Max Stackhouse, "The Continuing Importance of Walter Rauschenbusch," in *The Righteousness of the Kingdom*, ed. Water Rauschenbusch (New York: Abingdon Press, 1968), 13–59.

12. Ibid., 20–21.

13. Ibid., 23.

14. Robert T. Handy, *A Christian America: Protestant Hopes and Historical Realities* (New York: Oxford University Press, 1971), vii.

15. Marsden, *Religion and American Culture*, 96. See also Christopher Lasch, *The True and Only Heaven: Progress and Its Critics* (New York: W. W. Norton & Co., 1991), 46, 47–48.

16. H. Richard Niebuhr, *The Kingdom of God in America* (New York: Harper & Brothers, 1937).

17. Reinhold Niebuhr, *The Irony of American History* (New York: Charles Scribner's Sons, 1952); see also Richard Reinitz, *Irony and Consciousness: American Historiography and Reinhold Niebuhr's Vision* (Lewisburg, Pa.: Bucknell University Press, 1980).

18. Martin E. Marty, *Religion and Republic: The American Circumstance* (Boston: Beacon Press, 1987), 95–123.

19. James L. Ash Jr., "American Religion and the Academy in the Early Twentieth Century: The Chicago Years of William Warren Sweet," *Church History* 50:4 (December 1981), 451–52.

20. Ibid., 455–56.

21. Nathan O. Hatch, *The Democratization of American Christianity* (New Haven, Conn.: Yale University Press, 1989), and Jon Butler, *Awash in a Sea of Faith: Christianizing the American People* (Cambridge: Harvard University Press, 1990). Perhaps the most important book that challenges the "consensus historians' " account of "Protestant America" is R. Laurence Moore's *Religious Outsiders and the Making of Americans* (New York: Oxford University Press, 1986).

22. See John F. Wilson, *Public Religion in American Culture* (Philadelphia: Temple University Press, 1979).

23. See Marty, *Religion and Republic*, 47; Mark Noll, *A History of Christianity in the United States and Canada* (Grand Rapids: Wm. B. Eerdmans Publishing Co., 1992), and idem, *One Nation under God? Christian Faith and Political Action in America* (San Francisco: Harper & Row, 1988).

24. Roger Finke and Rodney Stark, *The Churching of America, 1776–1990: Winners and Losers in Our Religious Economy* (New Brunswick, N.J.: Rutgers University Press, 1992).

25. George Lindbeck, *The Nature of Doctrine: Religion and Theology in a Postliberal Age* (Philadelphia: Westminster Press, 1984), 123–24; Milbank, *Theology and Social Theory*, 101.

26. See, for example, James Gustafson's critique of my work (and Lindbeck's) in "The Sectarian Temptation: Reflections on Theology, the Church, and the University," *Catholic Theological Society Proceedings* 40 (1985); 83–94. For my response, see my *Christian Existence Today: Essays on Church, World, and Living in Between* (Durham, N.C.: Labyrinth Press, 1988), introduction.

27. See Ralph E. Luker, *The Social Gospel in Black and White: American Racial Reform, 1885–1912* (Chapel Hill, N.C.: University of North Carolina Press, 1991).

28. See Richard Fox, *Reinhold Niebuhr: A Biography* (New York: Pantheon Books, 1985), esp. 41–61.

29. See Rauschenbusch, *A Theology for the Social Gospel* (Nashville: Abingdon-Cokesbury Press, 1945).

30. Charles Brown reports on Niebuhr's reading of Troeltsch in his biography, *Niebuhr and His Age: Reinhold Niebuhr's Prophetic Role in the Twentieth Century* (Philadelphia: Trinity Press International, 1992), 32.

31. Ronald Stone, ed., *Professor Reinhold Niebuhr: A Mentor to the Twentieth Century* (Louisville, Ky.: Westminster/John Knox Press, 1992), 68–70; the tapes of Niebuhr's course are available.

32. H. Richard Niebuhr, "Ernst Troeltsch's Philosophy of Religion" (diss., New Haven, Conn.: Yale University, 1924); and idem, *Christ and Culture* (New York: Harper & Brothers, 1951).

33. See, for example, Benjamin A. Reist's review, "Five Troeltsch Studies," *Religious Studies Review* 17 (October 1991), 323–27; and Hans-Georg Drescher's *Ernst Troeltsch: His Life and Work* (Minneapolis: Fortress Press, 1993).

34. See Hans W. Frei, "Niebuhr's Theological Background," in *Faith and Ethics: The Theology of H. Richard Niebuhr*, ed. Paul Ramsey (New York: Harper & Brothers, 1957), 9–64.

35. Sydney E. Ahlstrom, *A Religious History of the American People* (New Haven, Conn.: Yale University Press, 1972), 779.

36. William Hutchison, *The Modernist Impulse in American Protestantism* (Durham, N.C.: Duke University Press, 1992), 295–98.

37. See Lindbeck, *The Nature of Doctrine*, 31.

38. Newman Smyth, *Christian Ethics* (New York: Charles Scribner's Sons, 1882).

39. Edward LeRoy Long Jr., *A Survey of Christian Ethics* (New York: Oxford University Press, 1967), and James Gustafson, *Christian Ethics and the Community* (Philadelphia: Pilgrim Press, 1971), 23–82.

40. Walter Muelder, *Foundations of the Responsible Society* (Nashville: Abingdon Press, 1959).

41. Ahlstrom, *A Religious History of the American People*, 788.

42. See Robert Bruce Mullin, *Episcopal Vision/American Reality: High Church Theology and Social Thought in Evangelical America* (New Haven, Conn.: Yale University Press, 1986).

43. See, for example, J. David Hoeveler Jr., "The University and the Social Gospel: The Intellectual Origins of the 'Wisconsin Idea,' " *Wisconsin Magazine of History* (summer 1976): 282–98.

44. Barton Bledstein, in his *The Culture of Professionalism: The Middle Class and the Development of Higher Education in America* (New York: W. W. Norton & Co., 1976);

for what remains the best single account of the power of the expert in modernity, see Alasdair MacIntyre, *After Virtue* (Notre Dame, Ind.: University of Notre Dame Press, 1984), 79–87.

45. Gustafson argues much the same thesis in his *Protestant and Roman Catholic Ethics: Prospects for Rapprochement* (Chicago: University of Chicago Press, 1978).

46. For example, *The Church against the World* (Chicago: Willett, Clark & Co., 1935), introduction.

PART IV

LIBERAL AND PROGRESSIVIST THEOLOGIES

9

ROMAN CATHOLIC
MORAL THEOLOGY

FR. CHARLES E. CURRAN

Catholic moral theology involves the systematic, thematic, and critical scientific reflection on the Christian moral life from the Roman Catholic perspective. The Catholic Church has always been interested in how Christians should act, and from earliest times has reflected on the implications of faith and the gospel for Christian life and actions. A truly systematic and scientific theology as such arose in the twelfth and thirteenth centuries, as illustrated in the work of Thomas Aquinas (d. 1274). Moral theology as a discipline separated from dogmatic theology began in the seventeenth century with the manuals of moral theology that continued in existence until Vatican II.[1]

Despite the significant changes and developments in recent Catholic moral theology, distinctive characteristics of the Catholic tradition continue to shape Catholic moral theology today — mediation, catholicity, with a small c, opposition to individualism, and the relationship to the life of the Catholic Church. The emphasis on mediation sees the divine as mediated in and through the human, with the acceptance of a fundamental goodness of the human and of human reason, as illustrated in the traditional acceptance of natural law understood as human reason directing us to our end in accord with our human nature. To discover what God is asking, one does not go immediately and directly to God, but to the reason and creation made by God. Catholicity with a small c involves a concern for all aspects of human life in this world and for a catholic and universal perspective that deals with the good of humankind as a whole. The Catholic approach rejects any sectarianism that sees the church as cut off from the rest of society. Mediation and catholicity ground the Catholic emphasis on a "both/and" approach rather than an "either/or." The Catholic tradition insists on faith and reason, grace and works, scripture and tradition, Jesus and the church. The distinctive Catholic approach opposes individualism by insisting that the person is by nature social and political, called to live in political society and striving for the common good and not merely for one's own individualistic good. The relationship to the church sees the moral life in the context of the church, with special emphasis on the life of the sacraments such as penance, and in relation to the hierarchical teaching office with its authoritative teaching role in matters including morality.

The manuals of moral theology in existence before Vatican II (1962–1965) were textbooks that prepared future priests to be judges in the sacrament of penance. According to the Council of Trent (1545–1563), the Catholic faithful had to confess their mortal sins according to their number and kind once a year. The practice of the sacrament of penance played a very significant role in the life of the Roman Catholic Church before 1965. These textbooks prepared future priests for their role as judges in the sacrament of penance by explaining what acts were sinful and their degree of sinfulness. These manuals employed a legal ethical model, with law, including the eternal, the natural, civil, and ecclesiastical laws, constituting the objective norm of morality; whereas conscience, which strives to conform to the law, constitutes the subjective norm of morality. The model of the Ten Commandments was often used to explain the morality of particular acts in the part of the discipline called special moral theology as distinguished from fundamental moral theology, which treated of those aspects (e.g., law and conscience) common to all human actions. These textbooks of moral theology were cut off from systematic or dogmatic theology, spiritual theology, contemporary philosophy, and the empirical sciences, and followed an approach that was legalistic, minimalistic, forgetful of the subject of morality, and casuistic. An important aspect of Catholic moral theology in the middle of the twentieth century concerned the increased role of the papacy in determining and authoritatively deciding the morality of particular acts, especially in the area of sexual and medical morality. Pope Pius XII spoke out on many issues in medical ethics, such as abortion, anesthesia, conflict situations, death and dying, sterilization, and selling blood. Whenever the pope spoke out, the issue was closed.[2]

The popes in the late nineteenth and twentieth centuries insisted that Catholic philosophy and theology follow the teaching and method of Thomas Aquinas. Neoscholasticism became the Catholic approach. Although the manuals of moral theology claimed to be following the approach of Aquinas, their narrow focus and legal model was not Thomistic. Catholic philosophers (e.g., Jacques Maritain) developed and applied the ethical approach of Thomas Aquinas. In the course of the twentieth century some Thomists and some followers of the Tübingen school (emphasizing a life-centered and biblically oriented approach) criticized the manuals of moral theology, but these textbooks remained basically unchanged and were used in Catholic seminaries until Vatican II.[3] This council and the 1968 encyclical *Humanae vitae* significantly affected the development of Catholic moral theology.

VATICAN II AND ITS AFTERMATH

Vatican II did not devote a specific document to moral theology, although the Pastoral Constitution on the Church in the Modern World dealt with aspects of social ethics, but the basic approach of the Council deeply affected moral theology in a number of important areas—focus, model, method, integration of scripture and theology, emphasis on the person, ecumenism, and dialogue with the world, and others.

Vatican II insisted on the universal call of all Christians to holiness.[4] Christians must take a greater responsibility for their world and work in all areas to bring about a better human condition. Thus the scope of moral theology could no longer be limited to the training of judges in the sacrament of penance with its emphasis on the minimal and what is sinful. Moral theology became life-centered and not sin-centered.

Bernard Lonergan, a very significant Catholic systematic theologian and philosopher, maintained that the primary change effected by Vatican II was a shift from classicism to historical consciousness. Classicism tends to see reality in terms of the eternal, immutable, and unchanging, and often uses a deductive approach. Thus, a pre–Vatican II theology began with the definition of terms (e.g., What is a human being; What is political society) that was true for all times and all places and deducted moral considerations from these premises. Vatican II proposed a historically conscious approach, which gives more emphasis to the particular, the contingent, and the changing while still insisting on continuities with the past and employing a more inductive approach.[5] The Pastoral Constitution on the Church in the Modern World began its discussion of important social areas not with an abstract definition true in all circumstances, but with the signs of the times (nn. 47; 54–56; 63; 73; 77). Without abandoning the Catholic emphasis on universality and catholicity, this method greatly transformed Catholic theology. Such a move made it easier for later developments to begin with the experience of the poor and the marginalized or with the experience of women. The emphasis on a more inductive approach means that the discipline will not expect as firm and great a certitude with regard to its moral decisions and conclusions as with a deductive approach, for historical developments might also bring about new situations and changes.

Vatican II insisted on the need to overcome the split between faith and daily life.[6] The Council also stressed the need to make scripture the soul of theology and to give the scripture a very significant place in the liturgy and in the spiritual life of Catholics.[7] The earlier natural law approach to moral theology so emphasized the roles of reason and nature that scripture was reduced at best to a proof text which was occasionally used to prove a conclusion that had been based on natural law reasoning. Since that time Catholic theologians in dialogue with others have been discussing the proper role and function of the scriptures in moral theology, with many recognizing a significant role of the scripture in forming the personal and communal identity of Christian people and in describing the attitudes and virtues of the Christian. On specific issues, the direct involvement of the scriptures is much less significant, since these issues depend heavily on reason and contemporary realities. The need to make moral theology more theological responded to the Council's call for faith to have a more immediate effect on daily life in the world. In keeping with the traditional Catholic emphasis on mediation, however, most Catholic moral theologians recognize that scriptural and theological concepts must be mediated in and through the human.[8]

The recognition of the need to incorporate scripture and theology into moral theology raised a question that has been widely discussed in the subsequent years: What is distinctive or unique about Catholic ethics and morality? I maintain there are many distinctive aspects about Catholic morality, but Catholics or Christians in their daily lives in this world are not called to act in ways that no other human beings are called to act in working for a better society. There is no unique Christian moral content for life in the social, political, and economic orders of human existence in this world.

Vatican II gave greater emphasis to the person and the subject as distinguished from the natural and objective. In keeping with the traditional Catholic "both/and" approach, however, the emphasis on the subject does not do away with a proper role for the objective. The Declaration on Religious Liberty of Vatican II (n. 1) based its acceptance of religious freedom, which represented a significant change from past teaching, on the dignity of the human person, which has been expressing itself more and more deeply on the consciousness of contemporary human beings (note also the shift to historical consciousness). The older denial of religious freedom rested on the objective nature of truth, but the shift to the person and the subject resulted in a different approach to religious freedom.

The emphasis on the person, together with a call to holiness, had a significant effect on moral theology's emphasis on the moral growth and development of the person. Bernard Häring, the primary international figure in the renewal of moral theology before and after Vatican II, insisted on the importance of conversion (note the biblical influence). Conversion calls for a fundamental change of heart and the need to deepen and grow through continual conversion.[9] Karl Rahner, probably the most significant Catholic theologian in the twentieth century, developed an anthropology that distinguished the core freedom of the person from categorical freedom. His theory of fundamental option insisted on the basic orientation of the person in the depths of one's core freedom, which is expressed and developed through concrete categorical actions, but the goodness of the human being as distinguished from the rightness of the act comes from this basic orientation.[10]

Such emphasis on the subject and the person changed the understanding of the important Catholic distinction between moral sin and venial sin, and the understanding of the sacrament of penance. Moral sin breaks one's relationship with God and makes one deserving of eternal damnation in hell, whereas venial sin offends God but does not break the basic relationship. The pre–Vatican II approach saw sin primarily as an act against the law of God. Thus many different moral acts were often described as grave sins, although in reality they should have been called grave matter. In the perspective of the fundamental option, sin involves the changed fundamental option or orientation and cannot be reduced just to the external act itself.[11] Some, including Pope John Paul II in his encyclical *Veritatis splendor*, have criticized the fundamental option for downplaying the importance and significance of the external act.[12] The proper response to these objections appeals to an important distinction. The particular or categorical act can be described as morally right or wrong, but whether or not moral sin is present depends on the fundamental orientation or the conversion of the person.

Vatican II's Decree on Ecumenism encouraged ecumenical dialogue with Christians and other religions. Before the Council, the Catholic Church saw itself as the one true church of Christ primarily in opposition to and distinguished from Protestantism. The initial ecumenical enthusiasm of the Council has waned, and institutional ecumenism has not really developed, but ecumenism deeply influences Catholic moral theology today. Catholic theologians read and dialogue with Protestant theologians. One cannot properly do Catholic theology today without such a dialogue. Ecumenical societies of moral theology exist in which Protestants and Catholics together discuss the aspects of their discipline.

Vatican II especially emphasized dialogue with the modern world and purposely avoided any condemnations.[13] Such an approach contrasted strongly with the pre–Vatican II era with its defensive position with regard to modern culture, frequently resulting in a ghetto posture. Subsequently many have criticized Vatican II for being too optimistic about the modern world, but the emphasis on dialogue remains. The emphasis on dialogue has greatly affected Catholic theology in general and moral theology in particular. In the late nineteenth and early twentieth century the popes insisted on Thomism as the Catholic theology and philosophy, in an attempt to prevent dialogue with other contemporary methods and approaches. Since Vatican II, moral theology has been open to learn from and utilize many different philosophical approaches. No longer can one speak of a monolithic method in Catholic moral theology, but certain traditional Catholic moral emphases continue to be present.

HUMANAE VITAE *AND ITS AFTERMATH*

Humanae vitae, the 1968 encyclical letter of Pope Paul VI reiterating the Catholic teaching condemning artificial contraception in marriage, constitutes a second very significant event that shaped the development of Catholic moral theology in the last three decades.

Before 1963 there had been no article in a theological journal calling for a change in the Catholic teaching on artificial contraception. In the church atmosphere of the early twentieth century this teaching was not questioned. The changed atmosphere brought about by Vatican II occasioned the questioning of this teaching both by Catholic couples and by theologians. In June 1964, Pope Paul VI publicly called attention to a special commission appointed earlier by John XXIII to study the question of artificial contraception and took the issue out of the competency of the Council in the light of this commission. However, during the Council there were some discussions that touched on contraception. The long fifth session of the commission showed that the vast majority favored a change in the teaching, and documents to this effect were leaked to the press in 1967.[14] However, on July 29, 1968, Paul VI publicly issued his encyclical. "The church, calling men back to the observance of the norms of the natural law as interpreted by their constant doctrine, teaches that each and every marriage act must remain open to the transmission of life. . . . Indeed, by its intimate structure, the conjugal act, while most closely uniting husband and wife, capacitates them for the generation of new lives, according to laws inscribed in the very being of man and woman."[15]

The papal encyclical has continued to echo in the life of the Roman Catholic Church, and basically set the future agenda for moral theology in four important areas—sexual ethics, natural law, the existence and grounding of norms, and dissent from authoritative hierarchical teaching.

The papal and hierarchical teaching have continued to employ in sexual ethics the basic criterion found in *Humanae vitae*, that the nature and purpose of the sexual faculty call for sexual acts that are both open to procreation and expressive of love union. On this basis the hierarchical magisterium has continued to condemn masturbation, homosexuality, and pre- and extramarital sexuality, as well as artificial contraception.[16] The majority of Catholic moral theologians reject the teaching on artificial contraception. Roman Catholicism has witnessed the same debate over homosexual genital acts that has transpired in other Christian churches and in the broader society. The papal teaching and other theologians continue to condemn homosexual genital acts, even within the context of a loving union striving for permanency. Some theologians justify these acts on the basis of the loving commitment of the two parties. A third position justifies such acts in this context but sees them as falling short of the ideal. Sexuality has continued to be an area of strong disagreements within Roman Catholicism.[17]

Humanae vitae has also touched off a continuing discussion about natural law.[18] From a theological perspective, natural law refers to the fact that the Catholic approach has traditionally recognized human reason and not just revelation as a source of ethical wisdom for the discipline. The philosophical aspect of the question refers to how one understands the meaning of natural and the meaning of law. The papal teaching follows the older, Thomist understanding that human reason discovers the three levels of basic human inclinations—those shared with all living things (the inclination to continue in existence); those shared with all animals (procreation and the education of offspring); and those proper to humans as rational beings (to know God and to live together in human society). These inclinations are morally normative.[19]

Catholic revisionist moral theologians object to this understanding from two different perspectives.[20] First, they accuse *Humanae vitae* and this approach to natural law of physicalism, which makes the physical or biological morally normative and forbids human reason to interfere in these physical and biological processes. The human can and should interfere in the physical process if this is for truly human good. The physical is just one aspect of the human, and at times can and must be sacrificed for the good of the total human. In other areas, for example, killing, the moral aspect of the act (murder) is distinguished from the physical aspect of the act (killing). Not all killing is murder. The anthropology of the encyclical makes the physical or the animal aspect morally normative, in conformity with an anthropology that sees the human being as a rational animal.

Second, the revisionist understanding rejects the faculty approach to natural law, which makes the nature and purpose of the faculty the moral criterion. Rather, the faculty must be seen in relation to the person and to the marital relationship. Thus, for the good of the marriage or the good of the person one can and should interfere with the purpose of the faculty. Notice here the effect of giving greater emphasis to the person as the ultimate moral criterion.

More radical criticisms of the manualistic natural law approach have also arisen, coming especially from the recognition of historicity and historical consciousness. The emphasis on history and God working through history contrast with the view that God works through nature. A historically conscious approach will also be more inductive than the deductive approach of the manuals of moral theology. The older natural-law approach did not give enough importance to diversity and pluralism. Emphasis on praxis and starting with the experience of the oppressed and marginalized have also challenged the more universal and neutral starting place of natural law. Even those in the Catholic tradition who challenge natural law still recognize such basic realities in the Catholic tradition as the role of reason, the need for mediation, and the possibility of some type of universal ethic permitting a dialogue among all people.

Whereas most revisionist approaches to natural law or challenges to it support positions often at odds with hierarchical teaching in the sexual area, Germain Grisez and John Finnis have been proposing a modified natural-law theory which strongly supports the papal teaching on artificial contraception. This newer approach to natural law denies that the natural teleology of human functions demands absolute moral respect. They likewise appear to reject the basic teleology of the Thomist approach in general, with their insistence on the role of practical reason with its self-evident knowledge of certain basic human goods that one can never go against but that can be ordered in different ways. Procreation is one of these basic human goods that one can never directly go against.[21] Thus the discussion about natural law continues with different approaches—some strongly defending the view found in Aquinas and in the hierarchical teaching, others modifying this understanding of natural law, and others even rejecting and proposing a different methodology

Humanae vitae also set the stage for the ongoing debate in Catholic moral theology about the existence and grounding of moral norms, which is sometimes described as the debate about intrinsically evil acts.[22] Dissenters from *Humanae vitae* point out the fallacy of physicalism in the encyclical, which identifies the human moral act with the physical or biological structure of the act. Revisionist Catholic theologians thus distinguish between moral evil and premoral evil (also called ontic, or physical). By its very nature something that is described only in terms of the physical structure or aspect of the act cannot ipso facto be morally normative. In this light, revisionist theologians disagree with the hierarchical teaching on contraception, sterilization, artificial insemination, and the principle of the double effect, which has been employed in the Catholic tradition to solve problems in which one act has effects that are both good and bad. The crucial condition of the principle of double effect is that the good effect must follow equally immediately as the bad effect, or in other words that the bad effect cannot be produced by means of the good effect. Thus one could not abort a fetus (presumed to be a living human being) in order to save the life of the mother. One could, however, remove a cancerous uterus that was pregnant because the physical act does not immediately target the fetus as a means to save the mother but targets the diseased uterus itself. In this approach the physical causality or physical structure of the act is morally normative.

In the light of the problem of physicalism, many revisionist Catholic moral theologians have developed a theory often called proportionalism. One may do a physical or premoral evil if there is a proportionate reason. However, these proportionists also want to avoid the opposite danger of a total consequentialism or utilitarianism. Thus, in weighing the good against the bad they propose various ways of avoiding such a total consequentialism. The Catholic proponents of proportionalism generally hold on to the condemnation of bombing cities or civilian targets in order to shorten the war. Disagreement about the exact meaning of a proportionate reason necessary to do a premoral evil remains, but all attempts strive for a middle way between the older Catholic approach and total consequentialism or utilitarianism.

Pope John Paul II, in his encyclical *Veritatis splendor* (nn. 71–83), strongly condemns proportionalism. Some Catholic theologians agree with the condemnation. Grisez and others also strongly oppose proportionalism on the basis of their theory of certain basic human goods that one can never directly go against, and thereby agree with the particular positions taken by the hierarchical magisterium.[23]

A fourth issue precipitated by *Humanae vitae* concerns the legitimacy of dissent from papal teaching and the proper relationship between the hierarchical teaching authority in the church and theologians. Before Vatican II, the Roman Catholic Church had become more centralized and authoritarian than ever before in its history. Recall the many pronouncements of Pope Pius XII (1939–1958) on moral issues, which ended any further theological discussion. Vatican II in theory called for a less authoritarian understanding of the church and its teaching office and saw the hierarchical magisterium in service of the total people of God. In the light of these developments some Catholic theologians openly dissented from the teaching of *Humanae vitae* condemning artificial contraception.[24]

The dissenters then and now justify their action by appealing to the nature of authoritative noninfallible teaching.[25] This term only came into existence in the latter part of the nineteenth century, after the definition of papal infallibility. In the light of the circumstances of twentieth-century Catholicism, with its defensiveness and authoritarianism (recall the condemnations of Americanism and modernism at the turn of the century), dissent had never been discussed in any depth. Authoritative noninfallible teaching does not belong to the core of faith. Most of the moral teachings or issues involved (contraception, principle of double effect) are based on reason and not on faith and the gospel. Also the moral issues involve a great deal of complexity and specificity, in the light of which one cannot claim a certitude that excludes the possibility of error. These teachings on specific moral issues might be wrong. The assistance of the Holy Spirit given to the hierarchical magisterium does not mean that the hierarchical teaching authority does not have to do all the homework in striving to arrive at moral truth. History also shows that many such specific moral teachings (e.g., slavery, the rights of the accused, usury, religious freedom, the justification for the marital act) have changed over the years. Even early proponents of the nineteenth-century terminology of authoritative noninfallible teaching admitted the possibility of error in such authoritative noninfallible teaching.

However, the papal teaching office has never publicly and explicitly acknowledged the legitimacy of such dissent. The hierarchical magisterium has not changed its teaching on any of the controverted issues and has taken action against some dissenting theologians. John Paul II wrote his encyclical *Veritatis splendor* (n. 5) to address the crisis in the church constituted, not by occasional unlimited dissent, but by an overall and systematic calling into question of traditional moral teachings on the basis of certain ethical and anthropological presuppositions. The discussion within the Roman Catholic Church continues with regard to dissent from such authoritative noninfallible teaching and about the proper roles of theologians and the hierarchical magisterium.

A very few Catholic theologians (e.g., Grisez) have maintained that the teaching on contraception is infallible, on the basis of the ordinary infallible magisterium of pope and bishops' always and everywhere teaching something as a matter of divine faith to be held definitively by the faithful.[26] The vast majority of Catholic theologians disagree, holding that such issues were not taught as a matter of faith to be held definitively by all the faithful. However, Pope John Paul II in his encyclical *Evangelium vitae* of 1995 condemns murder, direct abortion, and euthanasia by using a formula that some could interpret as claiming these teachings are infallible by reason of the ordinary magisterium of pope and bishops.[27]

All recognize that a restorationist approach in recent documents of the hierarchical magisterium wants to tighten things up in the Roman Catholic Church, especially with regard to moral theology. In my judgment, this attempt cannot and will not be successful in the long run, but the tensions are very prevalent at the present and for the immediate future. I appeal to the traditional Thomist and Catholic understanding of an intrinsic morality—something is commanded because it is good, and not the other way around. The hierarchical magisterium must conform itself to what is good and true, and by itself it can never make something good that is not good.

Within Roman Catholicism, those who like myself dissent from some of the past papal sexual and medical moral teachings generally are quite supportive of the hierarchical social teachings. At the same time, some who disagree with the social teachings as being too liberal are in agreement with the papal sexual and medical teachings. In my judgment this points to a difference in approach between the two areas of papal teaching.

Almost by definition, the social teachings as found in the papal social encyclicals dealing with political, economic, and cultural aspects of existence in national and global society are not troubled by the problem of physicalism. Such a problem comes to the fore only in personal moral issues of sexual and medical ethics.

In addition, much change and development has occurred in papal social teaching even in the twentieth century. Pope Leo XIII at the end of the nineteenth century downplayed freedom, equality, and participation, whereas Paul VI made these important aspects of his social teaching. Nineteenth-century papal social teaching strongly condemned individual freedom, whereas twentieth-century evaluations of such freedom were much more positive. In light of the growth of totalitarianism in the twentieth century, papal social teaching defended the dignity, freedom, and rights of the individual. John XXIII in 1963 for the first time in papal social documents developed a Catholic understanding and defense of human rights.[28]

Papal social teaching shows a definite development toward the emphasis on the person, historicity, and historical consciousness. The acceptance of religious liberty by Vatican II well illustrates this development. The underlying and perhaps more significant issue in the religious liberty debate of Vatican II centered on change or development in church teaching. The nineteenth-century papal teaching strongly condemned religious freedom. How could the church now accept this teaching? The historical circumstances changed so that what was true in the nineteenth century was no longer true in 1965.[29] As a result, the papal social teaching had a historical hermeneutic to justify change and development that is not present in the sexual and medical teaching. In order to support its teaching in the sexual and medical areas the papacy continues to cite the older teachings of Pius XII, which emphasized the more classicist approach not open to development and change. Thus significant methodological differences exist between the papal approach to sexual and medical morality and its approach to social morality.

However, Vatican II's acceptance of a historical hermeneutic to explain the changed teaching on religious liberty is quite problematic. Such an approach is inadequate. One has to recognize at least somewhere along the line that the older teaching was in error. The Council fathers were unable and unwilling to admit that previous church teaching had been wrong. If the Council had clearly faced the possibility and reality of error in authoritative noninfallible teaching, there might never have been a *Humanae vitae*. Paul VI in 1968 recognized that the primary reason for reiterating the condemnation of artificial contraception was the past teaching proposed with constant firmness by the hierarchical magisterium.[30] Sooner or later—and we hope it is sooner—the hierarchical magisterium must recognize error in its teachings.

TWO OTHER PUBLICS:
SOCIETY AND THE ACADEMY

This chapter has considered Catholic moral theology in the twentieth century in terms of its relationship to the Catholic Church. In addition, moral theology also relates to two other publics—society as a whole and the academy. These relationships have also influenced the development of Catholic moral theology.

In many ways society and developments within society propose the agenda for moral theology. The discussions about sexuality mentioned above came from societal developments emphasizing planned parenthood and the so-called sexual revolution. The global population problem has increased the pressure on the hierarchical teaching on contraception. In the whole area of sexuality, however, the disciplinary actions taken by the Roman authorities against Catholic theologians writing on these topics has obviously influenced many other Catholic theologians not to write in these areas.

The last twenty-five years have witnessed the growth of a new discipline—bioethics. Before 1965, Catholic moral theologians were about the only ones who were interested in medical ethics going back to such concerns as the professional obligations and responsibilities of doctors and the important distinction between impotence and sterility in marriage legislation. Since medicine and morality before 1965 had the same basic criterion; that is, the good of the individual patient, there was no need for a special discipline. However, new technological developments raised significant new questions and also for the first time posed the possibility of harming the individual person to help others, as in questions of experimentation or transplantation. The Catholic tradition has made a significant contribution to the broader bioethical discussions with its teaching in a number of areas, such as the obligation to use only ordinary means to conserve life. Abortion has been a controversial area in society in general and also within the Catholic Church, with some Catholic theologians dissenting from the hierarchical position. Without doubt, the discussion over euthanasia will become more heated in society in the immediate future.

In terms of social issues in the world, the plight of the two-thirds world has come to the fore. Catholic theologians in South America (e.g., Gustavo Gutiérrez, Luis Segundo, Leonardo Boff) writing from a praxis perspective and not an academic setting have developed a theology of liberation with emphasis on a preferential option for the poor. Some have accepted a Marxist sociological analysis to develop such a theology. The Vatican has twice addressed the issue of liberation theology, pointing out some problems, but this remains the most widespread theological development since Vatican II. The emphasis on a *preferential* option for the poor coheres with the traditional Catholic emphasis on inclusivity and universality, so that others are not excluded. Note that liberation theology involves a different methodological approach to theological ethics, and not just another area of theological study.[31] Significant relationships exist between liberation theology, which has spread from Latin America across the globe, and black liberation theology, which emerged from the black Protestant experience in the United States.

In economic ethics the Catholic tradition has historically disagreed with both socialism and capitalism. The papal social encyclicals in this century have moved from espousing a third way to a critical approach to existing economic structures. The popes condemned the atheism, materialism, and sacrifice of the person to the totality in Marxism. Although official Catholicism was a strong opponent of communism, dialogue superseded condemnation from the time of John XXIII and Vatican II. Perhaps Catholics could find a Marxist sociological analysis to be helpful.[32]

Catholicism has moved from a rather blanket condemnation of liberalism and the Enlightenment in the nineteenth century to an appreciation of some of its emphasis on freedom, equality, and human rights. However, the papal approach in particular and the Catholic tradition in general will always oppose a one-sided individualism, based on its more communitarian and social understanding of the human person. The traditional Catholic emphasis on the common good calls for limits on capitalism and the need for all to work together for the good of humankind and the environment. Although Catholicism has learned important aspects of social issues from the Enlightenment, it can never accept individualism.[33]

In the United States, the Roman Catholic bishops in 1986 published a pastoral letter on the economy insisting on economic rights as well as political rights, and seeing the fulfillment of the basic needs of the poor as of the highest priority.[34] However, some American Catholics (e.g., Michael Novak, George Weigel, and lately Richard John Neuhaus) have taken a different tack by insisting that the Catholic tradition has not given enough importance to the productivity of wealth, and have adopted a much more positive view of the American economy.[35] In the political sphere, as mentioned earlier, as the twentieth century progressed the official Catholic teaching became more open to basic political rights and to recognizing democracy as the best form of government.

In many parts of the globe, including the United States, questions have arisen about the best way for the church and the Christian to address the issues facing our pluralistic societies. Before Vatican II the Catholic approach generally used a natural law method based on human reason and human nature that Christians share with all humankind, thus facilitating dialogue with everybody. The Vatican II insistence on relating faith more directly to daily life has resulted in more theological and Christian symbols and concepts. In using such distinctively Christian approaches in a pluralistic society, however, one must try to make them understandable to others who do not necessarily share these beliefs.

A particularly divisive topic in many countries concerns the relationship between law or public policy and morality.[36] With the acceptance of religious liberty the Catholic church recognized that the freedom of individuals in society should be recognized as far as possible and curtailed only when necessary.[37] The debate about abortion laws has erupted in many countries. Many Catholic theologians, together with the pope, insist that civil law must protect the rights of the unborn, the most vulnerable of people in society. I have reasoned, however, that because of the existing doubts and debates in society at large about the personhood of the fetus, law should give the benefit of the doubt to the freedom of the mother.[38]

Ecological and environmental concerns have come to the fore in the last few decades. These significant issues and reflection on them have called on moral theology to change and adjust its own method and self-understanding. Moral theology after Vatican II moved to an emphasis on the subject and historicity, but environmental ethics reminds us of the need not to forget the objective and the natural. Post–Vatican II moral theology has become too anthropocentric, and it needs to develop more of its older emphasis on creation and nature to deal more adequately with environmental issues.[39]

Feminism constitutes an important social issue that has received much attention in the academy. Feminist thought in general and feminist ethics have challenged the perspective of a disinterested neutral observer approach and insisted on beginning with the experience of women in a patriarchal society. Likewise, the differences between feminist, womanist, and *mujerista* approaches have surfaced. Catholic women have strongly and rightly attacked the patriarchy in the church, whose effect is seen today especially in its denying women access to priesthood and leadership. Despite their strong protests about existing structures in church and society and their insistence on starting with the experience of the oppression of women, Catholic feminists generally insist on the need for an inclusive morality that involves all. Here their catholicity with a small *c* comes through despite the starting point of their ethical considerations.[40]

Especially in the United States, the academy has become the primary home of moral theology, as distinguished from the seminary in the pre–Vatican II period. Catholic colleges and universities include moral theology as an academic discipline to be treated the same as other disciplines. This shift in location grounds the emphasis, especially in the United States, that academic freedom protects the rights and responsibilities of Catholic theologians in the academy. Vatican officials have been wary about accepting the academic freedom of Catholic theologians in United States colleges and universities, precisely because of losing control over these academics.[41]

The academic standards of the academy have improved the discipline of moral theology. More articles and books are being written now than fifty years ago. Especially in the United States, with its large number of Catholic colleges and universities, there are many more moral theologians than in the past. The shift of the locus of moral theology to the academy as contrasted with the seminary has had beneficial results for the discipline.

The complexity of the matter to be studied and the academic nature of the enterprise call for specialists in specific, particular areas. No longer will one person be able to claim competency in the many different areas of moral theology. Thus individuals specialize in moral theology and bioethics; social, political, and economic ethics; business ethics; legal ethics; the ethics of the professions; environmental ethics; and so on. However, despite or perhaps in part because of inclusion in the academy, the interdisciplinary aspect of moral theology has not developed as much as it should have.

Without doubt, philosophical ethics remains the primary dialogue partner for moral theology because of sharing the same subject matter and many of the same methodological concerns. This dialogue takes place in many different ways. The debate over the existence and grounding of exceptionless norms has brought moral theology into dialogue with contemporary deontological and teleological theories. The dialogue between Catholicism and liberalism has already been mentioned. Philosophers often distinguish different approaches to ethics—principled, virtue, or casuist approaches, for example. Catholic moral theology in its historical development and by virtue of its distinctive inclusive character has tended to see these approaches as complementary. All three aspects belong to moral theology in my judgment, although one approach might receive greater emphasis from a particular author.

At the present time postmodernism has become prominent in philosophical circles. The Catholic tradition shares some of its problems with modernism, but the traditional Catholic commitment to human reason and its insistence on a catholic, small *c*, morality embracing all humankind resists some of the more decentering aspects of postmodernism. In this connection some postmodernist ethicists reject foundationalism, according to which all ethics is grounded in one foundational reality. The Catholic natural law theory, with its basis in human anthropology, well illustrates a foundational approach. Catholic theologians are just beginning to grapple with these issues, with some theologians accepting the criticism of foundationalism and employing a more pragmatic approach.[42] Here again the Catholic tradition stands for the need to have some type of possible dialogue and criticism that represents all human beings on our planet.

It is impossible to predict the future development of moral theology, but it will occur in moral theology's relationships with its three publics—the church, the academy, and society. By its very nature, the relationship with the church has been and will continue to be the most significant. In addition, the distinctive aspects of the Catholic moral theology tradition—mediation, catholicity with a small *c*, and opposition to individualism—will continue to direct the discipline.

NOTES

1. No definitive history of moral theology exists. For the best available study, see Louis Vereecke, *Storia della teologia morale moderna*, 4 vols. (Rome: Accademia Alfonisiana, 1980). These volumes are mimeographed notes provided to students, but are available to the general public. For a very helpful study in English, which does not claim to be an exhaustive history, see John Mahoney, *The Making of Moral Theology: A Study of the Roman Catholic Tradition* (Oxford: Clarendon Press, 1987).

2. Mahoney, *Making of Moral Theology*, 22–36, 156–64.

3. John C. Ford and Gerald Kelly, *Contemporary Moral Theology,* vol. 1: *Questions in Fundamental Moral Theology* (Westminster, Md.: Newman Press, 1958), 42–103.

4. Pastoral Constitution on the Church, nn. 39–42, in Austin Flannery, ed., *Vatican Council II: The Conciliar and Post-Conciliar Documents*, rev. ed. (Collegeville, Minn.: Liturgical Press, 1992), 396–402. Subsequent references in the text of this chapter will just give the paragraph numbers of the documents cited.

5. Bernard Lonergan, "A Transition from a Classicist Worldview to Historical Mindedness," in *Law for Liberty: The Role of Law in the Church Today,* ed. James E. Biechler (Baltimore: Helicon, 1967), 126–33.

6. Pastoral Constitution on the Church in the Modern World, n. 43; in Flannery, *Vatican Council II*, 943.

7. Dogmatic Constitution of Divine Revelation, nn. 21–26, in Flannery, *Vatican Council II*, 762–65.

8. William C. Spohn, *What Are They Saying about Scripture and Ethics?* rev. ed. (Mahwah, N.J.: Paulist Press, 1995).

9. Bernard Häring, "La Conversion," in *Pastorale du péché,* ed. Ph. Delhaye (Tournai, Belgium: Desclée, 1961), 65–145; see also Walter Conn, *Christian Conversion: A Developmental Interpretation of Autonomy and Surrender* (Mahwah, N.J.: Paulist Press, 1986).

10. Josef Fuchs, a very prominent figure in contemporary moral theology, who taught in Rome, has developed and employed the Rahnerian approach in his moral theology. For an early discussion of fundamental option, see Josef Fuchs, *Human Values and Christian Morality* (Dublin: Gill & Macmillan, 1970); for more recent illustrations of his use of fundamental option, see Josef Fuchs, *Christian Morality: The Word Becomes Flesh* (Washington, D.C.: Georgetown University Press, 1987).

11. Timothy E. O'Connell, *Principles for a Catholic Morality,* rev. ed. (San Francisco: Harper & Row, 1990), 89–102.

12. John Paul II, *Veritatis splendor*, nn. 65–70, in *Origins* 23 (1993): 316–18.

13. John W. O'Malley, *Tradition and Transition: Historical Perspectives on Vatican II* (Wilmington, Del.: Michael Glazier, 1989).

14. For the historical development, see Robert Blair Kaiser, *The Problem of Sex and Religion: A Case History in the Development of Doctrine* (Kansas City, Mo.: Sheed & Ward, 1985).

15. Pope Paul VI, *Humanae vitae* (Washington, D.C.: United States Catholic Conference, 1968), nn. 11, 12.

16. Congregation for the Doctrine of the Faith, "Declaration on Certain Questions Concerning Sexual Ethics," *Catholic Mind* 74, n. 1302 (April 1976): 52–65; Pope John Paul II, *Familiaris Consortio· The Role of the Christian Family in the Modern World* (Boston: St. Paul Editions, 1981).

17. Anthony Kosnik et al., *Human Sexuality: New Directions in American Catholic Thought* (New York: Paulist Press, 1977), 99–239. This book was the report of a committee established by the Catholic Theological Society of America. The board of directors of the Society "received" the report. For the negative Vatican response to the book, see "Congregation for the Doctrine of the Faith on Anthony Kosnik et al., *Human Sexuality,* July 13, 1979," in Charles E. Curran and Richard A. McCormick, eds., *Readings in Moral Theology,* No. 8: *Dialogue about Catholic Sexual Teaching* (Mahwah, N.J.: Paulist Press, 1993), 483–90.

18. Charles E. Curran and Richard A. McCormick, eds., *Readings in Moral Theology*, No. 7: *Natural Law and Theology* (Mahwah, N.J.: Paulist Press, 1991). This series, now consisting of nine volumes, has dealt with the primary moral considerations in contemporary Catholic thought.

19. Thomas Aquinas, *Summa theologiae* (Rome: Marietti, 1952), I, II, q. 94. The manuals of moral theology understood Thomas's inclinations as absolute norms and not merely as direction-giving principles.

20. For my approach, see Charles E. Curran, *Directions in Fundamental Moral Theology* (Notre Dame, Ind.: University of Notre Dame Press, 1985), 119–72.

21. Germain Grisez, *The Way of the Lord Jesus*, vol. 1: *Christian Moral Principles* (Chicago: Franciscan Herald Press, 1983), 3–274; John Finnis, *Natural Law and Natural Rights* (Oxford: Clarendon Press, 1980). For an accurate condensation of the Grisez position, see Germain Grisez and Russell Shaw, *Fulfillment in Christ: A Summary of Christian Moral Principles* (Notre Dame, Ind.: University of Notre Dame Press, 1991).

22. For an overview of the debate that is favorable to the revisionist position, see Bernard Hoose, *Proportionalism: The American Debate and Its European Roots* (Washington, D.C.: Georgetown University Press, 1987). For studies of Richard A. McCormick, who has been the foremost American contributor to this discussion, see Paulinus Ikechukwu Odozor, *Richard A. McCormick and the Renewal of Moral Theology* (Notre Dame, Ind.: University of Notre Dame Press, 1995); Charles E. Curran, ed., *Moral Theology: Challenges for the Future: Essays in Honor of Richard A. McCormick, S.J.* (Mahwah, N.J.: Paulist Press, 1990).

23. Grisez and Shaw, *Fulfillment in Christ*, 60–74.

24. For the reaction to *Humanae vitae*, see Joseph A. Selling, "The Reaction to *Humanae Vitae:* A Study in Special and Fundamental Theology" (S.T.D. diss., Catholic University of Louvain, 1977).

25. For the recent discussion on dissent in Roman Catholicism, see Charles E. Curran and Richard A. McCormick, eds., *Readings in Moral Theology*, No. 6: *Dissent in the Church* (Mahwah, N.J.: Paulist Press, 1988).

26. Germain Grisez, "The Ordinary Magisterium's Infallibility," *Theological Studies* 55 (1994): 720–32.
27. Pope John Paul II, *Evangelium vitae*, nn. 57, 62, 65, in *Origins* 24 (1995): 709–11, 712.
28. See Charles E. Curran, *Directions in Catholic Social Ethics* (Notre Dame, Ind.: University of Notre Dame Press, 1985), 5–69.
29. Richard J. Regan, *Conflict and Consensus: Religious Freedom and the Second Vatican Council* (New York: Macmillan Co., 1967), 38–48.
30. Paul VI, *Humanae vitae*, n. 6.
31. Alfred T. Hennelly, ed., *Liberation Theology: A Documentary History* (Maryknoll, N.Y.: Orbis Books, 1990).
32. Arthur F. McGovern, *Marxism: An American Christian Perspective* (Maryknoll, N.Y.: Orbis Books, 1980).
33. R. Bruce Douglass and David Hollenbach, eds., *Catholicism and Liberalism: Contributions to American Public Philosophy* (Cambridge: Cambridge University Press, 1994).
34. National Conference of Catholic Bishops, *Economic Justice for All: Pastoral Letter on Catholic Social Teaching and the United States Economy* (Washington, D.C.: National Conference of Catholic Bishops, 1986).
35. For a position different from the United States bishops' and espousing a more conservative position, see *Toward the Future: Catholic Social Thought and the U.S. Economy: A Lay Letter* (New York: Lay Commission on Catholic Social Teaching and the U.S. Economy, 1984).
36. Mary Segers, ed., *Church Polity and American Politics: Issues in Contemporary American Catholicism* (New York: Garland Publishing, 1990).
37. Declaration on Religious Liberty, n. 7, in Flannery, *Vatican Council II*, 805.
38. Curran, *Directions in Catholic Social Ethics*, 127–45.
39. Kevin W. Irwin and Edmund D. Pellegrino, eds., *Preserving the Creation: Environmental Theology and Ethics* (Washington, D.C.: Georgetown University Press, 1994).
40. Charles E. Curran, Margaret A. Farley, and Richard A. McCormick, eds., *Readings in Moral Theology*, No. 9: *Feminist Ethics and the Catholic Moral Tradition* (Mahwah, N.J.: Paulist Press, 1996).
41. George S. Worgul, ed., *Issues in Academic Freedom* (Pittsburgh, Pa.: Duquesne University Press, 1992).
42. Francis Schüssler Fiorenza, "Systematic Theology: Task and Methods," in *Systematic Theology: Roman Catholic Perspectives*, ed. Francis Schüssler Fiorenza and John P. Galvin (Minneapolis: Fortress Press, 1991), 1:1–87.

10

CORRELATIONAL THEOLOGY AND THE CHICAGO SCHOOL

WERNER G. JEANROND

Correlational theology is the name for a current movement in theology that promotes a mutually critical dialogue between theological thinking and other forms of critical thinking. Correlational theology acknowledges that genuine insight into the mystery of God's presence in this universe may not only be found within the framework of a classical theological exploration of the Christian tradition, but may also be gained through a mutually critical co-operation between theologians and other interpreters of the human condition, such as philosophers, anthropologists, sociologists, psychologists, literary scholars, legal scholars, natural scientists, and others. Thus, correlational theology is methodologically aware both of its own limits and of the potential contribution by nontheological forms of thinking to the constructive work of the theologian.

As such, correlational theology stands firmly within the long theological tradition of establishing a relationship between Christian learning and the wider culture. Scholars such as Origen, Augustine, Thomas Aquinas, and Friedrich Schleiermacher have all attempted to engage in some form of correlational theology, i.e., to link theological learning with the wider intellectual culture of their time—without, however, undermining the distinctive character of the theological enterprise. Theology may learn, for instance, from philosophy without therefore becoming philosophy. Distinctiveness, but also openness toward conversation with other branches of knowledge, are the signs of that tradition of theological discourse out of which the correlational theology of our time has emerged.

In contemporary theology the term "correlational theology" is usually associated with the works of Paul Tillich, David Tracy, Langdon Gilkey, Hans Küng, Edward Schillebeeckx, among others, in spite of the important differences between their respective theological projects. But, at times, correlational theology functions also as a description of the so-called Chicago School of theology, and thus refers to the particular emphasis that Chicago theologians, notably David Tracy, put on the significance both of the interdisciplinary study of religion and of interreligious dialogue for Christian theological thought.

In this chapter I shall first offer a brief account of the emergence of correlational theology. Second, I shall present David Tracy's theological method as a paradigm of current correlational thinking in Christian theology. Third, I shall discuss the correlational methodologies of Edward Schillebeeckx and Hans Küng and point to some further aspects of the reception of correlational theology. I shall conclude with a brief assessment of the potential of correlational thinking in theology.

THE EMERGENCE OF
CORRELATIONAL THEOLOGY

The term "correlational theology" was introduced into the theological debate by Paul Tillich. In the first volume of his *Systematic Theology* (1951) he described his own method as "correlational."[1] By this he meant that there existed a relationship between the general existential horizon of modern human beings and the particular response formulated by theologians on behalf of the Christian tradition of faith in the triune God. The existential horizon suggests human questions that find their authentic answers ultimately only in Christian faith.

> In using the method of correlation, systematic theology proceeds in the following way: it makes an analysis of the human situation out of which the existential questions arise, and it demonstrates that the symbols used in the Christian message are the answers to these questions. The analysis of the human situation is done in terms which today are called "existential."[2]

This relationship advocated by Tillich does not work as a both-way correlation, however; rather it describes a one-way movement from existential questions to Christian answers. An interdisciplinarity in Tillich's method can be detected only as far as the assessment of the horizon of modern men and women are concerned. "The analysis of existence, including the development of the questions implicit in existence, is a philosophical task, even if it is performed by a theologian."[3] But the response to this analysis of existence is the sole prerogative of Christian theology. Neither the question of pluralism in theological thinking nor the fuller impact of interdisciplinary thinking in general was yet dealt with in their own right by Tillich and, as a result, they remained outside his methodological framework. Nevertheless, Tillich fostered an increased cooperation between contemporary philosophical and theological concerns.

Tillich's theological program was to exert a strong influence on North American theology in general and on theology at the University of Chicago Divinity School in particular long beyond his death in Chicago in 1965. Chicago theologians Langdon Gilkey and David Tracy have developed their respective theologies initially in critical dialogue also, though not only, with Tillich's work.

Gilkey has moved beyond Tillich's method of correlation in a number of ways: (1) He insists on a thorough methodology properly informed by phenomenological and hermeneutical consideration.[4] (2) He explores the presence of the divine in secular culture and in other religions and assesses the significance of that presence for Christian faith. (3) He then attributes ultimate enlightening significance to the reinterpreted Christian witness. His thesis is that

> the Christian awareness of God grows out of the wonder and the ambiguity of the ordinary life of man in the world, but that it is an awareness that

is finally brought to conscious and definitive form by the central experience of illumination and renewal that comes in the community that witnesses to the Christ.[5]

Gilkey calls his own method correlational[6] in the sense that his theology aims all along at linking an interpretation of human existence under the conditions of modernity with a reinterpreted Christian message.[7] It is certainly Gilkey's great achievement to have freed correlational thinking from the narrow confines established by Tillich and to develop it creatively in his own theological project. "Theology . . . is the enterprise of understanding reflectively and thus, in our own cultural terms, the contents of the Christian faith or, correlatively, of interpreting the human situation in its widest extent in the light of that faith."[8]

Among David Tracy's conversation partners on his way to developing a broader and self-critical correlational theology we find not only Paul Tillich and Langdon Gilkey, but also the Canadian philosopher Bernard Lonergan, who insisted on a critical rationality for all adequate theological methodology and who was informed by traditional Thomist, phenomenological, and American pragmatist concerns.[9] Tracy shares all these concerns but has complemented them with a vigorous attention to hermeneutical developments in modern and postmodern philosophy. The question of interpretation has assumed a guiding role in Tracy's theological discourse. And his insights into both the necessarily subjective aspect that accompanies all interpretative efforts and the resulting pluralism of interpretations have made him search for a dialogical model for theology. But a true dialogue must be mutual, and a critical dialogue must be prepared to follow truth wherever it may lead, notwithstanding the possible institutional commitments of the theologian. Hence, Tracy has developed a correlational method for theology that is both critical and self-critical, that listens to the other as other without attempting to subordinate the conversation partners to one's own agenda.[10] Unlike Tillich's one-way correlational theology, Tracy's correlational method works both ways—it insists on a *mutually* critical correlation.

Tracy has taught at the University of Chicago since 1969. His cooperation with the French philosopher Paul Ricoeur, with the late Romanian historian of religion Mircea Eliade, and with numerous thinkers from many fields within the humanities has deepened his awareness of the constructive possibilities of a mutually critical conversation between theology and other disciplines in the academy. Tracy's theological work provides ample evidence of the genuineness of his dialogical form of thinking.

TRACY'S THEOLOGICAL METHOD AS A PARADIGM OF CORRELATIONAL THEOLOGY

In *Blessed Rage for Order: The New Pluralism in Theology* (1975), Tracy presented his theological methodology, which he then further refined in *The Analogical Imagination: Christian Theology and the Culture of Pluralism* (1981), in *Plurality and Ambiguity: Hermeneutics, Religion, Hope* (1987), as well as in a number of programmatic articles.[11] Tracy proposes a revisionist model of theology:

> The revisionist theologian is committed to what seems clearly to be the
> central task of contemporary Christian theology: the dramatic confronta-
> tion, the mutual illuminations and corrections, the possible basic recon-
> ciliation between the principal values, cognitive claims, and existential
> faiths of both a reinterpreted post-modern consciousness and a reinter-
> preted Christianity.[12]

This definition underscores the significance of interpretation in Tracy's methodology. Both our contemporary consciousness and our Christian tradition are in constant need of interpretation. "All authentic reflection, all reflection where the
subject matter and not the subject determines the questioning, has a properly
hermeneutical character."[13] Hans-Georg Gadamer, Paul Ricoeur, and Jürgen Habermas have been Tracy's chief conversation partners on his way to developing a critical and self-critical hermeneutics.[14] From Gadamer, Tracy has adopted the
emphasis on conversation, from Ricoeur the concern for proper methodological
strategies, and from Habermas the attention to the communicative conditions in
which rational discourse occurs. A theological project committed to a process of
refinement through continuing conversation can only be revisionist. Although one
may regret Tracy's choice of such a loaded term as "revisionism," there can be no
doubt as to the programmatic nature of this term: According to Tracy no form of
theology and no theological method can ever be considered final; all theology is in
constant need of reinterpretation and refinement through critical conversation. That
is how Tracy defines his "move to the normative paradigm of conversation."[15]

According to Tracy, Christian theology has two principal sources, and these are
"Christian texts" and "common human experience and language."[16] The results of
the investigations of these two sources are to be critically correlated by the theologians who then must determine the truth status of their investigations by employing "an explicitly transcendental or metaphysical mode of reflection."[17]

This first presentation of his method has been further refined by Tracy in subsequent publications. There he has widened the scope of the two sources of theology significantly. The Christian tradition does not manifest itself only in texts.
Rather, a living religious tradition expresses itself in a great variety of forms besides linguistic inscriptions—for instance, ritual, symbol, experience, liturgy, music, art, architecture, or lifestyle.[18] All these forms require, however, the kind of
theological attention, reflection, and interpretation that Tracy has called for already in *Blessed Rage for Order*.

The concept of a common human experience is also significantly enlarged and
problematized in Tracy's subsequent work when he pays particular attention to the
feminist critique of traditional forms of rationality and discourse and to the
hermeneutics of suspicion articulated by Ricoeur in the aftermath of such masters
of suspicion as Karl Marx, Sigmund Freud, and Friedrich Nietzsche.[19] Although
Tracy continues to insist on the need for any critical theology to engage in the project of developing an adequate rationality, he sees this demand no longer met as
easily as he once suggested in *Blessed Rage for Order*. "I am not as sure as I once
was that modern reason can produce so unproblematically the kind of uncompli-

cated metaphysical and transcendental arguments needed for fundamental theology."[20] The insights into the postmodern critique of modern rationality and the indepth appreciation of plurality and ambiguity as basic categories of any adequate rationality have made Tracy very sensitive to the fuller reality of the modern project. "Ambiguity . . . is not simply a negative term. Ambiguity involves both truth *and* falsehood, goodness *and* evil, and even, in the religious dimension, the holy *and* the demonic. The modern project surely has involved all these realities."[21] Tracy continues to argue that we should not cease to devote our energies, thoughts, and actions to the yet unfinished Enlightenment project of human emancipation. But at the same time we need to reflect on the ambiguities of this project which have been highlighted by more recent postmodern critiques. Thus, in spite of a number of significant improvements and clarifications, there can be no doubt that Tracy has remained faithful to his basic model of a critical and self-critical correlational theology.

Tracy distinguishes between three related disciplines in theology, all of which are committed to the correlational model: fundamental, systematic, and practical theology.[22] *Fundamental theology* reflects on the conditions of human rationality in general and theological reasoning in particular. It is concerned with identifying religious dimensions and experiences in human reality and with discussing their truth claims. Fundamental theology is thus intrinsically related to the general human search for truth and the development of an appropriate methodology. Obviously, its primary place is in the academy. *Systematic theology* interprets the particular religious tradition to which the theologian belongs. It will "ordinarily assume . . . the truth-bearing character of a particular religious tradition . . . [and] thereby focus upon reinterpretations and new applications of the tradition for the present."[23] It is primarily, though not exclusively, related to the church. *Practical theology* is concerned with the practical transformation of both individual practitioners of a religious tradition and communal, social, and political structures in the light of the insights gained by both fundamental and systematic theologies. Hence it primarily reflects on the social dimension of religious praxis.

Paul Tillich, on the one hand, is generally considered a poor methodologist in terms of explicitly developing his theological method. Moreover, his explicit statements on method do at times not even do justice to the much richer material treatment of concrete theological issues and concerns, such as being and God, existence and Christ, life and the Spirit, reason and revelation, and history and the kingdom of God.[24] Tracy, on the other hand, has already offered a rich and extensive methodological treatment of Christian theology at the interface of modern and postmodern culture, though so far has not yet presented larger theological applications of his method, although he has proposed exciting outlines.[25] In terms of his own program, Tracy has concentrated most on fundamental theology, that is, on that aspect of theology which is most concerned with the current conditions of theological rationality. And here he has especially emphasized the public nature of the Christian discourse on God.

Theology is a public exercise; it is concerned with all aspects of our reality.

Any Christian theology is finally and radically theocentric. This insight into the universal character of the divine reality that is the always-present object of the Christian's trust and loyalty is what ultimately impels every theology to attempt publicness. For God as understood by the Jewish, Christian and Muslim believer is either universal in actuality or sheer delusion. Theology in all its forms is finally nothing else but the attempt to reflect deliberately and critically upon that God.[26]

Only a public theology can be really correlational. A theological discourse that insists on a special prerogative to the recognition of truth excludes automatically the possibility of a mutuality in the search for truth. Moreover, Tracy trusts that the classic manifestations of meaning and truth, including those from within the Christian tradition, will continue to resist any temptation to domesticate them.[27] Classic texts, such as the Bible and postbiblical expressions of Christian thinking and devotion, will in their own right claim public attention and an ongoing conversation about their message. "If the religious classics are both classics and religious at all, they should be intelligible to all."[28] But Tracy also reminds us that "[a] conversation is a rare phenomenon."[29] Regardless of whether we wish to engage in a conversation with a text or in a conversation with other readers about a text, we are confronted by otherness and its challenge to our self-understanding.

Conversation in its primary form is an exploration of possibilities in the search for truth. In following the track of any question, we must allow for difference and otherness. . . . Otherness and difference can become, however, genuine possibility: the *as* other, the *as* different becomes the *as* possible.[30]

Hence, for Tracy only a public theology can guarantee that sort of conversation which is genuinely open to the recognition of otherness and difference, and thus to the possibilities of new and creative insights into the manifestation of truth.[31]

In the second part of *The Analogical Imagination*, as well as in a number of articles and in his preparatory work toward a forthcoming book on God, Tracy has outlined how his correlational theology may take concrete shape with regard to the great Christian topics such as God, Jesus Christ, the Spirit, church, and the nature of evil. Again and again he insists that a mere theology of proclamation is not acceptable. Rather, he demands attention to both manifestation and proclamation from all adequate Christian theology.[32] The entire cosmos in all its dimensions can be considered to be a place of possible divine manifestation; in other words the so-called secular has been "disclosed as religiously significant."[33] And more specifically, "this demand for both manifestation and proclamation is incumbent upon all Christians who recognize the reality of Jesus Christ as the Christian classic, i.e., as the decisive re-presentation in both word and manifestation for our God and our humanity."[34] The theological task will then be to provide new interpretations of God's self-disclosure in history appropriate to the tradition and intelligible for the situation. But in order to understand the tradition and our own situation, the theologian needs to employ the best available hermeneutical strategies of reception as well as of ideology critique. Interpretation requires critical theory in order to allow for genuine interpretation to happen. Thus, Tracy sums up the theological task: "A mutually critical correlation occurs in any individual theology between the theologian's interpretation of the event and the tradition in the particular situation and the theologian's interpretation of the situation by means of the event."[35]

Tracy sees the Christ-event as the central manifestation of Christian faith, but cautions that no interpreter can reach this event without going through the process of an analogical imagination. "We understand one other through analogies to our own experience and we understand ourselves through our real internal relations to and analogous understandings of the other."[36] Hence, there is not only no theological shortcut beyond this hermeneutical condition directly to Jesus Christ, but there is the possible enrichment of any analogical perspective through the necessary conversation on the significance of the Christ-event for our understanding of God and for our understanding of ourselves in the light of our theological insights. It is therefore not appropriate to state that either Jesus Christ or the Bible can function as *absoluta norms* for any adequate Christian theology, since even such norms can only be approached through analogical imagination in a hermeneutical process. And, as we have already seen, this process in turn calls for conversation.

> Conversation remains the ideal of any analogical imagination in any tradition. Conflict is just as often the reality. Nor should conflict be feared as the analogical imagination's own internal demand for ever-new negations of its always tentative order, its similarities-in-difference, must recognize.[37]

Tracy's model of a correlational theology is the result of his hermeneutical insights into the conditions of understanding and self-understanding. He approaches the necessary pluralism of interpretation that emerges from such a hermeneutical model by emphasizing both the claim to truth of the Christian and non-Christian classics and the need for a public and mutually critical conversation on any such claim. Neither the classic nor the model of conversation is any longer depending on the typically modernist trust in the autonomous self, which reaches objective cognition in the Christian tradition or the contemporary situation.[38] Hence, correlational theology remains Tracy's approach to the challenges of the postmodern condition of thinking and acting.

RECEPTION AND IMPACT
OF CORRELATIONAL THEOLOGY

The limits of Paul Tillich's correlational method have already been discussed above. Insofar as Tracy developed his own correlational method partly in reaction to Tillich's, one can say that Tracy's development of a new and mutually critical theological method is itself part of the reception history of correlational theology. But Tracy's model is not the only one. The Belgian theologian Edward Schillebeeckx and the Swiss-German theologian Hans Küng have presented their own particular correlational theologies.

Edward Schillebeeckx, professor emeritus at the University of Nijmegen in the Netherlands, has developed a correlational approach to Christology. In his magisterial works, *Jesus: An Experiment in Christology*; *Christ: The Experience of Jesus as Lord*; and *Church: The Human Story of God*, Schillebeeckx has attempted to correlate our contemporary situation with the knowledge of Jesus Christ that the Christian tradition discloses to its critical interpreter.[39] Moreover, in his *Interim Report on the Books* Jesus & Christ, he provided an explicit discussion of his methodology.[40] Here he formulates his correlational project more succinctly:

> What we are concerned with is . . . a mutually critical correlation in which we attune our belief and action within the world in which we live, here and now, to what is expressed in the biblical tradition. This correlation therefore requires: 1. an analysis of our present world or even worlds of experience; 2. an analysis of the constant structures of the fundamental Christian experience about which the New Testament and the rest of the Christian tradition of experience speak, and 3. the critical correlation and on occasion the critical confrontation of these two "sources."[41]

Thus, Schillebeeckx, like Tracy, calls for a method that does justice to the hermeneutical fact that any recourse to earlier layers of the Christian tradition is always already conditioned by present-day experiences. Moreover, Schillebeeckx claims that his kind of "critical correlation between religion and human experience already appears in scripture."[42] Hence, in all periods of the Christian tradition we can observe this relationship between message and situation whereby new experiences help us to understand our own Christian experience and knowledge, "just as, conversely, the specifically Christian experiences and explanations as they are expressed in scripture and the long tradition of Christian experience have their own original force in explaining our experiences in the world in a critical and productive way."[43]

This critical correlation put into praxis suggests that the symbol of Jesus as Lord is evocative for our own human experiences:

> It discloses our own existence to us; it illuminates what authentic human life can be when we are aware that we are safe in the hands of the living God and can accept it as a challenge. . . . At the same time, the transforming power of this representative symbol calls us to a conversion in faith; in other words, this correlation is achieved in *metanoia* or conversion, and not in a single alignment.[44]

It is interesting to note that later on Schillebeeckx expresses some doubt as to the suitability of the term "correlation." He continues to hold that the however volatile Christian identity of meaning can be found only "on the level of the corresponding relation between the original message (tradition) and the always different situation, both in the past and in the present."[45] But instead of speaking of "correlation," he finds it better to speak of " 'the encounter of cultures,' a 'culture-shock,' or confrontation of cultures that draw their vitality from the Christian gospel and acclimatize it in their own cultural forms."[46] Thus, while remaining committed to a correlational method, Schillebeeckx wishes to highlight more the difference of cultural incarnations in which Christian faith occurs and the confrontation that might arise when biblical and nonbiblical cultures and traditions meet.

In this context it is also important to note that Schillebeeckx has qualified his hermeneutical strategies in his later writings. While in *Jesus* he employed primarily historical-critical tools of reconstructing the best picture of the historical Jesus, in *Christ* his method turns more toward a literary-critical reading of New Testament texts, and then shifts toward an ethical reading of the Christian demands for solidarity, conversion, and transformation at the end of *Christ* and in *Church*. "Man as the subject of an ethical demand is therefore the presupposition for the understanding of the Christian proclamation of faith."[47]

Hans Küng voices his general agreement with Schillebeeckx's method of correlation, but, as we shall see now in more detail, calls for a sharpening of the criteria that need to be applied when a confrontation between biblical and contemporary experiences occurs.[48]

Küng, professor emeritus at the University of Tübingen, has developed yet another version of correlational theology. In general terms his theological work may be characterized in at least four respects (1) Küng has offered thorough discussions on ecclesiology, always attempting to correlate the tradition of understanding the Christian church with the demands of modern historical-critical thinking. (2) In his published work Küng has tackled all major aspects of Christian faith in such a correlational way. (3) Moreover, he has been engaged in a number of interreligious conversations. And (4) he has presented programmatic studies of the relationship between Christian faith and culture; in more recent times concentrating especially on the religious situation of our time and on the related project of global responsibility. Within the framework of this chapter I cannot deal with all these aspects of Küng's theological work.[49] Instead I wish to discuss his own explicit statements on theological method.

Like Tracy and Schillebeeckx, Küng has been acutely aware of the need to find a new paradigm for contemporary theology; and like Tracy and Schillebeeckx, he has proposed a correlational method. Küng identifies two poles of Christian theology: (1) God's self-disclosure in the history of Israel and in the history of Jesus and (2) our own human world of experience. With regard to the former pole, Küng underlines that God's revelation can be recognized only through human experience,[50] and with regard to the second pole he stresses that our everyday, common human and ambiguous experiences need interpretation, more specifically they "need the meaning giving [*sinngebend*], religious, Christian interpretation."[51] "It is the task of theology to elaborate a critical correlation between the tradition of Christian experiences on the one hand and our contemporary experiences on the other,"[52] But unlike Tracy and more than Schillebeeckx, Küng wonders how to deal with a possible emergence of conflict between biblical and contemporary experiences. What should we do when the two poles of Christian theology contradict each other and "when contemporary 'experiences' offer us once again a 'Führer' or some kind of political 'movement of salvation'? . . . Does not then the critical 'correlation' necessarily need to become a critical 'confrontation'?"[53]

Küng therefore demands a sharpening of the method of critical correlation in the direction of establishing a Christian norm that can adjudicate such a possible confrontation. He attributes "normative significance" to "the special Christian experiences, or better: the Christian message, the gospel, Jesus Christ himself."[54] Jesus Christ himself is the center of scripture, he whom "the first Christian community experienced as the Christ and who in the New Testament is originally witnessed to as the living Jesus, as he stands for God and the human being."[55] Therefore Küng insists on the lasting normative character of the New Testament ("norma normans") for all postbiblical tradition. Moreover, for Küng, as for Schillebeeckx, correlational thinking points to a way forward beyond the narrow doctrinal positivism of their Roman Catholic Church context: to establish a critical correlation between a newly reconstructed biblical faith on the one hand and the current situation in church and society on the other.

Therefore Küng considers the historical-critical reconstruction of the Jesus of history to be an essential requirement of any critical theology.[56] Hence, for him the historical-critical work of the Christian exegete is foundational for systematic theology and constitutive for any adequate interpretation of the Christian tradition. Thus, Küng appreciates the historical-critical method as providing us with a privileged access to the truth of Christian faith, and not only as one among many necessary correctives of any merely dogmatic formulation of Christian tradition. Küng's method of correlation stands, therefore, somewhat in between Tillich's and Tracy's. With Tracy, Küng affirms the need for critique of any dogmatic formula that claims to represent authentic Christian faith. With Tillich, Küng affirms the demand for secure access to Christian normativeness. Of course, all serious Christian theologians will want to agree on the normative status of the original Christian witnesses. But how one treats of these original Christian witnesses is a different question.

Tracy rejects the claim that the historical-critical method could function in terms of securing a constitutive criterion of authentic Christian faith. "Historical-critical methods (like such other methods as ideology-critique, womanist and feminist theology and genealogical methods) are corrective to, but hermeneutically not constitutive of, all properly theological interpretations of scripture."[57] Tracy has no difficulty agreeing with Küng on the general importance of the historical-critical method for truthfulness. But Tracy rejects any suggestion that this method be "allowed to constitute the truth of the central Christian theological claims for Jesus Christ."[58] For Tracy, there is no possibility of a shortcut around the laborious and often detoured hermeneutical journey of interpreting the Christian tradition in all its plurality and ambiguity. There is no access to any pure layer of the Christian tradition of believing in Jesus Christ. Tracy stresses that Christians "believe *in* Jesus Christ *with* the apostles."[59] But even the very first apostolic witness is permeated by distortions. Moreover, according to Tracy, the question of a truthful interpretation of the biblical and postbiblical texts of the Christian tradition is not identical with the question of the truth of the Christian religion as such. Therefore, Tracy suggests that Küng may develop his earlier work on critical rationality and existential trust as outlined in Küng's magisterial work *Does God Exist?*[60]

in the direction of establishing a set of criteria for assessing truth in theology and in interreligious dialogue.[61]

In *Plurality and Ambiguity*, Tracy has suggested a hermeneutical model of understanding truth in terms of disclosure/concealment.

> Truth manifests itself, and we recognize its rightness. More technically stated, truth is here understood, on the side of the object, as the power of disclosure and concealment in the object itself; and that disclosure is related to truth as an experience of recognition on the side of the subject. There is, in every true manifestation, an intrinsic, that is dialogical, interaction between the object's disclosure and concealment and the subject's recognition. That interaction is conversation.[62]

Tracy's concept of correlation is thus much wider than Gilkey's, Küng's, and Schillebeeckx's. It includes the global search for truth as manifestation. However, this insistence on the dialogical search for truth through a public conversation, here about the self-disclosure of God in Israel and in Jesus Christ, is not shared by all contemporary theologians. Tracy's theological vision and method are severely criticized by some eminent representatives of the so called postliberal school of theology.

Postliberal theology is a movement usually associated with Yale University and theologians such as George A. Lindbeck and the late Hans W. Frei, although its increasing popularity can now be traced to many other North American and some European universities. Though here I cannot treat of this movement in any detail, I wish to point to some major differences between postliberal and correlational theology.[63]

George A. Lindbeck rejects the basic insight of correlational theology into the need to participate in a global dialogue on the truth of contemporary (religious) experiences and of those religious experiences that are mediated through the Christian tradition. He is not concerned with the hermeneutical task of identifying the meaning of certain texts and experiences in changing historical, linguistic, and cultural circumstances. Rather, he promotes a cultural-linguistic model which stresses "the degree to which human experience is shaped, molded, and in a sense constituted by cultural and linguistic forms."[64] Hence Lindbeck claims that he, like Tracy and other promoters of correlational theology, "emphasizes the experiential and existential side of religion, though in a different way."[65] For while Tracy, Schillebeeckx, and Küng ultimately aim at discussing the rationality and truth of Christian faith and of its expressions throughout its history, Lindbeck wishes to discuss the function of doctrines (e.g., church teachings). "The function of church doctrines that becomes most prominent in this perspective is their use, not as expressive symbols or as truth claims, but as communally authoritative rules of discourse, attitude, and action."[66]

According to Lindbeck, a religion functions like a language game. Religion makes experience possible, not experience, religion. Thus, he does not favor mutually critical correlations between the interpretation of human experience and the interpretation of the Christian tradition. Rather, for Lindbeck the Christian understanding of all reality is determined by the biblical narratives. Therefore he wishes to propagate a theology firmly rooted in the center of Christian religion, which means for him a theology rooted in Holy Scripture and not supported by philosophical foundations. He rejects all theoretical attempts to establish foundations for the Christian faith in God, as well as any effort, such as metaphysical, existential, phenomenological, or hermeneutical, to uncover universal principles or structures with the help of which one could understand religion. "The grammar of religion, like that of a language, cannot be explicated or learned by analysis of experience, but only by practice."[67] Instead of redescribing the faith in new concepts, postliberal theology "seeks to teach the language and practices of the religion to potential adherents."[68] Hence Lindbeck's theology differs from Tracy's, Küng's, and Schillebeeckx's not only in terms of method, but also in terms of aim. Lindbeck wishes to explicate Christian faith inside the (actual or potential) Christian movement, while the correlational theologians attempt to develop a public rationality of that faith.

Hans W. Frei too was concerned with the biblical foundations of theological thinking and the resulting Christian self-description. "Theology is an aspect of Christianity and is therefore partly or wholly defined by its relation to the cultural or semiotic system that constitutes that religion."[69] Theology is thus not a reflective-critical discipline that treats of the different religious manifestations and church documents from the standpoint of a critical distance from church praxis. Such a scientific distance, which makes possible a critical and self-critical interpretation of the faith community, as well as of its texts, traditions, and paradigms of action, is not of interest to Frei. Rather, Frei—like Lindbeck and, for that matter, Karl Barth—finds fault with the very call for such a critical distance and considers this call a hubris on the part of the theologian and a sellout of theology's independence from all other sciences and disciplines.

Unlike correlational theology, postliberal theology is exclusively centered around the biblical texts. "It is the text, so to speak, which absorbs the world, rather than the world the text."[70] Moreover, unlike correlational theology, postliberal theology puts all its hope in the Christian community thus absorbed by the biblical text. The text and its community determine the nature of postliberal theology, not the question of whether the claims to truth made by the text and its community are understandable and justified or not. While correlational theology emphasizes the need for a global dialogue and all available critical and self-critical strategies to deal with the question of religious truth, postliberal theology has abandoned this kind of search for truth in favor of discussing a given communitarian praxis of narrating and living the Christian story. Hence, in order to fulfill its theological objectives, postliberal theology does not need the close cooperation with philosophical and other academic disciplines beyond the occasional "ad hoc" contacts.[71]

While postliberal theology rejects the basic orientation of correlational theology, the emancipatory theologies that have emerged since the 1960s have a lot, though not everything, in common with the methodology of correlational theology. Political theology, liberation theology, feminist theology, ecological theology, and contextual theology all employ correlational thinking insofar as they link their interpretation of some aspects of the current global situation with their interpretation of the Christian tradition. All these theological movements discuss the oppressive and emancipatory features with the Christian tradition itself and then correlate the emancipatory potential of that tradition with their reading of their respective context in order to move toward strategies of transformative action. Thus, the correlational nature of these theological movements is beyond question. Moreover, Christian theologies all over the world have been thoroughly enriched by these theologies' new insights both into the situations and into the tradition, and by their courageous correlation.

However, we would need to reflect more deeply than is possible here on the precise nature of the actual correlations and the question of critique and mutuality in these correlations. Therefore, some questions may clarify some potential problems: How critical and how mutual are these emancipatory movements in terms of their correlational theologies? Do the needs of the specific context or situation determine or condition the theological reflection? Are the various rereadings of the tradition fully subjected to the needs of the context or are the reinterpretations of the tradition also allowed to challenge the interpretation of the particular situation? And do the theological interpreters of both tradition and situation claim a hermeneutical prerogative that would then no longer be subject to the ongoing conversation about the truth claims of Christian faith? In other words do these and other even more recently emerging theologies of emancipation, gay and lesbian theologies for instance, accept a self-critical position of mutuality in their correlative way of thinking, or do they retreat into a new kind of one-way theology, where the existential context of the theologian has priority over the reinterpretation of the theological claims of the Christian tradition? If the latter is the case, then this form of correlation would be very much like Paul Tillich's, with the sole difference that Tillich accorded priority to the Christian message over the situation, while such new forms of correlational reflection would now accord priority to the situation over the message. The reductionist nature of the latter position has been the horror scenario to which Frei and colleagues have drawn attention:

> Liberation theologians frequently invoke the term "hermeneutics" to indicate a general view on the relation between theory and practice under the priority of the latter, and then authorize biblical interpretation under this view, demonstrating the amenability of the Bible's contents to the understanding with which they approached it.[72]

David Tracy too warns against any reduction of the hermeneutical task to say just what the reader may wish to hear. But he warns with equal strength against any reluctance to listen to the readings that the poor and the oppressed fellow humans have to offer to the global conversation on the Christian tradition today. He insists, however, that this

> is not to say that option for the poor is translatable into the distinct claim that only the poor can provide proper readings of these [scriptural] texts,

any more than it suggests that only the poor can experience revelation or find salvation or only the poor are the objects of that radical love of neighbor that is the heart of the Christian gospel. That option does not translate into the position that says, once the poor make their interpretations, all others are to sit back and passively receive them.[73]

Tracy stresses that no emancipatory program exhausts Christian salvation. But he adds that "Christian salvation, rightly understood, cannot be divorced from the struggle for total human liberation—individual, social, political, and religious."[74]

The most promising strategy to fight all forms of hermeneutical prerogatives is self-criticism[75] and a radical openness to discover otherness. Therefore, it is also wrong to claim that only believers can interpret the religions. In Tracy's terminology, such a position would rob the religious classics of their claims to truth.[76]

Hence, Tracy's concept of a mutually critical correlation must reject any claim to hermeneutical privilege, however well-intended a defense of Christian self-description or however well-intended a defense of the emancipatory needs of any particular context it comes from.[77] All claims to Christian identity and hermeneutical authenticity are subject to the mutuality principle of critique.

THE POTENTIAL OF
CORRELATIONAL THEOLOGY

The potential of any theology committed to critical correlations between an interpreted context and an interpreted tradition depends, as we have seen, to a significant extent on the theologian's willingness to engage in mutual critique and self-critique. Moreover, the ideal framework for such a mutually critical reflection is a global conversation on the meaning and truth of religion—in our case, on the meaning and truth of Christian faith.

Such a theological project committed to mutually critical correlations, however, will never be able to offer a very strong criterion of identity as it is demanded both by postliberal theologians on the one hand and by a number of correlationally thinking theologians not committed to mutuality on the other hand. For a theology operating with mutually critical correlations, Christian identity is a task and not a starting point.[78] Moreover, identity can only be understood as an implicit project that is not promoted by excluding other voices from the conversation. Rather, any voice claiming to contribute to a critical and self-critical conversation on the meaning and truth of Christian faith will need to be considered. This process of coping with otherness in dialogue is a messy process and will never satisfy a thinker who aims at quick confirmations of Christian identity and authenticity. And finally, this global conversation on the meaning and truth is on the grounds of its own hermeneutical presuppositions endless: all potential voices will need to be heard and considered.

Faced with a great variety of theological projects and methods, the theology student of today might take into consideration whether she or he wishes to enter this messy and endless conversation in the hope of finding a deeper sense of Christian meaning and truth or opt instead for speedier and either more limited or potentially more authoritarian resolutions of the question of Christian identity and authenticity.

NOTES

1. Paul Tillich, *Systematic Theology*, vol. 1 (Chicago: University of Chicago Press, 1951), 60: "The method of correlation explains the contents of the Christian faith through existential questions and theological answers in mutual interdependence."
2. Ibid., 62.
3. Ibid., 63.
4. Langdon Gilkey, *Naming the Whirlwind: The Renewal of God-Language* (Indianapolis: Bobbs-Merrill Co., 1969), 266–84; and idem, *Reaping the Whirlwind: A Christian Interpretation of History* (New York: Seabury Press, 1976), 134–39.
5. Gilkey, *Naming the Whirlwind*, 486.
6. Cf. Gilkey, *Reaping the Whirlwind*, 147; and idem, *Message and Existence: An Introduction to Christian Theology* (New York: Seabury Press, 1979), 54.
7. See the programmatic title of Gilkey's book *Message and Existence*.
8. Gilkey, *Message and Existence*, 53f.
9. See Bernard Lonergan, *Method in Theology* (New York: Seabury Press, 1979). For a discussion of the philosophical and theological influences behind Tracy's methodology, see Jennifer L. Rike, "Introduction: Radical Pluralism and Truth in the Thought of David Tracy," in *Radical Pluralism and Truth: David Tracy and the Hermeneutics of Religion*, ed. Werner G. Jeanrond and Jennifer L. Rike (New York: Crossroad, 1991), ix–xxvii.
10. For a more detailed assessment of David Tracy's theological method, see Werner G. Jeanrond, "Theology in the Context of Pluralism and Postmodernity: David Tracy's Theological Method," in *Postmodernism, Literature and the Future of Theology*, ed. David Jasper (London: Macmillan Publishers; New York: St. Martin's Press, 1993), 143–63.
11. David Tracy, *Blessed Rage for Order: The New Pluralism in Theology* (New York: Seabury, 1975; reprint, with a new preface, Chicago: University of Chicago Press, 1996); idem, *The Analogical Imagination: Christian Theology and the Culture of Pluralism* (New York: Crossroad, 1981); idem, *Plurality and Ambiguity: Hermeneutics, Religion, Hope* (San Francisco: Harper & Row, 1987; reprint Chicago: University of Chicago Press, 1994); idem, *Dialogue with the Other: The Inter-Religious Dialogue* (Louvain: Peeters, Eerdmans, 1990); idem, *On Naming the Present: God, Hermeneutics, and Church* (Maryknoll, N.Y.: Orbis Books, 1994). For a bibliography of Tracy's work up to 1991, see Stephen H. Webb, "Bibliography of David Tracy," in Jeanrond and Rike, eds., *Radical Pluralism and Truth*, 286–93.
12. Tracy, *Blessed Rage for Order*, 32.
13. Tracy, *The Analogical Imagination*, 102.
14. Cf. Werner G. Jeanrond, *Text and Interpretation as Categories of Theological Thinking*, trans. Thomas J. Wilson (New York: Crossroad, 1988).
15. Tracy, *The Analogical Imagination*, 102.
16. Tracy, *Blessed Rage for Order*, 43.
17. Ibid., 52.
18. Cf. Tracy, *The Analogical Imagination*, chap. 5.
19. See esp. Tracy, *Plurality and Ambiguity*, 76–78, and Tracy's new preface written in 1995 to the 1996 reprint of *Blessed Rage for Order*, xiii–xvi.

20. New preface to *Blessed Rage for Order*, xiv.
21. Ibid., xv.
22. Cf. Tracy, *The Analogical Imagination*, 54–82.
23. Ibid., 58.
24. Cf. Tillich, *Systematic Theology*, 1:66–67. See also John Clayton, *The Concept of Correlation: Paul Tillich and the Possibility of a Mediating Theology* (Berlin: de Gruyter, 1980).
25. See, for instance, his outline for a future Christology in pt. 2 of Tracy, *Analogical Imagination*, 248–338; and his outline for a new theological discourse on God in idem, *On Naming the Present*, 27–58, and "The Hermeneutics of Naming God," *Irish Theological Quarterly* 57 (1991): 253–64. See also idem, "Evil, Suffering, Hope: The Search for New Forms of Contemporary Theodicy," in *CTSA Proceedings* 50 (1995): 15–36.
26. Tracy, *The Analogical Imagination*, 51.
27. Tracy, *Plurality and Ambiguity*, 15.
28. Ibid., 103. For a discussion of Tracy's notion of the classic, see Jeanrond, *Text and Interpretation as Categories of Theological Thinking*, 133–42.
29. Tracy, *Plurality and Ambiguity*, 18.
30. Ibid., 20f.
31. Cf. ibid., 28.
32. Tracy, *The Analogical Imagination*, 218.
33. Ibid.
34. Ibid.
35. Ibid., 433.
36. Ibid., 452.
37. Ibid., 453.
38. Cf. Jeanrond, "Theology in the Context of Pluralism and Postmodernity," in Jasper, ed., *Postmodernity, Literature and the Future of Theology*, 159–61.
39. Edward Schillebeeckx, *Jesus: An Experiment in Christology*, trans. Hubert Hoskins (New York: Seabury Press, 1979); idem, *Christ: The Experience of Jesus as Lord*, trans. John Bowden (New York: Seabury Press, 1980); idem, *Church: The Human Story of God*, trans. John Bowden (London: SCM Press, 1990).
40. Edward Schillebeeckx, *Interim Report on the Books* Jesus & Christ, trans. John Bowden (New York: Seabury Press, 1980).
41. Ibid., 50–51.
42. Ibid., 53.
43. Ibid., 55.
44. Ibid., 60.
45. Edward Schillebeeckx, "The Role of History in What Is Called the New Paradigm," in *Paradigm Change: A Symposium for the Future*, ed. Hans Küng and David Tracy, trans. Margaret Kohl (New York: Crossroad, 1989), 307–19; quote, p. 313.
46. Ibid., 312.
47. Edward Schillebeeckx, *Christ*, 660. For a more detailed comparison of David Tracy's and Edward Schillebeeckx's methodologies, see Werner G. Jeanrond, "På väg mot en kristologi i dag," in *Jesustolkningar idag: tio teologer om kristologi* (Stockholm: Verbum, 1995), 235–62.
48. Hans Küng, *Theologie im Aufbruch: Eine ökumenische Grundlegung* (München: Piper, 1987), 129–52. All translations of quotations from this book are mine.
49. For an assessment of Küng's theological work, see Jeanrond, "The Rationality of Faith: On Theological Methodology," in *Hans Küng: New Horizons for Faith and Thought*,

ed. Karl-Josef Kuschel and Hermann Häring, trans. John Bowden (London: SCM Press, 1993), 104–21.

50. Küng, *Theologie im Aufbruch*, 135.
51. Ibid., 145.
52. Ibid., 146.
53. Ibid., 151.
54. Ibid.
55. Ibid.
56. See here also Hans Küng, *On Being a Christian* (Garden City, N.Y.: Doubleday & Co., 1976).
57. Tracy, "Truthfulness in Catholic Theology," in *Hans Küng: New Horizons for Faith and Thought*, 81–92, quote, p. 85.
58. Ibid.
59. Ibid.
60. Hans Küng, *Does God Exist? An Answer for Today*, trans. Edward Quinn (Garden City, N.Y.: Doubleday & Co., 1980).
61. Tracy, "Truthfulness in Catholic Theology," 90.
62. Tracy, *Plurality and Ambiguity*, 28.
63. For a more in-depth presentation and assessment of postliberal theology and comparison with correlational theology, see Werner G. Jeanrond, "The Problem of the Starting-Point of Theological Thinking," in *The Possibilities of Theology: Studies in the Theology of Eberhard Jüngel in His Sixtieth Year*, ed. John Webster (Edinburgh: T. & T. Clark, 1994), 70–89.
64. George A. Lindbeck, *The Nature of Doctrine: Religion and Theology in a Postliberal Age* (Philadelphia: Westminster Press, 1984), 34.
65. Ibid., 35.
66. Ibid., 18.
67. Ibid., 129.
68. Ibid., 132.
69. Hans W. Frei, *Types of Christian Theology*, ed. George Hunsinger and William C. Placher (New Haven, Conn., and London: Yale University Press, 1992), 2.
70. Lindbeck, *The Nature of Doctrine*, 118.
71. Cf. Frei, *Types of Christian Theology*, 70–91.
72. Ibid., 120.
73. Tracy, *Plurality and Ambiguity*, 103.
74. Ibid., 104.
75. Cf. ibid., 105.
76. Cf. ibid., 110.
77. Cf. ibid., 141, note 56.
78. See Werner G. Jeanrond, *Theological Hermeneutics: Development and Significance* (New York: Crossroad, 1991), chap. 7.

11

PROCESS THEOLOGY AND
THE PRESENT CHURCH STRUGGLE

JOHN B. COBB JR.

The term *process theology* can include all streams of theology, such as the Hegelian, that emphasize process over against substance. Usually, however, it is limited to theologies informed by a naturalistic philosophy rather than an idealist one. Within this limitation, the term has two overlapping meanings. Sometimes it refers to the "Chicago School." At other times it refers to all theology significantly influenced by Alfred North Whitehead and Charles Hartshorne. I will deal chiefly with the latter, but because of the importance of the context at Chicago where process theology was most developed, I begin there.

The Chicago School developed in the context of two controversies in the final decade of the nineteenth century: the social gospel and the theory of evolution. The former challenged the dominant individualistic interpretation of salvation. The latter forced a reappraisal of human self-understanding and biblical authority.

The social gospel arose among pastors in urban centers who became aware of the suffering of industrial labor. They saw that this was due not to individual irresponsibility but to socioeconomic structures. Hence, unless these were changed, there could be no salvation within history. The early exponents of the social gospel did not carry their theological reflections very far. Their emphasis was on the urgency of reorienting the church's preaching and programs so that they would be relevant to pressing social needs. It was only after World War I that the social gospel achieved its full theological expression in Walter Rauschenbusch's *A Theology for the Social Gospel.*

Reflection about church and society led, at the Divinity School of the University of Chicago, to rereading Christian history in sociological terms. Christianity came to be understood as a sociohistorical movement or process. Inspired by Jesus, it adjusted to and transformed the social context in which it found itself. Ideas that worked well in one period became obstacles in another. The task in each age is to deal effectively and credibly with the problems at hand. In an industrial and democratic society, both feudal and monarchical images of the past and the heightened individualism of more recent centuries should be replaced.

Evolutionary biology was not the first challenge from the sciences to the worldview of the Bible, but it was the most intense. Whereas Western Christians had located themselves above nature, evolutionary thinking placed them fully within it. Also, it conflicted with the story of creation in the Bible.

German theology had followed Kant in locating its work among the humanities, understood to be quite independent of the natural sciences. It had solved in advance the problem of conflict between science and religion by viewing them as mutually irrelevant. The authority of the Bible was located exclusively on the side of human affairs. Critical biblical scholarship developed in the context of this dualism of humanity and nature.

The Chicago scholars, such as Shirley Jackson Case, learned from this tradition but did not accept its dualistic assumptions. They believed that Christian thinking must be recast in naturalistic terms. Hence they were interested in the thinking of those scientists who interpreted the human meaning of evolution as well as quantum and relativity theories.

This kind of openness to science was widespread among progressive Christians, and the recasting of Christian thought in relation to the new science came to be called "modernism." It received its most systematic and sustained expression in the Chicago School, under the leadership of Shailer Matthews. From the point of view of modernists, affirmation of the best insights of the culture was required by faith. Clinging to past formulations only hampered the work of the church.

Obviously, this position was controversial. The strongest reaction was the rise of fundamentalism, and the modernist-fundamentalist controversy painfully divided many denominations. But most Christians were uncomfortable with both extremes.

Neoorthodoxy gained its following in this country from this middle group. Its Kantian separation of the realm of faith from empirical and historical knowledge offered a way of renewing the fullness of inherited faith while avoiding controversy with scientists and historians. The Genesis account of creation could be understood to be theologically true, while biologists were free to provide, in another sphere, scientific information about the rise of species. Historians could affirm what they found most plausible about Jesus, but theological affirmations of the incarnation of God in Jesus could not be touched by their work.

The leading theologians in the United States who introduced neoorthodox ways of thinking were not close followers of Karl Barth. In retrospect, indeed, it is hard to view the Niebuhr brothers and Paul Tillich as neoorthodox at all! Nevertheless, they encouraged a shift of attention to the continental thinkers. Modernism had gained much of its political strength in the church from the impression that it was the only way to avoid controversy with science and history. When American Christians found in the dualism of neoorthodoxy a sophisticated alternative way of avoiding such controversy while preserving much more of the traditional language and wisdom of the tradition, modernism lost most of its prestige and following. During the 1940s and 1950s, and until the mid-1960s, neoorthodoxy dominated Protestantism in both church and school.

At Chicago, however, the major features of modernism were retained. Whereas neoorthodoxy appealed to an ungrounded act of faith as the basis of theology, the Chicago Divinity School thinkers held that faith should be based on the best knowledge available. Faith is trust in that which evidence and experience show to be trustworthy. Further, humanity is part of the natural world, and Christian belief is to be set in the context of all obtainable information about that world.

The most influential thinker at Chicago during the 1930s and 1940s was Henry Nelson Wieman. For Wieman the primary religious question is that of identifying that which we can trust completely, that is, God. In his most influential phase, he insisted that this must be done in a purely empirical way, although the meaning of "empirical" for him was by no means limited to sense experience. Wieman proceeded to analyze how human good grows through a process of creative interchange. That process, he showed, cannot be managed, but it can be trusted. Indeed, it *should* be trusted and served, because otherwise it cannot do its full creative and redemptive work. He spelled out the implications of this trust for many areas of society. The resulting theology was called neonaturalism.

Although what came to be known as "process theology" owes much to Wieman and other empiricists, it takes its departure especially from the influence on the Chicago faculty of the work of Alfred North Whitehead. Whitehead was first appreciated as one of those scientists who reflected on the relation of science to the problems of human meaning. His book *Science and the Modern World* won him a premier place among such scientists. His next book, *Religion in the Making*, moved in a more theistic direction than most of the Chicago faculty was prepared to go. His theism was further developed in *Process and Reality*.

Wieman was initially quite appreciative of Whitehead, but he became increasingly opposed to Whitehead's speculative method. Bernard Meland was associated with Wieman in the development of the empirical emphasis, but he enriched it through his cultural and historical sensitivity.

Charles Hartshorne joined the philosophy faculty at about the same time that Wieman came to the Divinity School, and he held a joint appointment in the Divinity School. He had been Whitehead's assistant at Harvard, and although he had developed his own philosophy quite independently, he greatly appreciated Whitehead. Whereas reflection about God was at the periphery of Whitehead's thought, it was central to Hartshorne's. Insofar as process theology is identified with a particular doctrine of God, it is often that of Hartshorne.

Hartshorne related his work to the sciences and made his own contributions to the fields of psychology and ornithology. But his reflections about God did not arise, as did Whitehead's, from a cosmology revised to take account of changes in the natural sciences. He formulated his doctrine as a rationally required revision of classical theism, and he dealt extensively with the traditional arguments for the existence of God. His style and approach, therefore, were quite different from the Chicago School. Whereas metaphysics had been alien to that school, and was sharply opposed by Wieman, Hartshorne reintroduced it.

Hartshorne believed that the loss of credibility of a metaphysically real God in the nineteenth and twentieth centuries was due, not so much to intrinsic difficulties with metaphysics, as to the incoherence involved in classical doctrines of God. These doctrines were developed in the patristic period as a synthesis of biblical and Greek ideas. This synthesis achieved its culminating form in St. Thomas. But as in many syntheses, fundamental tensions remained unresolved, and by the modern period the doctrine ceased to be convincing. Hartshorne proposed a neoclassical synthesis which, by suitably revising the classical one, could once again make evident the reality of God.[1] This bold proposal, along with Hartshorne's brilliant execution of the program, fascinated many students in the Divinity School.

Hartshorne taught that the problem with classical doctrines is their one-sidedness. They see, for example, that God must be immutable, since a merely mutable being would not be worthy of trust or worship. But they fail to notice that a merely immutable being cannot be affected by anything that happens in the temporal world. This means either that time is ultimately an illusion or else that God is indifferent to what happens in time. Aristotle could hold this without discomfort, but it is alien to the Bible and forces Christians into confused inconsistencies.

Hartshorne proposed a solution that, once grasped, seems simple and persuasive. The immutability that is important is unchanging character. In the Bible, God is presented as faithful to God's promises. In Jesus' teaching, God unfailingly loving. But this does not mean that what happens in time makes no difference to God. On the contrary, God is affected by all temporal occurrence, taking account of everything that happens.

God is, therefore, not immutable in all respects, but God is immutable in some. God's nature or character is immutable. On the other hand, being responsive to everything that happens, God is radically mutable. Hartshorne distinguished God's abstract essence and God's concrete actuality. The former is immutable, the latter, ideally responsive and, hence, mutable. Thus God is eternal in some respects and temporal in others.

It is important to add that the mutability of God never entails loss. It consists in the addition of current happenings to the divine experience. All that God has known and been in the past remains everlastingly part of the divine life.

For Hartshorne, this is a matter of deepest religious import. The values of life are bound up in a temporal passage that soon consigns them to oblivion. If we reflect only on the endless passage of the vast sea of events, those which constitute our little worlds lose significance. But if all that we have been and done is forever present and real in God, its importance is secure. This is our immortality, and it suffices.

Hartshorne revises the doctrine of omniscience as well. Classically this doctrine was interpreted to imply that God knows the future as well as the past and present. Hartshorne argues that this is a mistake. To be omniscient in the sense of possessing ideal knowledge is to know the past and the present. But it is not to know the details of the future, because these are not now settled. Ideal knowledge includes the probability of different future events. But to "know" that a particular event will occur, when its occurrence is now uncertain, would be an error and, therefore, cannot belong to omniscience.

This argument assumes the genuine indeterminateness of the future. This is based, in Hartshorne, on doctrines about causality generally, including the role of God in the world. With regard to causality, Hartshorne again points out the one-sidedness of so much traditional teaching. Often this assumes that an event is either caused by its past or not, whereas in fact it is determined in some but not all respects. No event is either unaffected by its past or completely determined by it. Much about the future is now determined, but much is also to be determined by the future events themselves.

God's role is not that of one causal agent among others. On the contrary, God decides how fully the past determines the present by establishing the most fundamental principles of order. If there is too much determination of the present, creatures are mere automatons, and there is a loss of all significance. If there is too little, the ensuing chaos prevents the emergence of meaningful events. God ensures that balance of regularity and freedom which allows for the achievement of the greatest complexity and richness of creaturely experience.

The traditional doctrine against which Hartshorne argues most polemically is divine omnipotence. He believes that this idea is incompatible with human freedom and with divine goodness. It implies either that God actually determines everything that happens or that God could do so but refrains. The latter formulation opens some space for freedom, but it leaves the problem of evil unsolved. Furthermore, all doctrines of omnipotence are based on erroneous notions of power.

Power, as Hartshorne understands it, is inherently relational. The more powerful the one causally affected, the greater the power of the cause. The idea of omnipotence, on the other hand, implies that the affected is powerless. To have an effect on what is powerless expresses no significant power.

For example, if we suppose that matter is purely passive and that God acts only on this, we attribute no significant power to God, whatever form God imposes. If we suppose that human beings have considerable power and that God profoundly affects us, then we attribute much greater, but not *all*, power to God.

The Christian tradition has attributed omnipotence to God under the mistaken impression that this is the highest degree of power. We *should* attribute optimum power to God. But that, in Hartshorne's view, is the power to set optimum conditions for creaturely existence. This power is significant because the creatures who are affected by it have great power of their own.

Since Hartshorne referred appreciatively to Whitehead in support of all these theological revisions, his students did not at first recognize the differences between the two thinkers. But over the years these have become increasingly apparent, and have led to debates. Whitehead came to his doctrine of God quite differently and gave a different account of God's role.

Whitehead begins with an analysis of the actual entities that make up the world. He understands them as events, rather than as substances. The events of which we normally speak, he shows, can be analyzed into much smaller units, which he calls actual occasions. A momentary human experience and a quantum happening are both such actual occasions. His actual entities resemble Leibnizian monads in some respects, but they are temporally atomic and constituted by real relations to others.

He argues that to be an actual occasion is to be something for itself as well as something for others. It is something for itself in the moment of its occurrence—a subject/agent—and something for others as soon as it has occurred—a datum/cause. Every actual occasion is both subject and object.

This runs counter to the modern division of the world between human subjects and natural objects. Human experience is an example of the events that constitute nature. It is an unusual and remarkable example. For instance, it typically includes conscious feelings, whereas most actual occasions do not. But the basic structure—reception from the past, self-constitution, and causal influence on the future—is common.

Whitehead engages in detailed analysis of how the occasion is informed by its past and supplements that past creatively. It is with regard to the latter activity that he speaks of God. The present occasion includes elements of the past as that past gives itself to be included. This is the work of efficient causality, and it is massive. If this were the whole story, there would be what William James called a "block universe." There would be neither subjectivity nor agency. Because we know in ourselves that there are subjectivity and agency, we know this is not the whole story. But how is this possible?

Whitehead proposes that we think of each actual occasion as dipolar. In one of its poles it is formed by its past. This is its physical role, and it is this that provides the massive order that is the necessary background for self-determination. The relation to each element in its past is a physical prehension.

But each occasion also transcends the causality of the past by responding to it with more or less originality. This requires that the physical prehensions are supplemented by "conceptual" ones. Thus, in addition to prehending past events, an occasion also takes account of possibilities ingredient in those events or closely related to them. Just how it relates these possibilities to the actualities it feels is its "decision." This means that in a situation that is inherently indeterminate, there is a determinate outcome. Other possibilities are cut off.

For those habituated to thinking in dualistic terms of human subjects surveying an objective nature, the generalization of elements in human experience to all actual entities appears misleading. But for those who seek a nondual metaphysics, all actual entities must be, like us, subjects as well as objects, agents as well as patients. On the other hand, it is important not to generalize characteristics of human experience that depend on peculiarly human reality and to understand that the actual entities are the unitary events, such as a momentary human or animal experience and a quantum of energetic activity, not stars and animal bodies. These are vast societies of such events.

Attributing "conceptual" prehensions and "decisions" to quantum events does not entail supposing that they have conscious experience. Consciousness arises only in events of extraordinary complexity, such as the souls of animals, and even there highlights only limited aspects of experience. Unlike Hartshorne, Whitehead never thought of this as "panpsychism." The idea that each event prehends possibilities as well as actualities assumes, in Whitehead's view, that there is a realm of such possibilities ordered in their relevance to the actual world. This establishes the basic structures or "laws" of the world, but also generates freedom within those structures. This ordering is divine: and God thus plays a role in Whitehead similar to that in Hartshorne.

Nevertheless, there are differences. The ordered novelty and novel order of the world are made possible in Whitehead's view by God's persuasive lure exercised through relevant possibilities. Also, this is the work of what he calls the Primordial Nature of God, constituted by envisagement of all the pure possibilities, a concept not paralleled in Hartshorne.

Similarity recurs with respect to the preservation of the past. Like Hartshorne, Whitehead believes that the ultimate evil, though not always the most pressing, is the fading of all that occurs into the forgotten past. This threatens all human meaning. Like Hartshorne, Whitehead sees God as the answer to this threat. What is lost in the world remains forever vividly present in the Consequent Nature of God.

Although the effect of God in the world chiefly emphasized by Whitehead is similar to that proposed by Hartshorne, Whitehead notes an additional possibility. In the closing passage of *Process and Reality*, he speaks of a particular providence for particular occasions. This suggests that in the prehension of God, occasions may be lured not only in terms of the general structures of order and novelty, but also by quite particular divine purposes related to quite specific circumstances. Another difference between them is found in Whitehead's distinction of God and creativity. His rhetoric at times subordinates God to creativity and declares creativity, rather than God, ultimate. There is nothing like this in Hartshorne.

The difference diminishes when Whitehead's meaning is analyzed. He does not think of creativity as an actuality greater or more fundamental than God. On the other hand, it is not a mere abstraction. It has the role in his thought played by prime matter in medieval Aristotelian theology. In that tradition, every creature is an instance of matter with a particular form. Whitehead breaks with this tradition in two ways. First, his "material cause," far from being passive, is activity itself. It is the many becoming one, an act apart from which there is nothing at all. Secondly, God is not exempted from the principle that every actuality is an embodiment of this creativity. God is, therefore, the primordial and everlasting embodiment of creativity, providing the forms for all other instantiations. God is not the creator of creativity, since creativity is not the sort of thing that could be created.

Among the claims made for process theology, whether Hartshornean or Whiteheadian, is that it resolves the problem of theodicy in a satisfactory way. If the difficulty of reconciling the evil in the world with belief in a good God has been a major reason for the rise and growth of atheism in the Western world, this is no small claim. Barry Whitney and R. Maurice Barineau are among those who have dealt with this. David Griffin has provided the most extensive development of the argument in *God, Power, and Evil: A Process Theodicy* and *Evil Revisited*.[2]

The most basic difference between the two philosophers is with regard to their fundamental projects and their understanding of what they have done. Hartshorne's project is a doctrine of God internally consistent and coherent with the rest of human knowledge. The reality of God will be made manifest through the revision of traditional arguments, especially the ontological. Whitehead's project is to provide the most probable account of the overall nature of the world, in light of what is known from the sciences and human self-experience. Imaginative insight and speculation replace coercive argument. He emphasizes the inadequacy of language and thought generally to the completion of this task, and he assumes that whatever is achieved today will be surpassed in the future.

The differences between Hartshorne and Whitehead have generated debates among their followers on many topics, including the doctrine of God. Some, such as

Donald Sherburne and Robert Mesle have called for reformulating Whitehead's philosophy without God. Others, such as Lewis Ford and David Pailin, have reworked their ideas extensively into quite original doctrines of God. Still others, such as Robert Neville, have appreciated much of process philosophy, while critiquing every form of theism associated with it and offering quite different alternatives.

In the climate generated by the dominance of neoorthodoxy, all this appeared irrelevant to real theology. For process theology, the ontology of God and the possibility of religious knowledge were the main themes. These discussions were viewed by the majority as a branch of philosophy of religion rather than as Christian theology. The modernist style of such Chicago thinkers as Bernard Meland and Bernard Loomer tended to confirm this view. However, over the years the situation changed. Although process theologians such as Anna Case-Winters have continued to write about God, others have addressed a wide range of theological topics. As they do so, it becomes apparent that the use of similar categories and a similar understanding of God can issue in quite varied views of Christ or the church.

The one Chicago professor who deeply engaged the ongoing theological discussion was Daniel Day Williams. In *God's Grace and Man's Hope*,[3] he reformulated Wieman's vision in theological language. In *The Spirit and the Forms of Love*,[4] he offered a comprehensive theology from a Whiteheadian perspective.

Norman Pittenger, although not part of the Chicago School, early appropriated the categories of Whitehead's philosophy for his theological work. He has written highly readable books on dozens of theological topics.

Schubert Ogden's publication of *The Reality of God* in 1960 reformulated Hartshorne's arguments in conversation especially with existentialists. He argued that our inescapable sense of the meaningfulness of existence gives evidence of an implicit faith in God that a Hartshornean doctrine of God makes explicit. He followed this up with *Christ without Myth*, in which he brought together a radical version of Bultmann's kerygmatic Christology with Hartshorne's doctrine of God.

David Tracy's call for revisions of the traditional doctrine of God in *A Blessed Rage for Order* closely followed Hartshorne's. But even more than Ogden, for the fuller development of his theology he drew on other sources. Indeed, Tracy is truly catholic in his use of the fruits of theological reflection, but his work continues to be compatible with process theology.

In 1965 I published *A Christian Natural Theology*. This developed the outlines of an anthropology and ethics based on Whitehead's thought and discussed issues dealing with the doctrine of God. I followed this with *The Structure of Christian Existence*, in which I used Whiteheadian categories to locate what is distinctive about Christian existence in a historical and comparative context, and with *Christ in a Pluralistic Age*, in which I formulated a Whiteheadian Christology in view of the religiously plural context. These books reflect both my Whiteheadian commitments and my judgment that Christian theology should be written with keen awareness of other religious options.

Over the years there have also been specialized studies of particular doctrines. Don Browning and David Wheeler have written on the atonement; Blair Reynolds, on pneumatology; Susan Nelson, on sin; Jean Lambert, on forgiveness; Paul Sponheim, on faith. Several books have been published on spirituality, such as those by Francis Baur, Martha Rowlett, Carolyn Stahl, and Barry Woodbridge.

As I look back, it is striking that in the 1950s and 1960s many process theologians were particularly attracted to existentialists as conversation partners. This relation usefully highlighted one side of process thought, the accent on the subject/agent and its self-constitution. But the result was a neglect of other aspects of the heritage of process thought.

Process theologians were recalled to their naturalistic roots by the emergence to general attention of the ecological crisis symbolized by Earth Day, 1970. Our philosophical and modernist forebears had displayed sensitivity in these issues, but our engagement with anthropocentrically oriented theologians has led us away from them. When these concerns were forced on our attention, we had the tools for early response.

Whereas many theologians were informed by the Kantian separation of the human and the natural spheres, our tradition had held them together, teaching that all events have intrinsic as well as instrumental value. Further, it had emphasized the intricate interconnectedness of all things. Hence we were able to engage directly in Christian reflection about the relation of human beings to other creatures. For the most part this has been ecologically oriented, but Daniel Dombrowski and Jay McDaniel have also dealt with our responsibilities to individual animals.

The relevance of our sociohistorical heritage became clear through the impact on the theological scene of such thinkers as Altizer, Pannenberg, and Moltmann. The shift of emphasis from existence to history was reinforced by black theology and Latin American liberation theology. A few black theologians, such as Henry Young and Theodore Walker, found positive value in process ideas. Delwin Brown's *To Set at Liberty* relates process thought to Latin American liberation theology, and others have responded to black and liberation theologies in a friendly and supportive way. Nevertheless, these have been significant challenges.

Process theology had participated with most other forms in assuming that the theological task was to give expression to Christian faith generally. It was no more sensitive than were most others to the distortions introduced by the social location of the writers. Although those influenced by Whitehead, such as Williams, emphasized that all thinking is perspectival, this had to do more with intellectual traditions and cultures than with socioeconomic location, gender, or race. Genuinely assimilating the implications of the latter has been difficult.

Furthermore, process theology inherently resists the full particularization of theology proposed by some of the newer movements. Even when it fully recognizes the particularity of its own perspective, it still seeks to use that recognition in order partially to transcend it and to aim at a more adequate perspective. To place multiple theologies, representing the diverse experiences of different groups, alongside one another without seeking to mediate their differences is against the deep commitment of process theology to dialogue and synthesis.

The relation to feminist theology has been different. A few women, such as Marjorie Suchocki, were process theologians before the rise of contemporary feminism. They moved quite naturally into feminism without abandoning their earlier perspective, as can be seen in Suchocki's *God, Christ, Church.* The feminist critique of dualism and individualism, the objection to a deity with stereotypically masculine characteristics, the call to replace hierarchical with reciprocal relations, and the understanding of power as persuasive, empowering, and receptive, rather than controlling, have been common to process and feminist theology. Ecofeminism has shared the understanding of humanity as fully a part of the natural world. What was affirmed theoretically and abstractly in process thought has taken on practical and concrete meaning in feminism. This has been pure gain.

Earlier forms of process thought, however, had provided no analysis of gender and little of culture. Accordingly, even those feminists most influenced by process theology depend on other sources, especially the experience of women, and develop their thought in the context of the feminist conversation. Catherine Keller and Rita Brock are among the best known of those process theologians who are feminists first.

Process theologians have concerned themselves with interreligious discussion. Clark Williamson and Bernard Lee have dealt especially with Christian anti-Judaism. I have worked in the Buddhist-Christian dialogue. Joseph Bracken has written *The Divine Matrix.* Schubert Ogden has published *Is There Only One True Religion or Are There Many?*

One of the strengths of the earlier sociohistorical school was the collaboration of theologians and historians, especially biblical scholars. As this school gave way to empirical, rational, and speculative emphases, this collaboration waned. Amos Wilder and John Knox were the last of the biblical scholars of the earlier generation to maintain the connection. Will Beardslee, David Lull, Ted Weeden, Russell Pregeant, and Ronald Farmer have worked to renew it in New Testament studies.

Whereas much theology has accepted the fragmentation of academic disciplinary boundaries, Whiteheadian theology seeks to be informed by all areas of human thought and, in turn, to inform them. Hence, much of the work of process theologians has not been narrowly theological. Some of this has dealt with areas of ministry. Daniel Day Williams wrote extensively on ministry. Gordon Jackson has done the most systematic work with regard to pastoral counseling, while Seward Hiltner, Archie Smith, James Lapsley, Robert Brizee, Robert Kinast, Larry Graham, and David Roy have contributed. In Christian education, Randolph Crump Miller and Mary Elizabeth Moore stand out. Ronald Allen has written on preaching.

Some of those relating theology "secular" fields to theology also follow the process tradition. Ian Barbour has been the premier such thinker in relating science and religion. His contributions have culminated in the first volume of his Gifford Lectures, *Religion in an Age of Science.* Frederick Ferré and John Haught have made valuable contributions. In biology, Charles Birch has been the leader; in mathematics, Granville Henry. In Germany, Christoph Wassermann has taken the lead.

Process theologians have worked on issues of sociology, politics, and economics as well. Examples of these in sequence are Widick Schroeder, Franklin

Gamwell, and Douglas Sturm. A good example of process theology focused on a particular contemporary issue is Warren Copeland's *And the Poor Get Welfare*. I have teamed up with the economist Herman Daly to write a critique of standard economic theory from the perspective of process theology: *For the Common Good*.

In the past decade or so much of the energy of religious studies has been captured by deconstructive postmodernism. There are many similarities with Whiteheadian thought, such as the deconstruction of the Western understanding of the self and, in general, the critique of the Enlightenment. Indeed, "postmodern" had been used by process theologians before its appropriation by the French school. Whitehead's *Science and the Modern World* depicted both modern science and modern philosophy as bankrupt, and proposed new beginnings. Like deconstruction and related movements, he challenged the effort to find a secure starting point for thought in epistemology—or anywhere else. Still, deconstructive postmodernism continues the Kantian tradition over against the naturalism of process thought. Its rejection of "presence" continues that tradition's tendency to separate the knower from immediate contact with the known. Whitehead's answer to Hume expresses the process response.

Deconstruction concludes that we must do without any orienting ideas or inclusive vision, whereas Whitehead strove to create a new cosmology. However far he went in deconstructing inherited categories, his goal was constructive. David Griffin has captured this point in labeling his new program, supported by process theology, "constructive postmodern thought." He has drawn into discussion under this rubric many who are not students of Whitehead but who share the desire to build a livable home out of the new discoveries of the sciences, the contributions of primal and Eastern religions, ecological sensitivity, and liberationist commitments.

The influence of deconstruction on scholars of religion has widened the gulf between the church and the study of religion in the university. Process theology strives to participate in both. Its commitment to the church handicaps it with respect to full acceptance in religious studies, and its commitment to complete openness and radical revision handicaps it with respect to the church. Both those who reject Christianity and those who affirm it typically prefer that Christianity be understood in terms of what it has been in the past, rather than as itself in process. Until recently process theology was a North American phenomenon, and this chapter has dealt with this. But now a significant body of literature has been published in German. There is theological interest also in England, France, Belgium, Switzerland, Germany, Eastern Europe, Japan, Korea, and China. In these contexts it takes on new forms.

The process theology I have described has been Christian. But process categories can be attractive to thinkers in other traditions as well. Scholars such as William Kaufman and Sandra Lubarsky are developing Jewish versions. John Yokota and Ryusei Takeda use process categories in their expositions of Buddhism. The Chicago School has flourished for a century largely because of its processive character. Its style and focus have changed repeatedly. The sociohistorical school went into eclipse after World War II and gave way to neonaturalism and the empirical emphasis. All are alive and well in quite new forms. The rational and speculative theologies that emerged in the '50s, and whose fortunes I have been following, may by now have made their contributions to the doctrine of God, but Whiteheadian theology has taken new life in relating to a wide range of fields and interacting with other current movements. Through such metamorphoses energy is renewed. Whether process theology will long continue as such or merge into new movements called constructive postmodernism, or ecofeminism, or American naturalism, or creation spirituality remains to be seen.

NOTES

1. Charles Hartshorne, *Man's Vision of God and the Logic of Theism* (New York: Harper & Brothers, 1941).
2. David Ray Griffin, *God, Power, and Evil: A Process Theodicy* (Philadelphia: Westminster Press, 1976); idem, *Evil Revisited: Responses and Reconsiderations* (Albany, N.Y.: State University of New York Press, 1992).
3. Daniel Day Williams, *God's Grace and Man's Hope* (New York: Harper & Brothers, 1949).
4. Daniel Day Williams, *The Spirit and the Forms of Love* (New York: Harper & Row, 1968).

12

EMPIRICAL THEOLOGY AND ITS DIVERGENCE FROM PROCESS THOUGHT

ROBERT S. CORRINGTON

The movement of empirical theology has deep roots in early nineteenth-century German liberal Protestantism and late nineteenth-century American pragmatism. It is important to state at the outset that there is no direct correlation between contemporary empirical theology and eighteenth-century British empiricism, which operates under a highly abstract and truncated account of human experience. Hume's understanding of atomic sense data, tied to a deep skepticism about any religious claims, plays little if any role in current analyses of the forms and dynamics of human experience. For Hume, all complex experiences are products of primary, and ultimately simple, sense experiences that are brought together through resemblance, contiguity (closeness), and habit. Consequently, he held that any complex experience was to some degree arbitrary. Contemporary empirical theology has a much broader epistemology, governed by social theory, that honors the stretch and elasticity of all experience, especially religious. It rejects the idea that all complex experiences can or must be broken down into constituents. Its epistemology takes on the whole of experience in all its ambiguity while honoring its infinitely diverse connective tissue. In the tradition of William James, empirical theology takes relations to be as real as *relata* (thing) and struggles to find the divine or the holy within the relations that gather up the fragments of the world.[1]

Perhaps the true founder of empirical theology is Friedrich Schleiermacher (1768–1834), whose careful descriptions of all phases of experience culminated in a brilliant phenomenological description of the unique features of religious experience as it opens the self to God.[2] Schleiermacher refused to see experience in purely subjective terms, insisting that finite human experience is what it is because its intentional object is what *it* is. That is, we can have a religious experience, specifically, the experience of sheer or absolute dependence (*das schlechthinige Abhängigkeitsgefühl*), only because the infinite opens itself to the finite in a direct way. Contrary to neoorthodox misreadings of Schleiermacher, his perspective insists that the woof and warp of human experience are driven by orders and powers outside itself.[3] One can feel absolute dependence only because an actual and living infinite enters into subjectivity and shapes it around *its* infinite reality.

Given this kind of robust affirmation of the self-disclosure of divine realities, Humean skepticism is utterly out of place. The *telos* of human experience is to enter into the most pervasive and powerful orders of the world, which, by definition, are religious (although this point will be refined and challenged in the subsequent history of empirical theology). There remains a tension within Schleiermacher's thought that continues to appear and reappear in the ongoing evolution of empirical theology. It becomes manifest in his 1799 essays, *On Religion: Speeches to Its Cultured Despisers.*[4] This tension involves the relation between a kind of universalistic understanding of experience and the particular positive or historical needs of a given community that shapes experience around texts, founders, and traditions that are unique to it alone. Put simply: just how generic is experience, and does it point to a kind of universal, perhaps romantic, religion that can dispense with conditions of origin in all their particularity?[5]

Schleiermacher felt pulled in both directions, the generic and the particular, and never fully resolved this tension. Perhaps the genius of empirical theology is just this refusal to land fully on either side of this great divide. The infinite, as an unconditional ground, has no finite or particular traits, while its historical appearance may, some — most notably Hegel — would say *must*, take on finite traits. There are tensions within contemporary empirical theology that mirror those already emergent in 1799. Is empirical theology necessarily Christian, or is it in a position to become a truly universalistic perspective? As we will also see, there is a tendency within some empirical theologians (e.g., Jerome Stone, Donald Crosby, and Charles Hardwick) to put pressure on the concept of divinity itself, thus giving us something that Schleiermacher would never have endorsed: namely, religious experience without a corresponding divine object.

The second historical trajectory animating contemporary empirical theology is classical American pragmatism. Here we see a more diverse and tension-filled antecedent horizon, which has flowered in various ways in the contemporary movement of empirical theology. One way to delineate these branches is to trace them back to specific figures from whom current categorical frameworks are derived. For the majority of contemporary empirical theologians (e.g., William Dean, Nancy Frankenberry, Jerome Soneson, and E. J. Tarbox), inspiration comes from William James (1842–1910) and John Dewey (1859–1952), both of whom integrated the Darwinian turn into biological and social accounts of experience. James is far less social than Dewey and more open to forms of psychopathology within experience, yet both thinkers radically broadened our understanding of what occurs when the self is placed within a shifting and often hostile natural environment.

Thinkers more attuned to James tend to work with a pluralistic and open-ended account of the mobile horizons of experience as they create a kind of personal, or even private and subjective, understanding of matters religious. Thinkers more attuned to Dewey stress social reconstruction and a strong organic model of organism-environment transaction at the foundation of whatever might be held to be religious.[6] Followers of James can retain the more classical language of consciousness and the subconsciousness, whereas followers of Dewey are far less likely to speak of consciousness at all, preferring to simply use the very broadly construed word "experience." James is open to a kind of pluralistic theism which speaks of centers of vitality in an emerging universe. Dewey, on the other hand, comes very close to affirming a deep naturalistic agnosticism and views the concept of God as little more than a kind of Kantian regulative Ideal that transcends the ethical or aesthetic, but which denotes nothing really ontological.

A third, and thus far less developed, branch derives its inspiration from C. S. Peirce (1839–1914), founder of pragmatism and semiotics (the theory of signs and their function).[7] While Jamesians and Deweyans distance themselves from systematic metaphysics, thinkers friendly to Peirce (e.g., Douglas Anderson, Robert Corrington, Robert Neville, and Michael Raposa) recast the concept of religious experience within a more generic framework, which attempts to show the structure of nature and its relation to an ontologically real God. Yet Peirceans also tend to distance themselves from process metaphysics, which is held to be too romantic and idealistic in its delineations of the primordial and consequent dimensions of God. In addition, the Peircean trajectory moves toward a form of pansemioticism that affirms that everything that can be in any way discriminated by the self is manifest as signs that can be translated into other signs. Yet such perspectives also deny that there can be anything like a superorder of meaning or some kind of divine supersign.

Less influential, but still of great conceptual import, is the later thought of Josiah Royce (1855–1916), the absolute idealist who dominated the philosophy department at Harvard during its so-called golden age.[8] Royce created a brilliant synthesis of Peirce's early (1860s) semiotic theory with his own understanding of the nascent theology of Paul and its relation to the communities of the early church. For Royce, Paul had the profoundly difficult task of weaving the fragmentary sayings of Jesus into a coherent theology and theory of community (as the body of Christ) that could give some self-consciousness to the very fragile communities that he established around the Mediterranean. From Royce's perspective, Paul became the first hermeneut of the church, and showed us how to use signs to interpret the inner workings of the Spirit in history.

There is thus an intimate relation between semiotics and the concept of community. Most empirical theologians, unless they embrace an extreme Jamesian relativism, locate religious experience within what are hoped to be emancipatory communities that live as the locus of signs-in-process.[9] Royce's more idealistic and absolutistic elements have been dropped, while his semiotic eschatology has been regrounded in naturalism and empiricism. The empirical element can be found in the hermeneutic theory that is directly tied to signs within finite, but community-based, experience.

The classical American thinkers all worked out of what can be broadly construed as a naturalistic perspective. The kind of empiricism that is found in contemporary empirical theology is usually located within a naturalism that is distinctive to the American philosophical scene. While it is impossible to trace the full contour of a term as broad in scope as "naturalism," it is possible to give some indication of fairly stable and recurrent traits that, as a cluster, are unique to naturalism. The most important commitment of a naturalist, in this American sense, is to the idea that there can be no supernatural realm disconnected from nature. Whatever is in whatever way it is, is in and of nature. It follows that God must be fully within nature, even if that same God can also, but in a different dimension, sustain nature.

There is only one nature, a nature that cannot be bound or contained in an order larger in scope than itself. Two other general conceptions usually go with this rejection of anything like a supernatural order. The first is a refusal to specify any kind of basic "what" for nature. That is, nature is best seen as the constant availability of orders, and as those orders themselves. Each order will have some unique traits, and no one trait can be found in all orders. Therefore it makes no sense to posit some primitive substrate, such as spirit, matter, substance, or energy, as being pertinent to all orders in all respects. The second general conception that usually accompanies naturalist perspectives is what the recent American philosopher Justus Buchler has called "ontological parity."[10] This doctrine asserts that nothing can be more or less real than anything else. Contrasted to this is the recurrent position known as "ontological priority," which asserts, either explicitly or implicitly, that something — say God — is more real than something else. Naturalists generally refuse to see nature as a hierarchy or orders each manifesting some kind of diminishing or deepening participation in the real. From the standpoint of ontological parity, God is no more or less real than a fictional character or a passing thought.

Paradoxically, for a true naturalist, it makes no sense to even talk of nature per se, as if it were a *discriminandum* or object over and against the self. It makes more sense to see the word "nature" as functioning as a kind of precategory, rather than as a term that could have a contrast. While we *can* speak of the contrast of God and nature, we cannot speak of something "nonnatural" that would contrast with nature. The precategory of nature refers to whatever is in whatever way.

Given this rejection of supernaturalism, it follows that the classical doctrine of *creatio ex nihilo* is put under profound pressure.[11] God is either coemergent with the other orders of nature, or is a later emergent. To talk of a creator prior to creation or, more precisely, of a creator who *becomes* the creator in the very act of creation, is to posit by fiat some reality that is discontinuous with all other realities. Such an ad hoc deity, according to naturalism, actually has no ontological location rather than in the realm of human language. Naturalists in general are suspicious of any concept of divine omnipotence, although their criticisms are different from those of a process thinker like Hartshorne. For a naturalist, God cannot be omnipotent, because God is one order, perhaps the supreme one, within nature. These other orders each have their own sphere of power which is other to the divine power. For most process thinkers, on the other hand, there is a crucial sense in which God still transcends and envelops nature (the position known as panentheism). For them, nature cannot be greater than God. For naturalists, on the other hand, it is almost as if nature is the genus of which God is the species. Put differently, nature cannot be plurally located (since it spawns all locations in its dimension of *nature naturing*), while God can be and is so located.

When naturalism is wedded to the radical concept of experience that comes jointly from the liberal German theological tradition and the classical American philosophical tradition, a powerful epistemology and metaphysics emerge that can recast many of the antecedent doctrines of theology. To take one important example, the classical doctrine of sin is recast in a variety of ways to show that the human process is not so much in rebellion or in disobedience as it is in a state of woundedness, which is a direct result of the indifference of the nature from which the self has been ejected. It is important to note here that this rethinking of the concept of sin runs parallel to current feminist and nonfeminist deconstructions of patriarchy.[12] What makes empirical theology distinctive is that it makes its own deconstructions and reconstructions out of a much more generic and compelling metaphysical horizon which locates race, class, and gender analyses within categorial delineations of greater scope. Put differently, social conflicts are in and of an indefinitely ramified nature, from which it is impossible to prescind such crucial realities. Empirical theology avoids many of the provincial and polemical debates that can reduce theology to a war of finite powers, or of self-positioning narratives.

With the concept of sin transformed in this way, it follows that the concept of grace must be recast. For a naturalist and an empirical theologian, grace is manifest as a natural process that can appear in the qualitative consummation of experience or in the pulsations of nature that have no ultimate whence or whither. Natural grace, the sense that any order is rather than is not, is ubiquitous. Such grace is, of course, beyond good and evil. The ebola virus is sustained by natural grace in the same way that a great creative product is. This grace is not a gift from a divine being, nor is it tied to history in a special way. This is not to say that there may not also be a special form of divine grace that is a unique presence within nature. God's grace has very different relational features than natural grace, although some empirical theologians remain skeptical about this divine and more particular form of grace.[13]

It is safe to say that almost all empirical theologians would call themselves naturalists. Yet naturalism has several species-variations, and each one carries with it a distinct tone.[14] The form that is most removed from traditional religious conceptions is what could be called a *descriptive naturalism* (e.g., Dewey, Santayana, Buchler). This form stresses the utter scope and utter indifference of nature to the needs of the human process. At the same time, it works out of the contemporary neo-Darwinian synthesis and focuses on antecedent causal relations. Teleology is introduced only in sparing ways, and any concept of panpsychism (mind being more basic than matter in the universe) is firmly rejected. A second form of naturalism can be labeled *honorific naturalism* (e.g., Emerson, Heidegger). This form focuses on spiritual momenta within nature and sometimes has a strong eschatological flavor. For an honorific naturalist, nature may or may not be fundamentally mind or spirit, but at the very least it is the locus for world-transforming energies that have been most adequately described by the great religions. Process thought seems to belong to the family of naturalisms, but it is disqualified because of its panentheism, that is, its nature is too small while God is too big. Finally, there is what might be called an *ecstatic naturalism* (e.g., Peirce, Tillich, Corrington[15]), which stresses the utter indifference of nature in the dimension of *nature natur- ing*, while affirming some finite and fragmentary prospects of transcendence within the dimension of *nature natured* (creation).

All three forms of naturalism, the descriptive, honorific, and ecstatic (with process thought being a kind of quasi naturalism), are empirical in methodology. Again, this special sense of the word "empirical" has nothing to do with the tradi- tion associated with Locke, Berkeley, and Hume, each of whom imposed a strait- jacket on experience and reduced it to a pale shadow of itself. For the contemporary empirical theologian, in contrast, empiricism entails the view that experience is a medium in and through which the various orders of the world be- come manifest in all their complexity. There is no such thing as a drive to boil down the objects of experience to some kind of alleged simple. Indeed, empirical theology rejects the very idea that nature could even contain such simples.

The question suggests itself as to whether or not this fairly wholesale recon- struction of experience, nature, and the divine can play a positive role in the Chris- tian church or, by implication, in reformed or reconstructive forms of Judaism? It is fair to say that empirical theologians remain divided on this key issue. Some, such as Neville, feel very much at home within the Christian perspective and find no fundamental tension between their naturalism and the symbols and claims of either Christianity or Judaism. The church, in such a view, consists of those for whom transforming and creative experiences bind them around the historical and natural appearances of the Christ, or of the covenant. Authority still derives from finite but shared human experience, rather than from antecedent texts or doctrinal formulations. Thus, a number of empirical theologians can claim membership in a positive and historically based religion, even if the locus of authority has shifted.

Yet for other empirical theologians, there is a strong need to move to the edges of Western monotheism. This takes place for two main reasons. The first is that of the growing pressure felt in the encounter with world religions. By definition this relativizes the truth claims of exclusivistic, and some might say, tribal, monothe- ism. Empirical theologians claim to have an advantage over doctrinal theologians precisely because they can meet representatives of other religions on the ground of common human experience, even though that common ground is, of course, shaped by cultural forces as well. The second reason put forward for moving to the edges of our Western monotheism is that the philosophical resurrection of na- ture, after its forced abjection for many centuries, makes it impossible to go back to particularistic and self-serving religions that are deeply wedded to structures of origin and power that have no generic import. Simply put, naturalism conveys a breadth of vision that compels a move toward a universalistic, but nonimperial, understanding of religion.

The actual historical situation is, of course, more ambiguous. Most empirical theologians would have to admit that their driving categories and metaphors come from both Judaism and Christianity, even if they are stretched, or even broken, to serve a vision that insists on being generic and nonexclusivistic. This situation is reminiscent of that facing the young Schleiermacher as he tried to balance the

claims of natural religion (a religion of pure universal reason without the alien in-
trusion of revelation) with a positive religion (that has its founder, text, tradition,
and unique symbol system). Empirical theology is no stranger to this tension, but
has evolved after the crises of evolutionary theory and the big bang cosmology,
thus moving it farther away from positive claims that are tied to speciesism or an
anthropocentric view of the cosmos. If anything, the new cosmology makes it increasingly hard to cling to claims of private or group-specific textual revelation.
Living in an expanding universe, and immersed in a biosphere driven by natural
selection, random variation, and self-organization, it is an insult to prop up a cosmology that would privilege one religion and its history over time. Put in stark
terms, entropy (the tendency of any closed system toward heat loss and loss of order over time) will someday make all life on our biosphere impossible. Eschatological dreams are always devoured by an indifferent nature.

Using Wesley's quadrilateral of reason, experience, scripture, and tradition, it
is clear that empirical theology privileges reason (in a humbled form) and experience (in an expanded form). Reason is humbled from its seventeenth-century form
with its quest for universal sufficient reasons. Experience is expanded from its
eighteenth-century form to include anything that could impact on human awareness in any way. The human process assimilates much that it cannot render conscious, yet this too is a nascent form of experience. For example, one may
assimilate the effects of gossip without being conscious of them. Some possibilities may emerge and some actualities may change, all shaping the *general* tenor
of experience.

Empirical theology is thus a naturalism and a radicalized empiricism. Tradition
is held by most empirical theologians to be the presence of the powers of origin,
and hence slightly demonic. Scripture is sometimes held to be a slightly heteronomous body of insufficiently generic positions. This is not to say that empirical theology must be antitraditional or hostile to the biblical witness, but that it
moves more decisively in the direction of fresh and open experience that rides on
the back of a self-transforming nature. Like Kant, who judged the Bible according to the canons of pure and practical reason, the empirical theologian will place
the Bible against the infinite book of nature. This larger book dwarfs all human ar-
tifacts and shows us that history, no matter what its glories, is a mere species of
nature. Hence, empirical theology, at least in its most radical forms such as that
found in ecstatic naturalism, shows that history is a subaltern configuration *within*
nature.[16] From this perspective, an overemphasis on tradition or scripture is anti-
naturalistic, and hence a form of idolatry.

The focus on pragmatic and finite reason, on the one hand, and a radicalized account of experience on the other, received a new dynamism and richness in the
twentieth-century movement known as the "Chicago School of theology." This
loosely defined movement, held together by a common commitment to Deweyan
pragmatism and Whiteheadian process thought, expanded philosophical categories in the direction of a church-related theology that struggled to integrate
metaphysics and practical church life.[17] What is interesting about this so-called
school is that it shied away from a more robust metaphysics in the process vein,

insisting that the basic process categories, like that of creativity, must work in a less architectonic and, therefore, more pragmatic context. Hence, Whitehead's concept of cosmic creativity, as separate from God, becomes translated into creative processes within nature and human culture that sustain and enhance value.

Perhaps the most important figure of the Chicago School, at least for the philosophical theologian, is Henry Nelson Wieman (1884–1975), whose own daring reconstruction of both Dewey and Whitehead paved the way for later innovators who wished to render theology into evolutionary and empirical terms.[18] For Wieman, value exists as a real force in the world, that is, it is not reducible to human projection, and God is the power of creativity working, not to create the world out of nothing, but to sustain the growth of value in an evolutionary context. Like Dewey, who also taught at the University of Chicago (although not in the Divinity School), Wieman wants the religious impulse to be thoroughly naturalistic and embedded in finite evolutionary structures that surround and shape human culture. For Wieman, as for the other empirical theologians, supernaturalism is antireligious because it cuts us off from the real values that must operate under the shifting and ambiguous events of nature. Insofar as members of the Chicago School ventured to say something of the "what" of nature, it was understood to be the "sum" of energy/events that harbor some genuine novelty and some fairly robust forms of teleology (the process element).

The focus on value moved the Chicago School dramatically away from continental positivism, with its insistence that value is only a matter of human preference projected onto an inert and value-free realm of nature. Rather, value, embodied in goods that are enjoyed by individuals and their communities, is that part of nature that participates in divine creativity in an intimate way. Writing in 1946, Wieman says:

> We shall try to demonstrate that there is a creative process working in our midst which transforms the human mind and the world relative to the human mind. We shall then show how transformation by this process is always in the direction of the greater good. The human good thus created includes goods, satisfaction of human wants, richness of quality, and power of man to control the course of events. . . . Throughout the writing that follows we shall take as our guide the creative event, which produces qualitative meaning.[19]

Thus there is no ontological abyss separating divine value from human and natural value. God is nothing if not manifest within those creative events of nature that enhance our enjoyment of qualitative meaning. Here we see Wieman articulating a form of the naturalist commitment to ontological parity. No value is less real than another, and no creative event is more real than another. God cannot be more real than the various loci of divine appearance within nature, and no humanly enjoyed value can be in any way less real than God.

The process component of Wieman's perspective is evident in the optimistic sense that there will be an increase in the complexity and enjoyment of value over time. His language is more honorific than Dewey's, who always stressed the equal status of the precarious and the stable. For a Deweyan descriptive naturalist, there is no room for any kind of eschatology, other than a minimalist communal hope for positive democratic reconstruction. For the empirical theologian of the Chicago School, the goods of nature are also divine goods which we were meant to enjoy even under the strenuous conditions of evolutionary ramification, a process that allows for expansion and teleological growth around instantiated values. Within the travail of evolution, the creative process, greater than the "sum" of finite creative events, has saving and transforming power, a power that is rooted in God, not in mere collective or cultural projection.

For Wieman, we are called by the creative momentum of the divine to enter fully into the tensions of our evolutionary context. He called this process one of "appropriate awareness" that goes beyond mere cognition and awakens all aspects of the self-world correlation. As is often the case in naturalist and empiricist frameworks, social and aesthetic categories seem to usurp strictly religious ones. Yet the empirical theologian can rightly ask: Just what does one mean by the "strictly" religious? For a naturalist or empiricist (in this special sense of the term) there can be no such detached sphere or removed order that has allegedly unique features. Rather, there is a continuum connecting the most "ordinary" experience with all other types. Perhaps the religious experience has a special intensity and a special object, but it is fully permeable to the social, ethical, and aesthetic dimensions of the self-world relation. Hence, our "appreciative awareness" of divine creative energy and value is one that utilizes all dimensions of experience. There is a direct correlation between antisupernaturalism and the rejection of something like a unique and quarantined religious experience.[20]

The Chicago School brought both metaphysical and social categories to bear on theological issues. Its radical immanentism, tied to an appreciation of science as a privileged form of inquiry, advanced theological reflection by tying it to issues in general culture. However, it must not be assumed that empirical theology is simply another form of apologetic theology that has as *its* task the translation of theological structures into ones held to be congenial to the surrounding culture. The drive within empirical theology is far more radical, precisely because it wishes to push to the edges of established monotheisms to gauge how the human process can encounter nature face-to-face.

In line with this momentum, the concept of revelation becomes dynamized to incorporate future elements. Empirical theology refuses to acknowledge something like an antecedent repository of so-called extranatural wisdom. Revelation is moved into the open future and becomes a form of education or learning within an infinite nature that has no obvious whence or whither.[21] In *ecstatic naturalism* revelation is understood to be something akin to Tillich's ecstatically transformed reason. In no case will an empirical theologian see revelation as a form of information or as a command. The issue of the covenant is more complex. In Robert Neville's quasi-process naturalism, the concept of the covenant is central to explaining the self-world bond as sustained by an indeterminate God (as being-itself) that becomes determinate in the act of creation. For most empirical theologians, however, the concept of the covenant is muted. Perhaps the alternative metaphor is that of mourning, a feeling-tone that points directly to the infinite and heterogeneous momentum of nature from which all things come, and into which all things return. In this view, the human process has the status of a foundling rather than that of an image of God that participates in God's glory.

Once that self becomes a foundling it must negotiate between and among the innumerable orders of creation. On this side of the great divide (between *nature naturing* and *nature natured*) there are a number of intrinsic relations and connections that bind the self to nature's orders. Empirical theology, especially in its Jamesian forms, insists that the universe is filled with dynamic continua that grow and change. Any item in the universe will connect with innumerable others. Only process thinkers, however, will go so far as to insist that a given item (actual occasion) will be related to all other past realities. For an empirical theologian, there are genuine discontinuities in the heart of nature, and all continua must admit tears in their fabric. By the same token, there can be no ultimate continuum of continua. Nature is the constant availability of continua, not an overarching unity. Unities come and go in a nature that cannot support all that it spawns.

Is this view of nature pessimistic, especially when contrasted with the Judeo-Christian conception of a good creation? For the empirical theologian, nature cannot be anything other than what it is; namely, the indifferent generative source of whatever is in whatever way it is. To call "it" either good or evil is to make a profound category mistake. Goods come and go, as do demonic eruptions. If nature is the genus of which God is the species (although nature must be beyond all genera), then it cannot be the result of a divine creative act out of nonbeing. Hence God cannot put a unique moral/ontological stamp on the innumerable orders of the world. Perhaps a much more fruitful image than that of the "goodness" of creation is that of the unconscious of nature, an unconscious that is prior to any predication or moral evaluation.[22] It is not often noticed that there is a deep mystical strain in empirical theology, especially in its conjunction with generic forms of naturalism. By the term "mysticism" in this context is meant an awareness of the utter abyss and groundlike quality of *nature naturing* in its inexhaustibility. Justus Buchler coined the term "providingness" as an alternative to the term "providence."[23] This terminological shift represents a profound metaphysical sea-change. Nature has no special relation to providence, but is the providingness that makes each and every order possible. Providingness is without purpose, without consciousness, without moral intent, and without any understanding of time and time's flow. Yet it is indirectly available to the human process through its connection with the unconscious of the self. This connection is one that almost all empirical theologians are still a bit reluctant to make. After all, the classical American philosophical tradition, to name no other, was not friendly to depth psychology (James is only a partial exception to this claim, because of his stress on the transforming focus of consciousness rather than on the heterogeneous momenta of the unconscious). Hence, any connection between the depth of the human process and unconscious providingness of nature is looked at with some suspicion. However, I am persuaded that it is just this connection which remains the unthought within the heart of empirical theology.

This issue of the unconscious of nature can be traced back to the German philosopher F. W. J. Schelling (1775–1854), a contemporary of Schleiermacher. It is well known that Tillich (whom I have called a precursor of ecstatic naturalism) wrote two dissertations on Schelling and that he remained indebted to him throughout his theological career. It is not often noted, however, that Tillich pulled away from some of the more radical aspects of Schelling's theory of nature in order to domesticate it within the context of systematic theology. On the American side, one of the most important sources for contemporary empirical theology is in the writings of C. S. Peirce, who was also a slightly wayward disciple of Schelling. In the move to radicalize our understanding of nature, empirical theology has come close to affirming many of Schelling's key insights. Yet the openness into the utter ground of the world, which is in no way correlated to any Logos-like structure, has been restrained. At this stage in the evolution of naturalism it is important to engage in an emancipatory reenactment of Schelling so that this hidden side of nature, a side that is ultimately known through a kind of mystical experience, can appear. The text that I have in mind comes from his 1809 work *On Human Freedom*:

> Following the eternal act of self-revelation, the world as we now behold it is all rule, order and form; but the unruly [*das Regellose*] lies ever in the depths as though it might again break through, and order and form nowhere appear to have been original, but it seems as though what had initially been unruly had been brought to order.[24]

The unruly is that which is prior to any of the manifest orders of creation. Schelling even hints that it may be prior to God, as a kind of churning or striving that births even the divine. The unruly ground, as heterogeneous momentum, is the ultimate abyss (Plato's *chora* or Julia Kristeva's *material maternal*) out of which the world emerges. Nature is not just what is manifest to consciousness, but what appears in the rhythmic momenta of the unconscious. Here all images of sight, or of the mirroring of nature, break down. A special *kind* of experience takes over that brings the self face-to-face with the unruly depths of a nature that can never be encompassed by philosophy or theology, or perhaps even the divine.[25]

Not all empirical theologians would be happy with this nod to Schelling, yet there are clear antecedent hints within their various naturalisms that another and deeper trajectory must manifest itself in the self-nature-divine correlation. Suffice it to say that at this historical juncture, few competing perspectives have exhibited such metaphysical courage in an age that prefers piecemeal and self-congratulatory analyses to what Hegel called the "strenuousness of the concept." Empirical theology and its several naturalisms represents a distinctively American contribution to world theology and philosophy, perhaps precisely because it has strong roots in other traditions. In the end it asks us to have the courage to accept a smaller God so that we can become permeable to a much larger nature. At the same time, it asks us to let go of our cherished projections and desires in the face of an unruly ground that does not even know that they exist.

NOTES

1. On the issue of experience and religion, see Nancy Frankenberry, *Religion and Radical Empiricism* (Albany: State University of New York Press, 1987).
2. The locus for this phenomenological description is in the second edition (1830–1831) of his *Der christliche Glaube*, ed. and trans. H. R. Mackintosh and J. S. Stewart as *The Christian Faith* (Edinburgh: T. & T. Clark, 1928).
3. The chief example of such a misreading is Karl Barth's *The Theology of Schleiermacher*, ed. Dietrich Ritschl and trans. Geoffrey W. Bromiley (Grand Rapids: Wm. B. Eerdmans Publishing Co., 1982). The text is based on Barth's 1923/24 lectures given at Göttingen University.
4. There are several translations available of Schleiermacher's *Speeches*. An excellent one for teaching purposes, because of its fine introduction, is *On Religion: Speeches to Its Cultured Despisers*, trans. Richard Crouter (Cambridge: Cambridge University Press, 1988). This translation is based on the first (1799) edition.
5. See Roger A. Badham, "World Spirit and the Appearance of the God: Philosophy of Religion and Christian Apologetic in Schleiermacher's Early Thought," *The New Athenaeum* 5 (forthcoming).
6. For a contemporary defense of a Deweyan natural theology, see Jerome Paul Soneson, *Pragmatism and Pluralism: John Dewey's Significance for Theology* (Minneapolis: Fortress Press, 1993).
7. See Robert S. Corrington, *An Introduction to C. S. Peirce: Philosopher, Semiotician, and Ecstatic Naturalist* (Lanham, Md.: Rowman & Littlefield, Pubs., 1993).
8. See Robert S. Corrington, *The Community of Interpreters: On the Hermeneutics of Nature and the Bible in the American Philosophical Tradition* (Macon, Ga.: Mercer University Press, 1987). Second edition with a new preface, 1995.
9. For an increasing alternative perspective that stresses a strong relativism, see the work of J. Wesley Robbins, who comes out of a sustained dialogue with the thought of Richard Rorty. See Robbins's article "Pragmatism, Democracy, and God: A Reply to Rockefeller," *American Journal of Theology and Philosophy* 14:3 (September 1993): 279–85.
10. Justus Buchler's main metaphysical work is *Metaphysics of Natural Complexes*, 2d expanded ed., ed. Kathleen Wallace, Armen Marsoobian, and Robert S. Corrington (Albany: State University of New York Press, 1990).
11. One important exception to this divorce of naturalism and a radical doctrine of creation can be found in the thought of Robert C. Neville. His most important book in this connection is *God the Creator: On the Transcendence and Presence of God* (Chicago: University of Chicago Press, 1968). A second edition with a new preface has been published by State University of New York Press in 1992.
12. Among those thinkers who are working to combine aspects of feminist analysis with empirical theology are Sheila Davaney, Nancy Frankenberry, and Marjorie Suchocki.
13. For a physicalist account of grace, Charley D. Hardwick, *Events of Grace: Naturalism, Existentialism, and Theology* (Cambridge: Cambridge University Press, 1996). For a minimalist account, see Jerome A. Stone, *The Minimalist Vision of Transcendence: A Naturalist Philosophy of Religion* (Albany: State University of New York Press, 1992).
14. On the forms that naturalism can take, see William M. Shea, *The Naturalists and the Supernatural: Studies in Horizon and an American Philosophy of Religion* (Macon, Ga.: Mercer University Press, 1984), and Robert S. Corrington, *Ecstatic Naturalism:*

Signs of the World, Advances in Semiotics (Bloomington, Ind.: Indiana University Press, 1994). Shea's book details the rise of the Columbia University School of philosophical naturalism. This school, which has roots in Aristotle and Santayana, and was embodied in the work of Dewey, Woodbridge, Randall, and Buchler, is second in importance only to the classical period of pragmatism (roughly 1870–1930s). The Columbia School was somewhat indifferent to theological issues, yet has a great deal to say about how nature is to be envisioned.

15. For an analysis of ecstatic naturalism, see Roger A. Badham, "Windows on the Ecstatic: Reflections on Robert Corrington's Theonomous Naturalism," *Soundings* (forthcoming); and Todd A. Driskill, "Beyond the Text: Ecstatic Naturalism and American Pragmatism," *American Journal of Theology and Philosophy* 15:3 (September 1994): 305–23.

16. A very important exception to this is the unique historical naturalism found in the work of William Dean. Concerning this, see his two books *American Religious Empiricism* (Albany: State University of New York Press, 1986), and *History Making History: The New Historicism in American Religious Thought* (Albany: State University of New York Press, 1988).

17. An indispensable study of the whole of the empirical theology movement, with special focus on the Chicago School, is Randolph Crump Miller, ed., *Empirical Theology: A Handbook* (Birmingham, Ala.: Religions Education Press, 1992). See especially the chapters by Tyron Inbody and Nancy Frankenberry for an overall perspective. Other key figures in the Chicago School are Bernard Loomer and Bernard Eugene Meland.

18. An excellent introduction to Wieman's thought is Marvin C. Shaw, *Nature's Grace: Essays on H. N. Wieman's Finite Theism* (New York: Peter Lang, 1995). This book is the second volume in the ongoing series American Liberal Religious Thought, ed. Don Crosby and W. Creighton Peden.

19. Henry Nelson Wieman, *The Source of Human Good* (Carbondale: Southern Illinois University Press, 1946), 17. For a contemporary empirical theology that focuses on the centrality of value, see Frederick Ferré, *Being and Value: Toward a Constructive Postmodern Metaphysics* (Albany: State University of New York Press, 1996).

20. Another important anthology touching on many aspects of empirical theology is Creighton Peden and Larry E. Axel, eds., *God, Values, and Empiricism: Issues in Philosophical Theology*, Highlands Institute Series I (Macon, Ga.: Mercer University Press, 1989). This book is a product of the First International Conference on Philosophical Theology, held at Oxford University, and sponsored by the Highlands Institute for American Religious Thought. The Highlands Institute, founded in 1986, is devoted to research and publication in empirical theology and naturalism. In addition to the publishing series is their refereed periodical, the *American Journal of Theology and Philosophy*. A new anthology of original Chicago School writings, covering the period from 1906 to 1988, has been published in two volumes as *The Chicago School of Theology: Pioneers in Religious Inquiry*, ed. Creighton Peden and Jerome A. Stone (Lewiston, N.Y.: Edwin Mellen Press, 1996).

21. On revelation as learning, see Robert C. Neville, *A Theology Primer* (Albany: State University of New York Press, 1991).

22. For a slightly different take on this issue, see Donald C. Crosby's article "The Ultimacy of Nature: An Essay on Physidicy," *American Journal of Theology and Philosophy* 14:3 (September 1993): 301–14.

23. Buchler, *Metaphysics of Natural Complexes*, 3.
24. Friedrich W. J. Schelling, *On Human Freedom*, trans. James Gutman (La Salle, Ill.: Open Court, 1936); from the 1809 German text, *Über das Wesen der menschlichen Freiheit*.
25. See my article, Robert S. Corrington, "Nature's God and the Return of the Material Maternal," *American Journal of Semiotics* 10:1–2 (1993): 115–32.

PART V

LIBERATIONIST AND FEMINIST THEOLOGIES

13

INTERSTITIAL INTEGRITY
Reflections toward an
Asian American Woman's Theology

RITA NAKASHIMA BROCK

A recurring dream stole often into my childhood sleep, intruding about four years after I moved from Japan to Kansas. In the dream, I am fighting my way up a sharply pitched, forested Okinawan hillside. I burst in the door of my house and start screaming: "They have taken my mother! The Communists have kidnapped her and are brainwashing her!" I had run all the way from a distant house to which I had followed the kidnappers. To find her, it had taken me hours of stealing quietly between the neighborhood houses, scattered in tall, dark pine woods lit by a weak afternoon sun. She was tied to a chair in a locked house; I shouted through a closed window, "Mother, do you know me? Ayako! It's Rita!" Her blank stare frightened me. I felt as if all ground had dissolved under me and I was floating in a terrifying, opaque whirlpool.

I had lost my mother in my waking life too. She was emotionally remote, in a place I could not go. In the intervening years, I have decided the dream was as much about my own transition from Japanese to American society, when I was six, as it was about my distant relationship to my mother. It was a dream about my struggle to reconnect to a memory of being rooted and secure, a place lost forever. I struggled to reconnect to that lost self as I learned to cope with my American life.

By the time my dream ceased, Japan had become an "imaginary homeland,"[1] both vague and magnified in my imagination. It was a place where I felt loved and protected, a lush, mountainous world edged by sparkling seas, in stark contrast to the dry, brown prairies of Kansas and the hostile kids who called me "Jap." As the only small child in a large Japanese household, I had been shielded from the struggle and sorrow of post–World War II Japan—of my mother's life in Fukuoka, her abandonment by my Puerto Rican father, and her reasons for leaving after marrying my white American stepfather. In Kansas, we no longer spoke a language of mutual fluency, though I understood her silences and did not know I understood them. On my first return to Japan, when I was twenty-two, I was a stranger in my birthplace. Yet America did not feel like home. My identity as an Asian Pacific American is rooted in my configuration of Asia as an irretrievably lost home.

ASIAN PACIFIC AMERICANS

"Asian Pacific American" is a political, socially constructed identity, born of the two-and-a-half centuries of confluence of those whose ancestry links them to Asia and the Pacific Islands. Calling oneself Asian Pacific American comes from conscious reflection on the experience of living in North Atlantic society with the racial features of Asians and Pacific islanders and from knowledge of the history of Asian and Pacific peoples in the United States.[2] The complex and regionally varied mixes of cultures and consciousness that form Asian Pacific America have seethed from a volcanic cauldron of political forces: Columbus's search for Asia and its European colonization, American imperialism in the Pacific Basin, and racism in American society, where the heat of race erupts from a black and white fault line. The experiences of Asian Pacific Americans (hereafter referred to as APAs) cannot, of course, be melted into one homogenized experience. We have varied histories and experiences.

In 1965, the vast majority of us were second- or third-generation Americans, who had survived in the face of a viciously racist society that viewed all Americans of Asian ancestry as unwelcome foreigners. We endured forced labor, lynching, illegal and unconstitutional imprisonment, that is, we were exploited similarly to African Americans.[3] United States immigration policy maintained a social and legal hegemony from 1790 until 1952 that denied naturalized citizenship to virtually all except those who looked white; Congress rescinded the 1790 act only when it became embarrassingly evident that U.S. policy looked like Nazi policy.[4]

Our survival strategies and activism were constructed in response to U.S. foreign policy and its racist effects.[5] In APA communities, women have had to struggle with subordination, oppression, and invisibility as we have worked in solidarity with others in the struggle for justice and as we have worked to sustain our families, communities, and cultures. The APA women's movement emerged from women's frustration with male-dominated APA movements.[6]

APA women have found partners in the work for justice in the feminism of the dominant culture, in communities of other women and men of color, and in our ethnic communities. We often find strength in the experiences of our ancestors, grandmothers, mothers, and sisters and their legacies of survival, despite our ambiguous feelings about their lives. We tend to value our responsibilities to our families despite the difficulties.[7]

Part of the intensity with which APAs assert our Americanness, defend our civil rights, and distinguish ourselves from Asian nationals comes from the history of the treatment of APAs, politically, socially, and culturally—a history that is intricately tied to U.S. foreign policy, beginning with expansion toward Hawaii and Asia in the nineteenth century. The Pacific was treated as the "American Lake."[8] The Japanese bombing of Pearl Harbor in World War II and the subsequent Communist revolution in China prompted many Japanese and Chinese Americans to dissociate from their countries of origin. Non-Asians in America often hold to the misconception that APAs are responsible for the actions of governments in our ancestral lands, treating us as foreigners. Even as it interned Japanese Americans during World War II, the U.S. government tried to use nisei as translators, without understanding that only 3 percent spoke the language of their immigrant parents with any fluency. In the recent case of a Chinese American who was murdered by a Taiwan mercenary, the media treated the case as an inter-Asian problem, rather than as the slaying of an American citizen by a foreign national.[9] Unlike Europeans, who can assimilate after they lose any trace of a foreign accent, APAs continue to be regarded as "exotic" foreigners. The dominant culture continues to think we are interchangeable with Asians whose cultures may be as unfamiliar to us as European ones are to many white Americans.

Racism picks relentlessly at one's soul, a corrosive and often subtle wearing away of one's confidence and sense of well-being. The structures of racial hegemony in the United States create a double bind. Even as APAs struggle to retain a sense of our own distinctive and individual identity in the face of racist stereotypes, we struggle also to defend the group to which we belong. For women, our subordination within our ethnic communities and in the dominant malestream society complicates the question of identity and justice.

Other Americans often view APAs through the lens of exoticized, colonialist constructions of race and gender, captured by the term "Oriental." "Oriental" is a gendered term: Asian men are seen as either sinister villains or as obsequious, asexual servants. Female stereotypes of "Suzy Wong" or "Geisha Girl" are associated with prostitution and exoticized sexuality. The entertainment media created images of the evil Dragon Lady, as well as "Lotus Blossoms," submissive, attentive, and compliant women who serve their dominating white colonial men, a stereotype seen most recently in the musical *Miss Saigon.*[10] The current rise in sex tourism to Asia[11] and the U.S. demand for mail-order brides is fed by these stereotypes.

The APA struggles to claim our legal rights and equal treatment, to attain economic security and professional success, and to move beyond the persistent reminders of racism have made the questions of identity and justice central to APA communities. In addition, the 1965 immigration act has resulted in two-thirds of APAs now being first-generation immigrants, adding great numbers to our earlier migrations from Asia and the Pacific. This demographic shift has contributed substantially to the question of APA identity, a question never easy to answer. The political consciousness of justice for this newer group of APAs was galvanized in the mid-1980s by the racist murder of Vincent Chin, whose confessed killers never went to jail.[12]

With the current large proportion of first-generation APAs, questions of identity and the struggle with marginality have reemerged with new urgency. This new group of APAs has presented more clearly the influences of Asian cultures on our American identities, influences that create generational, political, and gender tensions in our communities. The demographic complexities of new APAs have also exposed more clearly the limits of conceiving identity based on nationalism and borders. It does not behoove women to adhere to the politics of male-dominated governments in constructing our identities—of accepting the legitimacy of either the "American Lake" or androcentric definitions of Asian nationalism and culture. We must guard against being pawns in the politics of patriarchies.

DISSONANT DIFFERENCES

The majority of Asians who emigrate to the United States come as Christians.[13] Because of North Atlantic hegemony in the United States, Asian Americans who are Christians have greater political power in a society deeply permeated by Christian discourse, but that does not mean that all aspects of Asian culture have been removed from Asian American Christianity. APA Christian churches incorporate into their communities elements of Asian religious festivals, such as New Year's celebrations and teriyaki chicken dinners during Obon. Korean American, Ilse (first-generation) Christian worship, especially in sermons and prayers, sometimes has resonances of the intense, explosive, spirit-filled shaman rituals of Korea, quite unlike the quiet intensity of some Japanese American issei services.

APA cultural preservation and our new demographics since 1965 lead me again to reflect on the differences between Asian and Western thinking, theory, and behavior. Even as I conceive such a dichotomy, I am aware that what APAs think of as Asian may bear little resemblance to what someone from Asia may understand about being Asian. Asian cultural implants in America find their life in a context that changes them, and Asians in Asia, especially Christians, are not free of Westernization. In fact, Asians trained in traditional missionary Christian theologies often have a more negative view of traditional Asian religions than do APAs. On the other hand, many second- or third-generation APAs were taught our ideas about Asia by the white male gaze that dominates the field of Asian studies.[14] Hence, how we construct our differences from North Atlantic hegemony may reflect a malestream, exoticized view of Asia. In addition, of course, regions of Asia differ from one another radically, and parts of Asia have undergone centuries of North Atlantic influences. Because our experiences are regional and diverse, I will restrict the remainder of this chapter to what I know best, Americans from East Asia, with the caution that this discussion represents only a segment of East Asian Americans and with the caveat that Asian American studies have been criticized because of the hegemony of East Asian scholars and voices. East Asia refers to the shared cultural roots in Confucianism, Taoism, and Buddhism of Korea, Japan, Taiwan, Okinawa, and China. Distinct regional differences also exist within these countries, in addition to their shared aspects. My caveats are intended to acknowledge my limits and avoid conveying a proprietary sense that I can speak for others less familiar to me.

There are times when my ways of thinking and perceiving cannot be easily grasped in English or categorized in terms of the Western education I have received. These intuitive impulses make me uncomfortable with and suspicious of polarization and dualism. The impulses come from outside my Western education, from an earlier linguistic grammar and structuring of reality. And one primary religious difference between much of East Asia and the United States lies in the tension between the unifying visions of nondualistic religions, such as Buddhism, and the dualistic dichotomies of monotheistic religions, such as Christianity. I was formed for five-and-a-half years within the first framework and educated thoroughly in the second.

The Western logic of either/or leads to polarizations in Christianity between good and evil, true and false, black and white, insider and outsider, and margin and center.[15] Western androcentric ideas of self value being uncompromised by relationships to the world. The male self is supposed to stand on principle and give priority to ideology through loyalty to the good side of the either/or divide.[16] This autonomous self parallels a theology that asserts an absolute being called God, who alone is good. Western monotheism provides categories of ultimacy that are primarily ethical, based on the either/or choices of moral dualisms. The classical Western absolute, based in an ontology of essentialism, is unambiguous, transcendent, and perfect, controlling all things, making distinctions between good and evil.

Rationality in secular Western culture has taken on similar attributes.[17] Priority is given to dispassionate knowledge and its verbal reification, rather than to engaged knowing in its many fluid, embodied manifestations.[18] Even postmodern, deconstructionist analyses tend to focus on forms of discourse and verbal constructions of hegemony. These emphases create dissonant differences between my own sense of Asian realities and Western religions.

INTERSTITIAL INTEGRITY

> Crisscrossing more than one occupied territory at a time, she remains perforce inappropriate/d—both inside and outside her own social positionings. . . . The interstice between the visual and the tactile is perhaps the (nothing)-spiritual conveyed above in the fragrance of mist—at once within and beyond the sense of smell. Within and beyond tangible visibility. A trajectory across variable praxes of difference, her (un)location is necessarily the shifting and contextual interval between arrested boundaries.[19]

The traditional Eurocentric and androcentric categories of theology are inadequate to capture the cross-cultural nuances and multidimensional intuitions that constitute Asian American religions. In addition, the nationalistic/arrested boundaries drawn by the politics of wars and race are too confining to make sense of the transpacific, multicultural experiences of APAs.

I propose interstitial integrity as an alternative category of theological anthropology. In shifting to interstitiality, I am pushing the social positioning of Asian Americans inside and outside theological uses of liminality by Fumitaka Matsuoka and marginality by Jung Young Lee. Neither liminality nor marginality adequately conveys the complexities of the spiritual journeys of APA women.[20] Both terms conceive APA identity in its relationship to the hegemony of the dominant culture. While such hegemony is a facet of our lives, it is not the whole of them. Interstitial integrity opens ways of speaking about the construction of complex cross-cultural identities that include subordination, but destabilize and contest it. Interstitiality speaks of the theological contributions of APAs, drawing from our fluid, multilayered, transversal experiences.

East Asian cultural roots are embedded in nondualistic metaphysics and religions. Nondualism allows for fluidity, flexibility, and multiplicity. The search for balance and harmony in the midst of multiplicity places ultimacy in aesthetic categories. The sacred is embedded in life's ambiguities, and the human task is to discern its power, for good and ill. Human goodness is found in the capacity to be wise and to negotiate relationships that maintain life and harmony. This more fluid sensibility does not lead to a total moral relativism, even as it acknowledges the inevitability of some forms of tragedy and evil. The most effective way of confronting evil, however, is not to remove oneself from knowledge of it. Cries of anguish against injustice and pain emerge also in Asian societies, and moral distinctions are made between good and evil. Nonetheless, the ontological status of these distinctions and strategies for obtaining justice and for creating moral societies differ from Western essentialist models, especially Christian models, which tend to equate innocence of evil and martyrdom with moral virtue.[21]

The sense of reality, based in APA sensibilities, is often grounded in paradoxical, both/and thinking. Both/and thinking understands that while at a particular, bordered moment A may not equal B, nonetheless, A can become B. And sometimes A *is* B. Margins and centers shift constantly, even when they seem fixed. Reality is constructed as fluid, transitional, and impermanent. This both/and thinking characterizes many APA women's struggles to live a transcultural, marginalized existence. But there is not one margin. As Trinh T. Minh-Ha puts it:

> In the colonial periphery (as in elsewhere), we are often them as well. Colored skins, white masks; colored masks, white skins. Reversal strategies have reigned for some time. *They* accept the margins; so do *we*. . . . The margins, our sites of survival, become our fighting grounds and their site for pilgrimage. . . . Without a certain work of displacement, again, the margins can easily recomfort the center in its goodwill and liberalism; strategies of reversal thereby meet with their own limits. . . . Marginal by imposition, by choice, by necessity. The struggle is always multiple and transversal—specific but not confined to one side of any border war.[22]

Out of Asian cultural roots, with a more fluid sense of reality, APAs find ourselves in between, in transition, and invisible. Our hybrid, transversal perceptions, based in a sense of the impermanence of reality, are viewed as a state of insecurity in a culture that values clarity and objective, rational truth. Matsuoka calls this "holy insecurity." He argues that holy insecurity drives the concern in APA communities for empathy for the disinherited, for dignity for the hopelessly uncredentialed, and for rights for the disfranchised. Holy insecurity rests partly in a different sense of selfhood than the Western autonomous individual has. Matsuoka found in APA religious communities an emphasis on the "intrinsically social and collective character of selfhood and the irreplaceable character of community for the well-being of Asian-American Christians."[23]

In Asian American communities there is a great emphasis on affecting human behavior by example. Praxis, storytelling, and experience take priority—all indirect methods of influencing human behavior. Direct confrontation with a person can be regarded as bad form (too egotistical) and a demonstration of one's lack both of social skills and of subtle intelligence.[24] Human beings are understood to prefer humane forms of behavior when given a fair choice. Ethical behavior is created far more by influence, by good models of virtue that are deeply internalized by mimesis, than by personal adherence to an ideology or to sound theory. Human goodness is created by social forces and grounded in community.

The emphasis on community can, however, have negative consequences for APA women and gays and lesbians, especially when our concerns for justice have been seen as creating undue conflict. Sexism and homophobia occur in APA communities and marginalize women, especially lesbians. Women experience a pressure not to break ranks and report crimes against them because they believe that they bring on their own afflictions, that they are victims of fate, or that they will bring shame on themselves and their families.[25] The pressures are strong to keep domestic violence, sexual abuse, and poverty hidden. Some APA women experience the ethnic communities of their parents as a confinement in traditional Asian heterosexist customs, for example in arranged marriage.[26] Assimilation into the dominant culture has been seen as a source both of alienation from Asian identity and of freedom from the constraints of traditional culture. However, North Atlantic feminist theories and methods have not been entirely embraced by APA women, partly because the racism, forms of discourse, and polemics in feminism alienate us from feminist communities, even when we find aspects of the theories helpful.[27] Where women connect across racial lines in American society, the connecting is achieved by the muting and marginalization of subordinated cultures.

To understand our experiences in several cultures at one time, APA women have been struggling with the fluid, complex demands of holy insecurity—to know what it means to construct a sense of selfhood. Our liminality is an experience of fluid, multiple selves. As Wendy Ho describes it,

> Mother, as well as daughter, develop multiple voices to encode or signify in language as a way of surviving in a racist, sexist world. . . . The daughter, as her mother before, and each in her own challenge and degree, attempts to disrupt and subvert the discourses which confine their potential. Both their stories and voices generate an interactive and multiple sense of their similarities and differences as mothers/daughters, of their possible complicity in traditional/dominant power configurations and strategies of appeasement, and of their subversive signifying strategies for survival. . . . There is no unified, centered tradition in her communities in America that allows [Maxine Hong Kingston] as a Chinese American woman to speak easily and forthrightly in her own person. The self is often fragmented, split and invisible to the self and is defined indirectly by a conflicting web of interpersonal relations and roles.[28]

There are many worlds in which APA women are subordinated and oppressed. We struggle to cope with conflicting and often fluctuating worlds. Our various worlds, both problematic and life-giving, pull in many different directions, but each has a social, intellectual, and spiritual structure that must be understood—and each is both criticized and appreciated. We shift constantly both inside and outside our own social positionings, in the interstices, "in the wilderness that we transverse."[29]

Strategies for survival and prosperity are valued in many Asian and APA societies because human life, despite its many sufferings, is understood to have intrinsic value. It is a great honor to be born human.[30] Survival depends on learning which spiritual powers and people require attention, at which times, under which conditions. Behavior is determined by the accurate discernment of one's relationships and the demands they make in relation to one's values and feelings. The dead never completely have, but remain, remembered under conditions related to how they lived. The older one gets, the more one has verification for having learned how to negotiate living among powerful forces so that one lives skillfully and well. Moral categories serve a greater aesthetic good, summarized as an adequate, dialectical harmony within human relationships and the larger natural world. In the interstices between ethics and beauty, between Asia and North America, I find insights into how better to complicate theology, to make it more interstitial, to open categories more adequate to APA women's spiritual sensibilities. In the spaces between oppression and liberation, sin and salvation, brokenness and wholeness, I find interstitial integrity.

Interstitial life often feels like a process of being torn among several different worlds that refuse to get along. It can, in its transcendence, however, feel as if one is following the rhythms of a migrating bird. The bird cannot rest long in one place, but it finds nourishment and strength to fly on. This refusal to rest in one place, to reject a narrowing of who we are by either/or decisions, or to be placed always on the periphery, is interstitial integrity. Interstitial refers to the places in between, which are real places, like the strong connective tissue between organs in the body that link the parts. This interstitiality is a form of integrity, not a state of being impaired or lesser than one whose identity is monocultural, as if such a thing ever really existed anymore except by self-deception. Integrity has to do with moments of entireness, of having no part taken away or wanting. Integrity is closely related to integration, to acts of connecting many disparate things by holding them together. Integr(ity)ation is ongoing renewal and restoration, learning how to live in the tensions of holding together all the complex parts of who we are.

Interstitial integrity is how many APAs, women and men, cope with marginality, the experience of feeling peripheral to the dominant, malestream culture. But interstitial integrity is more. Asian Pacific American life is not simply a reaction to oppression or a construction of racism and sexism. Interstitial integrity is the challenge that confronts anyone struggling to live amid transcultural forces who refuses to deny one part of her/his life and ancestry while struggling to maintain a sense of meaning and worth in life. It is, in contrast, the monumental task of making meaning out of multiple worlds by refusing to disconnect from any of them, while not pledging allegiance to a singular one. It allows space for the multiple social locations of identity in a multicultural context. "Instead of the self ever being fully solid, unified, or defined, it becomes a more shifting, fluid, decentralized notion of selfhood without hard, finite boundaries."[31] Interstitiality is not an integrity of yes or no despite the context, not a sense of honor that guards the self from relational influence that might corrupt its purity. This more narrow understanding of integrity implies that a morally superior state of being is to be uninfluenced and unchanged by relationships.[32]

Asian Pacific Americans participate in a variety of worlds, in some more central, in others more peripheral, sometimes both central and peripheral. This multi-sphered life allows for a transcendence that is an immanental, embodied form of transcendence. This transcendence involves both participation in a world and the bringing of critical judgment from a consciousness of other worlds one knows. Korean Americans refer to *nun chi*, literally "eye-measure," the capacity to observe, assess, and make judgments based on remaining unsubsumed by a particular context.[33] The awareness of living in multiple worlds and the self-possession that maintains a perspective of concern and compassion in every context are the places of interstitiality found in transcendence, maintained by the consistencies of memory and reflection on values and context.

In each of our various worlds, APA women describe feeling slightly ill at ease, not completely comfortable or at home, because we import the knowledge we gain from our other worlds, which makes us a little outside each one. For example, Maxine Hong Kingston finds immanental transcendence in her memoirs, *The Woman Warrior*.[34] She learns of the misogyny and sexism of Chinese culture as told her by her mother, Brave Orchid. But Brave Orchid also has her most powerful, confident moments in China as a successful healer, and her re-creation of Chinese myths of strong women, as well as stories of victimized women, give her daughter the same ambiguous power to talk-story. Kingston struggles to live in the world of ghosts, which is what her mother calls the American non-Chinese world. The ghosts confuse and silence her as she struggles to understand her mother's duplicity, which is "a way of life that protects the powerless, that ensures survival when one feels threatened or has something to hide from the powerful—whether we are speaking of jealous ghosts or a racist/sexist community or country."[35]

In the world of ghosts Kingston eventually finds her power to talk-story, to play on a barbarian reed pipe. Going home to her mother makes her sick with all the conflicts of her life, and still home is a source of who she is, a place she feels grounded to a power she needs, even as she transforms it. There is no unambiguous, singular place to be, only the increasing skill in learning to talk and to know herself through all her relationships.

Survival and healing come, as they do for Kingston, in life-giving moments lived in the interstices. Immanental transcendence, *nun chi*, requires the critical analysis of social/political/economic systems, which can become a life-saving spiritual act. Immanental transcendence is not otherworldly, not dissociated from embodiment, but is both being in and not being in a situation that allows us to awaken to both our victimization by and our participation in life-destroying systems.

Interstitial integrity allows us to evaluate our behavior and exercise moral discrimination and self-evaluation. But because we live in the interstices, we must also engage in solidarity with others who also live in the interstices. The relational selfhood and importance of community and family for Asian American women points to the social reality that no insight can be remembered and light the way toward new understanding without being told in a community, and no insight can be told without the listening that calls it forth. We find our impetus for social change or justice within political movements. We are women and human beings because we live in relationships, in all their ambiguity. We never outgrow our need to know ourselves in the mirror of other living beings, who open windows on larger worlds. This relational life, in all its difficulty, is the inescapable form of our existence. It is life in interstitial integrity.

In interstitial living, we turn to many cultural resources for our spiritual resources, resources that come from communities in which we participate. One such resource, which is the means by which we become attuned to spiritual presence, is silence.

When Silence Speaks

> There is silence that cannot speak. There is silence that will not speak. Beneath the grass the speaking dreams and beneath the dreams is a sensate sea. The speech that frees comes forth from that amniotic deep. To attend its voice, I can hear it say, is to embrace its absence, but I fail the task. The word is stone.[36]

Joy Kogawa's novel *Obasan* begins with this meditation on silence, which suggests the complexity of silence: its freezing of memory in inaccessible mystery, its signal of a stubborn refusal to speak, its indication of truth suppressed by fear, and its revelatory power beyond words.[37] Silence can hide realities we want to keep private, pain we are not ready to expose, or shame we cannot bear to bring to light.

In the American context of active protest against oppression, silence can mean acquiescence, withdrawal, and absence. I remember moments in my childhood, when my ears and heart burned at the sound of "Jap" and "Chink" words; I told no one and allowed the burning to be buried deeply. The silence with which many Japanese Americans endured the humiliation of the internment camps is often seen in this negative way, just as Maxine Hong Kingston experiences her mother's silence and half-disclosures about her misbehaving female Chinese ancestors as signs of shame and dishonor.

Mitsuye Yamada, a Japanese American poet who was interned in World War II in the desert, describes the anguish and anger of that injustice and her silence about it. In "Thirty Years Under," Yamada describes the three decades she kept her humiliation and wounds, "in a cast iron box/sealed it/labeled it/do not open . . . ever."[38] Sansei poet Janice Mirikitani writes searing indictments of this silence of absence and acquiescence to injustice: "The strongest prisons are built with walls of silence."[39] Mirikitani calls for the shattering of silence. Outspoken outrage at injustice against women, people in poverty, and people of color dominates Mirikitani's work, where silence signals resignation to oppression. But even such silence may be an active strategy, a deliberate refusal to speak in order to protect one's children, as Yamada admits to her daughter when she explains why she chose to shield them from exposure to racism and from the horrors of internment.[40]

The spiritual power of silence lies in its capacity to nurture mystery and presence, the power of the semiotic. When Yamada finally tells her daughter about the internment and her reasons for silence, the power of their emotional connecting goes deeper than words and lodges in tears and an embrace.[41] Silence as presence creates spaces squeezed out by words. Sitting in silence with oneself or with another nurtures complex emotions and experiences known only in the silent knowing of self and other.

I remember the power of silence from my early childhood in Japan. This Japanese linguistic and social structure shaped me for the first five-and-a-half years of my life and informs what I mean when I talk about relational human existence. I do not mean the volitional, emotional personal relationships of equality and mutuality sometimes idealized in feminist theologies, but an inescapable structure of human life that can produce serious forms of brokenness and life. Patriarchy and sexism can exist in relational understandings of the world. Relationality is not an answer to oppression, but a nondualistic way of understanding reality that helps us acknowledge the impact of our relationships at the core of our lives, for good and ill. Injustice, pain, and suffering are not the opposite of connection, but are manifestations of it. And without our relationships, the brokenness of oppression cannot be healed.

The healing of relationships can be known in silence. Silence has both a quiescent, reflective value based on attunement to the other and an active value in communicating oneself nonverbally. Silence is not always the absence of communication, but can be a deeper interrelational connecting. Silence allows many things to coexist without eliminating each other; it makes space for emotional complexity and ambiguity. In the West, where a more emphatic self-assertion is valued, silence is seen as overwhelmingly negative, as cowardice or passivity. Silence makes one invisible, even when one is attempting to communicate through it.

Silence has always lain at the root of my own spirituality and is the thing I find most often missing in Protestant worship. My sense of interstitiality, however, involves being socialized not only to Japanese silence, but also to Western words. And sometimes my own silences come from feeling centered and clear, while at other times I am silent because I am silenced by the disjuncture between my intuitive awareness and my words or by outside pressures that make me afraid. Discerning which silence is at work is a constant process of watching and deciding. This complex orientation toward silence is also part of the APA experience, as Matsuoka notes.[42]

In 1988, Yamada published new poems of connection, resistance, and healing. She describes her internment camp experience of the desert as a time when "I spent 547 sulking days. I watched the most beautiful sunsets in the world and saw nothing."[43] In a place where everything was done in silence, Yamada says, she was too young to hear silence then. She spent years hating the desert as a reminder of her pain, until a friend who loved the desert taught her to see it anew. In learning to love what she could not see before and in learning to connect to the desert's wild beauty, she was drawn to the memory of the Chinese men who built the Western railroad, buried in the sand in shallow graves, "the genetic code of Asian ancestral ties."[44]

Yamada writes of resistance, of the strengths and ambiguities of her family's legacy of women. In the final section on connecting, Yamada writes of laying her aging woman body spread-eagled on the ground, reaching toward the four points of a future in which "my home town this earth"[45] will be a place of life, like the desert she once could not see. In this collection of poems, Yamada describes herself as searching for her cultural heritage, which she finds in all the complex parts of a life stitched together by her poignant, compassionate caring and hoping. Her vision is one of attunement to the interstices, where connections are made. Remembrance and connecting are the roots of survival and healing. Hers is an interstitial silence that leads, in moments of ripeness, to poetic words.

Being with others in the silent process of healing is neither easy nor for the fainthearted, but one finds courage and hope. Silent presence opens the heart to compassion and life to grace. As Yamada discovers, life putters and sputters on, and moments of resistance to oppression and healing come in the midst of the puttering and sputtering. Silence that creates prisons must be shattered. The silence of listening must be respected. The restorative silence of the natural world and tacit, complex, unspoken holding of others in an embrace of care are received as grace. To heal is to speak and work against injustice *and* to listen to silence. The work of spiritual healing is grounded, finally, both in the solidarity of silence and in the words and actions that convey our vision of justice and wholeness.

Another recurring dream stole into my sleep during my childhood, around the same time as the dream in which I lost my mother. In the dream, I stood at the top of the stairs outside the door of our second-floor apartment in Ft. Riley, Kansas. I leaned headfirst toward the door at the bottom of the stairs, and as my weight shifted I drifted over the stairs and out the door. Like a bird, my body would glide over the ground at the level of the treetops outside. The sky was always a sunlit blue and the breeze a warm spring gust. I was never lost or frightened. I knew how to go home and, at the end, I swooped up the stairs in the air and landed my feet at the top before going inside. By flying around I saw a great deal and took delight in what I saw, but I was a little above, watching in my delight and a little sad at being alone. I always awakened with a poignant sense of freedom and joy. Perhaps I dreamt of the promise of interstitial integrity.

NOTES

1. Salman Rushdie, *Imaginary Homelands: Essays and Criticism 1981–1991* (New York: Viking Penguin, 1991).
2. Young Mi Pak, "Pan-Pacific Identity? A Skeptical Asian American Response," *Journal of Women and Religion* 13 (1995):15–24.
3. Gary Okihiro, "Is Yellow Black or White?" *Margins and Mainstreams: Asian Americans in History and Culture* (Seattle: University of Washington Press, 1994).
4. Ronald Takaki, *Strangers from a Different Shore: A History of Asian Americans* (New York: Penguin Books, 1989).

5. William Wei, *The Asian American Movement* (Philadelphia: Temple University Press, 1993), 11–43.

6. Ibid.; and Judy Chu, "Social and Economic Profile of Asian Pacific American Women: Los Angeles County," in *Reflections on Shattered Windows: Promises and Prospects for Asian American Studies*, ed. Gary Y. Okihiro, Shirley Hune, Arthur A. Hansen, and John M. Liu (Seattle: Washington University Press, 1988).

7. Asian Women United of California, *Making Waves: An Anthology of Writings by and about Asian American Women* (Boston: Beacon Press, 1989).

8. Pak, "Pan-Pacific Identity."

9. Tomoji Ishi, "Contemporary Anti-Asian Activities: A Global Perspective," in *Asian Americans: Comparative and Global Perspectives*, ed. Shirley Hune, Hyung chan Kim, Stephen S. Fugita, and Amy Ling (Pullman: Washington State University Press, 1991).

10. See the documentary film *Slaying the Dragon*, by Deborah Gee, available from National Asian American Telecommunications Association, 346 Ninth St., 2d floor, San Francisco, CA 94103.

11. Rita Nakashima Brock and Susan Thistlethwaite, *Casting Stones: Prostitution and Liberation in Asia and the United States* (Minneapolis: Fortress Press, 1996).

12. Wei, *The Asian American Movement*, 193–96.

13. Barry A. Kosmin and Seymour P. Lachman, *One Nation under God: Religion in Contemporary American Society* (New York: Harmony Books, 1993); 147–54.

14. Rudy Busto, "Framing Asian American Religions: Orientalism, Asiacentrism, and the Sound of One Hand Clapping," unpublished paper delivered at the 1996 Association of Asian American Studies meeting; and Wong and Manvi, "Asiacentrism and Asian American Studies," *Thinking Theory in Asian American Studies*, ed. Michael Omi and Dana Takagi, *Amerasian Journal* 21, 1–2 (1995): 137–47.

15. Nel Noddings, *Women and Evil* (Berkeley: University of California Press, 1989).

16. Catherine Keller, *From a Broken Web: Separation, Sexism, and Self* (Boston: Beacon Press, 1986); and Rosemary Radford Ruether, *Sexism and God-Talk: Toward a Feminist Theology* (Boston: Beacon Press, 1983).

17. James Hillman, *Re-Visioning Psychology* (New York: Harper & Row, 1975).

18. Trinh T. Minh-Ha, *When the Moon Waxes Red: Representation, Gender, and Cultural Politics* (New York: Routledge & Kegan Paul, 1991).

19. Ibid., 4.

20. Fumitaka Matsuoka, *Out of Silence: Emerging Themes in Asian American Churches* (Cleveland: Pilgrim Press, 1995); and Jung Young Lee, *Marginality* (Minneapolis: Fortress Press, 1995).

21. Noddings, *Women and Evil*.

22. Minh-Ha, *When the Moon Waxes Red*, 16–17.

23. Matsuoka, *Out of Silence*, 64.

24. Julia Matsui-Estrella, "From Hawaii to Berkeley: Tracing Roots in Asian American Leadership," *Journal of Women and Religion* 13 (1995):3–4.

25. Laura Uba, "Barriers to the Use of Mental Health Services," in *Asian Americans: Personality Patterns, Identity, and Mental Health* (New York: Guildford Press, 1994), 198–213.

26. Dana Y. Takagi, "Personality and History: Hostile Nisei Women," in *Reflections on Shattered Windows*.

27. Asian Women United of California, *Making Waves*; Rita Nakashima Brock and Naomi Southard, "The Other Half of the Basket: Asian American Women and the Search for

a Theological Home," *Journal of Feminist Studies in Religion*, vol. 3, no. 2: 135–49; and Shirley Geok-lin Lim, "Asian American Daughters Rewriting Asian Maternal Texts," in *Asian Americans: Comparative and Global Perspectives*, 239–48.

28. Wendy Ho, "Mother/Daughter Writing and the Politics of Race and Sex in Maxine Hong Kingston's *The Woman Warrior*," *Asian Americans: Comparative and Global Perspectives*, 225–38.
29. Ibid., 234.
30. Kwok Pui Lan, lecture, November 5, 1993, at the conference "Reimagining: A Mid-Decade Celebration of the World Council of Churches Ecumenical Decade of Churches in Solidarity with Women," available on tape from the Reimagining Community, 122 W. Franklin Ave., Minneapolis, MN 55403.
31. Ho, "Mother/Daughter Writing," 234.
32. Keller, *From a Broken Web*.
33. Information from Mary Paik, McCormick Theological Seminary, at a meeting of Asian American theologians, Pojara Dunes, Calif., April 29, 1995.
34. Maxine Hong Kingston, *The Woman Warrior: Memoirs of a Girlhood among Ghosts* (New York: Alfred A. Knopf, 1976).
35. Ho, "Mother/Daughter Writing," 237.
36. Joy Kogawa, *Obasan* (Boston: Godine Press, 1981); first page.
37. Lim, "Asian American Daughters."
38. Mitsuye Yamada, *Camp Notes* (San Lorenzo, Calif.: Shameless Hussy Press, 1976).
39. Janice Mirikitani, *Shedding Silence* (Berkeley, Calif.: Celestial Arts Press, 1987), 5.
40. Yamada's conversation with her daughter in the film, *Mitsuye and Nellie: Asian American Poets*, written by Allie Light (Light-Saraf Films, 246 Arbor St., San Francisco, CA 94131).
41. *Mitsuye and Nellie*.
42. Matsuoka, *Out of Silence*.
43. Mitsuye Yamada, *Desert Run: Poems and Stories* (Latham, N.Y.: Kitchen Table: Women of Color Press, 1988), 2.
44. Ibid., 11.
45. Ibid., 84.

14

BLACK THEOLOGY
IN AMERICAN RELIGION

JAMES H. CONE

More than ninety years ago W. E. B. Du Bois wrote in *The Souls of Black Folk* his classic statement of the paradox of black life in America.

> It is a peculiar sensation, this double-consciousness, this sense of always looking at one's self through the eyes of others, of measuring one's soul by the tape of a world that looks on in amused contempt and pity. One ever feels his twoness,—an American, a Negro; two souls, two thoughts, two unreconciled strivings, two warring ideals in one dark body, whose dogged strength alone keeps it from being torn asunder.[1]

The "two warring ideals" that Du Bois described in 1903 have been at the center of black religious thought from its origin to the present day. They are found in the heated debates about "integration" and "nationalism" and in the attempt to name the community—beginning with the word "African" and using at different times such terms as "colored," "Negro," "Afro-American," "black," and "African American."

In considering black religious thought, let us give clearer names to the "two warring ideals"—clearer, that is, from the point of view of religion. I shall call them "African" and "Christian." Black religious thought is not identical with the Christian theology of white Americans. Nor is it identical with traditional African beliefs, past or present. It is both—but reinterpreted for and adapted to the life-situation of black people's struggle for justice in a nation whose social, political, and economic structures are dominated by a white racist ideology. It was the "African" side of black religion that helped African Americans to see beyond the white distortions of the gospel and to discover its true meaning as God's liberation of the oppressed from bondage. It was the "Christian" element in black religion that helped African Americans to reorient their African past so that it would become useful in the struggle to survive with dignity in a society that they did not make.

Although the African and Christian elements have been found throughout the history of black religious thought, the Christian part gradually became dominant. The African element, though less visible, continued, however, to play an important role in defining the core of black religion, thus preventing it from becoming merely an imitation of Protestant or Catholic theologies in the West.

Of course, there are many similarities between black religious thought and white Protestant and Catholic reflections on the Christian tradition. But the dissimilarities between them are perhaps more important than the similarities. The similarities are found at the point of a common Christian identity, and the dissimilarities can best be understood in light of the differences between African and European cultures in the New World. While whites used their cultural perspective to dominate others, blacks used theirs to affirm their dignity and to empower themselves to struggle for justice. The major reason for the differences between black and white reflections on God is found at the point of the great differences in life. As white theology is largely defined by its response to modern and postmodern societies of Europe and America, usually ignoring the contradictions of slavery and oppression in black life, black religious thought is the thinking of slaves and of marginalized blacks whose understanding of God was shaped by the contradictions that white theologians ignored and regarded as unworthy of serious theological reflection. In this chapter, I will analyze black religious thought in the light of Du Bois's "warring ideals," which emerged out of the struggle for justice—beginning with its origin in slavery and concentrating mainly on its twentieth-century development in the civil rights and black power movements, culminating with the rise of black theology.

ROOTS OF BLACK
RELIGIOUS THOUGHT: SLAVERY

The tension between the "African" and "Christian" elements acted to reorder traditional theological themes in black religion and to give them different substance when compared to other theologies in Europe and America. Five themes in particular defined the character of black religious thought during slavery and in its subsequent development: justice, liberation, hope, love, and suffering.

No theme has been more prominent throughout the history of black religious thought than the justice of God. African Americans have always believed in the living presence of the God who establishes the right by punishing the wicked and liberating their victim from oppression. Everyone will be rewarded and punished according to their deeds, and no one—absolutely no one—can escape the judgment of God, who alone is the sovereign of the universe. Evildoers may get by for a time, and good people may suffer unjustly under oppression, but "sooner or later, . . . we reap what we sow."[2]

The "sooner" referred to contemporary historically observable events: punishment of the oppressors and liberation of the oppressed. The "later" referred to the divine establishment of justice in the "next world," where God "gwineter rain down fire" on the wicked and where the liberated righteous will "walk in Jerusalem just like John." In the religion of African slaves, God's justice was identical with the punishment of the oppressors, and divine liberation was synonymous with the deliverance of the oppressed from the bondage of slavery—if not "now" then in the "not yet." Because whites continued to prosper materially as they increased their victimization of African Americans, black religious thought spoke more often of the "later" than the "sooner."[3]

The themes of justice and liberation are closely related to the idea of hope. The God who establishes the right and puts down the wrong is the sole basis of the hope that the suffering of the victims will be eliminated. Although African slaves used the term "heaven" to describe their experience of hope, its primary meaning for them must not be reduced to the "pie in the sky," otherworldly affirmation that often characterized white evangelical Protestantism. The idea of heaven was the means by which slaves affirmed their humanity in a world that did not recognize them as human beings.[4] It was their way of saying that they were made for freedom and not slavery.

Black slaves' hope was based on their faith in God's promise to "protect the needy" and to "defend the poor." Just as God delivered the Hebrew children from Egyptian bondage and raised Jesus from the dead, so God will also deliver African slaves from American slavery and "in due time" will bestow upon them the gift of eternal life. That was why they sang: "Soon-a will be done-a with the troubles of the world."

Black slaves' faith in the coming justice of God was the chief reason why they could hold themselves together in servitude and sometimes fight back, even though the odds were against them.

The ideas of justice, liberation, and hope should be seen in relation to the important theme of love. Theologically, God's love is prior to the other themes. But in order to separate black reflections on love from a similar theme in white theology, it is important to emphasize that love in black religious thought is usually linked with God's justice, liberation, and hope. God's love is made known through divine righteousness, liberating the poor for a new future.

God's creation of all persons in the divine image bestows sacredness on human beings and thus makes them the children of God. To violate any person's dignity is to transgress "God's great law of love."[5] We must love the neighbor because God has first loved us. And because slavery and racism are blatant denials of the dignity of the human person, God's justice means that "He will call the oppressors to account."[6]

Despite the strength of black faith, belief in God's coming justice and liberation was not easy for African slaves and their descendants. Their suffering created the most serious challenge to their faith. If God is good, why did God permit millions of blacks to be stolen from Africa and enslaved in a strange land? No black person has been able to escape the existential agony of that question.

In their attempt to resolve the theological dilemma that slavery and racism created, African Americans turned to two texts—Exodus and Psalm 68:31.[7] They derived from the Exodus text the belief that God is the liberator of the oppressed. They interpreted Psalm 68:31 as an obscure reference to God's promise to redeem Africa: "Princes shall come out of Egypt, and Ethiopia shall soon stretch forth her hands unto God." Despite African American reflections on these texts, the contradictions remained between oppression and their faith.

BLACK RELIGIOUS THOUGHT,
THE CIVIL RIGHTS MOVEMENT, AND MARTIN LUTHER KING JR.

The withdrawal of the black church from politics and its alliance with the accommodation philosophy of Booker T. Washington created the conditions that gave rise to the civil rights movement: the National Association for the Advancement of Colored People (NAACP) in 1909, the National Urban League (NUL) in 1911, and the Congress for Racial Equality (CORE) in 1942. These national organizations, and similar local and regional groups in many parts of the United States, took up the cause of justice and equality of blacks in the society. They were strongly influenced by ideas and persons in the churches. Civil rights organizations not only internalized the ideas about justice, liberation, hope, love, and suffering that had been preached in the churches, they also used church property to convene their meetings and usually made appeals for support at church conferences. The close relations between the NAACP and the black churches have led some to say that "the black church is the NAACP on its knees."

Due to the deradicalization of the black church, progressive black ministers found it difficult to remain involved in the internal affairs of their denominations. Baptist ministers, because of the autonomy of their local congregations, found it easier than the Methodists did to remain pastors while also being deeply involved in the struggle for black equality in the society. Prominent examples included Adam Clayton Powell, Sr. and Jr., father and son pastors of Abyssinian Baptist Church in New York. Adam Jr. made his entrance on the public stage by leading a four-year nonviolent direct-action campaign, securing some ten thousand jobs for Harlem blacks. In 1944 he was elected to Congress.

Adam Clayton Powell Jr. embraced that part of the black religious tradition that refused to separate the Christian gospel from the struggle for justice in society. In his influential *Marching Blacks*, he accused the white churches of turning Christianity into "churchianity," thereby distorting the essential message of the gospel, which is "equality" and "brotherhood."

> The great loving heart of God has been embalmed and laid coolly away
> in the tombs we call churches. Christ of the Manger, the carpenter's
> bench, and the borrowed tomb has once again been crucified in stained-
> glass windows.[8]

Other influential thinkers of this period included Howard Thurman and Benjamin E. Mays. Howard Thurman wrote twenty-two books and lectured at more than five hundred institutions. He also served as dean of Rankin Chapel and professor of theology at Howard University; as dean of Marsh Chapel and minister-at-large of Boston University; and as minister and cofounder of the interdenominational Fellowship Church of San Francisco. His writings and preaching influences many, and in 1953 *Life* magazine cited him as one of the twelve "great preachers" of this century. Unlike most black ministers concerned about racial justice, liberation, love, suffering, and hope, Thurman did not become a political activist; he took the "inward journey" (the title of one of his books), focusing on a "spiritual quest" for liberation beyond race and ethnic origin. He was able to develop this universalist perspective without ignoring the urgency of the political issues involved in the black struggle for justice.[9]

Benjamin E. Mays, ecumenist and longtime president of Morehouse College, also made an important contribution to black religious thought through his writings and addresses on the black church and racism in America. He chaired the National Conference on Religion and Race in 1963.[10] Mays was an example of a black religious thinker who found the black church too limiting as a context for confronting the great problems of justice, liberation, love, hope, and suffering. Like Thurman and Powell, Mays regarded racism as anti-Christian, an evil that must be eliminated from the churches and the society.

Both Mays and Thurman influenced Martin Luther King Jr. the most influential religious thinker and activist in American history. The fact that many white theologians, and some black ones too, can write about American religion and theology with no reference to him reveals both the persistence of racism in the academy and the tendency to limit theology narrowly to the academic discourse of seminary and university professors.

Much has been written about the influence of King's graduate education on his thinking and practice, especially the writings of George Davis, Henry David Thoreau, Mahatma Gandhi, Edgar S. Brightman, Harold DeWolf, G. W. F. Hegel, Walter Rauschenbusch, Paul Tillich, and Reinhold Niebuhr.[11] Of course, these religious and philosophical thinkers influenced him greatly, but it is a mistake to use them as the primary basis for an interpretation of his life and thought. King was a product of the black church tradition: its faith determined the essence of his theology.[12] He used the intellectual tools of highly recognized thinkers to explain what he believed to the white public and also to express the universal character of the gospel. But he did not arrive at his convictions about God by reading white theologians. On the contrary, he derived his religious beliefs from his acceptance of black faith and his application of it to the civil rights struggle.

In moments of crisis, King turned to the God of black faith. From the beginning of his role as the leader of the Montgomery, Alabama, bus boycott to his tragic death in Memphis, King was a public embodiment of the central ideas of black religious thought. The heart of his beliefs revolved around the ideas of love, justice, liberation, hope, and redemptive suffering. The meaning of each is mutually dependent on the others. Though love may be appropriately placed at the center of his thought, he interpreted it in the light of justice for the poor, liberation for all, and the certain hope that God has not left this world in the hands of evil men.

King often used the writings of Tillich, Niebuhr, and other white thinkers to express his own ideas about the interrelations of love and justice. But it was his internalization of their meaning in the black church tradition that helped him to see that "unmerited suffering is redemptive." While the fighters for justice must be prepared to suffer in the struggle for liberation, they must never inflict suffering on others. That was why King described nonviolence as "the Christian way in human relations" and "the only road to freedom."[13]

To understand King's thinking, it is necessary to understand him in the context of his own religious heritage. His self-description is revealing:

> I am many things to many people; Civil Rights leader, agitator, trouble-maker and orator, but in the quietness of my heart, I am fundamentally a clergyman, a Baptist preacher. This is my being and my heritage for I am also the son of a Baptist preacher, the grandson of a Baptist preacher and the great-grandson of a Baptist preacher. The Church is my life and I have given my life to the Church.[14]

The decisive impact of the black church heritage on King can be seen in his ideas about justice, liberation, love, hope, and suffering. King took the democratic tradition of freedom and combined it with the biblical tradition of justice and liberation as found in the exodus and the prophets. Then he integrated both traditions with the New Testament idea of love and suffering as disclosed in Jesus' cross, and from all three King developed a theology that was effective in challenging all Americans to create the beloved community in which all persons are equal. While it was the Gandhian method of nonviolence that provided the strategy for achieving justice, it was, as King said, "through the influence of the Negro Church" that "the way of nonviolence became an integral part of our struggle."[15]

As a Christian whose faith was derived from the cross of Jesus, King believed that there could be no true liberation without suffering. Through nonviolent suffering, he contended, blacks would not only liberate themselves from the necessity of bitterness and feeling of inferiority toward whites, but would also prick the conscience of whites and liberate them from a feeling of superiority. The mutual liberation of blacks and whites lays the foundation for both to work together toward the creation of an entirely new world.

In accordance with this theological vision, he initially rejected black power because of its connotations of hate, and he believed that no beloved community of blacks and whites could be created out of bitterness. King said that he would continue to preach nonviolence even if he became its only advocate. It is significant that King softened his attitude toward black power shortly before his assassination, and viewed its positive elements as a much-needed philosophy in order to eradicate self-hate in the black community, especially as revealed in the riots in the cities. He began to speak of a need to "teach about black culture" (especially black philosophers, poets, and musicians) and even of "temporary separation,"[16] because he realized that without self-respect and dignity, black people could not participate with others in creating the beloved community.

A similar but even more radical position was taken with regard to the war in Vietnam. Because the Civil Rights Act (1964) and the Voting Rights Bill (1965) did not affect significantly the life chances of the poor, and because of the failure of President Johnson's War on Poverty, King became convinced that his dream of 1963 had been turned into a nightmare.[17] Gradually he began to see the connections between the failure of the war on poverty and the expenditures for the war in Vietnam. In the tradition of the Old Testament prophets and against the advice of many of his closest associates in black and in white communities, King stood before a capacity crowd at Riverside Church and condemned America as "the greatest purveyor of violence in the world today."[18] He proclaimed God's judgment against America and insisted that God would break the backbone of U.S. power if this nation did not bring justice to the poor and peace to the world. Vicious criticisms came from blacks and whites in government, civil rights groups, the media, and the nation generally as he proclaimed God's righteous indignation against the three great evils of our time—war, racism, and poverty.

During the severe crises of 1966–1968, King turned, not to the theologians and philosophers of his graduate education, but to his own religious heritage. It was the eschatological hope, derived from his slave grandparents and mediated through the black church, that sustained him in the midst of grief and disappointment. This hope also empowered him to "master [his] fears" of death and to "stand by the best in an evil time."[19] In an unpublished sermon, preached at Ebenezer Baptist Church, he said:

> I've decided what I'm going to do; I ain't going to kill nobody , , , in Mississippi   and , , , in Vietnam, and I ain't going to study war no more. And you know what? I don't care who doesn't like what I say about it. I don't care who criticizes me in an editorial; I don't care what white person or Negro criticizes me. I'm going to stick with the best. . . . Every now and then we sing about it: "If you are right, God will fight your battle." I'm going to stick by the best during these evil times.[20]

It was not easy for King to "stand by the best," because he often stood alone. But he firmly believed that the God of black faith had said to him: "Martin Luther, stand up for righteousness. Stand up for justice. Stand up for truth. And lo, I will be with you even until the end of the world."[21]

King combined the exodus-liberation and cross-love themes with the message of hope found in the resurrection of Jesus. Hope for him was not derived from the optimism of liberal Protestant theology, but rather was based on his belief in the righteousness of God as defined by his reading of the Bible through the eyes of his slave foreparents. The result was the most powerful expression in black history of the essential themes of black religious thought from the integrationist viewpoint.

> Centuries ago Jeremiah raised a question, "Is there no balm in Gilead? Is there no physician?" He raised it because he saw the good people suffering so often and the evil people prospering. Centuries later our slave foreparents came along and they too saw the injustice of life and had nothing to look forward to, morning after morning, but the rawhide whip of the overseer, long rows of cotton and the sizzling heat; but they did an amazing thing. They looked back across the centuries, and they took Jeremiah's question mark and straightened it into an exclamation point. And they could sing, "There is a balm in Gilead to make the wounded whole. There is a balm in Gilead to heal the sinsick soul."[22]

BLACK RELIGIOUS THOUGHT,
BLACK POWER, AND BLACK THEOLOGY

From the time of its origin in slavery to the present, black religious thought has been faced with the question of whether to advocate integration into American society or separation from it. The majority of the participants in the black churches and the civil rights movements have promoted integration, and they have interpreted justice, liberation, love, suffering, and hope in light of the goal of creating a society in which blacks and whites can live together in a "beloved community."

While integrationists have emphasized the American side of the double consciousness of African Americans, there have also been nationalists who rejected any association with the United States and instead have turned toward Africa. Nationalists contend that blacks will never be accepted as equals in a white racist church and society. Black freedom can be achieved only by black people's separating themselves from whites—either by returning to Africa or by forcing the government to set aside a separate state in the United States so blacks can build their own society.[23]

The nationalist perspective on the black struggle for freedom is deeply embedded in the history of black religious thought. Some of its proponents include Bishop Henry McNeal Turner of the African Methodist Episcopal Church; Marcus Garvey, the founder of the Universal Negro Improvement Association; and Malcolm X, of the religion of Islam. Black nationalism is centered on blackness, a repudiation of any value in white culture and religion. Nationalists reversed the values of the dominant society by attributing to black history and culture what whites had said about theirs. For example, Bishop Turner claimed that "we have as much right biblically and otherwise to believe that God is a Negro, . . . as you . . . white people have to believe that God is a fine looking, symmetrical and ornamented white man."[24] Marcus Garvey held a similar view:

> If the white man has the idea of a white God, let him worship his God as he desires. . . . We Negroes believe in the God of Ethiopia, the everlasting God—God the Father, God the Son and God the Holy Ghost, the One God of all ages.[25]

The most persuasive interpreter of black nationalism during the 1960s was Malcolm X, who proclaimed a challenging critique of King's philosophy of integration, nonviolence, and love. Malcolm X advocated black unity instead of the "beloved community," self-defense in lieu of nonviolence, and self-love in place of turning the other cheek to whites.[26]

Like Turner and Garvey, Malcolm X asserted that God is black; but unlike them he rejected Christianity, as the white man's religion. He became a convert initially to Elijah Muhammad's Nation of Islam and later to the worldwide Islamic community. His critique of Christianity and of American society as white was so persuasive that many blacks followed him into the religion of Islam, and others accepted his criticisms even though they did not become Muslims. Malcolm pushed civil rights activists to the left and caused many black Christians to reevaluate their interpretation of Christianity.

> Brothers and sisters, the white man has brainwashed us black people to fasten our gaze upon a blond-haired, blue-eyed Jesus! We're worshiping a Jesus that doesn't even *look* like us! Now just think of this. The blond-haired, blue-eyed white man has taught you and me to worship a *white* Jesus, and to shout and sing and pray to this God that's *his* God, the white man's God. The white man has taught us to shout and sing and pray until we *die*, to wait until *death*, for some dreamy heaven-in-the-hereafter, when we're *dead*, while this white man has his milk and honey in the streets paved with golden dollars right here on *this* earth![27]

During the first half of the 1960s, King's interpretation of justice as equality with whites, liberation as integration, and love as nonviolence dominated the thinking of the black religious community. However, after the riot in Watts (Los Angeles), in August 1965, some black clergy began to take another look at Malcolm's philosophy, especially with regard to his criticisms of Christianity and American society. Malcolm X's contention that America was a nightmare and not a dream began to ring true to many black clergy as they watched their communities go up in flames.

It was during the James Meredith "march against fear" in Mississippi (June 1966, after Malcolm's assassination in February 1965) that some black clergy began to question openly King's philosophy of love, integration, and nonviolence. When Stokely Carmichael proclaimed "black power," it sounded like the voice of Malcolm X. Though committed to the Christian gospel, black clergy found themselves moving slowly from integration to separation, from Martin King to Malcolm X.

The rise of black power created a decisive turning point in black religious thought. Black power forced black clergy to raise the theological question about the relation between black faith and white religion. Although blacks have always recognized the ethical heresy of white Christians, they have not always extended it to Euro-American theology. With its accent on the cultural heritage of Africa and political liberation "by any means necessary," black power shook black clergy out of their theological complacency.

Separating themselves from Martin King's absolute commitment to nonviolence, a small group of black clergy, mostly from the north, addressed the black power movement positively and critically. Like King and unlike black power advocates, black clergy were determined to remain within the Christian community. This was their dilemma: How could they reconcile Christianity and black power, Martin King and Malcolm X?

Under the influence of Malcolm X and the political philosophy of black power, many black theologians began to advocate the necessity for the development of a black theology, and they rejected the dominant theologies of Europe and North America as heretical. For the first time in the history of black religious thought, black clergy and theologians began to recognize the need for a completely new starting point in theology, and they insisted that it must be defined by people at the bottom and not at the top of the socioeconomic ladder. To accomplish this task, black theologians focused on God's liberation of the poor as the central message of the gospel.[28]

To explicate the theological significance of the liberation motif, black theologians began to reread the Bible through the eyes of their slave grandparents and started to speak of God's solidarity with the wretched of the earth. As the political liberation of the poor emerged as the dominant motif, justice, suffering, love, and hope were reinterpreted in its light. For the biblical meaning of liberation, black theologians turned to the exodus, while the message of the prophets provided the theological content for the theme of justice. The Gospel story of the life, death, and resurrection of Jesus served as the biblical foundation for a reinterpretation of love, suffering, and hope in the context of the black struggle for liberation and justice.

As black theologians have reread the Bible in the light of the struggles of the oppressed, the idea of the "suffering God" became important in our theological perspective. Our theological imagination has been stirred by Jürgen Moltmann's writing about the "crucified God" as well as Luther's distinction between the "theology of glory" and the "theology of the cross." But it has been the *actual* suffering of the oppressed in black and other third world communities that was decisive in our reflections on the cross of Jesus Christ. As Gustavo Gutiérrez said: "We cannot speak of the death of Jesus until we speak of the real death of people." For in the deaths of the poor of the world is found the suffering and even the death of God. The political implications of Luther's insight on this point seems to have been greatly distorted with his unfortunate emphasis on the two kingdoms. Many modern-day Lutheran scholars are even worse, because they turn the cross of Jesus into a theological idea completely unrelated to the concrete historical struggles of the oppressed for freedom. For most Lutheran scholars, the theology of the cross is a theological concept to be contrasted with philosophical and metaphysical speculations. It is a way of making a distinction between faith and reason, justification by faith through grace and justification by the works of reason.

But when the poor of North America and the third world read the passion story of the cross, they do not view it as a theological idea, but rather as God's suffering solidarity with the victims of the world. Jesus' cross is God's election of the poor by taking their pain and suffering on the divine person. Black slaves expressed this theological point in such songs as "He Never Said a Mumbalin' Word" and "Were You There When They Crucified My Lord?"

Modern-day black theologians make a similar point when they said that "God is black" and that "Jesus is the oppressed one." Our rejection of European metaphysical speculations and our acceptance of an apparently crude anthropomorphic way of speaking of God is black theologians' way of concretizing Paul's saying that "God chose what is foolish in the world to shame the wise, God chose what is weak in the world to shame the strong, God chose what is low and despised in the world, even things that are not, to bring to nothing things that are" (1 Cor. 1:27–28, RSV).

Another characteristic of black theology is its deemphasis, though not complete rejection, of the Western theological tradition and its affirmation of black history and culture. If the suffering of God is revealed in the suffering of the oppressed, then it follows that theology cannot achieve its Christian identity apart from a systematic and critical reflection on the history and culture of the victims of oppression. When this theological insight impressed itself on our consciousness, we black theologians began to realize that we have been miseducated. In fact, European and North American theologians have stifled the indigenous development of the theological perspectives of blacks by teaching us that our own cultural traditions are not appropriate sources for an interpretation of the Christian gospel. Europeans and white North Americans taught us that the Western theological tradition as defined by Augustine, Aquinas, Luther, Calvin, and Schleiermacher is the essential source for a knowledge of the Christian past. But when black theologians began to concentrate on black culture and history, we realized that our own historical and cultural traditions are far more important for an analysis of the gospel in the struggle for freedom than are the Western traditions, which participated in our enslavement. We now know that the people responsible for or indifferent to the oppression of blacks are not likely to provide the theological resources for our liberation. If oppressed peoples are to be liberated, they must themselves create the means for it to happen.

The focus on black culture in the light of the black liberation struggle has led to an emphasis on praxis as the context out of which Christian theology develops. To know the truth is to do the truth, that is, to make happen in history what is confessed in church. People are not poor by divine degree or by historical accident. They are *made* poor by the rich and powerful few. This means that to do black liberation theology one must make a commitment, an option *for* the poor and *against* those who are responsible for their poverty.

Because black theology is to be created only in the struggles of the poor, we have adopted social analysis, especially of racism and more recently of classism, sexism, and homophobia, as a critical component of its methodology. How can we participate in the liberation of the poor from poverty if we do not know who the poor are and why they live in poverty? Social analysis is a tool that helps us to know why the social, economic, and political orders are arranged as they are. It enables us to know not only who benefits from the present status quo, but what must be done to change it.

In our struggle to make a new start in theology, we discovered, to our surprise and much satisfaction, that theologians in Asia, Africa, and Latin America were making similar efforts in their contexts.[29] The same was true among other ethnic minorities in the first world and among women in all groups.[30] Black theology has been challenged to address the issues of sexism[31] and classism in a global context, and we have challenged them, especially Latin Americans and feminist theologians of the dominant culture, to address racism.

SECOND GENERATION OF
AFRICAN AMERICAN THEOLOGIANS

During the 1980s a new, younger group of theologians began to appear on the theological scene. The most creative and influential group is the womanist theologians. They have challenged not only the sexism of black male theologians, but also their one-sided emphasis on the theme of liberation, defined by the exodus event in the Bible, and the black church accent on the saving event of Jesus' cross. Womanist theologians emphasize the theme of survival and quality of life, defined by the biblical story of Hagar and the saving event of Jesus' life and resurrection. For many womanists, especially Delores S. Williams, there is no saving event in Jesus' suffering on the cross.[32]

A second generation of black male theologians, while building on the work of the first generation and also engaging womanist theologians, are carving out a distinctive theological path which focuses on the slave narratives and other indigenous resources in African American history. They are, therefore, in conversation with literary critics, comparative religions, and other postmodern discourses.[33]

Using an Afrocentric perspective, black biblical scholars are emerging as a significant intellectual and cultural force in black theological and church arenas. Cain Felder, author of the influential *Troubling Biblical Waters* and editor of the important *Stony the Road We Trod*, is the leading figure.[34] With the publication of the *African American Bible*, black theological discourse has begun to impact the black church.

The rise of the younger generation of black male and female theologians has reinforced and deepened with the focus on liberation. What many of us now know is that a turning point has been made in the theologies of black and third-world communities as radical as were Schleiermacher and Barth in the nineteenth and twentieth centuries in Europe. Let us hope that the revolution in liberation theology will change not only how we think about God, but more important what we do in this world so that the victims might make a future that is defined by freedom and justice and not slavery and oppression.

NOTES

1. W. E. B. Du Bois, *The Souls of Black Folk* (originally pub. 1903; Greenwich, Conn.: Fawcett Premier Book, 1968), 16–17.
2. A concise statement of the major themes in black religious thought, during and following slavery, is found in a 1902 sermon of an ex-slave and Princeton Theological Seminary graduate, Francis J. Grimke. See C. G. Woodson, ed., *The Works of Francis J. Grimke* (Washington, D.C.: Associated Publishers, 1942) 1:354.
3. For an interpretation of the slaves' idea of justice and liberation, see James H. Cone, *The Spirituals and the Blues* (New York: Seabury Press, 1972), esp. chap. 3. See also Albert J. Raboteau, *Slave Religion* (New York: Oxford University Press, 1978); Vincent Harding, *There Is a River* (New York: Harcourt Brace Jovanovich, 1981); and Gayraud S. Wilmore, *Black Religion and Black Radicalism*, rev. ed. (Maryknoll, N.Y.: Orbis Books, 1983).
4. For a fuller discussion of the idea of heaven in slave religion, see Cone, *The Spirituals and the Blues*, chap. 5. See also John Lovell Jr., *Black Song* (New York: Macmillan Publishing Co., 1972), esp. pp. 310–12, 315–74.
5. Woodson, *Works of Francis J. Grimke*, 354.
6. Ibid.
7. For an interpretation of these texts, see Albert J. Raboteau, " 'Ethiopia Shall Soon Stretch Forth Her Hands': Black Destiny in Nineteenth Century America," *The University Lecture in Religion at Arizona State University* (January 27, 1983).

8. Adam C. Powell Jr., *Marching Blacks* (1945; rev. ed., New York: Dial Press, 1973), 194.
9. Some of Howard Thurman's most influential writings include *Deep River* (1945), *The Negro Spiritual Speaks of Life and Death* (1947), *Jesus and the Disinherited* (1949), and *The Search for Common Ground* (1971).
10. For an account of that conference, see Mathew Ahmann, ed., *Race: Challenge to Religion* (Chicago: Henry Regnery, 1963). Influential works by B. E. Mays include, with Joseph W. Nicholson, *The Negro's Church* (1933); also *The Negro's God* (1938), *Seeking to Be Christian in Race Relations* (1957), and *Born to Rebel* (1971).
11. See esp. Kenneth L. Smith and Ira G. Zepp Jr., *Search for the Beloved Community: The Thinking of Martin Luther King, Jr.* (Valley Forge, Pa.: Judson Press, 1974); John J. Ansbro, *Martin Luther King, Jr.: The Making of a Mind* (Maryknoll, N.Y.: Orbis Books, 1982).
12. The importance of the black religious tradition for King's theology has not received the attention that it deserves from scholars. See Cone's "Martin Luther King, Jr., Black Theology—Black Church," *Theology Today*, January 1984. See also David Garrow's definitive biography of King published under the title *Bearing the Cross: Martin Luther King, Jr., and the Southern Christian Leadership Conference, 1955–1958.* It shows the important role of the black church tradition in his life and thought.
13. See Martin Luther King Jr., "Non-violence: The Christian Way in Human Relations," *Presbyterian Life*, February 1958; "Nonviolence: The Only Road to Freedom," *Ebony*, October 1966.
14. King, "The Un-Christian Christian," *Ebony*, August 1965: 77.
15. See King, "Letter from a Birmingham Jail," in his *Why We Can't Wait* (New York: Harper & Row, 1963), 90–91.
16. The best sources for King's affirmative emphasis on black power and pride are his unpublished speeches on the "Pre-Washington Campaign," recruiting persons for the Poor People's March to Washington. See especially his addresses at Clarksdale, Miss. (March 19, 1968), p. 7; Eutaw, Ala. (March 20, 1968), p. 3; Albany, Ga. (March 22, 1968), pp. 5f. See the Martin Luther King Jr. Papers at the Martin Luther King Jr. Center for Nonviolent Social Change, Atlanta, Ga.; also "Conversation with Martin Luther King," *Conservative Judaism*, vol. xxii, no. 3 (Spring 1968): 8–9.
17. See King, *The Trumpet of Conscience* (New York: Harper & Row, 1967), 75–76.
18. See Martin Luther King Jr., "Beyond Vietnam" (a pamphlet published by Clergy and Laity Concerned; 1982 reprint of his April 4, 1967, speech at Riverside Church, New York City), 2.
19. The most reliable sources for King's theology are the unpublished sermons at the King Center archives. They include "A Knock at Midnight," All Saints Community Church, Los Angeles, Calif. (June 25, 1967); "Standing by the Best in an Evil Time," Ebenezer Baptist Church, Atlanta, Ga. (August 6, 1967); "Thou Fool," Mount Pisgah Baptist Church, Chicago, Ill. (August 27, 1967); "Mastering Our Fears," Ebenezer Baptist Church (September 10, 1967).
20. "Standing by the Best in an Evil Time," 7.
21. "Thou Fool," 14.
22. This is an often-used conclusion of many of King's sermons. This quotation is taken from "Thou Fool."
23. For an excellent introduction to black nationalism, see Alphonso Pinkney, *Red, Black, and Green: Black Nationalism in the United States* (Cambridge: Cambridge University Press, 1976). See also John H. Bracey Jr., August Meier, and Elliott Rudwick, eds., *Black Nationalism in America* (Indianapolis: Bobbs-Merrill Co., 1970).

24. Edwin S. Redkey, ed., *Respect Black: The Writings and Speeches of Henry McNeal Turner* (New York: Arno Press, 1971), 176.

25. Amy Jacques-Garvey, ed., *Philosophy and Opinions of Marcus Garvey*, 2 vols. (New York: Arno Press, 1968), 44.

26. The best introduction to Malcolm X's philosophy is still *The Autobiography of Malcolm X, with the Assistance of Alex Haley* (New York: Grove Press, 1965).

27. Ibid., 222.

28. For an account of the origin of black theology, see James H. Cone, *For My People: Black Theology and the Black Church* (Maryknoll, N.Y.: Orbis Books, 1984). See also Gayraud S. Wilmore and James H. Cone, eds., *Black Theology: A Documentary History*, vol. 1, 1966–1979 (Maryknoll, N.Y.: Orbis Books, 1979, rev. 1993); vol. 2, 1980–1992 (Orbis Books, 1993). The best narrative history of black theology by one of its creators is Gayraud S. Wilmore, *Black Religion and Black Radicalism*, rev. ed. (Maryknoll, N.Y.: Orbis Books, 1983). James H. Cone, *Black Theology and Black Power* (New York: Seabury Press, 1969) and *A Black Theology of Liberation* (Philadelphia: J. B. Lippincott Co., 1970) were the earliest published books on black theology. They were followed by J. Deotis Roberts, *Liberation and Reconciliation: A Black Theology* (Philadelphia: Westminster Press, 1971), and Major Jones, *Black Awareness: A Theology of Hope* (Nashville: Abingdon Press, 1971).

29. For an account of black theologians' dialogue with theologians in Africa, Asia, and Latin America, see Wilmore and Cone, *Black Theology: A Documentary History*, vols. 1 and 2; Cone, *For My People*, 140–56. See also my chapters in the volumes that have been published from the conferences of the Ecumenical Association of Third World Theologians: "A Black American Perspective on the Future of African Theology," in *African Theology en Route*, ed. Sergio Torres and Kofi Appiah-Kubi (Maryknoll, N.Y.: Orbis Books, 1979); "A Black American Perspective on the Search for Full Humanity," in *Asia's Struggle for Full Humanity*, ed. Virginia Fabella (Maryknoll, N.Y.: Orbis Books, 1980); "From Geneva to São Paulo: A Dialogue between Black Theology and Latin American Liberation Theology," in *The Challenge of Basic Christian Communities*, ed. Sergio Torres and John Eagleson (Maryknoll, N.Y.: Orbis Books, 1981); "Reflections from the Perspective of U.S. Blacks," in *Irruption of the Third World: Challenge to Theology*, ed. Virginia Fabella and Sergio Torres (Maryknoll, N.Y.: Orbis Books, 1983); "Black Theology: Its Origin, Method, and Relation to Third World Theologies" in *Doing Theology in a Divided World*, ed. Sergio Torres and Virginia Fabella (Maryknoll, N.Y.: Orbis Books, 1985).

30. The dialogue between black theology and other ethnic theologies in the United States has taken place in the context of the Theology in the Americas. For an interpretation of this dialogue, see Cone, *For My People*, chap. vii; see also Sergio Torres and John Eagleson, eds., *Theology in the Americas* (Maryknoll, N.Y.: Orbis Books, 1976); and Cornel West, Caridad Guidote, and Margret Coakley, eds., *Theology in the Americas: Detroit II Conference Papers* (Maryknoll, N.Y.: Orbis Books, 1982).

31. See especially Wilmore and Cone, *Black Theology: A Documentary History*, vols. 1 and 2; J. Cone, *My Soul Looks Back* (Nashville: Abingdon Press, 1982); *For My People*, chap. vi. See also James H. Cone, *The Spirituals and the Blues* (Maryknoll, N.Y.: Orbis Books, 1972), 49.

32. See especially Wilmore and Cone, *Black Theology: A Documentary History*, vols. 1 and 2. Also, Delores Williams, *Sisters in the Wilderness: The Challenge of Womanist God-Talk* (Maryknoll, N.Y.: Orbis Books, 1993); Jacquelyn Grant, *White Women's Christ and Black Women's Jesus: Feminist Christology and Womanist Response* (At-

lanta: Scholars Press, 1989); Kelly Brown-Douglas, *The Black Christ* (Maryknoll, N.Y.: Orbis Books, 1994); Katie Geneva Cannon, *Black Womanist Ethics* (Atlanta: Scholars Press, 1988).

33. See esp. Dwight Hopkins and George Cummings, *Cut Loose Your Stammering Tongue: Black Theology in the Slave Narratives* (Maryknoll, N.Y.: Orbis Books, 1991); Dwight Hopkins, *Shoes That Fit Our Feet: Sources for a Constructive Black Theology* (Maryknoll, N.Y.: Orbis Books, 1993).

34. Cain Felder, *Troubling Biblical Waters* (Maryknoll, N.Y.: Orbis Books, 1989); idem, ed., *Stony the Road We Trod: African American Biblical Interpretation* (Minneapolis: Fortress Press, 1991). An important resource for the development of black theology since 1980 is Wilmore and Cone, *Black Theology: A Documentary History*, vol. 2, 1980–1992.

15

WOMANIST THEOLOGY
Dancing with Twisted Hip

EMILIE M. TOWNES

to be called beloved
is to be called by God
to be called by the shining moments
be called deep within deep

to be called beloved
is more than one plus infinity
more than the million breaths of loving
than the sounds of tomorrow's horizon

to be called beloved
is the marvelous yes to God's what if
the radical shifting of growth
mundane agency of active faith

to be called beloved
is to ask the question
    what would it mean
    what would it look like if we actually believed
    that we are washed in God's grace

to be called beloved
is to answer the question
    we are not dipped
    we are not sprinkled
    we are not immersed
    we are washed in the grace of God

to be called beloved
is to listen to the words of Baby Suggs
    holy
    who offered up to them (us) her great big heart
                        —Emilie M. Townes

"Here," she said, "in this here place, we flesh; flesh that
weeps, laughs; flesh that dances on bare feet in grass. Love
it. Love it hard. Yonder they do not love your flesh. They de-
spise it. . . . Love your hands! Love them. Raise them up and
kiss them. Touch others with them, pat them together, stroke
them on your face 'cause they don't love that either. *You* got
to love it, *you*! . . . This is flesh I'm talking about here. Flesh
that needs to be loved. Feet that need to rest and to dance;
backs that need support; shoulders that need arms, strong
arms I'm telling you. . . . So love your neck; put a hand on it,
grace it, stroke it and hold it up. And all your inside parts that
they'd just as soon slop for hogs, you got to love them. The
dark, dark liver—love it, love it, and the beat and beating
heart, love that too. More than eyes or feet.
More than lungs that have yet to draw free air. More than
your life-holding womb and your life-giving private parts,
hear me now, love your heart. For this is the prize.[1]

This admonishment/sermon to love one's heart is an individual and a communal
call to question the radical nature of oppression and devaluation of the self and
the community in the context of structural evil. This line of questioning can and
should take a multitude of directions because it addresses the nature of *systemic* evil,
not individual sin alone. My aim is to consider what it means for African American
society and culture to love our heart, to be called beloved, under the rubric of womanist theo-ethical concerns for wholeness. The search for wholeness—physical, spiritual, concrete, and theoretical—is the key concern found in womanist theology.

This search for wholeness shapes the nature of the roots of womanist theology
that are found in the African American writer Alice Walker's concept and definition
of womanist and the relationship of definition to Black women's traditions of biblical interpretation and theological reflection. In 1982, Walker gave the definitive understanding of womanist.[2] In her four-part definition of womanist, she begins with
the origins of the term, the Black folk expression "womanish" or more accurately
the phrase, "You're acting womanish." Young Black girls who were precocious, in-
quisitive, stubborn, ornery—or any combination thereof—were accused of being
womanish. It became an adult's way of warning about the dangers of Black girls
moving beyond prescribed cultural boundaries and socioeconomic determinants. A
womanish young Black girl must not only be in charge, a gatherer of knowledge, she
must also be serious about her task. Who she is makes her dangerous to hegemony.

Walker's next understanding of womanist is communal. The womanist cares
about her people—contemporary and historical. Here Walker challenges us on the
nature of how Black folk are with each other. We are sexual beings who are to be
loved, sexually or not. We are oppressed people who have had saviors in our

midst—sometimes women. We cannot divorce ourselves from each other without killing ourselves and signing the death warrant for our future generations. We must, the womanist must, recognize her location *and* responsibility in a community.

As Walker addresses the origin and the communal dimensions of a womanist witness, she turns next to the individual. The individual (as are the other aspects of womanist) is grounded in love. Love of self, love of community, love of the worlds of Black women, love of the Spirit. These are all held together for the womanist—regardless. Spirit, community, person are held together in a wondrous, if not faithful, circle pointing toward wholeness and hope. Like the flowers in Walker's mother's garden, there is a respect for the possibilities, and a staunch will to grasp them.[3]

Her final word of instruction is brief: "Womanist is to feminist as purple is to lavender."[4] This signals the move so many Black feminists have made away from feminist preoccupation with gender inequalities without adequate attention and analytical and reflective insight into the interstructured nature of race, gender, and class oppression—and other forms of oppression as well. The womanist project is to take a fuller measure of the nature of injustice and inequalities of human existence from the perspective of women—Black women.

The theological roots of womanist theology begin in African cosmology (the way traditional African religions view this world and the universe) that sees all of life as sacred. There was no secular-sacred split that was common in the Western world. Slaves did not convert to Christianity in any significant numbers until the First Great Awakening in the 1740s. Southern slaves and free Blacks in the North experienced a constant renewal of traditions and religions of Africa in the Americas. This renewal included oral history, drumming at funerals and dances, preserving the art of wood carving, and making reed baskets and mats.[5]

The religious world of the slaves during the 1600s and 1700s was a blend of West African religions with Christianity. Although White missionaries and ministers prohibited religious dancing and shouting, the slaves did so in secret.[6] From West Africa, slaves understood that both evil and good are natural forces in the universe and both were available for consultation and protection. From Christianity, the slaves found a God who would send a man to set the slaves free as Moses had confronted Pharaoh to set the Hebrew slaves free in the book of Exodus.

By the early 1800s, more Black women converted to Christianity in greater numbers than Black men. With the rise of the Second Great Awakening and its strong evangelical influence, Black women found a religion that helped instill and strengthen a sense of identity. The revivalism that also accompanied the Second Awakening blended with the strong evangelical impulse to produce a religion felt personally and bodily. Combined with the evangelicalism and revivalism of the era was the official end of slavery. This meant that Black women began to employ more Jewish and Christian symbols.

Black women developed a spirituality and a theology forged from African cosmology, evangelical piety, and revival fervor. This produced a theology that had a deep and personal relationship with God and Jesus. Jesus was the one who understood the trials and tribulations of Black people and promised salvation. It was through this intensely personal relationship with Jesus that Black women could find ways to transcend the inhuman structures that surrounded them in the slave South and the repressive North.

After slavery, Black women took this personal experience of the divine and the promise of salvation into the public realm to reform a corrupt moral order. Their theology was one that began from a strong sense of piety that sought perfection and then moved this search into the public to transform an unjust social order. These women formed moral reform societies to address the sins of licentiousness (the lust of men and the prostitution of women), the family, and Jim Crow laws that legalized segregation. Black churchwomen were active in the women's club movement of the era as a way to alleviate Black suffering and push for social equality. Through the clubs, women established kindergartens and day-care centers, they set up adult reading classes, agitated for antilynching laws and for temperance, established schools, and pushed for the ability of Black men and women to vote.

As these women approached the Bible, they saw Jesus as both "feminine and masculine, passive and aggressive, meek and conquering,"[7] which led them to see themselves as both humiliated and soldiers. They also identified with Esther, who acted as an intermediary for her race. Following these twin lines, Black women embraced Jesus and saw their ultimate allegiance resting in God, not men. They saw themselves as called by God to take their more domestic role of wife, mother, and comforter into the public arena to prophesy and spread the gospel.[8]

This theological world, one in which an active faith means an active witness, has a profound influence on womanist theology in the contemporary United States. This produces a radical ontology within womanist theology.[9] When combined with Walker's definition, womanist theology has as its primary concern concrete existence (lived life) and searches for an impetus for a coherent and unified relationship between body, soul, creation, and Creator. Womanist theology seeks to uncover and affirm ways in which life itself can be and should be held sacred. This search carries within it the knowledge of slavery, racism, classism, sexism, and other forms of oppression that have an impact on the lives of all of us and their particular manifestation in the lives of African Americans.

Because of the nature of its project, womanist theology rejects dualism and argues for wholeness. The subject-other *relationship* is held in the web of creation (or in my terminology, is-ness). This runs counter to the self-other *opposition* that underlies much of Western thought. This self-other opposition (or subject-other split) is intrinsic to Western culture. As such, it must be part of ontological reflection, for it is part of reality as a whole. While recognizing this opposition or split, womanist theology advocates the self-other *relationship*. It is in a relational matrix that wholeness can be found for African Americans. Therefore being or is-ness is physical *and* spiritual in womanist theology.

This concern for wholeness is shaped within the contemporary rise of postmodern discourse as it responds to modernist inadequacies. Postmodernism in theology is still unfolding. Theologians such as Rebecca Chopp, Sheila Davaney, Mark Lewis Taylor, and Cornel West are among those who seek to expand the theological worldview of classical theologies—liberal (e.g., Friedrich Schleiermacher and Adolf Harnack), conservative (e.g., Carl F. H. Henry and Clark Pinnock), neoorthodox (e.g., Paul Tillich and Karl Barth). The theoretical intent of postmodern thought is to call attention to and appropriate the experience of difference and otherness as legitimate discourse for critical theory and rigorous theo-ethical reflection.

The promise of postmodernism is that it provides a way for many to think their way into concrete knowledge of and contact with African American realities and the diversity of communities found within United States society—racial, ethnic, sexual, class, age, geographic, etc. However, when postmodern discourse remains only at the thinking stage (abstract), postmodernism can commit the same death-dealing errors found in modernist assumptions of universal rationality, objectivity, value-free established knowledge, individuals who create communities rather than being birthed/formed by community, institutionalized radical doubt, and knowledge as hypothesis. The challenge for postmodern theology is to push for theoretical reformulations that embrace the great diversity found within humanity and creation *and* practice a concrete concern for the lives of people and implications of the theologies we espouse.

Postmodern theology has a radical historicity in which plurality, particularity, locality, context, the social location of thought, and serious questioning of universal knowledge are key features. Such concerns are consonant with a theology of wholeness. Issues of diversity and context have long been problematic for African Americans in the United States. Black men and women writers, from Phyllis Wheatley to Claude McKay to Toni Morrison to Randall Kenan, have wrestled with what it means to be Other in our society. They have served as literary critics for how modernist constructs serve to deny, extinguish, and devalue the distinctive features of blackness and the critical comments of African Americans on United States' life and injustices.

Black writers have provided a way into the bounty of Black life in the United States. Their work has fed (and has been nourished by) African American intellectuals and also folks like Miss Nora and Brother Hemphill. The growing body of Black voices in our sociocultural matrix makes it difficult to maintain modernist protestations toward universalities. More than ever before, we are challenged to consider the radical nature of particularity as foundational for theo-ethical reflection.

Although this work has opened greater possibilities for cross-cultural dialogue and understanding, the notion that we are aware of another person's feelings and experiences only on the basis of empathic inferences from our own veers into solipsism. Self-consciousness and awareness of others are not natural dance partners. Understanding the Other is not predicated on how the individual (or the group) makes the shift from the certainty of her or his inner experiences to the unknowable person. This tenuous shift often produces two outcomes: romanticization and/or trivialization. African American women and men and children experience racism, sexism, and classism in a multitude of ways. This is borne out in the stereotypical images of blackness as equivalent to poverty and destitution. Such one-dimensional representations of Black life are narrow, constricting notions of African American life.

Postmodern discourse and analysis that obscure the true diversity of life in the United States for Black Americans collapse African Americans into one grand master narrative. This narrative makes no distinction between the experiences of male and female in our various cultures—and within African American society in particular, issues of race and racism, or economic exploitation and social class location. Black folk become one dark stroke across the landscape of hegemonic discourse. When the Other remains abstract, the promise of postmodernism fails its liberative agenda. The call by Baby Suggs to love our hearts is a pithy reminder that particularity is more than an abstract construct of a philosophical colloquy. Particularity, historicity, locality, and context all represent human beings. Concrete material existence and abstraction can and should meet in postmodernism. Perhaps Baby Suggs can help us toward such ontological wholeness in her call to love the "beat and beating heart."

"THE DARK, DARK LIVER"

Baby Suggs's words are pithy instructions for womanist theology:

> And no, they ain't in love with your mouth. Yonder out there, they will see it broken and break it again. What you say out of it they will not heed. What you scream from it they do not hear. What you put into it to nourish your body they will snatch away and give you leavins instead. No, they don't love your mouth. You got to love it.[10]

The search for wholeness found in womanist theology is found through a theological exploration of the dynamics of race, gender, and class as interstructured oppressions. As such, womanist theology is a response to sexism in Black theology and racism in feminist theology. Black theology began with a concentration on race and racism as theological and moral problems. Black theology has roots in the Black Power Movement that arose out of the Civil Rights Movement of the 1960s. The call for Black power was a rallying cry for Black nationalist groups that were more radical than those groups active in the struggle for civil rights.

Oppression and racism became the focus of those advocating Black power. James H. Cone's *A Black Theology of Liberation*[11] was the first thorough consideration of the theological importance of the call for Black liberation found within Black power. Cone's early and potent stress on the liberatory message of the gospel was yoked with the Black religious experience I have outlined earlier in this chapter.

Womanist theology arose when Black women realized that the themes of Black theology did not include Black women's experiences either in the sociopolitical struggle for survival or the theological implications of a liberation that also included sexism and classism. "The Black experience" was really the experience of African American men and boys. The crux of the debate has been the challenge issued by Black women (and some men such as James Cone and Garth Baker-Fletcher) to recognize that the liberatory message of Black theology was too narrow in its scope.

Although womanist theology agrees with Black theology's critique of white racism and the need for Black unity, it also raises an important critique of Black theology. If, in fact, God's action in the lives of Black people is liberating, then all forms of oppression—including those internal to the African American community—are to be exposed and eradicated. Therefore, womanist theology began a critical assessment on the nature of heterosexism, misogyny, sexual abuse and violence, and sexism. This was not confined to the history of White male abuse of Black women, but also the abuse Black women experienced from Black men.

These are not solely sociopolitical problems; they are theological problems as well. The very nature of how Black men and women understand themselves as whole people, people created in the image of God, is at stake. The search for wholeness is one that must encompass rigorous introspection and critique within the African American community of faith.

The work of Delores S. Williams joins the recent work of Katie Geneva Cannon, Kelly Brown Douglas, and Jacquelyn Grant as they continue to push the themes of Black liberatory discourse.[12] Williams's work serves to trouble the waters concerning God's liberatory activity for *all* the oppressed.[13] Her work with the Hagar-Sarah texts in Genesis and Galatians points out that the oppressed and abused are not always guaranteed nor do they always experience God's liberating power. Her challenge to Black theology is to read the Bible seeking to identify with the non-Hebrews who are female and male slaves. She contends that from this perspective, there is a nonliberative thread present in the Bible that African American men and women must consider.[14] Williams argues that the wilderness experience is much more inclusive of the struggle of Black men *and* women.[15]

TO LOVE OUR NECKS
UNNOOSED AND STRAIGHT

Womanist theology challenges the theological presuppositions and assumptions of feminist theology as well. Womanist theology is not purely academic (objective)—it is also personal (subjective). Womanist theology attempts to articulate a theoretical critique of cultural hegemony through a call for the reimaging of the roles of men and women in religious practices and also in secular society. Within a theo-ethical framework, it is inductive and based on praxis. The inductive approach taken by womanist theo-ethical reflection stresses experience as opposed to the deductive approach of classical theological models. Rather than deducing conclusions from principles established out of religious traditions and philosophies, like all theologies of liberation, it begins with lived experience. Within the Christian context, the gospel message is good news to people when it speaks to their needs and proclaims the challenges in a concrete manner.

Ideally, the theoretical constructs of feminist theology (which along with Black theology are the twin academic roots from which womanist theo-ethical reflection emerges) refuse to accept the social location we either allow ourselves to assume due to social mores and strictures or to which we may be assigned by those same forces. The task before feminist theology is to name the particular sin and be able to articulate the universal dimensions of it. Rather, the universal is *manifested* in the particular, but not exhausted by it. Feminist theology, at its best, attempts to be antiracist, antisexist, anticlassist, antiheterosexist—in short, antioppressist.

This movement to live into an antioppression analysis that is truly inclusive has been a part of much of Black and feminist theologies in recent years. This was done through contesting such language as "blackness/whiteness," "oppression/liberation," "sisterhood," "common oppression," "women's experience." This became crucial as more women of color, women whose religious experience is other than Christian, and women from the spectrum of class differences and sexualities joined the academy under the rubric of feminism and Black liberation. The power of analysis sharpened our ability to name, critique, and strategize against the interstructured nature of oppression. We began, slowly, not only to hear the great diversity of women's experiences and the demands this placed on our methodologies, but we also began to understand the benefits and the costs we all bore. Womanist theology challenged the sexism and classism found in Black theology in its universalization of an uncritical understanding of Black male experience as the norm of all the African American community. We believe it is really true that the *only* place solidarity comes before work is in the dictionary.

Yet, there is more work to do in forging an inclusive methodology that takes differences seriously and addresses those differences in an integrated and coherent analysis. The emergence of womanist, *mujerista*, Asian women's liberation theology, and liberation theology from African women are indicative that the name, feminism, is problematic. The media have defined it, the church has confined it, academia ignores it, and feminist scholars in religious studies are left to refine it so that it can be an ideology that is broad in the concrete.

We are caught in a major methodological flaw: an incomplete praxis. The action and reflection that are key to any liberatory methodology are impaired. The reflection done in feminist theo-ethical methodologies is not truly inclusive of women's experience*s*. Women's lives are not a tapestried monolith. The careful consideration of and methodological inclusion of the varying social locations of women are crucial to truly scholarly and rigorous feminist studies in religion. This must take place not only in our scholarship, but also in our day-to-day lives.

This methodological flaw has birthed a postmodern turn in feminist theology that is extremely troubling because of the way it represents a two-headed coin. The postmodern rejection of universal laws, "objectivity," linear views of history that legitimate patriarchal notions of subjectivity and social order, science and reason as direct correspondents with objectivity and truth, and totalizing feminisms are welcome additions to theological discourse. In its best sense, postmodern discourse challenges us to rethink master narratives and notions of culture. This side of the coin of postmodern feminist theology continues the project begun within feminist discourse, that to discover, recover, and uncover the fact that women of color, poor women, women from various religious traditions, women of various sexualities were at the table *at the beginning*. Some of us were simply not served, nor were we asked if we were hungry and needed something to eat.

The other side of the coin of postmodern feminist theology is worrisome because of the emerging voice of individualism embedded in this discourse, particularly that which relies heavily if not exclusively on the field of cultural studies.[16] The theoretical and methodological intent of cultural studies is *not* to provide a new rationale for an individualism that serves to relativize experiences in a way that reduces human lives to competing ideologies. However, when cultural studies omits progressive, transformatory political and prophetic dimensions, it *does* serve to do so. This individualism is distinct from referencing the individual. Questions of the self and the self in relation to the community are extremely pertinent for religious reflection. These questions and the exploration of them within feminist reflection have pushed us, both academically and within the lives of religious communities, into a greater faithfulness to live into a fuller humanity.

The individualism that is troubling manifests itself in the privileging of epistemology and aesthetics over ethics and politics. Yet, questions of knowing and taste are interrelated with questions of right action, values, and the ordering of our society. This individualism's understanding of power dynamics and relations is simplistic. It fails to understand that power functions through other than technologies of control and domination. This individualism fails to nuance the value of master or grand narratives. It is true enough that narratives that employ a single standard that is then universalized should be held in deep suspicion and eradicated. Grand narratives, however, often function as powerful tools for identity and solidarity *for* the dispossessed and the marginalized.

General feminist discourse has a new generation of, in bell hooks's words,

> young white privileged women who strive to create a narrative of feminism (not a feminist movement) that recenters the experience of materially privileged white females in ways that deny race and class differences, not solely in relation to the construction of female identity but also in relation to feminist movement.[17]

This impulse has moved within feminist studies in religion as well. When issues of race and class and sexualities challenge their feminist practice, their feminist theological reflection is often found wanting. The danger remains that when far too many feminist scholars in religion weave their vision of a new ordering of creation, women of color, lesbians and transgendered peoples, and poor women are either left out or mere addenda to the analysis. This would not be so troubling if feminist theological reflection was nascent. Youth can be forgiven many things, but feminist theology is a maturing discipline that has faced this challenge of a more broad-based inclusivity, in this generation, since the late 1970s.

Feminist theology that is authentic is more than a vague concept of civil rights within a capitalist and misogynist system. It is more than a further extension of tokenism to include more women in existing social structures. Feminism that is authentic seeks to transform radically the social structures and human relationships within that structure. The agenda of authentic feminism includes relationships between men and women, rich and overly exploited, white and peoples of color, old and young, abled and disabled, student and professor, heterosexual and homosexual, clergy and laity.

It is not enough for feminist scholars of religion to apply the increasingly threadbare apology that they are white, middle-class, and privileged and therefore cannot adequately address the concerns of women who are not from this social location, or fail to see that their experience is not universal and cannot be totalized in such a way that it is inclusive. The essence of our various social locations demands that we understand *how* sociocultural hegemony functions to create that location. There is, in the very construction of race, gender, and class a demand for feminist theology to take these seriously and to explore both the costs and the benefits of our places in the sociocultural order.

TO DANCE WITH TWISTED HIP

Perhaps postmodernist discourses can provide us with the tools in womanist theo-ethical reflection to continue to explore this bonding between body and spirit. However, the danger lies in abstraction. The notion of the Other is not always a helpful category to tease through the thorny, concrete issues of body and spirit. The Other, linguistically, seems too sterile a category for a people who have been told to love the "dark, dark liver." The Other can be a category of avoidance rather than radical being (ontology), a category of abstraction rather than concreteness. The Other can lean heavily toward reductionism and denial of truth, toward indignity and injustice. Like all human constructs, notions of Otherness and particularity and pluralism can become categories that objectify and possess rather than open new ground for genuine dialogue and transformation.

At the heart of womanist theology is the self-other relation grounded in concrete existence and succored in the flawed transcendent powers of our spirituality. The legacy of lynching, the siting of toxic waste dumps, the rise of influential Black neoconservative thought, and attempts at bridging feminist and womanist theologies each signals the need for a theology of wholeness in which the self-other relationship becomes primary. Although these are only four moments in the stream of Black life and lives of African American women in the United States, they indicate the kind of rending of body and soul that decimates African American society and culture.

We make ourselves the oppositional Other, we turn to forms of self-hatred and self-destruction. Instead of critiquing and then working to eradicate notions of individualism, we forget our African past and seek to establish our lives as separate from each other. To engage in solidarity discourse without working to understand the true meaning and issues of place can be death-dealing. To recognize the differences in the socioeconomic structure of Black life does not mean that African Americans are free to cut those who are not in our social class or gender adrift from our lives. To divorce civil rights from environmental concerns is to live in a deadly dualism in which there will be no air to breathe. To practice historical amnesia about the legacy of lynching in the United States is to doom all of us to find new material to construct postmodern nooses.

Perhaps these cautions will be enough to hold womanist theo-ethical reflection to a rigorous and articulate witness that avoids reductionism in articulating the experience of living and loving in African American life. Rather than intellectually tempting our work with the luxury of competing narratives, wholeness demands the whole truth—our lives are complex and have layers of experience in each moment.

To remember our fleshiness is to recognize that dualistic oppositions such as self-other, egoism-altruism, theory-practice, individual-community, and mind-body are interactive and interdependent in a theology of wholeness. Each is relational and historical as it informs the other. Awareness of this complexity of African American life helps guard against reductionistic claims about who Black folk are and what they do. A people who run the gamut from Phyllis Wheatley to Henry Highland Garnet to Booker T. Washington to W. E. B. Du Bois to Ida B. Wells-Barnett to Martin Luther King Jr. to Malcolm X to Angela Davis cannot be easily defined or understood.

Defining black people's otherness or subjectivity as victimization is a hollow and incomplete description of radical being (ontology). We have narratives of resistance and rebellion as part of our story as well. Yet we must not rush too quickly to celebrate the victory of our diversity. Resistance is not synonymous with self-actualization on an individual or collective level.

A womanist theology of wholeness is, finally, radically relational. The various narratives of African American life are constituents of the grand narrative of Black faith and hope in this land. This relational character calls us to moral responsibility and accountability for our lives and the life of all those who have survived the diaspora. We are, in the most basic sense, each other's keeper. Out of this, we recognize the preciousness of life and the deep interconnection between body and spirit that will help us be made whole.

As a people who survived fourteen generations of slavery and seven generations of emancipation, the blending of body and soul is crucial to understanding and then constructing what the next seven generations will hold. A womanist theology of wholeness is founded on the belief that values like hope, virtue, sacrifice, risk, and accountability have had a different cast in the Black community.[18] The reinterpretation of these values has helped to hold Black folk in their sanity and determination.

Such values must be brought to the fore again. Our postmodern culture is breeding a kind of passivity in which the story of Black self-destruction and hatred becomes a daily item on the news wires. Black society and culture have changed and we are quickly moving away from the relational character of Black life that has sustained us and into an individualistic, nihilistic morality with no meaning-filled ethical core. This loss of values is the inheritance we gain from separating body and spirit, from placing individual over against communal concerns.

However, in its advocacy for relationality, womanist theology must take care that relationality itself does not slip into the miasma of abstractions. This will lead womanist theology down the path of weak ethical reflection and practice.[19] A womanist theology measures its reflection against the backdrop of the sociohistoric reality of Black life in the United States. This means that its project is endless as it works to discover and rediscover the intricacies of African American life from past to present. This reveals a paradoxical legacy of passivity, accommodation, assimilation, and protest. The lessons learned will always be tempered by the lessons yet to come. This makes womanist theology a dynamic process. In the end, we will be forced to make hard ethical choices. In a cosmos filled with worlds of oppression, we have no other option. The task of womanist theology is to illuminate, question, and begin the eradication of radical oppression and devaluation of the self and the community in the context of structural evil. Such evil operates in the interstices of human existence and in the novelty of creation. Such moral wrongness is rooted in our sociohistorical ontology. Ultimately, we cannot accomplish this alone. Not only do we turn to our relational bonds with each other, we must also turn to the God who shapes our hands, feet, necks, and dark, dark livers.

To be called beloved is to ponder these things in our hearts which we are to grow big. Womanist theological reflection demands that we stand up and dance with sometimes twisted hip the rest of what our hearts are saying. The reality of Black folk will give us the music to the song we must dance. To be called beloved is to do theo-ethical reflection with the deeply held knowledge that we are not dipped, we are not sprinkled, we are not immersed, but we are washed in the grace of God.

NOTES

This chapter was previously published as "To Be Called Beloved," *Annual,* The Society for Christian Ethics (1993):93–115.

1. Toni Morrison, *Beloved* (New York: Alfred A. Knopf, 1987), 88–89.
2. Alice Walker, "Womanist," in *In Search of Our Mothers' Gardens: Womanist Prose* (San Diego: Harcourt Brace Jovanovich, 1983), xxii–xxiii.
3. Walker, "In Search of Our Mothers' Gardens," in *In Search of Our Mothers' Gardens*, 241–42.
4. Walker, "Womanist," xxiii.
5. Erskine Clarke, *Wrestlin' Jacob: A Portrait of Religion in the Old South* (Atlanta: John Knox Press, 1979), 7–8; Gayraud Wilmore, *Black Religion and Black Radicalism: An Interpretation of the Religious History of Afro-American People* (Maryknoll, N.Y.: Orbis Books, 1983), 15–17.
6. Albert Raboteau, *Slave Religion: The "Invisible Institution" in the Antebellum South* (New York: Oxford University Press, 1978), 291–311.
7. Evelyn Brooks, "The Women's Movement in the Black Baptist Church, 1880–1920" (unpublished Ph. D. diss., University of Rochester, 1984), 146. For a fuller picture of Black women's religious world, see Evelyn Brooks Higgenbotham, *Righteous Discontent: The Women's Movement in the Black Baptist Church, 1880–1920* (Cambridge: Harvard University Press, 1993).
8. Brooks, "The Women's Movement," 153.
9. Although Paul Tillich's work in *Systematic Theology*, vol. 1 (Chicago: University of Chicago Press, 1951), is helpful in addressing ontology rather than metaphysics, this is not my concern in this chapter. Tillich addresses two major dimensions of reality — the ontic and the ontological. For him, the ontic dimension deals with characteristics of object and beings in the subject-object constructs of spatial and temporal reality. Ontology deals with reality as it is before it has split or divided itself into subject and object. In Tillich's understanding, ontology is nondualistic and immanental. Therefore, for Tillich, ontology is the study of being.

10. Morrison, *Beloved*, 88.
11. James H. Cone, *A Black Theology of Liberation* (Philadelphia: J. B. Lippincott Co., 1970).
12. Kelly Brown Douglas, *The Black Christ* (Maryknoll, N.Y.: Orbis Books, 1994); Jacquelyn Grant, "The Sin of Servanthood and the Deliverance of Discipleship," in *A Troubling in My Soul: Womanist Perspectives on Evil and Suffering*, ed. Emilie M. Townes (Maryknoll, N.Y.: Orbis Books, 1993), 199–218; Katie Geneva Cannon, *Katie's Canon: Womanism and the Soul of the Black Community* (New York: Continuum, 1995).
13. Delores S. Williams, *Sisters in the Wilderness: The Challenge of Womanist God-Talk* (Maryknoll, N.Y.: Orbis Books, 1993).
14. Ibid.; see chap. 6, "Womanist God-Talk and Black Liberation Theology," 143–77, esp. 144–45.
15. Ibid., 153–61.
16. The field of cultural studies is an exciting and provocative emerging discipline. The focus of this discipline is the theoretical and methodological consideration of culture. The focus is less historically, sociologically, politically, or economically based. Rather, the focus is much more on the formation of ideologies within a culture. For a good introduction to this discipline, see John Storey, *An Introductory Guide to Cultural Theory and Popular Culture* (Athens: The University of Georgia Press, 1993).
17. bell hooks, *Outlaw Culture: Resisting Representations* (New York: Routledge & Kegan Paul, 1994), 102.
18. See Katie Geneva Cannon's creative and unctuous discussion of dominant ethics in *Black Womanist Ethics* (Atlanta: Scholars Press, 1988), 2–4.
19. For an illuminating discussion of relationality as it relates to women transracially, see Marcia Y. Riggs's chapter, "The Logic of Interstructured Oppression: A Black Womanist Perspective," in *Redefining Sexual Ethics: A Sourcebook of Essays, Stories and Poems*, ed. Susan E. Davies and Eleanor H. Haney (Cleveland: Pilgrim Press, 1991), esp. 99–100.

16

BURNING TONGUES
A Feminist Trinitarian Epistemology

CATHERINE KELLER

Feminist theology in the context of the United States in its first two decades circulated around the dilemma of the symbol of God, a dilemma first classically axiomatized by Mary Daly: "If God is male then the male is God."[1] Patriarchy on earth as it is in heaven: as long as the church holds to its unacknowledged biblical literalism regarding the sex of God, as we have suggested, it will continue to deprive itself of the full proclamatory gifts of women. A ｐｍｉｉｉｉｉｉｉｉｉｉｉ ｉｐｉｉｉｉｉｉｇ ｉ ｉ．ｉｉ ｕｕｉｉ ｉｉｉｉｉｉｉｉ ｉｉｉｉｉｉｉｉｇ ｐｏｉｉｔｌ．ｉ ｃｕｉｉｉｏｌ ｇｕｕｇｕ ｌｌｉｕ ｄｉｌ· ference of our contexts. Indeed, in order to share something of the present vitality of feminist church-related theology in the United States, I must for this chapter presuppose awareness of those basic correlations of theological language and hierarchy. For to belabor the above line of argumentation, already played out over more than two decades, sometimes yielding churchwide creativity and sometimes mere polarization, would bore this writer to silence. We few churchly feminists had become so enmeshed in theological gender politics on simultaneous symbolic and institutional fronts—struggling as to whether to desex, resex, or double-sex the divine, and as to which linguistic strategy would best serve the needs of female ordination and advancement in the churches—that certain underlying issues of theological epistemology, questions of what kind of "knowledge," of understanding, we exercise when we speak of divine attributes, had of necessity remained rather vague. I believe they must now come to the fore, not simply in order to replay old assertions of metaphoric as opposed to literalist uses of language, but in terms of theological criteria. Thus, institutional context frames the present inquiry into a Trinitarian epistemology, unfolded as a feminist economy of the Spirit. The point will be not to replace, but to enhance theology with epistemology, that is, to draw attention to certain dimensions of theological understanding—a particular kind of "knowing"—which direct our being and our doing, and therefore to enliven our personal and corporate consciousness, rather than letting God-language direct us into a transcendental vacuum, feminist or not. At the same time, such a strategy, which I do not offer in the name of the modern "new" (most of its moves may seen familiar, even old) but as an experiment, perhaps, in sophiological refocusing, will offer at least a framework in which I can survey major themes and texts of U.S. feminist theology.

In his quarrel with modernity, Karl Barth had criticized Christian "religion" as that which constructs "God" as an object of knowledge and use, serving human "interests." I cannot help but recognize that the feminist theological issue about the names of God becomes just such a project—and perhaps for this reason feels so tedious to many of us. Worrying about whether to name God as Father/Mother, as just Mother, as Goddess or God/ess, as Creator and Christ rather than Father and Son, as he, she, or a transpersonal it, we become almost stiffly self-conscious of the power dynamics of language; the sense of manipulating God-language for our group use (however liberating, however faithful) can therefore stifle its own purposes—its own disclosive, metaphoric life, its *Spirit*. The problem, of course, remains that those against whom we must make such arguments, those who like most Barthians would defend a masculinist linguistics of God, are themselves also guilty of just such "religion." The defense of the exclusively male names of the divine—once the power dynamics have been exposed—is given predictably and literalistically Trinitarian justifications. Yet these do not alter the fact that the obsessive restriction of the names of God to "Father," "Son," and "Lord" have served the interests of the sociological and "religious" subordination of women. In other words, the captivity of God in the imagery of the sex that just happened to be in control counts as a clear case of objectifying God-knowledge—even though Barth might have been incapable of this particular application of his theory.

At the same time, I do not like to see feminist theology hooked in some re-active inversion of the same idolatry: that creates tedium within, polarization without. Barth's own (early) inversion—that God is the Subject before whom we are objects—may be useful here if we read it through his later relationalism, influenced by Buber, in which of course no divine objectification of the human or human-to-human objectification is intended. I want in this context, however, to move somewhat differently: to claim that language about God in God's triune elements turns us first of all to the subject, that is, to a new accountability for our own subjective knowing. But this subjectivity proves to be nothing like the mod-ern, self-encapsulated subject of knowledge, who can only encounter the other as "his" object. On these terms God must always die. Rather, might it open us to a post-Feuerbachian realm of conscious, intersubjective relation, which then recip-rocally invites the images of divinity, which had prepared its way in the first place?

What sort of "knowledge" would such a relationalism entail? Certainly not the theocratic conflation of *pistis*, faith, with doctrinal propositions; and all the more certainly not the propositional truth methods of modernity, in which the act of knowing, freed from theological constraint, becomes an unadulterated power-drive: both objectify God along with the rest of creation. Yet no theology can long stand on the shifting sands of postmodern relativism, which, having with Foucault disclosed the pervasive modern internalization, in our very bodies, of "regimes of truth," would destroy "the will to knowledge" altogether: "All knowledge rests on an injustice."[2] But such an abdication becomes as disingenuous as the modern ar-rogance: if the former renders its world an object of control, the latter grants modernity its terms and so fails to take responsibility for its own production of knowledge. I think that as theology benefits from ongoing diagnosis of its own postmodern "condition" it will do well to take the opportunity for an epistemo-logical reflection looping together its traditions with its possible futures. Feminism poses the most powerful global challenge to that future and, as a new reformation of Christianity, has produced already not just new "knowledge" — a new corpus of texts, of propositions, of empirical analyses, of liturgical formulas and political codes — but a *way* of knowing, that is, it calls us anew as Christians to accountability for factoring in the specific perspectives, contexts, and styles by which we "know" whatever we know.

THE FIRST PERSON

Nothing in the post-Nicene tradition communicates more visibly the personality of the First Person that its sex, which seems, for the imagination, to assure personhood over thinghood more assuredly than any other human attribute; and it goes without saying within patriarchal civilization that this sex must then be masculine. But at the same time the Judeo-Christian God is explicitly characterized as supremely nonsexual by contrast to those pagan "fertility idols" we heard of in the titillating, cross-culturally ignorant polemics of our Old Testament courses, those "cult" demons who admit of either or multiple genders to the son of Yahweh, even when in Christianity he became the Father, was virtually never discussed as such. Always silently presupposed, left to the visual imagination, the metaphor of paternity congealed into the orthodox symbolism of the authoritatively unchanging. Of course, New Testament terms like "father" and "son" were used in context as fresh metaphors meant to open new relations, not Trinitarian dogmas meant to shut down possibilities, and if they were still used as such there would be no agonized discussion over "inclusive language" for the deity. But the original task of feminism — as book titles like *Beyond God the Father,* by Mary Daly; *Sexism and God Talk,* by Rosemary Radford Ruether; *Sex, Race and God,* by Susan Thistlethwaite; *The Body of God,* by Sallie McFague, suggest — lay in the mythoinstitutional confrontation with the First Person: at once to expose "him" as either *literally* a male, and thus an idol of masculine self-worship, or else as *linguistically a metaphor and not absolutely or necessarily male*; and to begin to propose alternatives (calling for either "inclusive language" or iconoclastic gynomorphism).

Whichever alternatives reveal themselves as most fitting in a particular community, it is the substitution of one ontological objectivism for another that I am questioning. Let me suggest that to shift strategies we (by which I now refer to any theologians, not just those who would call themselves "feminists") might lift up the implicit epistemology of such apparently ontological moves, and treat the divine attributes (person, father, creator, author, for example) as adverbs of human knowing rather than as mere substantives of divine substance. Thus, to try out this method: we might say that the theological episteme refracted through a feminist lens is less object-knowledge (knowledge of) than a way of knowing — therefore not knowledge of God as an object but rather, in ancient parlance, godly knowing. This means for the Trinitarian "First Person" that we seek to know, first of all, personally: that is, that knowledge of self, world, God must register first in our own experience as persons, as specific bodies of experience. We do not so much gaze at the divine personae, the "masks of God"; we look through them at our existence. The "personal"—a realm in which women have traditionally been rendered expert—is that which embodies its knowledge interpersonally; in "women's ways of knowing" it requires an epistemology of holistic integration of self with its experiences of others, thus of emotion and intuition with reason. Qualities of trust, of openness and commitment, taken on cognitive content, and thus factor what we call "faith" into understanding through a communalizing integration. At the same time this epistemological shift does not eliminate God as Person—rather, it lets God out of the objectified role of a literalized metaphor, out of the focus of the controlling Western epistemology for which reason dominated, even in the guise of "faith."

Let us consider now the attribute of Creator. While often creation theology has served merely to enforce the transcendent "sovereignty" (again the language of power-patriarchy) of a *creatio ex nihilo* long ago, feminist theology makes here the opposite gesture. It rediscovers the present immanence of the First Person— not "out of nothing" but "in the midst of everything." The response is what Rosemary Ruether has called "the conversion of the mind to the earth."[3] This was not easy. Theological feminists, who from the outset assumed the supposed biblical preference for history over nature as the site of divine revelation, readily joined the historicism of socialist feminists and other social justice movements in polarizing against the "naturalism" of the goddess movement, with its tendency to romanticize biology. Conversely, "goddess feminists" insisted that "feminist theology" was a contradiction in terms, that God in the biblical tradition is as irreversibly male as the conservatives claim "He" is. But the dialogue ripened, its maturation marked by the moment Ruether defined God as the "divine matrix of life," which she renamed "God/ess." This was no mere compromise, but a transcendence, forged in the flames of the planetary crisis of interlinked social and environmental injustice, of the binary opposition of culture and nature. Ecofeminism thus entered theology, and feminist theology leads the way for a greening of theology which in the 1980s had left John Cobb's Whiteheadian work on the connection of theological, cosmology to the ecological emergency almost the sole representative.[4] Cobb's process theology is itself of tremendous, if often unacknowledged, influence on feminist theology.

Epistemologically, then, this line of development suggests that the attribute of Creator of heaven and earth, apocalyptically redirected to the new creation, converts the character of human creativity. Our own works of creation (in which I include sermons, church school teaching, articles) no longer claim the pervasive enlightenment epistemology of the expert Knower in control of "his" knowable objects; the postmodern unmasking of the modern projects of empire and control, combined with the ecological horrors they unleashed, relativizes at once human and divine creativity. Neoorthodox attempts to relativize human object-knowledge to an absolute divine Subject anticipate in a certain ecclesiocentric sense the postmodern critique of the Enlightenment, yet they demonstrate little potential for influence beyond a closed ecclesial circle, as they fail to engage the complexities of cultural, let alone multicultural and ecological, conversation.

So *how* do we know in the light of the First Person of heaven and earth? We know *earthily*—that is, "adam-ically"; we know *ecologically*. That is, our processes of perception are recognized as thoroughly but not therefore reductively social and material: there is no epistemic process to which we have access that is not a matter of embodiment within an ecological niche. Theologically this means that spirit materializes: "the spirit of life" (Moltmann) is not the animating principle of some inherently dead matter, but the purposive vitality that matters, that becomes matter. Feminist theology presumes some psychoanalytic honesty regarding the patriarchal dread of matter, the matrix, as *mater*, but need not fixate itself on a Divine Mother. Rather, the emergence of maternal metaphors for the deity will depend on a biocentric knowing, a knowing of self and other as infinitely and irreducibly enmeshed—not thereby suffocated!—in the ecological vitalities of which God as Creator-Spirit symbolizes the widest interpretation. Such knowing massages our fragile modern ego-selves out of the ghostly constriction of individualistic power/knowledge. And of ultimately more importance, it relocates our fidelities to the project of the new creation: the renewing of the creation. Knowing the re-creator of heaven and earth becomes the epistemic praxis of re-creation of land, the ocean, and the atmosphere which are being apocalyptically devastated by the Western "dominion over the earth," a mockery of the adamic obligation to stewardship. Creaturely consciousness thus guides our ecological re-creation of the creation for which our species will be held accountable. To proclaim a Creator God who cares more about whether folk in the church are worshiping him with the right language than about what is happening to the planet must strike one as quaint blasphemy.

Yet such theological moves stimulate another attribute of the First Person, and thus another aspect of our own personhood: that of authority. Concepts of divine power flow preeminently from "God the Father," perfectly mirroring the power structures of millennia of what Schüssler Fiorenza calls the "kyriarchy"—the system of patriarchal domination by which male elites, now largely white, exercise dominion over everyone and everything else.[5] Feminist debate about whether to claim power for ourselves, to reject the idea of power, or to reconstrue power as empowerment (power for and in one another rather than power over another) seems not accidentally to parallel the theological debates about God-language: claim it for ourselves, reject it, or reconstruct it? Let me merely suggest in the present context that the Foucauldian feminist reading of power as in modernity, not that possessed by an authoritative, dominative Subject of Power at the top, but as "exercised," "capillary," flowing through our total network of social relations and internalized in our bodies, is proving most suggestive for feminist theological ethics.[6] While revolution loses its utopian allure in this model, promising no eschatological reversal, feminists may work the attribute of divine power as the epistemology of ethical attention to power. Knowing empoweringly means first of all attending to the power that we embody. Such power in women exercises intimate surveillance even over our own selves, in the internalized gaze of the "patriarchal connoisseur," and yet at the same time it lends us influence in our immediate life-world. To claim our own authority as women in religious communities and institutions means at once dethroning the patriarchal idol lodged in our personalities and taking seriously the power we already have. (Would this not hold of postpatriarchal men as well?) Power then becomes an exercise in the feminist ethics of mutuality laid out magisterially by Beverly Harrison: the empowerment of "right relations" as the work of justice.[7] For it is preeminently as a response to injustice that power becomes an issue: both in the exodus-prophetic tradition and in feminism. To know through the first persona is to know empoweringly, to register the interpersonal and the political currents of injustice and the mind-numbing consumerism that now supports it as cut through by potential force fields of spirit. In this mutual knowingness, no longer spreading pre-Auschwitz, pre-Hiroshima hoaxes about divine control over the course of history, we begin to take a new responsibility, which means to embody a new author-ity. Indeed, precisely as authors—as textual commentators, writers, and proclaimers of texts—we exercise an undeniable epistemological privilege.

So, then: personally, creatively, earthily, empoweringly, and authoringly, the "father" reread by feminism releases the epistemic space for an alternate construction of faith's knowledge. Has this transmission of the divine attribute into consciousness of relations proved after all Feuerbachian? I think, rather, it presupposes the modern disclosure of God-language as projection, without therefore reducing the space of a dismantled theological certainty to any new epistemological one.

THE SECOND PERSON

At the point of the Second Person, the Trinity really gets "personal." Only as Father of the Son does the monotheistic deity reveal himself *as* Father—and vice versa. And only as Son does divine Word become human flesh. For Christian feminism, the incarnation gives birth to at once great promise and great disappointment. It seems to restore the holiness of that human materiality drifting in patriarchy into an impure alienation as always "born of a woman," to open up *theosis* to all flesh. But inasmuch as Jesus is constructed as the great exception, he merely proves the rule—the rule of the immaterial Father. Christians are permitted this single point of divine immanence, concentrating in itself all the signals of transcendence. For women, the exceptional character of the incarnation has at once invited great intimacy with this archetypal "sensitive male," while reopening a relation to a paternity often felt as distant or abusive. At the same time the elevation of a Son to a status that by definition can never be attained by another, and therefore certainly never by a daughter, still functions to exclude Catholic women from ordination and Protestant women from a full vocation.

Feminist theology has therefore understood Christology as our great "thorn in the flesh." For only in the designation of the unique human manifestation of the divine does the Word of patriarchy become ultimate—the "last word." Thus Mary Daly surrendered any hope of a "second coming of women" under the banner of the Christian Logos, and led her 1970s exodus from the patriarchal church. But that Logos nonetheless has since inspired a wave of feminist Christologies, emphasizing the historical Jesus as a finite, charismatic Jewish male who gathered around him an egalitarian socio-spiritual movement; some feminist Christologies also stress the universality of the Christ-symbol as a cosmic eros or divine wisdom immanent in but transcendent of the historical Jesus, and thus capable of empowering women and other vulnerable flesh.

Out of the icon of the fleshly vulnerability of Jesus developed an orthodoxy of atonement, understood as redemption by innocent suffering. Precisely here have irrupted women's protests against the use of Christology to enforce an obediently suffering daughterhood: feminist Christology understands the crucifixion of that man as a result not of divine will, but of human sin. In the light of the astonishing data about the pervasion in U.S. family life of the physical abuse of children, including prominently the sexual abuse of girls, we have recognized in substitutionary and surrogacy constructions of atonement what Brock calls "cosmic child abuse": the imputation to the Father of the need for the physical torture, humiliation, and sacrifice of the perfectly innocent child. Womanist theology, sounding the difficult challenge of a truly pluralist and multitongued theology, shows that from a black woman's perspective as well, the atonement symbolism of surrogacy echoes slave mother's functions and thus sours Christology.[8]

Thus spurred both by the polyglossia of women's Christianities and by the maturation of our understanding of power as well, we are outgrowing the (white) feminist tendency to construct ourselves as the innocent victim. Instead Brock has proposed a "christology of erotic power."[9] Eros (not in the genital but in the cosmic sense linked to Tillich and Whitehead) here reanimates the Christ-symbol as a power of relation. Thus the point is to highlight not the heroism of an extraordinary individual, but the quality of relationships he generated around him. What matters is again not Jesus or the Christ as object, but the force field of christic relations and its power to animate a body of mutually implicated members as dissidents within the historical process.

Epistemologically, then, we know through the mask of the Second Person that whatever we know we know relationally; and this means erotically — with the fleshly, creative desire for connections to the others out of whose lives we come and whose future we transform just by being "members one of another." As daughters of God we are siblings of all creatures, seeking for them the justice that will allow mutuality for all; in this way we also maintain the perichoresis of the First and Second Persons. And third: the bodily knowing — "biblical knowledge" — of the incarnation thus infinitely overflows the single instance of Jesus; the Spirit was becoming flesh before and will be forever after him. Our bodily knowing is the knowing of social bodies: bodies which are themselves organic communities, enmeshed in endless socioecological networks beyond themselves. These relations become christological — indeed "atoning" — only as they become the subject of mutual attention.

Word: epistemologically, this christological personhood at once utters and incarnates the wisdom of the Jewish Hochma/Sophia. Thus Elisabeth Schüssler Fiorenza has developed a biblical theology of the historical Jesus as prophet and child of Sophia. Christology, as Moltmann and others argue, was originally inseparable from sophiology. But the convenience of the masculine Logos for the Fourth Gospel's designation of Jesus proved irresistible. Moreover, the growing privilege of the metaphor of Sonship over all other predicates—including, ironically that of Logos—which culminates in Nicene orthodoxy, neatly eclipsed this lingering female image of the divine. Schüssler Fiorenza's historicist rhetorical criticism well develops the exegetical basis for a Christology of Wisdom—as the prophetic praxis in the tradition of Jesus' "Jewish emancipatory movement" in which women figured so prominently. Yet the "critical praxis of reflective sophialogy" she then invites does not mean some new assumption of a "feminine" style of thinking "or a mode of theologizing from 'the woman's perspective.' "[10] "We must also consider that women, sometimes even more than men, have internalized cultural-religious feminine values and hence are in danger of reproducing the preconstructed kyriarchal politics of either womanly submission or feminine glorification in their own speaking and writing."[11] Yet I find Schüssler Fiorenza's absorption of poststructuralist antireferentialism—the assumption that "language" as a sociocultural phenomenon "does not reflect reality"—quite unwise; indeed, stifling not only the ecological promise of a sophiological Christology but the proclamatory work of women.[12] We cannot as women engage in proclamation of the word—the words spoken by and as female flesh—if we do not trust that our language refers, however clumsily and certainly only by way of our linguistic cultural conventions, to the "reality" of a suffering world. Reference within the field of endlessly shifting relations remains of necessity a matter of relative location. Wisdom thus offers herself as "a tree of life to those who lay hold of her" precisely within the destabilizing world of interfluent and untrustworthy powers.

Christologically I recommend something like Rebecca Chopp's own poststructuralist version of "proclamation" as a metaphor of women coming to voice, to authority, to authorship—to the Word. This "Word," unlike the repressive Word, "a figuration always ordered through the dominant discourse, . . . which has denied access of women to words and Word," refers to "reality" indeed. "This is a reality of Word as creative, interrupting, and transforming process—of Word that bridges chaos and creation, bringing light, earth, animals, plants, woman, man into physical being."[13] That theological knowing which has atoning power for feminists in the church will not keep silence: it knows proclaimingly. "While language in modernity reflects a monotheistic ordering, in feminist proclamation language constitutes an open possibility for transformation."[14] To know proclaimingly is then to know openly, transformingly, and polymorphically, for openness for Chopp references the force field of multiple voices in which the message to be proclaimed takes flesh and finds its tongues. Such a christological possibility moves with genderfluid ease to sophiology and back. Thus one might add that a sophiological epistemology, because it potentially breaks open the premodern and modern monoliths of a repressive One which inevitably produces and suppresses an Other, already moves beyond the dyads of gender into the Trinitarian epistemology of a manytongued Word of the world.

THE THIRD PERSON

It is "in the Spirit" that an alternative epistemology comes into its own medium. The charisms of the Spirit are precisely modes of knowing that were already in the first century deemed strange and disruptive: the ecstatic and prophetic gifts as well as those of teaching and interpretation, even of healing, are spirit-practices that cut against not only modern modes of cognition but classical conventions as well. The spirit empowers spontaneously embodied, communal, and empowering relations of subjects to other subjects in a manner resistant to the cognitive disciplines of the "kyriarchy," both within and without the church. Hence Paul's highly charged ambivalence about the Holy Spirit: "Never try to suppress the Spirit," he wisely warns (1 Thess. 5:19); but "Paul was worried by the direction [that] experiences of the Spirit were taking in Corinth."[15] Thus he hierarchically classifies the gifts according to his sense of communal order. New Testament scholar Antoinette Wire has set forth a persuasive scholarly argument that Paul's aggressive approach (threatening to come "with a stick," 1 Cor. 4:21) toward the Corinthians pertains especially to the women prophets. To these Corinthians the Spirit had granted far too much proclamatory public power for Paul (whose conversion did not fully dislodge his sexism) to tolerate.[16] Were these women's tongues burning like those of women called into leadership today?

If therefore we take into account the intriguing gender ambiguity of the Holy Spirit — its feminine *ruach* form, its elemental, nonanthropomorphic manifestations in fire, water, and wind, its frequent appearances in early Christianity, especially among the Syriac fathers, as nursing mother and power of new birth, its personhood invites feminist pneumatological speculation. The personhood of the Holy Spirit, always problematic for theological systematization — especially as supposedly proceeding from the Father and the Son, its own prechristological integrity thus suppressed by the Western imposition of the *filioque* clause — has been largely trivialized within the scholastic imagination. This is not surprising, given its in-spiration of nonscholastic and often revolutionary forms of knowledge and action. The spirit in modern Protestantism was left to flap around within the private pietisms of antirationalist traditions, often deeply associated with feeling and with women, but unable therefore to reshape the operative epistemologies of mainline faith and culture.

Yet, so far, the heavy and unambiguous masculinity for the First and Second Persons which controls ecclesial orthodoxy has proportionately preoccupied feminist theology. Mary Daly had dedicated her book *Pure Lust* to "the spirit" — but only after her metamorphosis into a decisively post-Christian prophet.[17] Feminist theologians have been rightly anxious about the disembodied and apolitical pietism of the "spiritual" traditions. Yet this anxiety has also repressed the pneumatological potential of the movement and thus locked us into the modern epistemologies characteristic of academic and political discourse. This pertains of course to the above question of the objectifying tendencies within feminism itself — what more epistemologically disobjectifying and interpersonalizing symbol than that of the Third Person? But the Roman Catholic theologian Elizabeth Johnson has finally broken the pneumatic barrier within feminism: her great work *She Who Is* unfolds a Trinitarian paradigm in which the Third Person becomes of necessity the first. Her moves are essentially sophiological, working the metaphor of Sophia at once for its gendered and for its ontological-relational connotations: thus Spirit-Sophia, named out of the clear intersection of those figures in the Wisdom of Solomon, initiates her systematic theology.[18] It then moves through Jesus-Sophia and Mother-Sophia: proposals not for male-exclusion (though readers nostalgic for the millennia of purely masculine God-talk often read a single text like hers as just such a threat) but for a delicate and biblically derived counterpoint.

The breezier openings of the Spirit into an alternative discourse beyond patriarchy has therefore only begun to be explored. The problem of its awkward Third Personhood—at once an "I" and an "it," a "thou" and a "he" or even "she," mediating between, reduced even to a kind of hypostasis of the relation between Father and Son, that is, the problem of the personhood of their interpersonality—might be nudged a bit through the epistemological move. That is, to know the Spirit is to know *spiritually* (Protestants, do not fear! you will not need to say the rosary); to experience the Spirit as person is not to objectify a third cosmic entity of some ghostly variety, but to personify the divine spirit, the very spirit of life, in one's own personhood. But then that personhood is *ipso facto* interpersonal, transpersonal, and ultimately theomorphic.

Nothing spooky there: the personhood of the Third Person reveals itself as the relation of relations, the dynamism of relation itself within a universe in which nothing is what it is in abstraction from the matrix of relations. This is, after all, a version of Augustine's pneumatology of "love itself." But the predicate of "love" is not here subordinated to the substantives of "lover" and "beloved": rather, any enduring personal hypostases are themselves discursive abstractions from the field of pneumatic relations constituting the creation. This spirit is God, the God who does not merely perform, but *is*, love. What matters, that is, what *materializes* love may well be called our spiritual practice, our spiritualized practices, in which through "gifts of the spirit" we cherish, enhance, and expand the boundaries of our social body. Not as the militant imperialism of any missionary body after Constantine, but as the *corpus christi*, whose main task in the world may be the *metanoia* for the devastating effects of the pathologized and institutionalized "body of Christ" on the body of creation: on the bodies of women, of Jews, of slaves, of the colored and the colonized, on the nonhuman matrix of life itself.

The task is so overwhelming as we approach the millennium, so fraught with apocalyptic resonances, that I am convinced that only revitalized spiritual practices (as opposed to the mere confessional verbiage of a Word abstracted from its Spirit) will empower the sustaining commitment needed for the New Creation. Christian defensiveness against critique by ourselves and by others, or against alternative spiritualities, will only enhance the likelihood of the "man-made apocalypse." For we as Christians need instruction from the old wisdoms of non-Western and indigenous traditions we had colonized; the former are more embodied in their spiritual practices around breath and meditation, the latter in their cosmologically and ecologically rich spiritualities. Only by evolving ecumenically Christian earth-spiritualities can we "ground the spirit" as a force of renewal rather than escape.[19] Because women have repeatedly been figured as that mother, home, earth whose embrace is to *be* escaped, such spirit-grounding serves at once as a feminist and an ecological practice. Thus, in the Trinitarian epistemology, which only the Spirit makes alive, the authority we claim from the First Person, itself relational, only lives as earth-flesh among us and only proclaims that word inasmuch as the community of the present charismatically authorizes it. Despite, or rather because of, its eschatological intensity, the Spirit in Christian form requires an intensive attention to its own immediacy. To know spiritually is to know presently—an embodiment of the possible in the now, only so enabling us to know spiritedly with enthusiasm, with vitality, in the energy without which proclamatory transformation collapses into the depressed dream of a dying church. An eminently epistemological persona, the Spirit recognizes itself in the cognition of any relation of knowing that energizes attention to the relations between relations, and therefore to the justice and the love through which relations seek to become consciously and spiritedly mutual. In the Trinitarian refraction beyond oneness or twoness, the polyglossia of Spirit sets tongues on fire. Yet such proclamation does not consume itself in single revelations, but burns in sustaining and sustainable community.

The privilege of the three, though not as such a biblical concern, does at least suggest for us always the dialectical movement of our own faith, as seeking understanding grounded in the endless complexity of relations. As Buber suggested, the "third" always attends to the "I" and the "thou" when they encounter each other in mutuality. Any biblically faithful epistemology will necessarily communicate "biblical knowledge"—that is, a knowledge suppressed by modern objectivisms and flooded by modern subjectivist reactions, the knowing of an intersubjective eros in which the relationship itself, as intrinsically valuable, at once becomes and reveals a Third. The Christian Trinitarian gesture, freed from its idolatrous objectifications of God, can then clarify the spiritual dynamic by which we try to make wise decisions amid the overwhelming suffering and complexity of cosmic and historical life at the turn of the millennium. Indeed, the Trinitarian rhythm of understanding may have a grounding effect, that is, if it provides a sense of oriented presence within our own bodily matrices of socionatural interaction. Feminist theology moves in many directions simultaneously, and so certainly will be better served by the triune than by monistic or dualistic models: inasmuch as the third functions always as the relation between all other relations—itself never merely one, but refracting into the polyvocal multiplicity of "tongues of fire."

NOTES

1. Mary Daly, *Beyond God the Father* (Boston: Beacon Press, 1973).
2. Michel Foucault, *The Foucault Reader*, ed. P. Rabinow (New York: Pantheon, 1984), 95.
3. Rosemary Radford Ruether, *Sexism and God-Talk: Toward a Feminist Theology* (Boston: Beacon Press, 1983).

4. Charles Birch and John B. Cobb Jr., *The Liberation of Life: From Cell to Community* (Cambridge: Cambridge University Press, 1981).
5. Elisabeth Schüssler Fiorenza, *Jesus: Miriam's Child, Sophia's Prophet: Critical Issues in Feminist Christology* (New York: Continuum, 1994).
6. C. W. Maggie Kim, Susan M. St. Ville, and Susan M. Simonaitis, eds., *Transfigurations: Theology and the French Feminists* (Minneapolis: Fortress Press, 1993).
7. Beverly W. Harrison, *Making the Connections: Essays in Feminist Social Ethics* (Boston: Beacon Press, 1985).
8. Delores Williams, *Sisters in the Wilderness: The Challenge of Womanist God-Talk* (Maryknoll, N.Y.: Orbis Books, 1993).
9. Rita N. Brock, *Journeys by Heart: A Christology of Erotic Power* (New York: Crossroad, 1988).
10. Schüssler Fiorenza, *Jesus: Miriam's Child*, 162.
11. Ibid., 188.
12. Ibid., 162.
13. Rebecca S. Chopp, *The Power to Speak: Feminism, Language, God* (New York: Crossroad, 1989), 29.
14. Ibid., 126.
15. José Comblin, *The Holy Spirit and Liberation* (New York: Orbis Books, 1989), 33.
16. Antoinette Clark Wire, *The Corinthian Women Prophets: A Reconstruction through Paul's Rhetoric* (Minneapolis: Fortress Press, 1990).
17. Mary Daly, *Pure Lust: Elemental Feminist Philosophy* (Boston: Beacon Press, 1984).
18. Elizabeth A. Johnson, *She Who Is: The Mystery of God in Feminist Theological Discourse* (New York: Crossroad, 1992).
19. Sharon Betcher, "Grounding the Spirit" (Ph. D. diss., Drew University, forthcoming).

MUJERISTA THEOLOGY
A Challenge to Traditional Theology

ADA MARÍA ISASI-DÍAZ

O ne of the reviewers of my book *En La Lucha* pointed out that I have spent the last ten years of my life working at elaborating a *mujerista* theology. When I read this, I realized the reviewer was right: the elaboration of *mujerista* theology has been and will continue to be one of my life-projects. Since I know myself to be first and foremost an activist, an activist-theologian, the reason why *mujerista* theology is so important to me is because to do *mujerista* theology is a significant and important way for me to participate in the struggle for liberation, to make a contribution to the struggle of Latinas in the United States.

What is *mujerista* theology? In the first part of this chapter, after a general description of *mujerista* theology, I will explain some of the key characteristics and elements of *mujerista* theology. In the second part I will deal with the challenges that *mujerista* theology presents to traditional theology. So, what is *mujerista* theology?

GENERAL DESCRIPTION

Allow me to start with the name: *mujerista* theology. To name oneself is one of the most powerful acts a person can do. A name is not just a word by which one is identified. A name also provides the conceptual framework, the point of reference, the mental constructs that are used in thinking, understanding, and relating to a person, an idea, a movement. It is with this in mind that a group of us Latinas[1] who live in the United States, and who are keenly aware of how sexism,[2] ethnic prejudice, and economic oppression subjugate Latinas, started to use the term *mujerista* to refer to ourselves and to use *mujerista* theology to refer to the explanations of our faith and its role in our struggle for liberation.[3]

A *mujerista* is someone who makes a preferential option for Latina women, for our struggle for liberation.[4] Because the term *mujerista* was developed by a group of us who are theologians and pastoral agents, the initial understandings of the term came from a religious perspective. At present the term is beginning to be used in other fields such as literature and history. It is also beginning to be used by community organizers working with grassroot Latinas. Its meaning, therefore, is being amplified without losing as its core the struggle for the liberation of Latina women.

Mujeristas struggle to liberate ourselves not as individuals but as members of a Latino community. We work to build bridges among Latinas/os while denouncing sectarianism and divisive tactics. *Mujeristas* understand that our task is to gather our people's hopes and expectations about justice and peace. Because Christianity, in particular the Latin American inculturation of Roman Catholicism, is an intrinsic part of Latino culture, *mujeristas* believe that in Latinas, though not exclusively so, God chooses once again to lay claim to the divine image and likeness made visible from the very beginning in women. *Mujeristas* are called to bring to birth new women and new men—Latino people willing to work for the good of our people (the "common good") knowing that such work requires the denunciation of all destructive sense of self-abnegation.[5]

Turning to theology specifically, *mujerista* theology, which includes both ethics and systematic theology, is a liberative praxis: reflective action that has as its goal liberation. As a liberative praxis *mujerista* theology is, first, a process of enablement for Latina women that insists on the development of a strong sense of moral agency and clarifies the importance and value of who we are, what we think, and what we do.

Second, as a liberative praxis, *mujerista* theology seeks to impact mainline theologies, those theologies which support what is normative in church and, to a large degree, in society—what is normative having been set by non-Latinas/os and to the exclusion of Latinas and Latinos, particularly Latinas.

Mujerista theology engages in this two-pronged liberative praxis, first by working to enable Latinas to understand the many oppressive structures that almost completely determine our daily lives. It enables Latinas to understand that the goal of our struggle should be not to participate in and to benefit from these structures but to change them radically. In theological and religious language this means that *mujerista* theology helps Latinas discover and affirm the presence of God in the midst of our communities and the revelation of God in our daily lives. Latinas must come to understand the reality of structural sin and find ways of combating it because it effectively hides God's ongoing revelation from us and from society at large.

Second, *mujerista* theology insists on and aids Latinas in defining our preferred future: What will a radically different society look like? What will be its values and norms? In theological and religious language this means that *mujerista* theology enables Latinas to understand the centrality of eschatology in the life of every Christian. Latinas' preferred future breaks into our present oppression in many different ways. Latinas must recognize those eschatological glimpses, rejoice in them, and struggle to make those glimpses become our whole horizon.

Third, *mujerista* theology enables Latinas to understand how much we have already bought into the prevailing systems in society—including the religious systems—and have thus internalized our own oppression. *Mujerista* theology helps Latinas to see that radical structural change cannot happen unless radical change takes place in each and every one of us. In theological and religious language this means that *mujerista* theology assists Latinas in the process of conversion, helping us see the reality of sin in our lives. Further, it enables us to understand that to resign ourselves to what others tell us is our lot and to accept suffering and self-effacement is not a virtue.

MAIN CHARACTERISTICS

Three main elements of *mujerista* theology that are closely interconnected are key to an understanding of this young theological enterprise.

Locus Theologicus

The *locus theologicus*, the place from which we do *mujerista* theology, is our *mestizaje* and *mulatez*, our condition as racially and culturally mixed people; our condition as people from other cultures living within the United States; our condition as people living on the borderlands, a reality applicable to the Mexican Americans, to the Cubans, the Puerto Ricans, and other Latino people living throughout the United States.

Mestizaje, which refers to the mixture of cultures as well as the mixture of the European white race and the Amerindian race, and *mulatez*, which refers to the mixture of cultures as well as the mixture of the European white race with the African race, are important for several reasons.[6] First of all, *mestizaje* and *mulatez* proclaim a reality.

Even before the new *mestizaje* and *mulatez* that are happening here in the United States, we all have come from mestizo and *mulato* cultures, from cultures where the white, red, and black races have been intermingled, from cultures where Spanish, Amerindian, and African cultural elements have come together and new cultures have emerged.

Mestizaje and *mulatez* are important to us because they vindicate "precisely that which the dominant culture, with its pervading racism [and ethnic prejudice], condemns and deprecates: our racial and cultural mixture."[7] *Mestizaje* and *mulatez* also point to the fact that "if any would understand us, they must come to us, and not only to our historical and cultural ancestors."[8] *Mestizaje* and *mulatez* are what make it "possible for our cultures to survive. 'Culture' is a total way of responding to the total world and its ever changing challenges."[9] Culture has to do with a living reality, and as such it must grow, change, adapt. And our new *mestizaje* and *mulatez* here in the United States are just that, our actual ongoing growing, based on our past but firmly grounded in the present and living into our future.

Finally, *mestizaje* and *mulatez* are our contribution to a new understanding of pluralism, a new way of valuing and embracing diversity and difference. Later, we will discuss the issue of differences in greater detail. Suffice it to say here that the kind of pluralism that does embrace differences is about distributing opportunities, resources, and benefits in an inclusive way. To embrace differences at the structural level goes well beyond recognizing the multiplicity of interests and identities that exist in this society, and their multiple claims on the institutions of the United States. Embracing differences, real pluralism, is first and foremost about making sure that institutional and economic elites are subjected to effective controls by the constituencies whose welfare they affect, that neither the enjoyment of dominance nor the suffering of deprivation is the constant condition of any group, and that political and administrative officers operate as guardians of popular needs rather than as servants of wealthy interests.[10]

Theologically, how do *mestizaje* and *mulatez* function? *Mestizaje* and *mulatez* are what "socially situates" us Hispanics in the United States. This means that *mestizaje* and *mulatez* as the theological locus of Hispanics delineate the finite alternatives we have for thinking, conceiving, expressing our theology.[11] For example, because *mestizaje* and *mulatez* socially situate our theology, our theology cannot but understand all racism and ethnic prejudice as sin, and the embracing of diversity as virtue. This means that the coming of the kin-dom[12] of God has to do with a coming together of peoples, with no one being excluded and at the expense of no one. Furthermore, *mestizaje* and *mulatez* mean that the unfolding of the kindom of God happens when instead of working to become part of structures of exclusion we struggle to do away with such structures. Because of the way mainline society thinks about *mestizaje* and *mulatez*, we cannot but think about the divine in nonelitist, nonhierarchical ways.

Mestizaje and *mulatez* for us Latinas and Latinos are not a given. In many ways they are something we have to choose repeatedly, something we have to embrace in order to preserve our cultures, in order to be faithful to our people, and from a theological-religious perspective, in order to remain faithful to the struggle for peace and justice, the cornerstone of the gospel message. Because we choose *mestizaje* and *mulatez* as our theological locus, we are saying that they are the structure in which we operate, from which we reach out to explain who we are and to contribute to what is normative in theology and religion in this society in which we live. *Mestizaje* and *mulatez* and the contributions they make to society's understanding of pluralism, therefore, are one of the building blocks of a *mujerista* account of justice.

Latinas' Lived-Experience
as Source of Theology

A second characteristic of *mujerista* theology is that it has as its source the lived-experience of Latinas. This means that most of *mujerista* theology's research is done in the barrios, the Hispanic neighborhoods. This characteristic of *mujerista* theology goes back to an old understanding of theology that unfortunately has been ignored now for many centuries. It was the understanding of St. Anselm of Canterbury in the eleventh century. For him, and for us *mujerista* theologians as well, theology is "faith seeking understanding." So our starting place is the lived-experience of Hispanic women, which, because our culture is one in which religion plays a very important role in our daily lives, in some ways is a religious experience.

Latinas' experiences, as all experiences, are social processes constituted not only by given actions but also by the evaluations (including ethical value judgments), tendencies, and perspectives of the subject-agent.[13] What constitutes Latinas' daily experiences, however, are not only particular reflective actions but also the social, economic, political, and cultural factors that frame such actions. Latinas' discourses on our experiences are not intended to provide objective historical facts, but rather are comprehensive narratives that reveal ways of self-interpretation—how we see and understand the world, and how we construct our selves, our communities, and the world at large.[14] These narratives show commonalities as well as particularities, bringing up the issue of whose experiences are to be taken into consideration in the elaboration of norms and how is the truth of one person's experience upheld in the face of another person's experience.

To deal with this issue we insist on the social character of experience, accepting the possibility that no perspective offers exclusive access to the truth and, therefore, that no "human perspective has a privileged access to ontological reality."[15] There is a communal aspect to experience, which in turn means that all experience is indeed socially located and connected to power, and "value-defined and interest-laden."[16]

The relative character of all experience points to the need to determine how to deal with differences and the grounds for determining whose experience to privilege at any given moment. Since *mujerista* theology is about the liberation of Latinas, it is precisely liberation, understood in a holistic sense of liberation at the structural as well as at the personal level, at the ideological level (which includes religious/theological perspectives) as well as at the historical level, that offers the basis for determining whose experience to privilege. The experiences of Latinas who benefit least in a material, psychological, or religious sense—these experiences with their particularities and specificities are the ones privileged by *mujerista* theology. The appeal then is to particular Latinas' experiences, to the experiences of Latinas that contribute to the struggles for liberation, to radical social change.

Does *mujerista* theology pay any attention to what scriptures tell us about God, what the doctrines and dogmas of our churches tell us about the divine, what theologians throughout the centuries have said about God? How does *mujerista* theology deal with the past? We certainly reject any and all regurgitation of the past. Reflexive use of the past is no good. But reflective use of the past is an important method in *mujerista* theology. Our communities have their own living religious traditions. The religious beliefs and practices of grassroots Latinas are not *ex nihilo*, but rather are rooted in traditions passed on from our ancestors and certainly rooted in Catholic and, more recently, in Protestant religious teachings.

Using the lived-experience of Latinas as the source of *mujerista* theology is an act of subversion. Our theology challenges the absolutizing of mainline theology as normative, as exhaustively explaining the Gospels and/or Christian beliefs. Our theology challenges the ongoing attempt by academic theology to consider itself the only valid theological enterprise because it is intellectual. Grassroots Latinas are admirably capable of explaining their religious understandings and practices. Latinas are "organic intellectuals," to use Antonio Gramsci's term, most capable of reflecting on their experience, of learning from it. This means that Latinas are not the object of *mujerista* theology. Latinas are the subjects, the agents of *mujerista* theology.

What, then, is the role of academically trained *mujerista* theologians? *Mujerista* theologians who are academically trained are not "more" or "better" theologians than grassroots Hispanic women theologians. We simply are theological technicians who have the ability to gather and report in writing theological understandings of grassroots Latinas. We are called to put our expertise at the service of our communities rather than at the service of institutional churches. And putting our expertise at the service of our communities means that we are accountable to them, an accountability that demands a precise practice, specific ways in which we are in ongoing relationships with them about what we are writing, what we are saying to the academy. This is what having an option for grassroots Latinas means for those of us who are academic *mujerista* theologians.

Lo Cotidiano

When in *mujerista* theology we talk about the lived-experience of Latinas we are referring to our liberative daily experience, to our experience of struggling every day, we are referring to *lo cotidiano*. *Lo cotidiano* has to do with particular forms of speech, the experience of class and gender distinctions, the impact of work and poverty on routines and expectations, relations within families and among friends and neighbors in a community, the experience of authority, and central expressions of faith such as prayer, religious celebrations, and conceptions of key religious figures.[17]

These key religious figures are not only those of Christianity, Jesus and Mary his mother, but also those more exclusively Catholic like the saints, and those of popular religion, such as the orishas of different African religions, and the deities of different Amerindian religions.

However, in *mujerista* theology *lo cotidiano* is more than a descriptive category. *Lo cotidiano* also includes the way we Latinas consider actions, discourse, norms, established social rules, and our own selves.[18] Recognizing that it is inscribed with subjectivity, that we look at and understand what happens to us from a given perspective, *lo cotidiano* has hermeneutical importance. This means that *lo cotidiano* has to do with the daily lived-experiences that provide the "stuff" of our reality.

Lo cotidiano points to "shared experiences," which I differentiate from "common experience." "Shared experiences" is a phrase that indicates the importance differences play in *lo cotidiano*. On the other hand, "common experience" seems to mask differences, to pretend that there is but one experience, one way of knowing for all Latinas.[19] And *lo cotidiano* points precisely to the opposite of that: it points to transitoriness and incompleteness.

Lo cotidiano is not a metaphysical category, it is not an attempt to see Latinas' daily lived-experience as fixed and universal. Rather it is a way of referring to the "stuff" and the processes of Latinas' lives.[20] *Lo cotidiano* is not something that exists a priori, into which we fit the daily lived-experience of Latinas. *Lo cotidiano* of Latinas is a matter of life and death, it is a matter of who we are, of who we become, and, therefore, it is far from being something objective, something we observe, relate to, and talk about in a disinterested way. Finding ways to earn money to feed and clothe their children and to keep a roof over their heads is part of *lo cotidiano* for Latinas. Finding ways to survive corporal abuse is part of *lo cotidiano*. Finding ways to effectively struggle against oppression is part of *lo cotidiano*.[21]

Besides its descriptive and hermeneutical task, *mujerista* theology appropriates *lo cotidiano* as the epistemological framework of our theological enterprise.

Therefore, *lo cotidiano*, the daily experience of Latinas, not only points to their capacity to know but also highlights the features of their knowing. *Lo cotidiano* is a way of referring to Latinas' efforts to understand and express how and why their lives are the way they are, how and why they function as they do.[22] Of course there are other ways of coming to know what is real; there are many forms and types of knowledge. Our emphasis on *lo cotidiano* as an epistemological category, as a way of knowing, has to do, in part, with the need to rescue Latinas' daily experience from the category of the unimportant.

Lo cotidiano has been belittled and scorned precisely because it is often related to the private sphere, to that sphere of life assigned to women precisely because it is considered unimportant. Or is it the other way around? In *mujerista* theology, then, *lo cotidiano* has descriptive, hermeneutical, and epistemological importance. The valuing of *lo cotidiano* means that we appreciate the fact that Latinas see reality in a different way from the way it is seen by non-Latinas. And it means that we privilege Latinas' way of seeing reality insofar as the goal of their daily struggle is liberation. This is very important for *mujerista* theology for, though for us *lo cotidiano* carries so much weight, it is not the criterion used for judging right and wrong, good and bad. It is only insofar as *lo cotidiano* is a liberative praxis, a daily living that contributes to liberation, that *lo cotidiano* is considered good, valuable, right, salvific.[23] Were we to claim *lo cotidiano* as an ethical/theological criterion, norm, or principle we would be romanticizing *lo cotidiano*. Yes, there is much that is good and life-giving in *lo cotidiano*, but there also is much that "obstructs understanding and tenderness, allowing to appear an abundance of postures of self-defense that are full of falsehoods, of lies, that turn *lo cotidiano* into a behavior that is not open to life."[24]

The importance we give to *lo cotidiano* steers *mujerista* theology away from any essentialism that would obscure precisely what is at the core of *lo cotidiano*: difference. At the same time, *lo cotidiano* moves us from the "add and stir" version of feminist theology. As an epistemological category *lo cotidiano* goes well beyond adding another perspective and points to the need to change the social order by taking into consideration the way Latinas see and understand reality. *Lo cotidiano* points to the fact that how we Latinas, women who struggle from the underside of history, constitute ourselves and our world is an ongoing process. It takes into consideration many different elements that we use to define ourselves as Latinas within the United States in the last years of the twentieth century.[25]

This does not mean, however, that *lo cotidiano* leads us to total relativism.[26] The fact that *lo cotidiano* is not the criterion, norm, or principle we use in *mujerista* theology does not mean that we use no criterion to judge right and wrong. As we have already said, we do recognize and hold liberation to be the criterion or principle by which we judge what is right or wrong, what is good or bad, what is salvific or condemnatory. By insisting as we have done on the "shared experiences" that constitute *lo cotidiano* we are trying to counter the isolationism inherent in individualism, the superiority inherent in claims of uniqueness, the hegemonic effect of false universalisms, all of which are intrinsic elements of absolute relativism. By saying that liberation is the criterion we use in *mujerista* theology, we are insisting

on making it the core element, yes, the essential element of Latinas' morality and
of all morality. In making liberation our central criterion, *mujerista* theology attempts to contribute to an elaboration of morality that revolves around solidarity
with the oppressed and the search for ways of an ever more inclusive social
justice.[27]

In no way is the specificity of *lo cotidiano* to be taken as an "anything goes"
moral attitude. That attitude is possible only by those who have power, by those
whose social-political reality is entrenched and who, therefore, do not feel threatened by the rest of humanity. That attitude is possible only in those who feel their
world is completely stable, that nothing needs to change and that nothing will
change. That is why *lo cotidiano* of Latinas is totally unimaginable for the dominant group; that is why they are totally disengaged from *lo cotidiano* of two-thirds
of the world; that is why they are incapable of conceiving new ideas, of creating
new ways of organizing society, even ways that would help them to perpetuate the
status quo.[28]

Our insistence on *lo cotidiano* indeed should be seen as a denunciation of inadequate and false universalisms that ignore Latinas' daily lived-experience. It
also is a denunciation of the oppression Latinas suffer. Our insistence on *lo cotidiano* is an attempt to make our Latinas' experience count, to question the "truth"
spoken by those who have the power to impose their views as normative. But our
insistence on *lo cotidiano* must not be read as denying the viability and need for
shared agendas and strategies. On the contrary, *mujerista* theology is anxious to
participate in developing those strategies for liberation which we know can grow
only out of real solidarity, and this, in turn, depends on a real engagement of differences rather than a superficial acknowledgment of them.

In *mujerista* theology *lo cotidiano* has made it possible to appeal to the daily
lived-experience of Latinas as an authentic source without ignoring social location. On the contrary, *lo cotidiano* makes social location explicit, for it is the context of the person in relation to physical space, ethnic space, social space.
Furthermore, *lo cotidiano* for Latinas points both to the struggle (*la lucha*) against
the present social order and to the liberating alternative that constitutes the core of
our historical project: community (*la comunidad*). This means that *lo cotidiano*
constitutes the arena where Latinas are confronted by the groups of which they are
members. This makes it possible for them to judge their own personal understandings, aspirations, ambitions, projects, and goals in their lives. So, *lo cotidiano* is where morality begins to play a role for Latinas.[29] *Lo cotidiano* becomes
the lived-text in which and through which Latinas understand and decide what is
right and good, what is wrong and evil.[30] As such *lo cotidiano* is not a private, individual category, but rather a social category. *Lo cotidiano* refers to the way Latinas know and what we know to be the "stuff" (*la tela*, literally, the cloth) out of
which our lives as a struggling community within the United States are fabri-
cated.[31]

Lo cotidiano for us is also a way of understanding theology, our attempt to explain how we understand the divine, what we know about the divine. I contrast this
to the academic and churchly attempts to see theology as being about God instead

of about what we humans know about God. *Lo cotidiano* makes it possible for us to see our theological knowledge as well as all our knowledge as fragmentary, partisan, conjectural, and provisional.[32] It is fragmentary because we know that what we will know tomorrow is not the same as what we know today but will stand in relation to what we know today. What we know is what we have found through our experiences, through the experiences of our communities of struggle. What we know is always partisan, it is always influenced by our own values, prejudices, loyalties, emotions, traditions, dreams, and future projects.[33] Our knowing is conjectural because to know is not to copy or reflect reality but rather to interpret in a creative way those relations, structures, and processes that are elements of what is called reality. And, finally, *lo cotidiano* makes it clear that, for *mujerista* theology, knowledge is provisional, for it indicates in and of itself how transitory our world and we ourselves are.[34]

A Specific Kind of Liberation Theology

The third characteristic of *mujerista* theology is that it is a liberation theology, a specific kind with its own characteristics. For us the unfolding of the kin-dom of God does not happen apart from history. We talk about "salvation liberation," believing that both are interconnected and that to work for liberation for us Christians, which has to do with establishing justice in concrete ways in our world, is not necessarily different from being good Christians. So our prime lens is liberation: how do religious practices and beliefs contribute to or hinder the struggle for survival, the struggle for liberation of our people?

Part of this understanding is the fact that for us theology is a praxis. By praxis I mean reflective, liberative action. To understand theology as praxis means that we accept the fact that we cannot separate thinking from acting. *Mujerista* theology is not reflection upon action but a liberative action in and of itself. The daily actions of our communities as they struggle to survive need intentional thinking, and religion plays a role in the thinking and the motivation for action, as well as in the kind of action done and the reason for doing it. Amplifying here what was mentioned above, the insistence that grassroots Latinas do *mujerista* theology, and that so doing is a liberative praxis, indicates that they too are intellectuals. The regular understanding of "intellectual" connotes a social function, a professional category. Unfortunately, however, this meaning is usually extended to mean that intellectuals, in contrast to nonintellectuals, are the ones who are capable of intellectual activity. In reality, however, although one can speak of intellectuals, one cannot speak of nonintellectuals, because nonintellectuals do not exist. . . . Each [one] participates in a particular conception of the world, has a conscious line of moral conduct, and therefore contributes to sustain a conception of the world or to modify it, that is, to bring into being new modes of thought.[35]

Women in general (but in particular poor women with little formal education, and even more so women whose first language is not English—as is the case with many Latinas) are commonly not considered quite capable of articulating what they think. Yes, many consider that Latinas' ability to think is at best limited. It is clear to see, then, why *mujerista* theology's claim that grassroots Latinas are "organic intellectuals," that their articulation of their religious understandings is an element of this theology, is in itself a liberative praxis.

Another important element of *mujerista* theology as a liberation theology is the part "the religion of the people" (popular religion) plays in it.[36] It is precisely this aspect of the religion of Latinas that provides the greatest impetus for our struggle for liberation. There is no way you can deal with Latinas and Latinos, study our culture or read our literature, without encountering the religion of the people (popular religion). After the Spanish language, the religion of the people (popular religion) is the most important identifying characteristic of Latinas, the main carrier of our culture. Latinas' Christianity is of a very specific variety. Its main vehicle, the signs and symbols that it uses, and a significant part of its theology are based on medieval Christianity, the pre-Reformation, sixteenth-century Christianity of southern Spain. But this sixteenth-century Spanish Christianity is mingled with the religious beliefs and rituals of African and Amerindian cultures as well.[37]

Now "dominant North Atlantic theology has generally regarded popular religion as a primitive force of religious expression needing to be evangelized."[38] *Mujerista* theology, as most of Latino theology, on the other hand, "recognizes popular religion as a credible experience of the . . . [divine]; and as a positive reservoir of values for self-determination."[39] In other words, in *mujerista* theology we insist on "the normative, graced, and even universal dimensions of the 'salvific' manifestations of non-Christian religions."[40]

The religion of the people (popular religion) plays a significant role in our struggles for survival and liberation. Many of us know from experience that it is mainly due to the religion of the people (popular religion) that Christianity is alive and flourishing among Latinas in spite of the lack of care and attention we have experienced from the churches. In the religion of the people (popular religion) we find a sense of embracing diversity that makes it possible for diverse elements to influence each other to the point where each element is reformulated, maintaining its own specificity but not without taking into consideration the specificity of the other elements.

CHALLENGES TO TRADITIONAL THEOLOGY

Let us now turn to deal with what I call "challenges" to traditional theology. In no way do I want to suggest that there is nothing good about traditional theology. But I do want to make it very clear that its relevance to what is going on in our world today is waning mainly because of the way in which it insists on dealing with tradition, and because theology seems to be content with seeing itself as accountable only, or at least mainly, to the institutional churches.

"Epistemological Vigilance"

The first challenge is born of a need we *mujerista* theologians recognize as primary: we must have "epistemological vigilance."[41] We need to be epistemologically vigilant, as indeed traditional theology should also be. But while we recognize this need and embrace it, traditional theology rejects it or simply ignores it. Now, what understandings are encompassed within this term of "epistemological vigilance"?

First, we *mujerista* theologians make a very serious and ongoing effort to be aware of our subjectivity. We need to have a "critical consciousness of the limits of our capacity to know reality, and of the 'concealing and distorting' tendencies of this same capacity."[42] We work hard at being aware of our ideological biases and, though it is not easy, we work hard at revealing such biases. This means that we have to be aware of how our own social situation colors our analysis of the religion of our communities and colors the way we say what we say in our theological writings.

Second, epistemological vigilance here refers to the constant need to evaluate how our theological enterprise contributes to the liberation of our people. And here I am referring not only to the results of our theology, our writings, but also to the way in which we conduct our research. The question, "Who benefits from this?" should never be far away from our minds. We need to apply a hermeneutics of suspicion to our constructive proposals, to our narratives, to our whole theological enterprise.

Third, epistemological vigilance refers to the need to avoid avoidance. *Mujerista* theologians need to be able to grapple with differences, with contradictions. We need to engage each other, to press each other for greater clarity, to question each other. In order to do this we need to work very hard at maintaining our sense of community, at not giving in to destructive competition or, what is worse, ignoring each other.

Now, all of this is a challenge to traditional theology because one of the key elements of traditional theology is its so-called objectivity, its so-called immutability, its sense of being "official" and, precisely because it is official, of being the only perspective that is correct.

Mujerista theology denounces any and all so-called objectivity. What passes as objectivity in reality merely names the subjectivity of those who have the authority and/or power to impose their point of view. So instead of objectivity, what we should be claiming is responsibility for our subjectivity. All theology has to start with self-disclosure. Self-disclosure as part of theology should give all those who in one way or another come into contact with our theological work our "actional route."[43] As a theologian I am obliged to reveal my concrete story within the framework of the social forces I have lived in. I am called to reveal the pivotal forces and issues that have formed me and that serve as my main points of reference. The idea in this kind of self-disclosure is to situate the subject, in this case myself, so that my discourse is understandable to others not only out of their own experience but insofar as they have the ability to go beyond the limits of their experience and see how my experience, because it is part of the processes of living, relates to and intersects with their experience, no matter how difficult both experiences are. In other words, the particulars of my life might not be something others can relate to easily, but, by knowing a little about them, others will be able to find some point of contact, at least because of similarities in the processes of our lives. Thanks to those points of contact, others will be able to understand me and assess what I say without necessarily agreeing with me or limiting me to the scope of their experience.

Because subjectivity embraces the question, "Who benefits from this *mujerista* theology?" it challenges the so-called objectivity of traditional theology that refuses to recognize that it often tends to benefit the status quo at the expense of those who are marginal in church and society. The status quo is not a natural arrangement but rather a social construct originating with and maintained mainly by white, Euro-American males. Traditional theology offers intellectual backing for religious understandings and practices at the core of our churches, and it is easy to see who are those in charge of our churches.

Finally, *mujerista* theology's insistence on recognizing and disclosing subjectivity challenges the official status of traditional theology that results in avoidance of engagement. Traditional theology has clothed itself with the immutability that it claims is God's. Or does perhaps not that traditional theology make God immutable because it makes God in its own image and likeness?

Theology as a Communal Task

Our second challenge to traditional theology has to do with the centrality that community has in our Latino culture and in our theology. This means that we will continue to use the lived-experience of our grassroots communities as the source of our theology. So the themes of our theology are those that are suggested to us by the religious understandings and practices of our communities and not by the doctrines and dogmas of our churches. The goal of *mujerista* theology is not to come up with a *Summa*, or with three volumes entitled "Systematic Theology #1, #2, #3." The themes *mujerista* theology deals with are those that are required by Latinas' struggle for liberation. Thus, in our first book we dealt with what grounds the struggle for many of us, our understanding of God. The second book dealt with issues of self-identity—of ethnicity—and of moral agency. And now we are working on issues of embodiment, for what is most commonly used against us, to oppress us, is our bodies.

Yes, we need to continue to approach theology from the perspective of the religious understandings and practices of our communities. This means that we must resist the temptation to do theology as usual, not only by our methods but also by resisting the temptation to follow the "regular" themes and divisions of traditional theology. In no way does this mean that our theology is not, should not be, rigorous. We owe to ourselves and our communities the very best theology that we can do. But good theology for us *mujerista* theologians has to do with a theology that helps our people in their struggle for survival, not a theology that receives the blessing of the status quo because it follows traditional patterns.

In a way traditional theology, even the best of traditional theology, by insisting on following the patterns established long ago in my opinion, closes itself to the ongoing revelation of the divine in our midst. Those who do traditional theology call their way of proceeding "faithfulness to the past." I call it "blindness to the present" and "ignoring the God-in-our-midst today."

The Importance of Differences

A third challenge *mujerista* theology presents to traditional theology has to do with *mestizaje* and *mulatez*, with how we understand and deal with diversity, with differences. For us differences are not something to be done away with but rather something to be embraced. In our theology we do not aim at assimilations, aim at making all that is different fit into some preconceived norm or center. That is not how we deal with diversity. Both in our understanding of *mestizaje* and *mulatez* as well as in our understanding of "the religion of the people" (popular religion) and how it functions in *mujerista* theology you can see what we mean when we talk about embracing diversity.

Let me explain this further. Usually in mainline discourse, in traditional theological discourse, difference is defined as absolute otherness, mutual exclusion, categorical opposition.[44] This is an essentialist meaning of difference in which one group serves as the norm against which all others are to be measured. Those of us who do not measure up are considered to be deviant, and our ideas are heretical.

Difference of opinion, difference of perspective, arising most of the time from different life-experiences, any and all differences are defined as a hostile and opposed position. This way of defining difference expresses a fear of specificity and a fear of making permeable the categorical boundary between oneself and the others, between one's ideas and those of others. Specificity tends to be understood as unique—lending it a certain air of "the unknown" of which one is afraid or which is romanticized as exotic.

In *mujerista* theology we posit embracing differences as a moral option. We work at seeing those who are different from us as mirrors of ourselves and what we think. Ideas that are different from ours are mirrors—not the only ones—we have for our ideas (similar ideas to ours, of course, also are mirrors of our ideas), for they do make us see our ideas in a new light, maybe even make it possible for us to better understand our own ideas, to clarify them for ourselves and for others, a result that might not be achieved if we were to ignore ideas different from ours.

To embrace differences we have to stop being lazy and have to know what others really think. But that requires self-conscious interaction, and we are afraid of interacting with those with whom we disagree. Also, to be able to interact with others we have to affirm difference as something positive, we have to affirm plurality, to make permeable the boundaries of our categories. All of this requires embracing ambiguity, something those of us who live at the margins know much about. But traditional theology is not willing to do that because instead of risking ambiguity it rests secure in its impermeable and immutable center.

In *mujerista* theology difference, then, means not otherness or exclusive opposition but specificity, variations, heterogeneity. Difference is understood as relational rather than as a matter of substantive categories and attributes. Difference is not then a description of categories, descriptions set one against the other across a barbed-wire fence. Rather difference points to the specificity of each description and seeks ways to relate those different descriptions, different because they come from people with dissimiliar life experiences.

Embracing difference, welcoming ambiguity, is not in any way to be conceived as wishy-washiness! We are not advocating total relativity. As a matter of fact, because *mujerista* theology is a strategy for liberation, there is a certain discipline of action that we demand of each other. Also, in Latino culture tradition is something very important. So tradition is taken into consideration. But the role of tradition is not to impose itself perennially without any changes. The role of tradition is to make present the wisdom of generations past which we are then called to evaluate and apply to the present in view of our need for survival, of our need for liberation. And, unfortunately, that is an understanding of tradition that traditional theology is not willing to consider.

In many ways what has guided *mujerista* theology from the beginning are those wonderful words of Miriam in the book of Numbers, "Has Yahweh indeed spoken only through Moses?" (Num. 12:2, RSV). Well aware of the fact that she suffered severe penalties for daring to scold Moses, for daring to claim that Yahweh also spoke to her and through her, our sister Miriam invites *mujerista* theologians to throw our lot with the people of God and to hope that, just as in her case, the authorities will catch up with us, that they will eventually also see that we have no leprosy, that we are clean. But their declaration of cleanliness is not what makes us clean, their saying is *not* what makes *mujerista* theology a worthwhile and important task for us. It is rather the fact that *mujerista* theology is part of the struggle for survival, of the struggle for liberation—that is what makes it right and just for us to pursue it. Doing *mujerista* theology is an intrinsic element of our struggle, of our lives, because indeed for Latinas in the United States to struggle is to live, *la vida es la lucha*.

NOTES

This chapter originally appeared in *Mujerista Theology: A Theology for the Twenty-First Century* (Maryknoll, N.Y.: Orbis Books, 1996).

1. There is no agreement among Latinas whether to refer to themselves as Hispanic women or as Latina women. My choosing to use Latina is done indiscriminately.
2. In *mujerista* theology heterosexism is understood to be a distinct element of sexism.
3. It is important to notice that we do not use the term *mujerismo* since it can be understood to indicate that Latinas' natural entity is based on being woman when in fact our natural entity as women is based on being human. See Raquel Rodríguez, "La Marcha de las Mujeres . . . ," *Pasos* 344 (Marzo–Abril 1991): 11, n. 6.
4. Though the rest of this chapter refers more directly to *mujerista* Latina women, we intend here to make explicit that Latino men as well as men and women from other racial/ethnic groups can also opt to be *mujeristas*.
5. Rosa Marta Zárate Macías, "Canto de Mujer," in *Concierto a Mi Pueblo*, tape produced by Rosa Marta Zárate Macías, P.O. Box 7366, San Bernardino, CA 92411. Much of this description is based on this song composed and interpreted by Rosa Marta in response to several Latinas' insistence on the need for a song that would help to express who they are, and which would inspire them in the struggle. For the full text of her song in English and Spanish, see Ada María Isasi-Díaz, "*Mujeristas*: A Name of Our Own," *Christian Century* (May 24–31, 1989): 560–62.

6. These original meanings have been expanded; these words also refer to the mixing of Latinos in the United States with those of other races-cultures who live in this country, and the mixing among ourselves, Latinos coming from different countries of Latin America and the Caribbean.

7. Justo L. González, "Hispanics in the United States," *Listening—Journal of Religion and Culture* 27, no. 1 (Winter 1992): 14.

8. Ibid., 15.

9. Ibid.

10. Michael Parenti, *Power and the Powerless* (New York: St. Martin's Press, 1978), 28.

11. Otto Maduro, *Religion and Social Conflict* (Maryknoll, N.Y.: Orbis Books, 1982), 42–43.

12. I use kin-dom to avoid using the sexist and elitist word "kingdom." Also, the sense of family of God that kin dom represents is much in line with the centrality of family in our Latina culture. I am grateful to Georgene Wilson, O.S.F., from whom I learned this word.

13. Donald L. Gelpi, *The Turn to Experience* (Mahwah, N.J.: Paulist Press, 1994), 121–57. I point out specifically value judgments because I think evaluations do not necessarily include value judgments. For example, actions can be evaluated in view of monetary profits without necessarily having in mind ethical values.

14. Ellen M. Ross, "Spiritual Experience and Women's Autobiography," *Journal of the American Academy of Religion* 59, no. 3 (1994): 527–28.

15. Sheila Greeve Davaney, "The Limits of the Appeal to Women's Experience," in *Shaping New Vision*, ed. Clarissa W. Atkinson, Constance H. Buchanan, and Margaret R. Miles (Ann Arbor: University of Michigan Research Press, 1987), 43–44.

16. Ibid., 46.

17. Daniel H. Levine, *Popular Voices in Latin American Catholicism* (Princeton, N.J.: Princeton University Press, 1992), 317.

18. Ibid.

19. This has very serious methodological implications for *mujerista* theology. See Ada María Isasi-Díaz, *En La Lucha: Elaborating a Mujerista Theology* (Minneapolis: Fortress Press, 1993), chap. 3.

20. Sharon Welch, "Sporting Power—American Feminists, French Feminists and an Ethic of Conflict," in *Transfigurations: Theology and the French Feminists*, ed. C. W. Maggie Kim, Susan M. St. Ville, and Susan M. Simonaitis (Minneapolis: Fortress Press, 1993), 174.

21. I want to make absolutely clear that *lo cotidiano* is not to be understood as housekeeping chores in the sense that work is usually conceptualized: cleaning, doing laundry, driving the children to extracurricular activities. However, neither do I wish to diminish the importance of those kinds of tasks.

22. Otto Maduro, *Mapas para la Fiesta* (Buenos Aires: Centro Nueva Tierra, 1992), 17.

23. In *mujerista* theology, salvation and liberation are intrinsically united. There can be no salvation without liberation. The realization of the kin-dom of God, which is what salvation refers to, begins to be a reality in history, and that is what liberation is. Liberation has to do with fullness of life, a prerequisite of the full realization of the kin-dom of God. For a fuller explanation, see Isasi-Díaz, *En La Lucha*, 34–45.

24. Ivone Gebara, *Conhece-te a ti misma* (São Paulo, Brazil: Ediciones Paulinas, 1991), 24.

25. For an explanation of the elements that are key to the self-understanding of Latinas, see Isasi-Díaz, *En La Lucha*.

26. My main dialogue partners for these following paragraphs have been Margaret Farley and Leonardo Boff, whom I cite below. See Margaret Farley, "Feminism and Universal Morality," in *Prospect for a Common Morality*, ed. Gene Outka and John P. Reeder (Princeton, N.J.: Princeton University Press, 1993), 170–90.

27. Leonardo Boff, "La postmodernidad y la miseria de la razón liberadora," *Pasos* 54 (Julio–Agosto 1994): 13.

28. Ibid. I am reminded here of one of the reasons Míguez Bonino gives for the preferential option for the poor and oppressed. According to him, since they have nothing to gain from the present structures, the poor and the oppressed are capable of imagining a different future, something those who are set in protecting the present are not capable of doing. See José Míguez Bonino, "Nuevas tendencias en teología," *Pasos* 9 (Enero 1987): 22.

29. Cecilia Mino G., "Algunas reflexiones sobre pedagogía de género y cotidianidad," *Tejiendo Nuestra Red* 1, no. 1 (Octubre 1988): 11–12.

30. To claim *lo cotidiano* as lived-text is in no way to say that it is a moral criterion.

31. Though I do not agree with all of Mary McClintock Fulkerson's ideas, she gives much to think about in our own *mujerista* theological enterprise. See her book *Changing the Subject: Women's Discourses and Feminist Theology* (Minneapolis: Fortress Press, 1994).

32. Maduro, *Mapas para la Fiesta*, 137.

33. And in *mujerista* theology we are very clear about our partisan perspective. We make a clear option for the perspective of Latinas, based on the fact that we believe the Christian message of justice and peace is based on an option for the oppressed.

34. I have here adapted Maduro's synthesis about knowledge. See his *Mapas para la Fiesta*, 136–38.

35. Antonio Gramsci, *Prison Notebook*, ed. and trans. Quintin Hoare and Geoffrey Norwell Smith (New York: International Publishers, 1975), 9.

36. After some discussion, several of us have started using "the religion of the people" instead of "popular religion" because the word "popular" seems to qualify whatever it modifies as something less important. This was the same reason why a while back we stopped using "popular religiosity."

37. At present certain Pentecostal elements are beginning to be integrated into Latino people's religion.

38. Arturo Bañuelas, "U.S. Hispanic Theology," *Missiology* 20, no. 2 (April 1992): 290–91.

39. Ibid.

40. This quotation is taken from unpublished notes of Orlando Espín and Sixto García for a presentation they made at the Catholic Theological Society of America. An edited version of their presentation/workshop can be found in the *Catholic Theological Society of America Proceedings* 42 (1987): 114–19.

41. This term is used by Maduro. In his work it refers mainly to the meaning I notice in the next paragraph. See Maduro, *Religion and Social Conflict*, 27–29.

42. Ibid., 27.

43. Mark Kline Taylor, *Remembering Esperanza* (Maryknoll, N.Y.: Orbis Books, 1990), 1–18.

44. I am indebted to the work of Iris Marion Young on the issue of diversity. See Iris Marion Young, *The Politics of Difference* (Princeton, N.J.: Princeton University Press, 1990), particularly chap. 6.

PART VI

DECONSTRUCTIONIST
A/THEOLOGY

[18]

THE END(S)
OF THEOLOGY

MARK C. TAYLOR

> Now I'm going to tell you how I went into that inexpressiveness that was always my blind, secret quest. How I went into what exists between the number one and the number two, how I saw the mysterious, fiery, line, how it is a surreptitious line. Between two musical notes there exists another note, between two facts there exists another fact, between two grains of sand, no matter how close together they are, there exists an interval of space, there exists a sensing between sensing—in the interstices of primordial matter there is the mysterious, fiery line that is the world's breathing, and the world's continual breathing is what we hear and call silence.
>
> —Clarice Lispector, *The Passion According to G. H.*

A theorem proposed between the two . . . what exists between the number one and the number two . . . between two notes . . . between two facts . . . between two grains of sand . . . an interval . . . nothingness . . . impermanence . . . the world's breathing . . . the world's continual breathing. . . .

The end of theology is approaching . . . has always been approaching . . . approaching from the beginning . . . even "before" the beginning . . . approaching without ever arriving . . . approaching "before" the beginning and without end. The endless approach of the end of theology might, however, harbor an end that is not merely an end of theology but another end . . . a different end that is not the end of difference. This alternative end implies the irreducible opening of the a/theological imagination. The task of thinking at the end of theology is to think beyond theology's end by thinking the "beyond" of an end that is not theological. This "beyond," which is neither simply immanent or transcendent, has been left unthought throughout the Western theological tradition. Indeed, theologies traditionally have been constructed in order not to think this strange end. It is precisely the unthought-of theology that today beckons our thought.

These reflections might seem to be something like what Friedrich Nietzsche labeled "untimely meditations." More precisely, the declaration of the end of theology might have been more timely a quarter of a century ago. For a brief period in the sixties it seemed as if Nietzsche's declaration of the death of God were being realized in Western history and culture. In his widely acclaimed book *The Secular City*, Harvey Cox argued: "The age of the secular city, the epoch whose ethos is quickly spreading into every corner of the globe, *is* an age of 'no religion at all.' It no longer looks to religious rules and rituals for its morality or its meanings."[1] Twenty years later, events forced Cox to revise his assessment of the religious situation in our age. The result was a new book, *Religion in the Secular City*, in which Cox examined "the dramatic reappearance of traditional religion throughout the world, from the grassroots fervor of Christian communities in Latin America to the rise of fundamentalism on network television."[2]

One of the most surprising developments of the past several decades has been the widespread return of traditional religious belief and practice. For many years social scientists have been arguing that modernization and secularization go hand in hand. As the forces of modernization wax, the influence of religion wanes. Max Weber long ago observed that modernity brings in its wake the disenchantment of the natural world and human life. With the rise of modern science and technology, what once had seemed to be the kingdom of God becomes the province of humanity. When the principles of scientific investigation are turned toward human beings, religious belief is demystified through what Paul Ricoeur labels "the hermeneutics of suspicion." Rather than disclosing the truth about the cosmos and human existence, *masters of suspicion*, such as Karl Marx, Sigmund Freud, and Nietzsche, interpret religion as a problematic expression of primordial economic, psychological, and biological laws and forces. The hermeneutics of suspicion extends the project of enlightenment, which Immanuel Kant accurately describes as humanity's struggle to emerge from "self-incurred tutelage." Sounding more like an Enlightenment philosopher than the founder of psychoanalysis, Freud writes: "The voice of the intellect is a soft one, but it does not rest till it has gained a hearing. Finally, after a countless succession of rebuffs, it succeeds."[3]

Although sophisticated analyses of the secularization process and the imaginative elaborations of the hermeneutics of suspicion have done much to illuminate our understanding of religious thought and conduct, it is becoming increasingly clear that they do not tell the whole story of our era. Religion has proved more persistent than its critics anticipated. The last three decades have given increasing evidence of what might be described as the disenchantment with disenchantment. For many the world and life in it are more mysterious than secularists allow. Moreover, the rigorous analyses growing out of the hermeneutics of suspicion suggest that the obsession with demystification must itself be demystified. Critics of religion often approach their task with a fervor that borders on the religious. Religion, it seems, is more complex and multifaceted than reductionistic critiques acknowledge.

Nowhere is the disenchantment with disenchantment more evident than in the recent rise of religious fundamentalism. The term "fundamentalism" comes from a series of booklets titled *The Fundamentals*, published between 1910 and 1915. In these tracts different writers asserted what they took to be the basic beliefs of Christianity that were being eroded by "modern" theology's effort to reach an accommodation with the "modern" world. Fundamentalism, in all varieties, grows out of the deep sense that something is wrong with modernity. The revival of religious fundamentalism is one of the most significant social, cultural, and political phenomena of our time.

It is important to appreciate the complexity and diversity of today's fundamentalism. The revival of religious fundamentalism is not limited to the United States. Fundamentalism is an international phenomenon of considerable significance. From Western and Eastern Europe to the Middle and Far East; from North to Central and South America; from Christianity, Protestant as well as Catholic, to Judaism, Islam, Buddhism, and Hinduism, to say nothing of countless esoteric cults, fundamentalism is exercising enormous attraction and power. In years to come I suspect this religious revival will be regarded as more important than either the first or the second Great Awakening. One of the reasons for the overwhelming significance of this religious revival is its political dimension. Although religion and politics are always closely related, this alliance can be more or less explicit. In the last several decades religion has directly entered into a not-so-holy alliance with a variety of political programs. We need only consider the interplay of religion and politics in the United States, Nicaragua, Brazil, Poland, Israel, Iran, Pakistan, Tibet, Afghanistan, Sri Lanka, and elsewhere to recognize that labels such as conservative, liberal, and radical are not interchangeable in the religious and political domains.

Given the extraordinary diversity of these traditions and cultures, is it possible to identify a common thread uniting various forms of fundamentalism? Fundamentalism, in all of its guises, I would suggest, involves the search for secure foundations to ground thought and action. Fundamentalism, in other words, is foundationalism. From this point of view, religious belief can be used to legitimize social and political actions as different as civil rights marches, abortion clinic sit-ins, opposition to right- or left-wing regimes, nonviolent protests, and violent resistance.

Those of us in the academy should not think that we are immune to these developments. Although less obvious, our struggle with foundationalism is no less important. The so-called crisis in the humanities underscores the currency of academic issues related to the question of foundationalism. The heated debates triggered by Allan Bloom's outrageous book, *The Closing of the American Mind,* as well as former Secretary of Education William Bennett's attacks on higher education and the criticisms of the humanities registered by Lynne Cheney, of the National Endowment for the Humanities, reflect the "back to basics" attitude that pervades much of our culture. This attitude is, in my judgment, pernicious and should be vigorously resisted. Fundamentalism or foundationalism is essentially reactionary. In the wake of the confusion and uncertainty brought by the pluralism and relativity of modern culture, there is a pervasive nostalgic longing to return to the peace and security of a world in which truth seemed knowable and morality doable. But there is no going back. As Wallace Stevens tells us, these simpler times never really existed. Like the houses of our mothers, "they never were. . . . Were not and are not." The question we now face is not how to fashion an antimodern reaction to modernism but how to develop an effective postmodern response to modernity. Something has gone wrong—terribly wrong—in modernity. In this the fundamentalists or foundationalists are right. Nevertheless, their solution compounds the problem. We are not called to reestablish foundations but to think their fault.

In an effort to think this fault, I would like to rethink certain developments in modern theology. The trends we have been considering notwithstanding, the most significant turn in modern theology is what Nietzsche labeled "the death of God." The death of God marks the end of theology. In this context, "end" obviously does not mean the cessation of theology as such. Theology continues, even though it might already have reached its conclusion or achieved its fulfillment. The question that lingers in the wake of the death of God is how to think "beyond" the end of theology.

Twentieth-century theology is, in large part, an elaboration and extension of questions asked and problems posed in the nineteenth century. The most important theological thinking in the last century takes as its point of departure the seminal debate between G. W. F. Hegel and Søren Kierkegaard. Hegel attempts to develop an all-inclusive System in which human beings achieve Absolute Knowledge. This System is supposed to present the philosophical articulation of the truth represented by the Christian religious imagination. Absolute Knowledge is total self-consciousness, in which God and self are perfectly united. In this union each comes to completion in and through the other. Kierkegaard, however, remains suspicious of Hegelianism's totalizing propensities. Kierkegaard's relentlessly nonsystematic critique of the System is a concerted effort to recover the difference and return the otherness that philosophy and philosophical theology repress. To think beyond the end of theology is to unthink repression in a way that allows the return of the repressed. This unthinking admittedly poses certain dangers, intellectual as well as social.

Twentieth-century theology begins with a resounding "No!" proclaimed in 1918 by Karl Barth in his book titled *The Epistle to the Romans*. Barth's "No" grows out of his effort to recover what Kierkegaard described as "the infinite and qualitative difference" between God and humanity that post-Hegelian theology had erased. Having begun with this "*Nein*," contemporary theology has remained implicitly or explicitly preoccupied with the related problems of transcendence, difference, and otherness. It would be correct to insist that, for most of this century (and not only for this century), theological reflection has been suspended, perhaps even hung up, between immanence and transcendence. Barth's "No" represents a rejection of every form of theological liberalism and all variations of cultural Protestantism in which divine presence is regarded as immanent in historical, social, and cultural processes. Barth argues:

> Religion compels us to the perception that God is not to be found in religion. Religion makes us to know that we are competent to advance no single step. Religion, as the final human possibility, commands us to halt. Religion brings us to the place where we must wait, in order that God may

confront us—on the other side of the frontier of religion. The transformation of the "No" of religion into the divine "Yes" occurs in the dissolution of this last observable human thing.[4]

As this text suggests, Barth presents a thoroughgoing critique of culture. He views all human constructions—social, political, moral, and religious—with suspicion. Barth's neoorthodox theology does not, however, involve a return to fundamentalism but is, instead, a radical attack on all foundationalism. The historical situation in which Barth formulated his critique makes his suspicion of humankind's cultural constructs not only understandable but even persuasive. By saying "Yes" to a radically transcendent God, Barth says "No" to the culture that left Western Europe in ruins.

The force of the neoorthodox critique of culture and society has decreased as the distance from world wars has increased. The most significant index of this development is the death-of-God theology that emerged in the 1960s. The death-of-God theology remains one of the most significant theological movements of this century. I would even go so far as to argue that modern theology reaches a certain end in the death of God theology. Any postmodern theological reflection that does not fall into antimodernism will have to pass through the "fiery brook" of the death of God. In this country the most influential proponent of the death-of-God theology is Thomas J. J. Altizer. Altizer's program must be understood in the context of the neoorthodoxy that dominated theological discourse during the first half of this century. When Altizer declares the death of God, it is really the death of the Barthian God he proclaims. Altizer's "No" to Barth's "No" is at the same time a "Yes" to a radical immanence in which all vestiges of transcendence are erased. In the Hegelian terms Altizer repeatedly invokes, the negation of negation (that is, the negation of radical transcendence) issues in a total affirmation that overcomes every trace of unreconciled otherness. Within Altizer's apocalyptic vision, the death of God is the condition of the possibility of the arrival of the Parousia. When the kingdom of God is at hand, authentic presence is totally realized here and now.

If we are to understand where Altizer departs from and remains bound to the presuppositions and conclusions of classical theology, then it is necessary to reformulate several crucial points in his position. By declaring the death of God, Altizer does not call into question the traditional understanding of Being in terms of presence. On the contrary, he insists that to be is to be present and to be fully is to be present totally. Although never stated in these terms, Altizer's argument implies that the mistake of traditional theism, of which Barthianism is but the most problematic variation, is not that it misunderstands Being as such but that it identifies the locus of true Being as transcendent to, rather than immanent in, the world of space and time. From Altizer's perspective, the total presence of God in the incarnation marks the death of the otherness that inhibits the very possibility of enjoying presence in the present. To cling to the belief that the divine is in any way other or transcendent is to suffer the disappointment brought by the delay or deferral of the Parousia. Precisely this delay or deferral, Altizer argues, ends with the life and death of Jesus.

Following Hegel, Altizer maintains that what is implicit in Jesus becomes explicit in the course of the historical process. With the death of God, transcendent presence becomes totally present in space (that is, here) and time (now). When the identity of the divine comes to completion in the identity of the human, difference and unreconciled otherness are overcome.

> Distance disappears in total presence, and so likewise does all actual otherness which is not the otherness of that presence itself. Difference can now be present only insofar as it is fully embodied in speech. When difference speaks, and fully speaks, it becomes present in speech, and wholly present in that speech. That speech is not simply the presence of difference, or the voice of difference. It is far rather the self-identity of difference, and its fully actualized self-identity, a self-identity in which difference embodies its otherness in the immediacy of a real and actual presence.[5]

With the incorporation of difference in identity, Altizer reinscribes the identity of identity and difference, which, as the Alpha and Omega of reflection, constitutes the very foundation of Hegel's System.

The question that remains after Hegel and after the theological reappropriation of his System is how to think otherwise than being by thinking a difference that is not reducible to identity. As I have suggested elsewhere, this is precisely the task that Kierkegaard sets for himself in his philosophical fragments and unscientific postscripts. In our day the question of difference has been taken up again by, among others, Jacques Derrida. Situating his own interrogation in relation to Hegel's System, Derrida maintains:

> As for what "begins" then—"beyond" absolute knowledge—*unheard-of* thoughts are required, sought for across the memory of old signs. . . . In the openness of this question *we no longer know*. This does not mean that we know nothing but that we are beyond absolute knowledge (and its ethical, aesthetic, or religious system), approaching that on the basis of which its closure is announced and decided. Such a question will legitimately be understood as *meaning* nothing, as no longer belonging to the system of meaning.[6]

To think beyond absolute knowledge (or, perhaps, to think the beyond "of" absolute knowledge) is to think after the end of Western theology and metaphysics by thinking what that tradition has not thought. In his influential essay "The End of Philosophy and the Task of Thinking" Martin Heidegger explains, "What characterizes metaphysical thinking that grounds the ground for beings is the fact that metaphysical thinking departs from what is present in its presence, and thus represents it in terms of its ground as something grounded."[7] Heidegger insists that metaphysics and what he identifies as the ontotheological tradition "does not ask about Being as Being, that is, does not raise the question of how there can be presence as such."[8] The task of thinking, in the strict sense of the term, is to think the unthought-of ontotheology, which answers the question of how there can be presence as such. One of the ways Heidegger characterizes this unthought is as "the *difference* between Being and beings" or, more concisely, "difference *as* difference." This difference should not be confused with the presence of any specific difference. Heideggerian *Differenz*, which is the condition of the possibility of all presence and every present, is not a presence and hence can never be properly present; yet neither is it simply absent. What neither philosophy nor theology has thought (because neither can think such an "unheard-of" thought without ceasing to be itself) is that which lies between presence and absence, identity and difference, being and nonbeing. Neither representable in nor masterable by traditional philosophical and theological categories, this margin is the trace of a different difference and another other. Is this other other Stevens's "theorem proposed between the two"? Perhaps.

No one has questioned this strange difference with greater rigor than Derrida. In Derrida's texts Heidegger's *Differenz* returns with a difference as *différance*. The neologism *différance*, which Derrida admits "is neither a word nor a concept," trades on the duplicity of the French word *différer*, which can mean both "to differ" and "to defer." Suspended between differing and deferring, *différance* involves the becoming-time of space and the becoming-space of time. The time of this difference and the difference of this time open unheard-of spaces in which the a/theological imagination can err. To glimpse the time–space of such erring, it might be helpful to return to my all too schematic outline of twentieth-century theology.

I have suggested that, since at least 1918, theologians have wavered between emphasizing divine transcendence and stressing divine immanence. Whereas Barth attempts to reassert divine transcendence, which calls into question all human achievement, Altizer is concerned to reestablish divine immanence, which is supposed to overcome every form of alienated consciousness. When situated historically, Altizer's critique of Barth can be read as a reversal of Kierkegaard's critique of Hegel. From this point of view, Altizer's "No" to Barth's "No" supplants Kierkegaard's dialectic of either/or with Hegel's dialectic of both/and. After this reversal of reversal, we must ask, What have Barth and Altizer not thought? What does the alternative of transcendence and immanence leave out? Is there a nondialectical third that lies between the dialectic of either/or and both/and? Might this third be neither transcendent nor immanent? Does this neither/nor open the time–space of a different difference and another other—a difference and an other that do not merely invert but actually subvert the polarities of Western philosophical and theological reflection?

To begin to respond to such questions, we must try to think the unthought and perhaps unthinkable difference, which I name with the improper name "altarity," by rethinking the death of God. Instead of leading to the total presence constitutive of the complete realization of both God and humanity, the death of God calls into question the very possibility of fulfillment by forever deferring the realization of presence. The infinite deferral of the end harbors an end that is not the end of theology. An end that is not the end of theology would be an end that is never present—an end that does not, indeed, cannot arrive. Such an endless end is what Maurice Blanchot describes as "the disaster."

The disaster is not an apocalypse. It is not a matter of vision, sight, or insight. The nonsite of the disaster is not a scene of knowledge or self-consciousness. No veils are stripped, no curtains raised. The disaster "reveals" nothing. This nothing is not, however, the nothing of Western philosophy and theology. The nothing of the disaster is neither the no thing that is the fullness of being nor the absence of things that is the emptiness of nonbeing. The nothing that both philosophy and theology leave unthought is "between being and nonbeing." It neither is nor is not; it is not present without being absent. Nothing approaches by withdrawing and withdraws by approaching. Through its approach, nothing ends ending by ensuring that nothing ends.

The disaster, then, is the nonevent in which nothing happens. The eventuality of nothing ruins all presence by interminably delaying the arrival of every present. In one of his most provocative accounts of the disaster, Blanchot writes:

> The disaster ruins everything, all the while leaving everything intact. It does not touch anyone in particular; "I" am not threatened by it, but spared, left aside. It is in this way that I am threatened; it is in this way that the disaster threatens in me that which is exterior to me—an other than I who passively become other. There is no reaching the disaster. Out of reach is he whom it threatens, whether from afar or close up, it is impossible to say: the infiniteness of the threat has in some way broken every limit. We are on the edge of disaster without being able to situate it in the future: it is rather always already past, and yet we are on the edge or under the threat, all formulations that imply the future—that which is yet to come—if the disaster were not that which does not come, that which has put a stop to every arrival.[9]

The nonarrival or absence of the end has a retroactive effect on the beginning, even as the inaccessibility of the beginning harbors an aftereffect for the end. If God is the Alpha and the Omega, then the death of God marks the end of the beginning as well as the end. In the presence of this twofold absence, religion itself must be refigured.

Religion is a binding (*ligare*) back (*re*) that is supposed to bind together. The return to the origin that constitutes the end holds out the promise of unifying human life by reconciling opposites and overcoming strife. But what if, as the poet Wallace Stevens avers, "It is an illusion that we were ever alive."[10] If the origin is always missing . . . If the end never arrives . . . If God is dead, then religion binds back to nothing. When *re-ligare* fails by returning all to nothing, it must be repeated. Through repetition, binding back is transformed into a rebinding that creates a double bind. This double bind is the trace of the nothing that is betrayed by the death of God. To be bound to and by nothing is not to be free but to be entangled in a double bind from which there is no escape. In the aftermath of the death of God, religion no longer heals wounds by binding together the opposites that tear apart. On the contrary, religion exposes wounds that can never be cured. The "re-" of religion marks a repetition (compulsion) that neither solves nor heals but re-marks the devastating space that is the dead time of the nonapocalyptic disaster.

A/theology struggles to inscribe the failure of religion in what Edmond Jabès describes as "wounded words." As Jabès points out,

> One crack and the building crumbles and initiates the endless reading of ruins.[11]

Lispector captures the drift of Jabès's wounded words:

> I return with the unsayable. The unsayable can be given to me only through the failure of my language. Only when the construct falters do I reach what I cannot accomplish.[12]

Faltering constructions—linguistic and otherwise—expose the fault of foundations and the error of every fundamentalism. This crack, this fault, lies "beyond" the end of theology. To write this "beyond" is to write the lack of language that is a nothing other than the nothing of silence. Neither speech nor silence, this lack of language remains in and as the failure of words. The wound of words is a tear that cannot be mended—a tear that can never be wiped away. This tear or tear, which interrupts the system of exchange, is neither exactly inside nor outside the text. As such, it eludes the economy of representation. That which is neither outside nor inside cannot be represented either referentially or self-reflexively. To write the "beyond" that is not the end of theology, it is necessary to write in a way that is nonreferential without being self-reflexive.

In an effort to describe the distinguishing features of this alternative a/theological writing, I have borrowed a term from Freud: parapraxis. A psychical parapraxis, Freud explains, "must be in the nature of a momentary and temporary disturbance. The same function must have been performed by us more correctly before, or we must at all times believe ourselves capable of carrying it out more correctly. If we are corrected by someone else, we must at once recognize the rightness of the correction and the wrongness of our own psychical process."[13] A parapraxis, then, involves a failure, slip, error, or mistake. The slip of the tongue or pen underscores the irreducible errancy of parapraxis. In this case, error betrays. Such betrayal always takes place along a border—at the limits of language. "Para," J. Hillis Miller points out, "is a double antithetical prefix, signifying at once proximity and distance, similarity and difference, interiority and exteriority, something inside a domestic economy and at the same time outside it, something simultaneously this side of a boundary line, threshold, or margin, and also beyond it."[14] Parapraxical writing is the praxis of the "para." This praxis involves the inscription of the boundary, threshold, margin, or limit. To write parapraxically is to write the limit rather than to write about the limit. The "para" inscribed in parapraxis is "inside" the written text as a certain "outside" that cannot be internalized. Thus parapraxical writing falls between referential and self-referential discourse. There is an inescapably performative dimension to parapraxis. In contrast to performative utterance, however, which always does *something* with words, parapraxis struggles to do nothing with words. It succeeds by failing. By doing nothing with words, para-praxical writing stages the withdrawal of that which no text can contain, ex-press, or re-present.

It is important to stress that parapraxis is not simply a latter-day version of clas-sical negative theology. The nothing toward which parapraxis is drawn is not the nothing of negative theology. Whereas negative theologians tend to regard noth-ing as the binary or dialectical opposite of being, the a/theologian interprets noth-ing as neither being nor nonbeing. Parapraxis, therefore, is no more positive than negative. Instead of employing a strategy of simple negation, parapraxis engages in what Kierkegaard labels "indirect communication." That which is unrepre-sentable cannot be approached directly but must be approached indirectly through linguistic twistings and turnings that can never be straightened out. As Michel de Certeau explains, this indirection "denatures language: it removes it from the func-tion that intends an imitation of things. It also undoes the coherence of significa-tion . . . it torments words in order to make them say that which literally they do not say."[15]

To undo the coherence of signification, it is necessary to think beyond repre-sentation by thinking after the "theological" age of the sign. Words are wounded when language goes astray. The nonsynthetic imagination employs aberrant syntax to create a text that lacks semantic plenitude. Errant language entails lin-guistic abuse through which the writer attempts to say the unsayable by allow-ing language to undo itself. The unsaying of language is not the same as mere silence. By simultaneously inscribing and erasing, parapraxis allows the with-drawal of language to approach in and through the tangled lines of the text. "That which must be said," de Certeau insists, "can only be said in the fissure of the word."[16] The fissure of the word is the fault that remains to be thought—the fault that theology has left unthought or that theology has been constructed not to think.

When language falters nothing happens. This nothing, which is neither the pres-ence of the no thing that is the ground of everything nor the absence of all things, is forever elusive and thus can never be experienced. It is the limit of experience. To approach this limit of experience is to undergo the irreducible experience of the limit. This experience of limit is a liminal experience in which an other that is, in effect, sacred is glimpsed. It is important to realize that this sacred is not God but is that which remains and approaches when gods fail . . . fail to arrive, to be present, or to be present again in our representations. The failure of God betrays the sacred. The site of this betrayal is the text inscribed in parapraxis. The a/theo-logical writer strives to restage the sacrifice of the Word. This sacrifice is radical; it is an expenditure without return in which negation is not negated. The sacrifice of the Word in writing is the betrayal of language that mourns the death of God. In the wake of this mourning, nothing is left . . . nothing remains . . . always re-mains. To write after the death of God . . . to write beyond the end of theology is to betray nothing.

In his posthumously published collection of fragments, *The Will to Power*, Nietzsche writes:

> Nihilism stands at the door: whence comes this uncanniest of all guests? Point of departure: it is an error to consider "social distress" or "physiological degeneration" or, worse, corruption, as the *cause* of nihilism. Ours is the most decent and compassionate age. Distress, whether of the soul, body, or intellect, cannot itself give birth to nihilism (i.e., the radical repudiation of value, meaning, and desirability). Such distress always permits a variety of interpretations. Rather: it is in one particular interpretation, the Christian-moral one, that nihilism is rooted.[17]

Nietzsche's claim is startling. Nihilism, he argues, is not the result of the decline of religion and morality but actually grows out of religious and moral beliefs. By establishing an opposition between good and evil, true and false, here and beyond, what is and what ought to be, religion and morality effectively alienate the self from itself, divide people from each other, and separate self and world. So understood, the affirmation of the foundational principles of religion and morality involves a nay-saying that is profoundly nihilistic. Such nihilism lurks in the midst of contemporary religious and political fundamentalism. History teaches us that such nay-saying, which disguises itself as religious affirmation, often becomes violent. The forms of such violence are not always obvious but frequently are very subtle. This tendency toward violence increases when one is convinced that his or her cause is just, vision is true, and way is divinely sanctioned. Certainty harbors repression. As repression spreads, violence grows. This violence inevitably is directed toward the other who is regarded as a threat. Security—be it national or personal—seems to require the mastery, if not the elimination, of the other. This struggle for mastery is nihilistic.

The nihilism that Nietzsche detects at the heart of morality and of certain forms of religion cannot be overcome by a simple reversal of nay-saying in a yea-saying that affirms what is and denies what ought to be. Such a reversal is characteristic of the death-of-God theology. The death of God issues in the divinization of humanity and the sanctification of the world. When what is, is what ought to be, one must embrace reality rather than seek ideality. This radical affirmation approaches what Hegel describes as Absolute Knowledge and Nietzsche labels Gay Science. All too often, however, there is a curious similarity between the nay-saying of the religious and moral struggle for mastery and the yea-saying of Absolute Knowledge and Gay Science. In each case, otherness and difference seem to be intolerable. The death of the transcendent God is the disappearance of the absolute difference which establishes every difference that cannot be reduced to the same and every other that cannot be made my own.

In the postmodern world, nihilism is, in a certain sense, unavoidable. It cannot be overcome by returning to a premodern search for foundations or the modern affirmation of presence. By thinking beyond the end of theology, by thinking the "beyond" of an end that is not theological, we approach the possibility of thinking otherness otherwise and thinking difference differently. One of the most pressing problems we face—indeed, have always faced—is the difficulty of remaining open to a difference we cannot control and an other we can never master. It is, perhaps, naïve to believe that a/theological thinking can contribute to our psychological, social, and political struggles with difference and otherness. I would hope, however, that this naïveté is, in Ricoeur's terms, a "second naïveté," a naïveté that has been tempered by reflection and its inevitable failure.

The sacrifice of the Word inscribed "in" the text as an exteriority that cannot be internalized creates a wound that never heals. This wound marks the opening of opening itself. The wound of the Word implies another space in which difference can approach differently. The task confronting us is to affirm difference without negating it—to accept otherness without denying it.

The end is approaching . . . has always been approaching . . . approaching from the beginning. Still, it seems closer today than ever before. We are on the edge of disaster, under its threat. That threat is real, and we delude ourselves by trying to deny or repress it. Can disaster be delayed? Will it be deferred? We cannot be sure. If there is hope, then it lies not in certainty but in uncertainty, not in security but in insecurity, not in foundations but in their faults, not in cures but in wounds— wounds that sometimes are inflicted on and by the Word. In "the twilight of the idols," we linger—linger with the wound that is not precisely ours. That wound might be our hope. Small hope. Fragile hope. Nothing more. *Nothing* more. Wound of the Word . . . a theorem proposed between the two . . . between the number one and the number two . . . between two notes . . . between two facts . . . between two grains of sand . . . interstices of primordial matter . . . nothingness . . . impermanence . . . the world's continual breathing. . . .

NOTES

This chapter originally appeared in *Theology at the End of Modernity,* ed. Sheila Davaney (Valley Forge, Pa.: Trinity Press International, 1991).

1. Harvey Cox, *The Secular City* (New York: Macmillan Co., 1966), 3.
2. Harvey Cox, *Religion in the Secular City: Toward a Postmodern Theology* (New York: Simon & Schuster, 1984), introduction.
3. Sigmund Freud, *The Future of an Illusion*, trans. W. D. Robson-Scott (Garden City, N.Y.: Doubleday & Co., 1964), 158.
4. Karl Barth, *The Epistle to the Romans*, trans. E. C. Hoskyns (London: Oxford University Press, 1968), 242.
5. Thomas J. J. Altizer, *The Self-Embodiment of God* (New York: Harper & Row, 1977), 81.
6. Jacques Derrida, *"Différance,"* in *Speech and Phenomena and Other Essays on Husserl's Theory of Signs*, trans. D. Allison (Evanston, Ill.: Northwestern University Press, 1973), 87.
7. Martin Heidegger, "The End of Philosophy and the Task of Thinking," in *On Time and Being*, trans. J. Stambaugh (New York: Harper & Row, 1972), 56.
8. Ibid., 70.
9. Maurice Blanchot, *The Writing of the Disaster*, trans. A. Smock (Lincoln, Neb.: University of Nebraska Press, 1986), 1.
10. Wallace Stevens, "The Rock," in *The Collected Poems of Wallace Stevens* (New York: Alfred A. Knopf, 1981), 525.

11. Edmond Jabès, *The Book of Questions: El, or The Last Book*, trans. R. Waldrop (Middletown, Conn.: Wesleyan University Press, 1984), 104.
12. Clarice Lispector, *The Passion According to G. H.*, trans. R. W. Sousa (Minneapolis: University of Minnesota Press, 1988), 90.
13. Sigmund Freud, *The Standard Edition of the Complete Psychological Works of Sigmund Freud*, trans. James Strachey (London: Hogarth Press, 1953–74), 6:239.
14. J. Hillis Miller, "The Critic as Host," in *Deconstruction and Criticism*, ed. Harold Bloom et al. (New York: Seabury Press, 1979), 219.
15. Michel de Certeau, *La fable mystique: XVI–XVII* (Paris: Gallimard, 1982), 195.
16. Ibid., 200.
17. Friedrich Nietzsche, *The Will to Power*, trans. W. Kaufman (New York: Random House, 1968), 7.

INDEX